Early Modern Europe

Early Modern Europe

THE AGE OF RELIGIOUS WAR, 1559–1715

Mark Konnert

Originally published by Broadview Press, 2006

LIBRARY AND ARCHIVES CANADA CATALOGUING IN PUBLICATION

Konnert, Mark William, 1957–
Early modern Europe: the age of religious war, 1559–1715 / Mark Konnert.

Includes bibliographical references and index.
ISBN 1-44260-004-1
(Previous ISBN 1-55111-588-3)

1. Europe—History—1517–1648. 2. Europe—History—1648–1715.
I. Title.

D246.K66 2006 940.2'2 C2006-903051-0

We welcome comments and suggestions regarding any aspect of our publications—please feel free to contact us at the addresses below or at customerservice@utphighereducation.com/ www.utphighereducation.com.

North America
5201 Dufferin Street,
North York, Ontario, Canada M3H 5T8

2250 Military Road,
Tonawanda, New York, USA 14150
TEL (416) 978-2239; FAX (416) 978-4738

UK, Ireland, and continental Europe
NBN International
Estover Road
Plymouth, PL6 7PY, UK
TEL (01752) 202300; FAX (01752) 202330;
EMAIL enquiries@nbninternational.com

EMAIL customerservice@utphighereducation.com

Higher Education University of Toronto Press gratefully acknowledges the financial support of the Government of Canada through the Book Publishing Industry Development Program for our publishing activities.

Cover & Interior by Liz Broes, Black Eye Design.

Printed in Canada

10 9 8 7 6 5 4 3 2 1

CONTENTS

LIST OF ILLUSTRATIONS

Maps

Figures

INTRODUCTION

Very quickly in their study of history, students learn (or at least ought to learn) that in the final analysis, any attempt to divide history up into periods (what historians call periodization) is ultimately artificial. It is, however, a necessary tool for studying the past, since the whole scope of history is obviously beyond any single person's capacity to comprehend. Thus, if we must impose ultimately artificial periods on the past, we must at least make sure that the periodizations we use make some sense, that is, that they are useful tools for coming to grips with the vast amount of data we have accumulated about past times.

The periodization I have chosen for this book coincides with my own interests and areas of research and teaching. Although it is certainly not the only way of dividing the past into manageable chunks, it is, obviously, one that I feel is useful and justified on a number of different grounds. The period from 1559 to 1715 in Europe was one of almost continual warfare, both civil and international (indeed the two are often difficult if not impossible to distinguish). The organizing principle of this book is that in large part this warfare was, at least until the mid-seventeenth century, largely driven by the religious division brought about by the Protestant Reformation of the early sixteenth century. Even after religion ceased to be a (if not the) major cause of war in Europe, the effects of a century of religious war still played an enormous role.

The year 1559 is a convenient starting point for a number of different reasons. First of all, it allows me to treat the religious division of Europe as an established fact. By that year, at least a whole generation of people had reached adulthood never having known the religious unity of western Europe under the Catholic Church. Thus, by beginning where I do, I can evade treatment of the causes and course of the Protestant Reformation, issues that are fascinating and vital, but tangential to my main concerns here.

That year also saw the signing of the Treaty of Cateau-Cambrésis between the two most powerful monarchs in Europe, King Henry II of the ruling Valois dynasty of France, and King Philip II of the Habsburg dynasty, whose most important possessions were the Spanish kingdoms of Castile and Aragon, but whose possessions also encompassed the Netherlands, parts of western Germany, large parts of Italy, and of course the Spanish colonial empire in the New World. Since 1494, rulers of the Valois and Habsburg dynasties had fought a more or less continual series of wars for supremacy in Europe. Wealthy and populous, but politically weak and disunited, Italy was at once their major battlefield and the major prize to be won. In 1559, both rulers decided that peace was in their best interests. Both kingdoms were financially and militarily exhausted by generations of warfare. Moreover, both kings were concerned about the growth of heresy in their domains, a problem that was difficult if not impossible to tackle while they were involved in major foreign wars. Philip II was the major beneficiary of the treaty since it recognized his control of large parts of Italy, but this must be accounted a Pyrrhic victory, since Spain was only marginally less exhausted than France. Nevertheless, Cateau-Cambrésis marked the beginning of a century of Spanish dominance in European affairs.

In terms of domestic politics as well, 1559 and the few years on either side of it also mark a kind of "changing of the guard" for many European states. The Habsburg Holy Roman Emperor Charles V (simultaneously King Charles I of Spain) began to abdicate his titles in 1555. Recognizing that the empire he had inherited through a series of dynastic marriages and accidents of birth, death, and inheritance was too large and complex to be governed by one man, he divided his territories into two parts. To his eldest son Philip (King of Spain, 1556-98), he bequeathed the Spanish kingdoms and their overseas empire, the Netherlands, the Free County (Franche-Comté) of Burgundy, and the Italian possessions consisting primarily of the Duchy of Milan in the north and the Kingdom of Naples in the south. To his younger brother Ferdinand he left the title of Holy Roman Emperor with theoretical authority over Germany, as well as the hereditary Habsburg lands of Austria, Hungary, and Bohemia. Ferdinand died in 1564 and was in turn succeeded by his son, Emperor Maximilian II (r. 1564–76). In France, King Henry II died prematurely in an unfortunate jousting accident and was succeeded by his eldest son, who became King Francis II (r. 1559–60). He would be followed by two of his younger brothers, neither of whom had legitimate male heirs to succeed them. (A fourth brother would die before having his chance to ascend the throne.) In England, after a long period of instability and religious uncertainty, Elizabeth I came to the throne in 1558.

The other end of the period is marked by similar watersheds in rulership and diplomacy. In 1713 the Treaty of Utrecht brought to a close the wars incited by the ambitions of King Louis XIV of France and established the balance of power that would dominate European diplomacy until the age of the French Revolution and Napoleon. It also marked the beginning of an age in which wars would be fought for more limited, and therefore more attainable, objectives. Louis XIV of France died in 1715, having reigned since 1643 and actually governed since 1661, succeeded on the throne by his great-grandson as Louis XV. In England, the last of the Stuart dynasty, Queen Anne, died in 1714. She was succeeded by an obscure and petty German prince, the Elector of Hanover, who became King George I of

England. Charles II, the last Habsburg king of Spain, died in 1700, replaced on that throne by a grandson of Louis XIV, who became King Philip V, the first of the Spanish Bourbon dynasty. In far-off Russia, Peter the Great died in 1725, having forcefully westernized Russia's elite and brought the weight and power of that vast country to bear on European affairs.

In the internal political development of European states, the dividing lines are not quite so neatly drawn. In general, I will focus on two broad trends: centralization and absolutism. The origins of both go far back into the Middle Ages, and both will continue beyond our period, but the century and a half under consideration here saw significant developments in both. By centralization I mean the continual if sometimes erratic tendencies of central governments to enhance and expand their control over their territories and their subjects. Absolutism refers to the form of that central government, to the question of who wields the power within the central government. As we shall see, absolutism continued to develop in the sixteenth and seventeenth centuries out of the disorders and violence of religious warfare and the continual need for governments to raise ever more revenue through taxation of their subjects, what some historians have called the "warfare state." In early modern Europe the two processes usually progressed hand-in-hand, but they need not. For example, by 1715 there was in England a highly efficient central government, which was nevertheless a partnership between the monarchy and the wealthy elites represented in Parliament.

In the realm of religion, 1559 or thereabouts also serves as a convenient point of departure. The initial impulse of the Reformation in Germany, that initiated by Martin Luther, had largely played itself out. In Germany, the two sides had fought each other to a stalemate, embodied in the Peace of Augsburg of 1555 with its principle of *cuius regio, eius religio*. Luther himself had died in 1546, and Lutherans became increasingly divided among themselves regarding theological issues. After the middle of the sixteenth century, Lutheranism was no longer a dynamic and expanding movement.

On the other hand, the version of reformed Christianity preached by John Calvin (1509–64) was just coming into its own by 1559. In many ways, 1559 represents Calvinism's entry onto the international religious stage. That year saw the final and definitive edition of Calvin's theological masterwork, *The Institutes of the Christian Religion*. It also saw the foundation of the Genevan Academy as a training institute for pastors and missionaries. It also saw the first meeting of the national synod of the Calvinist Reformed Church of France.

At the same time, the Catholic Church had, after a period of indecision and hesitation, decisively committed itself to a program of reform and fighting back against the Protestants. Like a great super-tanker, turning around a large and complex institution like the Catholic Church is a long and difficult process. The centrepiece of this process was the Council of Trent, which met off and on for a period of twenty years before finally concluding in 1562. It was these two movements, Calvinism and a reformed and resurgent Catholic Church, which provided the religious tension that in large part produced the religious warfare that would affect Europe over at least the next century.

Earlier generations of historians tended to discount the religious element of the wars that convulsed Europe in the sixteenth and seventeenth centuries. Surely, thought these largely secular and nationalistic historians of the nineteenth and early twentieth centuries, seemingly otherwise rational and educated people would not fight so hard, would not wreak so much havoc in the name of religion. Their real motives must have been other than religious: political, nationalistic, economic, or social. Religion was seen as a cloak, or a pretext, for their "real" motives. More recently, however, historians have been putting the religion back into religious wars. Certainly, there were other things at stake in these wars: territory, resources, wealth, or social conflict. But it is impossible to imagine that these wars would have lasted so long, and been so bitter and divisive, without their religious component. None of the disputes that caused the wars could be settled until the religious issue was settled in one way or another, or until people were willing to stop fighting about religion. This point was reached around 1648 with the Peace of Westphalia, marking the end of the Thirty Years' War, the most destructive and pointless of the religious wars. Thereafter, religion became largely tangential to diplomacy and warfare. It was a pretext, or an irritant, but it ceased to be a driving factor. Nevertheless, the Europe of the latter part of the seventeenth century was profoundly shaped by the religious wars of the previous 150 years.

Even as rulers and governments stopped fighting wars in the name of the "true religion," they still insisted on uniformity of religious belief and practice within their states. Several different elements come into play when examining religious life and practice. One is that governments—Protestant, Catholic, and indeed Eastern Orthodox—continued a centuries-long process of assuming greater control over the church in their lands and over the religious life of their people. Although this control progressed farther in Protestant areas than in Catholic, it was a difference of degree, not kind, and was part of the process of centralization discussed above. Political and religious leaders also attempted to reform the religious practices and beliefs of ordinary people. Again, this was common to Protestant and Catholic areas, although of course there were important differences. This reform had both a destructive and a constructive aspect. Destructively, reformers were concerned to purge popular practices of what they deemed to be "pagan" or immoral practices. Constructively, they wanted to inculcate in ordinary people the essentials of their faith, to make them into genuine Catholics, Lutherans, Calvinists, and so on. This is a process that historians call confessionalization.

So, in the realms of diplomacy and warfare, politics, and religion, the dates 1559 and 1715 (or thereabouts) mark convenient beginning and ending points. This is not as true of the other areas of human existence that will concern us: the economy, social structure, and intellectual and cultural life.

In all these areas, the major trends and developments have their origins well before 1559 and will persist long after 1715. In economic life our period is divided between two trends. The first is a period of economic and demographic recovery and expansion following the catastrophe of the Black Death in the mid-fourteenth century. First noticeable on a European scale in the mid-fifteenth century, it continued throughout the sixteenth, fuelled by gold and silver from the New World, and by a growing population. This recovery ran out of steam starting around 1600, although the timing and severity of the recession varied tremendously from place to place. This phase is characterized by stable or declining populations and economic stagnation and continued into the mid-eighteenth century, when fundamental changes in agriculture and industry, which we call the Industrial Revolution, removed previous limits on economic growth.

The structure of society and the nature of social relations are of course closely tied to economics. On the surface, European society in 1715 looked very similar to what it had been in 1559. Again, its origins go back into the Middle Ages, in particular to the late Middle Ages after the Black Death. European society was dominated by an aristocracy, mostly but not exclusively noble, whose preeminence was based on their control of land and agriculture. Supported by monarchy and church, it dominated a society made up overwhelmingly of rural peasants. But beneath the surface, we will see that significant changes had taken place in the nature of that aristocracy and the way it extracted wealth from the land, and hence in its relations with the peasants. These changes provoked a great deal of conflict and tension, manifested in numerous revolts and civil wars, as well as in phenomena such as the great witch hunts. The final evolution of these changes would not be seen until the Industrial Revolution and French Revolution when the economic dominance and political control of the aristocracy were overthrown.

In intellectual and cultural life, it is not as easy to generalize about the changes that take place, but it was an extraordinarily fertile period. This is the period of the Scientific Revolution, when the scientific legacy of Ancient Greece that had been transmitted through the Middle Ages was finally cast off. If received notions about something as basic as the nature of the universe had been shown to be so horribly wrong, what else might the ancients and the knowledge received from the past be wrong about? Certainly one of the most notable characteristics of elite thought in this period was a willingness to question authority of all kinds. Just as noticeable, however, was a kind of despair and a willingness to take refuge in the mystical, the magical, and the irrational. Going along with this at a more humble level was a general increase in education and literacy, fuelled largely by the efforts of religious reformers, but most of all by the printing press, which put literature within the reach of ordinary people. This too would ultimately result in a general questioning of authority. Religious reformers, who thought that education and literacy were the key to a genuine religious and moral revival soon discovered that once you have taught people to read, you could not control what they read, or wrote. As a result, European society was more secular in 1715 than in 1559, and although the major developments in this were still to come, the foundations were laid in our period.

This book is organized in four major sections. The first is largely analytical in nature and sets out the social and economic context of the events described in the following sections. The second deals with the period from 1559 to 1648 in

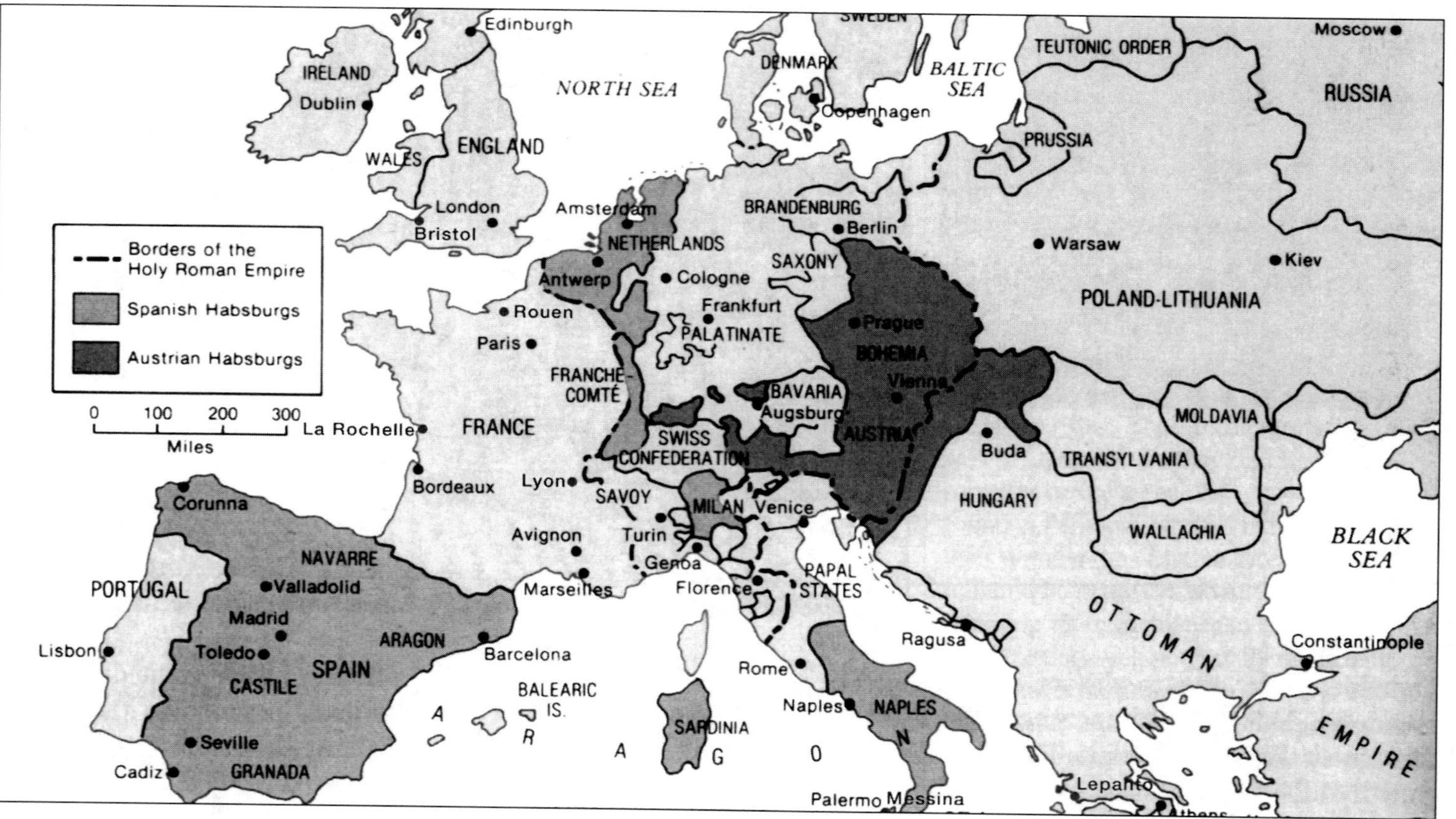

MAP 0.1 ✣ EUROPE IN 1559

western Europe and the religious wars that dominated. The third will examine the notion of a "seventeenth-century crisis" in European states and deals with the outcome of this crisis, largely through the further elaboration of royal absolutism. The fourth section deals with intellectual and cultural life, largely the dissolution of the old world-view and the construction of a new one.

Given the broad scope of this book, it is inevitable that some matters and areas receive either slight attention or none at all. Geographically, at least in parts two and three, I have concentrated on the major European countries of the period: France, the British Isles (concentrating mostly on England, with occasional glances at Scotland and Ireland where appropriate), Spain, the Holy Roman Empire, Sweden, Poland, and Russia or Muscovy. The Italian states are largely ignored, since there was no such thing as "Italy" capable of having a political history in this period, and because large parts of Italy were subject to foreign rule. Portugal is treated mostly in the context of the period of Spanish rule from 1580 to 1665, not because its history is not important or interesting, but because by this time Portugal had ceased to play an independently important role in European affairs. In terms of subject matter, unfortunately little attention is given to high culture, the world of literature, art and music, except where they relate to specific points and issues in other contexts, such as the golden age of Dutch culture in the seventeenth century, the artistic patronage of Louis XIV, or the specific qualities of seventeenth-century Spanish art. This neglect stems primarily from my own ignorance of these areas, as fascinating as I find them. In general, nothing makes one feel more like an impostor than writing a textbook. In my own case, this is especially so in the realms of high culture, and rather than expose my own lack of knowledge, I felt it better not to make the attempt.

PART ONE

Society and Economy in Early Modern Europe

CHAPTER ONE

Population and Demography

In the middle of the fourteenth century, the Black Death, or bubonic plague, killed between one-quarter and one-third of the people in Europe. In the aftermath of this catastrophe, Europeans established for themselves a demographic pattern that would persist until the Industrial Revolution of the eighteenth and nineteenth centuries, when the global population began an explosion that has continued into the present day. This pattern, moreover, had certain characteristics that distinguish it very clearly from most other pre-modern societies. Most notable among these characteristics were a relatively late age of marriage, a household made up of a nuclear family, and a relatively small number of children. In this chapter, we will look first at the overall numbers of people, at demographic trends and geographic variations; then at the distribution of the population; and finally at the patterns of birth, marriage, and death.

Numbers

All population figures for sixteenth- and seventeenth-century Europe are rough estimates, since early modern governments did not carry out censuses in the modern sense of the term. The first real censuses date from the late eighteenth and early nineteenth centuries: 1790 in the US and 1801 in Great Britain. Information about population therefore has to be pieced together from a number of different fragmentary and partial sources and then extrapolated to larger areas. Where early modern governments cared about numbers of people, it was almost always for purposes of taxation. Yet the basic unit of taxation was not the individual, as it is today, but rather the household. So, where sources have survived, it is often possible to say that there were a certain number of households in a jurisdiction, or whether there were more or fewer households, but this tells us little or nothing about the number of people. Information about household size comes primarily from parish records. Practically everyone was officially a member of the church, whether Protestant or Catholic, and many of the functions we associate with the state were carried out by the church. Generally, affairs of family, marriage, and inheritance were carried out under the auspices of the church rather than the secular government. In the course of the sixteenth century, most governments imposed on the parish priest or pastor the obligation of keeping accurate records of baptisms (not births), marriages, and funerals (not deaths). Thus in France, the Edict of Villers-Cotteret imposed on parish priests the duties of keeping such records. In England these duties were imposed on the clergy in 1538, and in the rest of Catholic Europe after the Council of Trent concluded in 1562. But the accuracy of these records of course depended on the interest and ability of the priest or pastor. Moreover, for most jurisdictions, there are nothing like continuous records before the seventeenth century at the earliest. Since they lacked accurate records, contemporaries' estimates varied widely and must be used cautiously. For example, sixteenth-century estimates of the population of Paris vary between 100,000 and 600,000.

Keeping these cautions in mind, we can still make some broad generalizations about the population of early modern Europe. Generally speaking we can distinguish three broad phases in European population. First, there was a sharp decline after the Black Death of 1348–50 and then a levelling off at a lower level. Following this, there was a recovery beginning in about 1450 and continuing through the sixteenth century. Finally, from about 1600 to about 1750, there is a mixed bag. There was a decline in some areas, stagnation in others, and slight increases in still others.

In the early fourteenth century, before the Black Death, there were likely 60 to 65 million people in Europe. As a result of the Black Death, the population dropped by between one-quarter and one-third, to somewhere between 40 and 50 million, and it remained at this lower level for about a century, until about 1450. From 1450 on we see a substantial growth, so that by 1600 the European population had surpassed its pre-plague level, likely to something like 85 or 90 million. At its peak in the late sixteenth century, the population of Europe broke down approximately as follows:

Germany	20 million
France	18 million
Russia	15 million
Italy	13 million
Spain and Portugal	9 million
Poland	8 million
British Isles	6 million
Low Countries	3 million
Scandinavia	2 million

For the next 150 years, the overall population remained relatively stable, but with significant regional variations. The population of France remained steady at 18–20 million, while that of England increased by about 30 per cent. Germany's population decreased by about 40 per cent as a result of the Thirty Years' War but began to recover later in the seventeenth century. The population of Spain declined by about 25 per cent, and that of Italy from 13 million to 11 million, a decline of 15 per cent. Overall, there was a shift in population south to north, and from east to west. For example, in 1600, the countries of southern Europe (Spain, Portugal, and Italy) accounted for about 33 per cent of Europe's population; in 1700, they accounted for about 30 per cent. In contrast, the British Isles, the Low Countries, and Scandinavia, went from 17 per cent in 1600 to 21 per cent in 1700.

Distribution

The people of early modern Europe lived overwhelmingly in the countryside, in villages that ranged in size from several dozen to 1,000 or even 2,000 in rare cases. In 1600 in western and central Europe, about 5 per cent of people lived in towns of 20,000 or more, and another 20 per cent lived in smaller towns; all the rest, 75 per cent, lived in country villages. In 1500, there were only four cities with more than 100,000 people: Paris, Naples, Milan, and Venice. By 1600, there were at least seven more: Antwerp, Seville, Rome, Lisbon, Palermo, Messina, and Amsterdam. Naples, Paris, and London each had over 200,000 inhabitants. By 1700, these three had 500,000 each, and Madrid, Vienna, and Moscow had grown to over 100,000.

Other than these largest cities, several regions were quite heavily urbanized. One of these was northern Italy where, besides the giants of Venice and Milan, other large cities included Florence, Genoa, and Bologna. Another such region was the Low Countries with towns such as Brussels, Ghent, and Bruges. Yet another was southwestern Germany, where we find Augsburg, Nuremburg, and a number of other smaller cities. In France, after Paris, the two largest cities were Rouen and Lyons, with between 60,000 and 70,000 people. After that, there were no towns with more than 30,000 people, although there were scores of towns with smaller populations. In England, after London, the next largest city was Bristol, with 20,000.

One of the major trends of the period was disproportionate growth in urban population. In England, the urban population doubled in the sixteenth century, mostly in London. In the province of Holland, between 1514 and 1622, the rural population grew by 58 per cent, but that of cities grew almost fivefold. As with population overall, this trend was more pronounced in northern and western Europe.

Birth, Marriage, and Death

Like many pre-modern societies, the birth rate in early modern Europe was high–much higher than is the norm in modern industrialized countries. In 2002, for example, the birth rate in France was approximately 12 per 1000; that is, for every 1000 people there were 12 live births per year. In Germany, it was 9 per 1000, and in the US, 14 per 1000. By way of contrast, the birth rate in the Democratic Republic of the Congo (formerly Zaire) is over 45 per 1000 (2002 estimate). In early modern Europe, the birth rate remained fairly constant at about 35 per 1000 people, which is about the natural maximum and which, although lower than the birth rate in the Congo today, is comparable to many Third World countries experiencing dramatic population growth.

In early modern Europe, population was kept from exploding by two factors—high rates of infant mortality and a relatively late age of marriage. Overall, about one-quarter of the babies born alive would die in infancy, while another quarter would die before puberty. So only about half of the babies born would reach adulthood and have children of their own. As a result of high rates of infant mortality, figures of life expectancy at birth can be misleading: about 28–30 years for men, a little higher for women. In other words, the vast numbers of children who died in infancy or childhood dragged down the statistical average. But if one survived to puberty, the chances of reaching adulthood, marrying, and having a family of one's own were fairly good. Although life expectancy was nowhere near as high as it today, many people lived to reach the age of 60, 70 or even 80.

In contrast to most other pre-modern societies, and contrary to much popular perception, Europeans did not tend to get married at very young ages. Although the average age at first marriage tended to fluctuate somewhat with economic and other conditions, the average age at first marriage was 25–26 for women, and two to three years older for men. In other words, the age at which people got married for the first time was almost exactly what it is today in the modern industrialized west. Popular perceptions of a very early age of marriage tend to come either from literary sources or from the example of the wealthy. For example, Shakespeare has Romeo and Juliet marrying when she is 14 and he is 16. The children of wealthy parents often tended to marry younger because there was significant property at stake, and marriages therefore tended to be arranged by the families. The children of wealthy families were also able to marry at younger ages because they did not have to work and save for years before acquiring enough money to establish their own household.

Another important distinction between early modern Europe and most other traditional societies was the pattern of household formation. The vast majority of people lived in nuclear, two-generation households, that is, one made up of parents and their children. This was directly related to the late age of marriage. Before setting up their own household, couples needed a degree of financial independence which, due to a lack of economic opportunities or most particularly during hard economic times, could take a number of years to achieve. Extended, multi-generational households were the exception, rather than the rule, although in some areas they were more common. Even fewer were joint households: two or more married couples and their children of the same generation. Households and families likely moved through cycles, just as they do today. At any given time the vast majority of households would be made up of nuclear families, but the same family would go through stages, starting out as just the couple and children, but a widowed parent (usually the mother) might move in for a time until her death.

Once married, a woman would become pregnant about every two years until menopause. In the circumstances of the times, this was very likely the maximum rate of conception, that is, without any form of artificial contraception. For one thing, poor nutrition inhibits fertility and makes miscarriages more likely. Indeed, severe malnutrition or famine may cause women to stop menstruating and ovulating altogether. Breastfeeding also inhibits fertility; thus a woman was less likely to conceive while still nursing her youngest child. If the average age at marriage for women was 25 and menopause came at 40, this meant an average of about seven pregnancies per fertile married woman. A number of these pregnancies would of course end in miscarriages or stillbirths. In the course of their childbearing years, therefore, most women would likely see only one or two of their children survive the perils of infancy and childhood and grow into adulthood. So not only did early modern Europeans live in two-generation nuclear households, but the average family size was between four and five. In other words, superficially at least, the demographic and household pattern of the sixteenth and seventeenth centuries looks a great deal like that prevailing in the modern industrialized west: marrying in one's mid- to late twenties, establishing a nuclear family household, and having between two and three children. It is, however, only a superficial resemblance. The late age of marriage was dictated by lack of economic opportunity, not a lengthy education. The relatively small family size was a function of high rates of infant mortality, not readily available artificial contraception.

Artificial contraception was exceedingly rare, if not completely unknown. A number of contemporary writers alluded to methods or concoctions designed to prevent pregnancy, but what these were, no one can say. Statistical evidence from several places indicates that couples were practising some kind of birth control, but in the absence of further evidence, it is likely that abstention and careful timing were the primary means, rather than any artificial method. Certainly much more common was the practice of abandoning unwanted infants, either to elements (which meant certain death) or on the steps of churches and hospitals (which was scarcely more promising).

It likely that most infants so abandoned were illegitimate. Yet it is surprising that the rate of illegitimacy was not higher than it was. One would suspect that such a late age of marriage (up to 12 or 13 years after the attainment of sexual maturity) would lead to rather high rates of premarital sex and illegitimate births. At least until the eighteenth century (when there is some evidence of an increase in illegitimate births), probably not more than 5 per cent of births were illegitimate, that is, occurring less than eight months after the wedding. This is likely explained by scarcity of resources: the coming of an extra mouth to feed before the resources were in place to sustain it could very well mean disaster for all concerned, not only the mother and father, but their respective families as well. There is also a good deal of evidence that while premarital sex may have been quite common, if a pregnancy resulted the man and the woman would quickly be married. In other words, premarital sex may have been common between men and women who had every intention of getting married. Once the woman's fertility was established, the wedding could then proceed.

These demographic patterns had a profound influence on family life. For one thing, grandparents were rare, which helps to explain the preponderance of nuclear families: there were simply not that many grandparents around with whom to form multi-generational households. Because men were usually older at marriage, and because their life expectancy was shorter in any case, there were many widows, but fewer widowers. Many widows would remarry rather quickly after their husband's death, often within months, if they were wealthy or attractive enough; this led to a large number of blended families—and all the conflict and tension that implies. (One has only to think of fairy tales and the stock figure of the wicked stepmother and step-siblings, as in Cinderella for instance.) On the other hand, many widows may have felt liberated by their husband's death and may not have been inclined to remarry, especially if they were able to take over and run the family farm or workshop, as was often the case.

In contrast to today, wealthier people tended to have more children than the average. Greater wealth generally meant better nutrition, which led to easier pregnancies and births. As a result, babies born to wealthy parents tended to survive at a somewhat higher rate. Children of wealthy families did not have to wait as long to get married, since they were already financially secure. As a result, women began their childbearing careers at a younger age and could potentially have more children. As mentioned above, when there was significant property at stake, wealthy families tended to arrange marriages for their children, usually at a younger age than the average. In the more humble levels of society, marriages were much less likely to be arranged. The blessing of parents or guardians was usually sought (as it is today), but parental approval was rarely withheld, and even when it was, it proved no obstacle, since the couple were already adults in their mid-twenties and had some economic security.

In 1960, the French historian Philippe Ariès published an influential book whose English title is *Centuries of Childhood*. In it he argued that early modern European society had no conception of childhood as we know the concept today. Children were thought of as little adults, and were treated callously and often cruelly. Infant and child mortality was so high, or so the argument went, that parents could simply not afford the emotional investment of love and affection in their offspring. The invention of childhood as a separate stage of life with its own unique needs and characteristics would not emerge until the nineteenth century.

Most historians of the family now reject this view as one-sided and misleading. True, there are many examples of cruel treatment of children in early modern

Europe, just as there are today. If one tried to define a norm for the treatment of children in modern western society, one would gain a very skewed picture by relying only on the files of the child welfare departments of local governments. Most of the evidence suggests that parents in sixteenth- and seventeenth-century Europe loved their children deeply and mourned their deaths keenly. Most of the practices usually produced to support Ariès's views have other and more convincing explanations. Child abandonment, as mentioned above, was rare and was almost always the result of an illegitimate birth, or of difficult circumstances on the part of the parents, who in many cases tried to retrieve their child once their fortunes had improved. Although the following, a note pinned to an abandoned baby in Rouen, comes from the late eighteenth century (1789), the sentiments expressed are no doubt typical of the sixteenth and seventeenth centuries as well:

> I was born today, January 7, of a legal marriage. My father and mother are suffering extreme poverty and do not have it in their power to have me christened or to render me the services my tender youth requires them to give me. It is only with the most mortifying distress and acute sorrow that they abandon me.

Infanticide was rare, punishable by death, and was almost always practised by desperate and isolated women, often domestic servants, who faced the loss of their job, reputation, and place in society, marginal as it was.

On the other hand, it is true that childrearing practices did differ from what is current today. Children, like everyone else, were believed to suffer from the taint of original sin and required strict moral discipline. (The idea of the child as innocent and pure until corrupted by society was a product of the Enlightenment of the eighteenth century.) Corporal punishment was the norm, based on the biblical principle "Spare the rod and spoil the child." Formal education, although it became more common in this period, was still expensive and was for the most part limited to the children of the elite. Children did work, often from a very young age. Especially in peasant households, their labour was needed in order for the family to survive and prosper. They would tend animals and perform other tasks appropriate to their age and strength. With a few exceptions, there is little evidence of the widespread economic exploitation of children that would later become common in the mines and factories of the Industrial Revolution, or in the Third World in the twenty-first century. Probably the most accurate assessment would be to say that parents in sixteenth- and seventeenth-century Europe loved and cared for their children no less than we do today, but that this affection was expressed in different ways.

Death

The three great causes of death in early modern Europe were war, famine, and disease. Of the three, war was the least important in terms of numbers. Few people (other than soldiers) died as a direct result of battle. But war, of course, had the result of worsening famines and epidemics. Before the later seventeenth century, armies were largely mercenary in nature, with little loyalty to king or country. With no regular means of supply, they lived off the countryside and its inhabitants. Having an army settle nearby meant disaster, especially in lean years. Soldiers were universally despised and feared for their depredations of the civilian population. Although armies themselves were not very large by modern standards, for every soldier there were approximately five camp followers: wives, mistresses, children, prostitutes, pawnbrokers, servants, or others. They lived in unsanitary conditions, leading to disease, which they spread when they moved on. Moreover, the terror spread by armies had the effect of driving people away, leaving fields untended and crops unharvested, bringing famine in their wake.

It is useful at this stage to examine the nature of warfare in this period. Military historians dispute whether or not there was such as thing as a "military revolution" in early modern Europe and, if there was, when it took place and what it consisted of. There can be no doubt, however, that the conduct of warfare underwent dramatic changes in the sixteenth and seventeenth centuries, whether or not these changes can be considered a revolution. In the Middle Ages, warfare was conducted on a rather small scale, and by mounted knights who fought each other in individual combat. In this world, warfare was a sort of noble sport conducted according to certain commonly understood rules. The advent of gunpowder changed all this, giving the lowliest infantryman the capacity to fell the most distinguished knight. The continued development of firearms and artillery brought a new element to the conduct of war. Now, the ability to organize and pay for large numbers of men for long periods of time became paramount. Most armies were made up of mercenaries commanded by contractors who put them at the disposal of the highest bidder. The Italian Wars of 1494 to 1559, the various wars of religion, and the Thirty Years' War were fought mostly by armies of this type. Often with no connection to the people or country where they were serving, and with no formal means of supply, they had to feed and clothe themselves, usually at the expense of the local population. If they were paid late, as they almost always were (some Spanish armies in the Dutch Revolt went unpaid for periods of years), the mutinous soldiers would "pay" themselves by pillaging any targets they could find.

By the late seventeenth century, however, armies were becoming more disciplined and orderly. The model of this new-style army was that of the Protestant Dutch Republic under Maurice of Nassau. Tactical developments dictated more stringent training and discipline to allow soldiers to fight in the new way. New standards were imposed for recruitment, training, and military discipline. Armies were better supplied and supervised by governments. It is ironic that while war became much more deadly on the battlefield because of continued improvements in weapons and tactics, it became much less deadly to non-combatants. By the eighteenth century, the conduct of warfare was much more refined and "civilized" than it had been in earlier centuries, and it ceased to have as disastrous an effect on civilian populations.

Although famine was widespread, few people actually starved to death; rather, hunger and malnutrition weakened them sufficiently for other causes of death to intervene, usually disease. The single biggest factor in provoking famine was the weather: a cool or wet summer could have disastrous consequences, something that happened again and again, particularly in the 1590s, 1660s, and 1690s. Even if the weather was fine, an isolated disaster like a flood or hailstorm could bring famine. Natural disasters were often compounded by man-made factors. Poor transportation infrastructure made trade in bulky and heavy items like grain prohibitively expensive. Thus one region might starve, while another, not far away, had plenty. But there was simply no practical way to get the surplus to where it was needed. Even within most countries, complicated systems of tolls and customs added to the expense and difficulty of transport. As mentioned above, the presence of soldiers and the disruptions of war also had disastrous effects.

Of course it was the poor who suffered most. Even at the best of times they lived on the edge of survival. In the cities, where ordinary people depended on purchasing their daily bread, a slight rise in prices meant hunger for most, while for the wealthy it simply meant a higher grocery bill. Hunger among the poor was an accepted fact of life; indeed, in 1558 a Roman newsletter reported, "Nothing new here, except that people are dying of hunger." Paradoxically, the countryside, where people grew their own food, often suffered worse. In cities, at least, there were some charitable institutions, and there were greater opportunities for begging or theft.

Epidemic disease was the greatest killer in early modern Europe. The most spectacular incident was of course the bubonic plague, the Black Death, which had wiped out up to one-third of the inhabitants of Europe in the mid-fourteenth century (the earliest cases of the Black Death occurred in 1347 in the seaports of southern France and northern Italy). There were no subsequent European pandemics on that scale, in part because the survivors now had immunity to the bacterium that caused the plague. But of course each new generation had people who were not immune and who were potential victims. Rather than Europe-wide epidemics, in the early modern period we see local or regional outbreaks, often very deadly, but limited in range. So in London for example, a 1563 outbreak of the plague killed a quarter of the population. It recurred again in 1603, 1625, and for the last time in 1665. In Amsterdam, plagues in 1624, 1636, 1655, and 1664 killed respectively one-ninth, one-eighth, one-seventh, and one-sixth of the population. And from 1596-1603 the "great Atlantic plague" killed one million people on the Atlantic coasts of France and Spain; the northern Spanish city of Santander lost almost 2,500 of its 3,000 inhabitants.

We now know that the plague is caused by the bacterium *Yersinia pestis*, which lives in the intestinal tract of a certain kind of flea. This flea typically infests certain types of rodents such as ground squirrels, who are able to coexist with it. Periodically, however, the bacterium will infect others species on which it has a lethal effect. In fact, the Black Death of the fourteenth century was in all likelihood caused by an outbreak among Asian black rats. These infected rats travelled westwards with Mongol armies to the Black Sea. (The black rat is a good climber, and probably a number of them found their way onto ships bound for Europe.) When a rat dies from the plague, the flea will seek another host, animal or human. When the flea bites the people, they are infected. The incubation period is between two and six days. Once infected, the victim develops a fever, chills, headache, fatigue, and painful swellings (buboes) in the lymph glands of the groin and neck. As the name of the plague suggests, death was a common outcome: as late as the early twentieth century, before the widespread availability of antibiotics, mortality rates were between 60 and 80 per cent. But once the infection reaches the lungs of the victims, it becomes known as pneumonic plague and can be spread directly from person to person without the intermediary of rats or fleas; in this form, it was almost always lethal.

None of this information, however, was known before the late nineteenth century. In early modern times, people understood that proximity to the ill somehow infected them but never made the connection between rats, fleas, and the plague. They did, however, attempt to quarantine and blockade stricken areas, occasionally successfully. More often, at the first sign of the plague, all who could flee did so, thereby inadvertently spreading the disease.

Like famine, the plague struck the poor disproportionately. The wealthy had the ability to flee to the countryside, and they lived in more hygienic conditions in the first place. In 1628, an observer writing of an outbreak in the French city of Lyons wrote, "only 7 or 8 people of quality died, and five or six hundred of lower condition." The plague also struck the cities harder than the countryside. Cities were centres of trade, and people came from all over to pursue their affairs, spreading the disease. Early modern cities were crowded and filthy, providing excellent rat habitat. The black rat was a city-dweller, unlike the native Europe brown rat, which preferred the country and was not as conducive a host for the plague bacillus.

The plague remained endemic in Europe for about 350 years, striking once or twice a generation. Although there were no more pandemics on the scale of the Black Death, Europeans could expect an outbreak of the plague about once a decade, regardless of where they lived. Then, in the early eighteenth century, it disappeared, the last major outbreak in Europe occurring in the French Mediterranean seaport of Marseilles in 1720. No one is quite sure it why it disappeared so abruptly. Some historians have posited a change in the rat population; the black rat may have been displaced by the gray rat, a more timid animal less likely to live in crowded cities. Better quarantine and isolation practices may have had some impact, as may changes in construction. For example, as stone and brick houses replaced wood, there were greater distances between human and rat populations. As thatched roofs were replaced by stone and shingles, rats had one fewer place to live. It is also possible that the plague may simply have run its course. We can say with certainty, however, that the disappearance of the bubonic plague was not due to any advance in medical science. People were just as ignorant of its causes in 1750 as they had been in 1350. Certainly the disappearance of the plague was a major factor in the increasing population of the later eighteenth century, since it removed one of the major sources of mortality in early modern Europe. Although the most spectacular, bubonic plague was far from the only killer disease: dysentery, smallpox, diphtheria, influenza, typhus, and typhoid also took a great toll.

The demographic pattern that had characterized Europe since the fourteenth century began to collapse in the course of the eighteenth, which saw the beginnings of the global population explosion that has continued into the twenty-first century. In addition to the disappearance of the bubonic plague removing one of the great sources of mortality, advances in agriculture, beginning in England and Holland, eventually provided ordinary people with more, better, and cheaper food. Better-nourished people have healthier babies, more of whom will live to adulthood to have children of their own. Improvements in agriculture and industry also led to a somewhat higher standard of living, which allowed couples to marry at a slightly younger age and begin their childbearing careers earlier. Therefore, by the time of the French Revolution at the end of the eighteenth century, Europeans were living in a new demographic universe.

CHAPTER TWO

Social Relations and the Structure of Society

Although in some ways the society of early modern Europe may seem distantly familiar to us, and was in many ways the ancestor of our own society, there are important differences. As we will see in this chapter, early modern Europeans thought about social organization differently than we do, and they had different attitudes toward social mobility. Following a discussion of social organization and social mobility, we will examine the various groups that made up early modern society, from the highest of the nobility to the lowliest beggar. During this period, the stability of the social order was threatened by forces that led to social stress and sometimes to violent rebellion. The roles and status of women are also examined, with a focus on both contemporary thought about women and the reality of women's lives. Finally, to discover what it reveals about this society, we will examine one of the most striking and distinctive phenomena of early modern Europe: the great witch hunts of the sixteenth and seventeenth centuries.

Social Organization and Social Mobility

Theories of Social Organization: a society of orders

Different societies in different times have had different ways of organizing themselves and of thinking about that organization. These schemes may or may not accurately reflect reality. Early modern European society was caught between two different types of social organization: that of class, and that of order (contemporaries also called it estate, or quality). I am not using the term *class* in its classic Marxist sense. Rather, I simply mean a view of society that sees people organized horizontally in social strata related first of all to their income and wealth, and secondarily to lifestyle, education, or occupation. This is admittedly a very non-theoretical view, but in part it reflects the contemporary North American discomfort in thinking about class at all. Unlike class, which divides society into horizontal layers, order (or estate, or quality) is a more vertical scheme of organization. In a society of orders, such as early modern Europe, power is exercised by those with status or prestige, rather than by those with great wealth. Of course, they were usually one and the same, but wealth usually followed status and prestige, rather than the other way around. Wealth by itself was no guarantee of prestige or power.

Medieval society had been thought of as consisting of three great estates or orders: those who pray (the first estate or the clergy), those who fight (the second estate, or the nobility), and those who work (the third estate, or the peasantry). Each was organized hierarchically, with each estate having its own rights and privileges, and each gradation having *its* own rights and privileges in turn. This scheme was based primarily on social rather than economic function, and it is highly doubtful that such a simple tripartite scheme ever accurately reflected reality. By the sixteenth century, it would have been obvious that society was not really organized so simply. Nevertheless, Europeans continued to think of society as being organized in orders, even if their schemes were much more complex.

To distinguish a society of orders from modern western industrial society, we must consider several important things. First, it is a view of social organization that enshrines inequality. Each order, each group, has its own rights, liberties, and privileges—its own marks of status and prestige—which it zealously guards and protects. These might be formally enshrined in law or might simply be sanctioned by custom and long usage. This made for endless squabbling among groups over who held what rights. Ceremonial occasions such as civic or religious processions, for example, were often the cause of serious and prolonged wrangling over who should precede whom, who should be received first, and so on. At other times, there were more concrete matters at stake. One of the most precious privileges to which people aspired was the right not to pay certain kinds of taxes.

The inequality of this society of orders was most visibly expressed in sumptuary laws prescribing what each group could or could not wear. It was also expressed in great attention to matters of protocol and deference: one's inferiors had to pay due respect, and in turn one had to pay due respect to one's superiors. There were elaborate codes that governed forms of address depending on a person's rank. Thus a duke was to be addressed as "Your Grace," while a count or baron might be addressed as "My lord." A humble country noble might be addressed as "squire" (*écuyer* in France), while a craftsman might be "maître" or "mister." Failure to employ the proper form, or insisting on a form superior to one's station was a cause for serious concern.

This social inequality was also expressed in many cases in legal inequality. Not everyone was subject to the same laws and legal procedures. In Catholic areas, clergy were often accountable to canon or church law, rather than the law of the secular ruler of the land. Nobles also were subject to different laws and legal procedures in many countries. For example, nobles of a certain rank had the right to be tried only by their peers, not by commoners. If found guilty of a capital offence, a noble was to be beheaded, whereas commoners were hanged, since beheading was usually a swifter and less messy form of execution, more suitable for the exalted of society. Unlike later times, when hanging became a science of sorts, and the scaffolding and rope were adjusted to break the condemned's neck, at this time many hanged convicts suffered a painful and protracted death from strangulation. On the other hand, beheading was not always as clean and swift. In France in 1626, the Count of Chalais was condemned to death for conspiracy against King Louis XIII and Cardinal Richelieu. His friends thought that they could delay the execution by kidnapping the axeman. Not to be deterred, the officials on the scene drafted a bystander to act as executioner. This amateur took more than thirty blows to sever the unfortunate count's head. Nor was legal inequality confined to the ranks of the clergy and nobility. Craft guilds had the legal right to govern the production and sale of their craft, and to discipline members for infractions. In Paris and elsewhere, university students were subject to the legal jurisdiction of the University, rather than that of the municipal government. Municipal authorities in Paris found themselves powerless to punish rowdy or criminal "students," many of whom still laid claim to that status long after finishing their studies.

A further distinction between early modern society and our own is that it was also a corporate scheme, unlike today's individualistic society. Orders, or estates, were groups that had a legally recognized corporate existence embodying its rights and privileges. They had oaths, initiation rights, and regulations that members were sworn to uphold. A person's rights, duties, and privileges depended on the groups to which he belonged. There was no sense of common citizenship or of obligations or rights that belonged to everyone equally.

One of the things that makes early modern European society so complex is the bewildering variety and nature of these orders. They could be geographical in nature; that is, residents of a certain province or region might claim or exercise rights not available to other regions or provinces within the same country. They could be occupationally based, such as guilds, universities, or law courts. They could be socially based, like the nobility or urban communes. They could be religious; indeed the Church as a whole was the preeminent order. But within the Church there were many orders and groups with their own corporate existence: monastic and mendicant orders such as the Benedictines, Franciscans, and Dominicans. There were also lay religious organizations—brotherhoods or confraternities. These organizations might be linked to a certain occupation, supplementing or supplanting guild structures. They might be geographically based—a village or city neighbourhood might have its own confraternity, often devoted to a particular patron saint. They could also be religious or devotional in nature—devoted to a certain saint, or a certain mode of devotion, or a charitable cause.

As if this were not complex enough, there are at least two further complicating factors. First, by the very nature of the system, people were members of more than one order at a time. A hypothetical tradesman could conceivably be a member of a guild, a religious confraternity, an urban commune, and part of a geographically based order. Second, the early modern period saw this whole structure subjected to numerous stresses and strains against which people reacted and protested. But the issues against which they protested, and who took what side, varied tremendously because of the variety and number of orders. A society such as this is capable of fracturing in innumerable ways, along various different fault lines. These stresses and strains came from two main sources: increased fiscal demands from royal governments, as they tried to reduce or eliminate fiscal privileges; and economic changes that fundamentally altered economic relations within society. At various times and under various circumstances, people were torn between different orders, or, as economic changes sped up, found themselves acting more on the basis of economic class interest—as peasants or workers for example—than as members of a recognized order.

Social Mobility

Early modern Europeans tended to think of social order as fixed and unchanging. There was, however, a great deal of social mobility in early modern Europe. But unlike today, contemporaries did not like to acknowledge it—it was seen as the exception rather than the rule. Again in contrast to today, when many people like to emphasize their humble beginnings in order to show how far they have come, in early modern Europe people frequently tried to disguise their humble origins. They would manufacture ancestors and pedigrees in order to show that their family had always been prominent, regardless of their actual origins.

In discussing social mobility, we need to keep several conceptual distinctions in mind. First of all, social mobility can work in both directions: there is upward and downward social mobility. Second, is it collective or individual mobility? That is, is it a question of a single individual or family moving up or down the social scale? Or is an entire group experiencing mobility? In our period, for example, several groups experienced collective social mobility. Actors and actresses experienced collective upward mobility, while clergy and professors experienced downward collective mobility.

In the case of individual mobility, is it intra-generational (within one person's lifetime) or inter-generational (across several generations)? In early modern Europe, the latter was much more common. To take a hypothetical case, a successful peasant might send one of his sons to live in a nearby town in order to sell his produce. His son, in turn, might be sent to a grammar school and then to university in order to prepare for a career as lawyer or civil servant. That son might accumulate enough wealth to live off his investments and would no longer practise an occupation. Instead, he would have acquired a country estate and be living the life of a leisured gentlemen. After several more generations, the family might acquire noble status, all the while attempting to cover up its peasant origins.

It is usually very difficult to track such social mobility, in large part precisely because people were so concerned with covering up their humble roots. It can also be difficult because the scheme of social stratification was itself changing over time. Wealth was always the essential precondition of social mobility, not primarily because people admired wealth so much, but because accumulated wealth was needed to live a lifestyle that conferred greater status. As we will see, this was an age of economic change and turbulence. As a result, wealth came into new hands, and left old ones, meaning that social mobility became easier for some and more difficult for others. Newly wealthy people and groups were shut out of status and power by those who already had it and wanted to keep it. Increasingly, we see a dysfunction between wealth, power, and status. It is these social antagonisms that lie behind much of the conflict of the period.

The Structure of Early Modern Society

The Nobility

As one would expect in a basically agricultural society, land was the chief source of wealth and status, and those who controlled the land were uppermost in society. At the top of the social hierarchy, therefore, was the nobility, which controlled most of the land, or at least a share of the land vastly disproportionate to their overall numbers. Nobles liked to pretend that they were a "race" or caste whose lines and boundaries were demarcated by blood and heredity. In fact, newcomers were being absorbed into the nobility all the time.

There were huge gradations within the nobility in terms of both wealth and status, and each rank had its own precise privileges and obligations and forms of address. At the top of the hierarchy were the high nobility, magnates, or grandees with huge landholdings and tremendous influence at court. They were the intimates of the ruler, the ones who attended him at court and (in theory anyway) fought beside him on the battlefield. They had independent political bases in their own regions and could and often did challenge their ruler's power. At the other end of the spectrum, we have the humble country squires. Often with minimal holdings, and these mortgaged to the hilt, they could often barely feed themselves and their families. In terms of wealth and lifestyle, they may be indistinguishable from the peasants around them. In France, such poor nobles were known as *hobereaux*, in Spain as *hidalgos*. Most nobles, of course, fell somewhere in the middle of these two extremes. If they had no grand pretensions to political power and influence, they were at least the big fish in their small local ponds.

What made a noble? What distinguished the nobility from everyone else? In theory, the nobility's *raison d'être* was warfare. According to the nobility's own self-definition, theirs was a warrior class and their nobility had been earned on the battlefield. Throughout the Middle Ages, when the king had needed an army, he had called upon his vassals, the nobility, who were obligated to fight for him by virtue of the personal and feudal ties between them. By the sixteenth century, however, this was almost completely a thing of the past. Changes in weapons and tactics, such as the use of gunpowder, had rendered the traditional noble knight obsolete. Rulers relied increasingly on professional armies, made up largely of mercenaries. It is true that many nobles found employment in these armies as officers and commanders, but warfare was no longer the centre of the noble world.

Nevertheless, noble culture retained much of its martial origins, and certainly many nobles saw in warfare their main occupation. Thus many nobles continued to pursue a military profession, but in a changed form.

Violence, however, continued as a key element in noble culture. Noble sons were taught to fence, to ride, and to shoot. Hunting remained a noble pastime and was seen as preparation for war. The many wars, civil wars, and rebellions of the period ensured that there was always employment. Indeed, a contributing cause of many of these disturbances was the existence of a large number of people who saw fighting as their vocation. Even when they were not at war, noble culture was a violent one. With nobles being ever sensitive to their and their family's honour, duels among them were a constant source of bloodshed. Kings and rulers issued decree after decree against duelling, but to very little effect. Nor were these duels the romanticized "pistols at dawn" sort of conflict portrayed in movies. Each combatant brought his friends and supporters, and the duels themselves often evolved into vast street brawls in which anything was fair game. In many remote areas, such as the mountains of central France, or in the north of England, where the king's justice was more theoretical than real, many nobles were not averse to careers of theft, banditry, and extortion. Indeed, the issue of noble violence and lawlessness is one of the key areas of conflict between kings and nobles throughout this period.

Nobles also distinguished themselves from the common herd by their lifestyle: they were expected to "live nobly." What this meant in the first instance was they were not to work. They were supposed to live off the revenues of their estates, their investments, and their positions and pensions held from the king. The stringency of this restriction on work varied from place to place and from time to time. For example, in France and Spain, nobles could participate in commerce only indirectly, as investors rather than as direct participants. If they violated this restriction, they ran the risk of *dérogeance*, or loss of noble status with its status and valuable privileges. Never as strong in England as on the continent, this opposition to commerce tended to lessen in the course of the seventeenth century as many governments tried to encourage noble participation in commerce and industry. On the other hand, agricultural work was generally permitted; things like estate management and improvement, selective breeding of plants and animals. In no case, however, was actual manual labour permitted.

Living nobly also involved being seen as magnanimous and generous, often to excess. Nobles were expected to engage in conspicuous consumption, to maintain large households, support numerous servants, and to entertain lavishly without concern for the cost. This aspect of living nobly involved displaying a kind of contempt for their wealth: only a money-grubbing merchant would stoop so low as to worry about the cost of things. Thus, many nobles impoverished themselves in maintaining a noble lifestyle. Although the economic fortunes of the nobility have been the subject of much debate among historians, there is no doubt that for many nobles, "living nobly" meant significant debt and declining wealth.

Yet another important component of nobility were the many privileges that went with membership in this order of society. Contemporaries paid great attention to matters of precedence and respect, depending on the rank of the individuals involved. Among noble privileges throughout Europe were the right to bear arms and the right to a coat of arms that displayed in precise heraldic terms a family's origins and status. On their own estates, many nobles possessed the right to mete out justice to their tenants. Powers of justice could be "low," "medium," or "high." The difference between low and medium justice concerned the maximum amount of the fines the lord's court could assess, while high justice consisted of the right to impose capital punishment. Nobles also claimed a kind of right of private justice to defend their honour, as expressed in the practice of duelling. There were various other sorts of legal privileges: the right to be tried by one's peers, or beheading instead of hanging if convicted of a capital offence.

Without question, the most important and concrete noble privilege was exemption from most forms of direct taxation. In theory this was justified by the concept that the nobility paid their taxes in blood; that is, that because they served the king by fighting for him, they had earned their tax exemptions. In France, for example, most nobles (and many townsmen as well) were exempt from paying the *taille*, the major direct tax,[1] although they did pay other sorts of taxes, including sales taxes. In the Spanish kingdom of Castile, nobles were exempt from all royal taxes. Although the details varied from time to time and place to place, all nobles claimed fiscal privileges of one sort or another.

The economic and political changes of the sixteenth and seventeenth centuries brought a great deal of change to the nobility, change that challenged their economic and political domination of society. These economic changes will be taken up in greater detail in a subsequent chapter. For now, suffice it to say that economic changes placed a premium on producing for the marketplace rather than for local consumption, and that first inflation and then stagnation changed the economics of estate management. As mentioned above, there has been a great deal of debate concerning the economic fate of the nobility in this period. All attempts at a general conclusion have proved futile, for there are enough exceptions to render any generalization useless. Many nobles were able to adapt to these changed circumstances, while many others were not. The important thing, however, is that conditions were changing and that nobles had to change as well if they wanted to maintain the wherewithal to live nobly.

Politically as well, nobles found themselves the object of far-reaching changes. Throughout the Middle Ages, rulers had always attempted to curb the independent political power of the nobility. This political power was derived from feudalism, where, in essence, royal power was contracted out to local warlords. As we have seen, by the end of the Middle Ages, feudalism had lost its military *raison d'être*, but the political legacy of feudalism remained—a nobility that exercised significant political power outside the direct command of the king. By the sixteenth century, rulers had made important strides in disciplining this independent political power, but its potential remained strong. At times of crisis, such as the

Wars of Religion or the Fronde in France, the nobility were more than willing and able to exercise this power in opposition to the royal government. Nobles tended to see themselves as the king's natural partners in governing rather than as his obedient subjects. They owed the king obedience when he was right, but when he was wrong they were permitted, even obliged, to disobey him. In most countries this right was assumed and customary, but in others, such as Hungary and Poland, it was expressly spelled out. Although it did not apply only to the nobility, this attitude is vividly displayed in the oath of allegiance sworn by the subjects to the king of the Spanish kingdom of Aragon: "We who are as good as you swear to you who are no better than we, to accept you as our king and sovereign lord, provided you observe all our liberties and laws; but if not, not."

Throughout the later Middle Ages, kings and rulers had come to rely on ministers and advisors who were not members of the traditional feudal nobility. This was a trend that continued and intensified during the sixteenth and seventeenth centuries. Kings preferred to rely on men who had no power base of their own, who were either not noble or who had been recently ennobled. Unlike the situation in the later Middle Ages in most European states this trend was coupled with significant growth in the royal bureaucracy. Thus, not only were the great nobles increasingly excluded from power at the centre of the government, but nobles found their power being infringed upon by non-noble or recently ennobled men in local government as well.

Indeed, service in the royal bureaucracy was the major avenue of social advancement for the middle class, a subject that will be examined when we look at the middle classes later in this chapter. Although these "new" nobles were in most ways legally equal to the traditional nobility, they were never quite accepted by the older nobles, who liked to pretend that their noble status stretched back centuries. In fact new nobles were being created all the time, and very few of the "traditional" or "feudal" nobility could trace noble lineage back more than several generations. Once noble status was achieved, the newcomers tried to pull the ladder up after themselves. Another major change that took place in the sixteenth and seventeenth centuries was that cash-strapped governments resorted to selling positions in the bureaucracy, which under certain conditions conferred nobility upon their owners. Less frequently, but more spectacularly, rulers sometimes simply sold titles of nobility outright. In 1611, King James I of England (1603–25) created the title and rank of baronet precisely to be sold to mobility-conscious commoners.

England was somewhat distinct when it came to the nobility, in that a much stricter distinction was made between the titled nobility or peerage, and the gentry. On the continent, all of the sons of a nobleman were themselves noble, although only one (usually the eldest) would inherit the title (if any) and the ancestral estate. In England, on the other hand, the rule of primogeniture was strictly enforced. That is, only the eldest son was himself noble, and the bulk of the father's holdings, including the title, passed only to him. The younger sons and their descendants were not noble, although many of them were still very wealthy and powerful. Nevertheless, they were not entitled to the same privileges as their older brother, including sitting in the House of Lords. Thus, the gentry (as they came to be known in England) were the functional equivalent of the lesser nobility on the continent. Accordingly, the pattern of social mobility differed somewhat as well. In England, it was relatively easier to move from the ranks of prosperous farmer or yeoman into the ranks of the gentry. The real barrier was between the gentry and the peerage or titled nobility. On the continent, on the other hand, it was more difficult to penetrate the ranks of the lower nobility, but relatively easier to acquire a title.

The Middle Classes or Bourgeoisie

The middle classes of early modern Europe were an enormously diverse group, hence the plural terminology. In many cases, they are defined by what they are not. Therefore, in the social terminology of the Middle Ages, they were neither noble nor peasant, hence the name "middle" classes. Unlike the peasants and nobles, who lived for the most part in the countryside, they resided in towns, hence the name "bourgeoisie." (In its original meaning, a bourgeois is someone who lives in a "bourg" or town.) Although there was a rural middle class, made up of enterprising capitalistic farmers, there was little interaction between them and the urban middle class, and they inhabited different worlds. To contemporaries, "rural bourgeoisie" would have been a contradiction in terms.

The "rising bourgeoisie" is one of the great explanatory myths in European history, one that has been invoked to explain almost everything from the Middle Ages through to the twentieth century. Like most myths, it helps to explain some things, but it also obscures others. It does have some truth to it, but not in the way one might expect. In fact, European bourgeois were continually rising from the twelfth through the nineteenth centuries, but as individuals, not as a group. The top levels of the bourgeoisie were continually being absorbed into the nobility. It was the aspiration of middle-class people to become noble, both to escape taxation and because of the status and prestige that nobility brought with it. It was really not until the nineteenth century that the bourgeoisie as a whole underwent collective upward mobility.

When we talk about the early modern bourgeoisie, we are talking about people who lived in cities and who were in charge of some economic activity or exercised a profession such as lawyers, physicians or civil servants, or who lived off their investments. We are not talking about the wage labourers or journeymen, but this group does include master craftsmen who owned and operated their own shops. It was, as mentioned above, the ultimate goal of the bourgeois to attain noble status. In order to achieve this goal, they needed to acquire a significant amount of wealth in order to leave their business behind, purchase land, and live nobly. The most common method of acquiring noble status was through office-holding in the government. In most of early modern Europe, cash-starved governments resorted to selling government positions for ready cash. This was known as venality of office, and the holders of these positions are referred to now as venal officeholders or venal bureaucrats. This practice was most pronounced and systematized in France but was present to a greater or lesser extent almost everywhere. Some of these positions conferred nobility upon their holder in and of themselves. In France, for example, the position of judge in a *parlement* or sovereign law court automatically conferred nobility on its holder. Other, less exalted positions might confer nobility under certain conditions, for example if the post was held in the same family for several generations, and its holders "lived nobly" all the while.

As soon as they could, therefore, aspiring bourgeois left trade and commerce behind in order to "live nobly," that is, without working in an ignoble occupation. Many of them lived as *rentiers*, that is, from the proceeds of their investments or *rentes*. Since all governments exceeded their means, they had to borrow money to fulfill their obligations. One means of doing this was through issuing what we would call bonds but were called *rentes* in France, *juros* in Spain, and other names elsewhere. While these *rentes* may have paid a relatively low rate of return, they were safe, or at least safer than many other investments, and were snapped up by socially ambitious bourgeois. Other kinds of *rentes* were private affairs, where a rich bourgeois might lend money to a poor peasant or nobleman with his land as collateral, a sort of mortgage or home equity loan. Often, the terms of such loans enabled the borrower to pay only interest installments, while the principal had to be repaid in a lump sum. This, of course, rarely happened. Bad luck, a bad harvest, or bad business decisions might lead to various fines for defaulting on payments, and ultimately often to the seizure of the property pledged as collateral. In this way the bourgeois might acquire the country estate he needed to live nobly. Those few bourgeois who succeeded were absorbed into the nobility, at least in terms of legal status, even if the "real" nobles did not fully accept them, seeing them as *nouveaux riches parvenus*. In several generations, however, the descendants of these new nobles themselves looked down on newcomers such as their own grandfathers or great-grandfathers had been.

Even among those bourgeois who were not yet successful in their noble aspirations, we see increasing stratification taking place. In towns and cities all over Europe, the wealthy and powerful bourgeois became a kind of urban patriciate, an oligarchy that dominated their city's social, economic, and political life. Increasingly, their horizons and ambitions went beyond their home town. They were involved in international trade and finance and had political, social, and economic ambitions beyond the town walls. As they moved up the social ladder, they tended to leave their businesses and trades behind. They sent their sons to university, acquired royal offices, and aspired to the leisurely life of a *rentier*.

Those left behind, the ordinary bourgeois, the master craftsmen, were increasingly on the outside looking in. Previously, they had all been part and parcel of the urban commune, belonging to the same craft or merchant guilds, and the same religious confraternities. Now, however, they were differentiated by wealth, power, status, and lifestyle. In short, whereas previously they had been bound together in the different orders of society (guild, commune, confraternity) that united their members in a vertical fashion, now they begin to behave more like horizontal economic classes than vertical orders. Urban patricians, no matter where their wealth came from originally, now had more in common with other patricians, both in their own towns and in others, than they did with members of their own trade or guild or urban commune. Likewise, the ordinary bourgeois found themselves increasingly united in their resentment at being shut out of meaningful participation in the fabric of urban life. What was true at this level was also true at the next level down in urban society, that of journeymen and urban wage labourers.

Urban Wage Labourers and Journeymen

Unlike the bourgeois examined above, the journeymen and wage labourers were in charge of no economic enterprise of their own, whether it be a vast international trading or financial empire, or a humble craftsman's shop. They were directly dependent upon being employed by others for their livelihood. In examining this stratum of urban society, we must make a fundamental distinction between skilled and unskilled labour. Skilled labour was organized in guilds, whereas most unskilled labour was not. Virtually every aspect of manufacturing and service was organized in guilds, from the still familiar—butchers, bakers, cobblers; to the less familiar—goldsmiths, coopers, sawyers, teamsters to the now completely obscure—such as *perruquiers* or wigmakers. Although guilds performed some of the same functions as modern labour unions, the comparison is completely misleading, since all the practitioners of the trade, bosses and employees alike, belonged to the guild. Guilds controlled quality, production, and consumption and decreed what kinds of items could be produced and sold at what prices. They also acted as charitable or benevolent associations, providing for widows and orphans of members, and they often lent a helping hand to members down on their luck.

Admittance to guilds was strictly regulated and controlled. An aspiring craftsman first had to serve as an apprentice for a period of years in a master's household, typically beginning at the age of 12 or 13. If he successfully completed his apprenticeship, that is, if he satisfied the requirements of his master and his guild, he then became a journeyman. As the name implies, he was expected to leave his hometown for a period of several years and practise his craft in other towns. As he moved from town to town, he would have to produce letters of reference from the guild in his hometown and from his previous employers attesting to his proficiency and his character. This facet of life in early modern Europe is reflected in the fairy-tale convention of the young man setting out to seek his fortune. In the normal course of things, journeymen could look forward to a more secure future once they became masters in their own right. Typically, in a somewhat idealized picture, becoming a master, getting married, and becoming a citizen all went together as rites of passage into adulthood and full participation in urban society. In order to become a master of his craft, the aspiring journeyman had to meet a number of qualifications. He usually had to post a bond committing him financially to the guild. He also had to provide evidence of satisfactory performance as a journeyman. And he had to provide evidence of proficiency in his craft in the form of a "masterpiece," which represented his very best work.

But just as the urban ruling class was separating itself from the ordinary bourgeois, so the ordinary bourgeois was trying to separate himself from the journeymen. Masters were continually making it much more difficult for journeymen to become masters in their own right. They might raise the bond necessary to practically unattainable levels, or they might assign more difficult and expensive masterpieces. In an age of rising population and economic changes, masters wanted to protect their own privileged position and keep their monopoly tightly controlled. Journeymen were increasingly relegated to being a permanent class of urban wage labourers, dependent on finding employment in a master's shop. This was a very insecure existence, a kind of permanent adolescence, which excluded journeymen from full participation in urban life. It was of course greatly resented by the journeymen, who formed their own associations, much like labour unions, with their own rituals, initiations, and network of contacts. Similarly, the masters of the various crafts found they had more in common with other masters of different crafts than they did with the journeymen in their own craft. Once again behaviour influenced by economic class crowded out behaviour according to order. So, wherever there was urban disorder in early modern Europe, journeymen were almost always in the forefront. They had a clear group consciousness and agenda, they were hostile to the urban ruling class and master craftsmen, and they were already organized.

Below the journeyman on the early modern social ladder were the unskilled labourers, often hired on a day-to-day basis with virtually no security. These were the unskilled construction workers who dug the foundations and carried the lumber and bricks, the ditch diggers, the water carriers, and so forth, who had nothing to sell, no skill on which to rely except their muscle power. In addition, a large number of the inhabitants of an early modern city were domestic servants: the cooks, laundry maids, and so forth. They were often economically quite secure, depending on the nature of their master or mistress, because they were housed and fed in their employers' household. Their social status, however, was very low. Not having an established residence of their own condemned them to a kind of perpetual childhood in the eyes of early modern Europeans.

The Peasants

As we have seen, the vast majority of people were peasants who lived in rural villages ranging in size from several dozen to several thousand in exceptional cases. There were, however, enormous variations in the nature of peasant and village life based on a variety of factors: the village's location, its soil, its proximity to a major centre and market for its produce, and so forth. At the level of the individual peasant family, the most significant variables were the size of the family's landholdings and the nature of their tenancy.

In the aftermath of the Black Death, those peasants who survived were in a relatively advantageous position. Because there were fewer people while the amount of arable land remained constant, land became cheaper while labour became more expensive. Most landlords found themselves having to grant their tenants favourable terms in order to obtain the labour they needed to cultivate their land. In western Europe, at any rate, this led to the elimination of serfdom. As the population, especially the urban population, revived in the late fifteenth and early sixteenth centuries, peasants (particularly those who lived near a city) were able to sell their produce on the market. Therefore, for most peasants the late fifteenth and early sixteenth centuries were a relatively good time: the average family's holdings increased in size, rents were low, wages were high, and there was money to be made selling one's produce in town.

Around the middle of the sixteenth century, however, the tide turned against peasants. Although the timing and severity of this shift varied from place to place, that it occurred on a wide scale is undeniable. The population came up against the limits of what was still primitive agriculture. As the population grew, landholdings were subdivided among generations to the point where many became too small to support a family. This meant that peasant families needed to find other work to supplement their income. But by this time, a rising population increased the supply of labour, thereby decreasing its price, that is, the wages paid to the labourer. Furthermore, the sixteenth century was a time of significant inflation, meaning that the goods peasants needed to buy on the market went up in price, just as real wages were declining. Peasants were caught in a vicious "scissors effect," or what one leading historian has called "the twin processes of pauperization."[2]

The legal nature of peasants' tenancy also varied tremendously. Although peasants had the right to farm their land to support themselves and their families, few could claim outright ownership of the land they farmed. In a sense, they "shared" ownership of their land with the lord of the manor. This was a vestige of the medieval past in which feudal lords were granted manors in order to provide for themselves and their families, and to provide them the resources needed to equip themselves for war. Although this is a very different concept of property ownership than we are accustomed to today, in some ways the two share some common features: although one may own a piece of land today, in most places what one may do with it is limited by such factors as covenants and zoning laws. In other words, just as we are not free to do whatever we wish with our land, the peasants of early modern Europe were governed by the tenancy restrictions and conditions of their landlord. These restrictions were often bewildering in their variety and complexity and differed tremendously from time to time and place to place. Typically, peasants had to pay various kinds of fees and dues to the lord. Some were paid in cash, while others were paid in produce. How these were paid, and how much, was determined by custom or negotiation. Peasants might also be obliged to obtain certain services from the lord—to grind their grain in his mill, press their grapes in his winepress, or bake their bread in his oven—for all of which they were charged.

Within the village lands, the lord also had land over which he had exclusive rights—the *demesne*. Typically, in earlier times, as unfree serfs, peasants had had to perform labour services on the lord's land. In France this was known as the *corvée*, while in Bohemia it was called *robot* and went by other names elsewhere. Whatever it was called, it was universally hated, since the lord's demands invariably came at times such as sowing and harvest, when peasants' labour was most urgently required in their own fields. By the sixteenth century, most peasants in western Europe were personally free and no longer serfs. Labour services were largely a thing of the past, but the various fees and other obligations lived on.

In a period of inflation, such as the sixteenth century, payments in cash lost value, so peasants who owed their lord cash generally made out better than those who owed him produce, but only if their tenancy was secure. In addition, because of growing populations, especially urban ones, tremendous profits were to be made in growing crops for the open market rather than local subsistence. Accordingly, landlords everywhere tried to renegotiate leases to get better deals for shorter terms. Or they might rent their *demesne* lands out to peasants, rather than cultivating it directly themselves. Another tactic was to assert the lord's rights over the village's common lands, such as meadows, pastures, and forests, which belonged to the community as a whole. These lands could be extremely important to the villagers: they might put a cow or a goat to pasture to supplement their diet with milk or cheese; or they might gather firewood or pick berries in the forest. In lean times, access to the common lands could mean the difference between survival and starvation. Everywhere, lords sought to "enclose" common lands to assert their rights of ownership. Often the land would be turned into pasture on which to graze sheep for their wool.

Besides the size of the family landholding, the other important variable on which the fortunes of peasants rested was the nature of their tenancy: that is, whether lords could easily break or amend the terms of peasant cultivation of the land, and whether the various dues and obligations were written and fixed or customary and therefore more susceptible to alteration. As we will see when examining the agrarian economy, the major change that took place in the sixteenth and seventeenth centuries was an increasing emphasis on production for the market rather than for subsistence. Who benefitted from this change, peasant or lord, depended to a great extent on the nature of the peasant's tenancy and on the ruthlessness or effectiveness of the lord.

Whatever the regional details, the broad trend was toward increased stratification in the countryside. There were large-scale rural capitalists who engaged in agriculture as a business from which they drew profit. Known in England as yeomen, in France as *fermiers*, they either owned their land outright (that is, free of feudal obligations), or leased it from a noble, or some combination of the two. Below these rural businessmen was a class of prosperous peasants, the village elite. Known as *laboureurs* in France, they grew enough food not only to feed themselves and their families, but also to sell on the market. As the elite of the village, from their ranks were drawn the mayors, the tax assessors and collectors, and the holders of other important local positions. Below the *laboureurs* were economically insecure peasants, the copyholders or *manouvriers*. Lacking enough land to support their families, they were dependent on sharecropping or on working for wages on someone else's land, whether a noble or bourgeois landlord, a *fermier*, or a *laboureur*. Below them were the landless labourers, entirely dependent on working for someone else as a hired hand or sharecropper.

In general terms, the social structure in the country was more fluid than in the city, at least up to the level of the gentry or the lower nobility. The primary distinction was wealth, unencumbered by guild regulations or ancestry. It was relatively common for peasants to advance to the rank of *fermie*r or yeoman, especially in England. But this also worked in reverse—for even the most secure peasant, only a few bad harvests, or a bit of bad luck, or the scourge of war stood between his family and destitution. Forced to rely on loans from bourgeois *rentiers*, many peasants lost their land and what little security they had and joined the population of the floating poor, the vagabonds, and the criminal underworld.

The Margins of Society

Below the level of wage labourers in both city and countryside there was a floating marginal population of paupers, beggars, bandits, thieves, and so forth. A large number of these (probably a majority) were genuine unfortunates who had fallen on hard times in changing economic circumstances. But there was also a permanent, more or less criminal underworld; in fact, the lines between criminal and legitimate behaviour were not always clearly demarcated. Both groups floated back and forth between city and countryside, but cities were magnets because of the opportunities for charity, begging or theft. Contemporaries were struck by the increase in the numbers of the poor, and saw a vast army of vagrants that threatened the established order. They did, however, distinguish between the deserving poor and the "sturdy beggars," that is, those capable of work but who preferred a life of begging or crime.

For the deserving poor, systems of poor relief, with workhouses, orphanages, and hospitals, were established. But the supply never came close to meeting the demand, and there was a universal sense of being overwhelmed by a vast army of the poor. In the early modern period, there was a fundamental shift in the conception and organization of charity and poor relief. In the Middle Ages, alms to the poor were seen as a good work, benefitting not only the recipient but also the donor. The recipient benefitted of course through the charity itself, allowing him to survive; the donor also benefitted in that giving alms assisted in his salvation. There was also a general understanding that the poor would pray for the spiritual welfare of their benefactors. Indeed, in their wills many people provided for the poor with the expectation that they would mourn at their funerals and pray for their souls. In any case, charity was a one-on-one affair, with a personal connection between the donor and recipient. Increasingly in the sixteenth century, there was a sense that such random acts of personal charity were insufficient for the task at hand.

This understanding and the changes that arose from it cut across religious lines. While Protestants of course denied the importance of good works for salvation, even many Catholics recognized that haphazard alms were not up the job. One of the advocates of a new approach to charity was the Spanish Catholic humanist Juan Luis Vives. In his 1526 book *De subventione pauperum* (*On the relief of the poor*), Vives proposed outlawing begging and establishing institutions such as hospitals, which would provide not only for the material needs of the poor, but also for their spiritual and moral needs. The chief motivation for charity was therefore not the desire to perform good works and thus attain salvation, but rather the fulfillment of one's moral and civic duty toward one's less fortunate fellows.

Consequently, there was a widespread movement to organize and systematize the delivery of charity. Many more conservative Catholics were alarmed by this, regretting the loss of the personal relationship that bound together beggar and donor, but ultimately the new impulse won the day. The organization of charity was almost everywhere a lay and governmental undertaking, rather than a religious or ecclesiastical one. In England, for example, the Elizabethan Poor Law of 1601 localized poor relief at the parish level. Begging was outlawed; the able-bodied were to be put to work in houses of correction, while children were to be apprenticed and the sick cared for at the expense of the parish. Most of the rest of Europe lacked the national direction seen in England: in most other places, the organization and delivery of poor relief were left entirely in the hands of local authorities. It was a rare town that did not have its own organization for managing charity and the poor.

Concurrent with this shift was an effort to improve the lot of the poor, rather than simply to provide for their immediate need for food or shelter. Orphanages were set up to care for and educate abandoned and orphaned children. Hospitals were set up to care for the sick or, in reality, to provide a place to die. Many historians who have studied this phenomenon have emphasized that this was simply another means of social control, that it was an effort to shut the poor up behind walls and closed doors, to get them off the streets, to "improve" them according to the prevailing norms of society. No doubt there was an element of truth in this: authorities everywhere recognized the danger posed to the social order by vagabonds and the destitute. On the other hand, many people in positions of authority undoubtedly were genuinely motivated by a sense of religious and civic obligation, and they were attempting to deal with a very difficult and intractable problem in the best way they knew how. It is certain, however, that their best efforts ultimately came nowhere close to meeting the need.

For the other sort—the undeserving poor or the "sturdy beggars," and the criminal underworld—there was no sympathy at all. In an age without established police forces and very rudimentary law enforcement, the authorities relied on making examples of those caught, meting out savage punishments to deter others. These included, but were not limited to, whipping, amputation of hands and/or feet, branding, cutting off noses or ears, and cutting out or drilling holes through tongues. An English law of 1572 prescribed harsh penalties for vagrancy: whipping and drilling through the ear for the first offence, being adjudged a felon for the second, and death for the third. In France, the theft of a loaf of bread was punishable by three years' rowing in the royal galleys, a virtual death sentence.

These marginal populations of thieves, beggars, and vagrants organized themselves in their own orders, with their own rituals and rights, a mirror image of "respectable society." In Rome for example, beggars organized themselves according to their preferred method of begging: purse-snatchers, those who pretended to be sick, those who claimed to be temporarily out of work, and so on. There were criminal gangs who terrorized city neighbourhoods in much the same way as modern organized crime. Large parts of the countryside were virtually ruled by bandits who preyed on both locals and transients. Some of these also acted as protectors of the locals and assumed a mythic status as "gentleman bandits" much like Robin Hood.

Change, Stress, and Rebellion

Popular revolts were a common occurrence in early modern Europe, whether in the cities or in the countryside. In the past, historians had tended to see peasant revolts as the primitive fury of a mindless mob striking out against their oppressors. Historical research, however, has dispelled this view; it was in large part a creation of those who were the targets of the revolts. The authorities saw these rebels as dangerous animals who could be dealt with only through violent repression, and it was their views that influenced later historians. In fact, it was not the lowest of the low, the landless poor and marginal population discussed above, who fomented and fought in the revolts. It was those who felt they had something to lose, not those who had nothing. What makes studying popular revolts so difficult is that sometimes they were undertaken to defend the rights and privileges of an order, sometimes of a class. This in turn depended in large part on where the perceived threat came from.

In general, revolts and rebellions were provoked by change, not by revolutionary or ideological aspirations. We can distinguish two kinds of triggers or causes: increased taxation and increased exactions from landlords. These causes in turn reflect two of the major changes taking place in this period: the growth of the centralized state with its bureaucracy and fiscal needs driven by warfare, and the changes in the rural economy driven by producing for the market rather than subsistence. In the case of the former, we are more likely to see an order-based revolt, with clergy, bourgeois, and nobles siding with the workers and peasants, since increased taxes hit everybody. In the latter case, it looks much more like class warfare, pitting the economic interests of the peasants against those of the landlords, whether noble, bourgeois, or clerical. The urban variant of this has journeymen and wage-labourers reacting against the urban oligarchies and masters who were restricting their rights and shutting them out of political power, as discussed above. In both cases, the rebels knew what they wanted, and their aims were generally conservative: to restore an often idealized past state of affairs.

The trigger for revolts was almost always an unpopular new measure: a new lease, a new tax, new regulations, enclosures, and so forth. The rebels wanted to restore the "good old days" even if they existed only in legend and the popular mind. Even as they resisted, and sometimes killed the king's agents and tax collectors, they averred their loyalty to the king himself. They were rebelling instead against the king's "evil advisors" or his greedy tax collectors or corrupt judges who were abusing the king's power. Once the revolts had broken out, the rebels adopted the forms and styles they were familiar with from their own popular culture. Thus, there was often an oath to the cause, similar to oaths of guilds and confraternities. The violence itself was often played out in ritualistic ways, adopted from the themes of popular culture. One of these was based on the theme of the "Land of Cockaigne," where everything is turned around: the expensive becomes ordinary and vice versa.[3] Peasant visions of plenty come true here: houses are thatched with pancakes, rivers run with beer, and pigs run around with forks conveniently stuck in their backs. This is closely related to the theme of the "world turned upside down," a typical theme in Carnival or Mardi Gras celebrations, where the traditional order of things was turned upside down, where disorder reigned. Carnival celebrations typically functioned as a safety valve, to allow people to blow off steam and escape the constraints of everyday life. They also served to re-emphasize the traditional order, in essence giving "ordinary" people a chance to have some fun before being reined in once again by those in charge. The line between traditional forms like Carnival and real rebellion is often very fine and indistinct. This fine line is exemplified in one of the best-studied popular revolts in early modern Europe, which took place in the southern French city of Romans in 1580. Preceded by several years of peasant unrest caused by increased taxation, and misery caused by warfare and local banditry, a cloth worker named Paumier seized control of the city. Frightened by the threat to the social order, and with their fears reinforced by the normal disorders of Carnival, the royal and civic authorities struck back, murdering Paumier and retaking control of the city and the surrounding countryside.[4]

With several exceptions, such as the various groups that arose during the English Civil War, early modern rebellions were not driven by revolutionary agendas, nor were they carried out by the truly desperate and destitute. They were the work of integrated members of their community, of peasants and journeymen who felt their tenuous position in society threatened by some new development: a new tax, increased rent for their land, new guild regulations that favoured the bosses, and so on. They were not a primitive mob striking in blind and illogical fury. They knew what they wanted and employed the means they were familiar with to get it.

The Roles and Status of Women

It is just as impossible to generalize about women's roles and status in sixteenth- and seventeenth-century Europe as it is in twenty-first-century western society. In both cases, there are substantial discrepancies between theory and reality. In our modern western world, women are legally equal to men in virtually all respects: women can vote, hold office, own and run a business, buy and sell property, attend university, choose their own occupation, and so on. Yet not many people would agree that this theoretical equality is perfectly realized in reality. Women still face substantial obstacles and prejudices in business, politics, and education. In early modern Europe, women were legally inferior to men. Indeed some thinkers questioned whether women should be considered human at all. Until they were married, they were under the legal control of their father, and afterward, of their husband. Generally speaking, they could not participate in political life, or buy and sell property on their own. In religion, women's roles were subservient to men's. Yet this legal and societal subordination was not perfectly realized in reality either: women did in fact do many of the things that they were not supposed to be able to. So, rather than talk about women's roles and status in general terms—since there is no blanket generalization that does justice to reality, then or now—we need to ask not about women generally, but about specific women and types of women.

Scientific and medical authorities (all men, of course) maintained that women were physically inferior to men in virtually all respects, although there were differences regarding details. Men were believed to be more rational, while women were more suspect to the influence of their bodily humours. (The word "hysteria" is derived from the Greek word for uterus.) Female reproductive organs were widely believed to be identical to the male, only turned inside out. Women were believed to be especially susceptible to sexual urges, and fear of unbridled female sensuality is widespread in the treatises of the day.

Women at all levels of society played an important role in economic life. For the vast majority of families who were peasants, women's roles and labour were essential to the family's survival. Although most tasks associated with growing grain, such as ploughing and harvesting, were the province of men, women took part by bundling the sheaves of grain or by gleaning the grain that had fallen to the ground during the harvest. Women were also responsible for much of the work that took place in or near the household, allowing them the flexibility required for their roles as caregivers for small children. Thus, a woman's tasks might include sewing and mending clothes, tending small animals such as goats or chickens, and tending the garden plot where she grew vegetables either for household consumption or for sale in a nearby town or market. Women also were intimately involved in the processing and sale of the products resulting from these tasks: making and selling cheese and butter, selling eggs, and so on.

The increased prominence of production for sale on the market and the proto-industrialization of the countryside (both discussed in Chapter 3) also affected the economic roles of rural women. On the one hand, increasing commercialization in the countryside opened up more economic opportunities for women, both as producers and as merchants. On the other hand, women's wages were generally about half of what men were paid for comparable work, since it was universally assumed that a woman's earnings were supplementary to her husband's or father's. Therefore many women laboured in the fields of landlords, tended olive groves or vineyards, or spun thread for urban cloth merchants, but they earned much less than men for the same work. Women were also very prominent as domestic servants in the households of better-off peasants, the gentry, and the nobility. In these positions, women could perform a variety of tasks, including laundry, child-care, cooking, and cleaning. These positions were generally held by younger women of families who could not otherwise afford a dowry for their daughters. The hope was that these young servant women would eventually be able to save enough for a dowry and then marry and establish a household and family of their own. Domestic service was thus a phase of life for many young women, rather than a life-long occupation.

In the cities, women's economic roles were more varied but were still strictly limited in both theory and practice. In the household of a master craftsman, the wife would often supervise the workers and servants. Indeed, there was at this time only a vague distinction between workshop and household. The journeymen in the master's shop, for example, were usually considered part of the household rather than strictly as employees in the modern sense. Depending on the ability and education of the woman, and the nature of the marriage and her husband, she might keep accounts, do the purchasing, sell the articles made, and invest the profits. Upon the death of her husband, she might operate the shop independently, pending her remarriage to another master of the same craft. Many guilds in many places allowed women to participate in the guild, but only very rarely on an equal basis with men. Women might, for example, continue making and selling wares but had no voice in the affairs of the guild, although they were usually still expected to pay the same fees and otherwise meet all the same obligations as male members.

Most urban women, of course, were not nearly so fortunate. Many women ran small retail enterprises, either in permanent shops or in stalls in the marketplace. They might sell items like pies and sausages that they made themselves, or eggs, cheese, and butter made in the country by other women. As in the country, domestic service was an important source of income and employment for women. According to some research, as many as one in twelve people were servants, and two-thirds of those were women. The textile industry also provided employment for many women, although as in most other cases, women were paid much less than men for similar or comparable work. Women might also work in, or even own or run, inns or taverns.

Many women, then as now, were forced to resort to selling their bodies in the form of prostitution in order to survive. In the Middle Ages and into the early modern period, many in positions of authority thought of brothels and prostitutes as necessary evils. If prostitutes were not available, young men might assault and rape "honourable" women or, even worse in the eyes of many, resort to homosexual relations. So many towns had official brothels, where prostitutes were licensed, taxed, and inspected for venereal diseases. The impact of the Protestant and Catholic Reformations and the attendant attempt at the moral reform of society (see Chapter 4), eventually did away with these official brothels, but not, of course, with prostitution itself. Prostitution and prostitutes thus became increasingly criminalized and marginalized. Few occupations were exclusively female. Prostitution was one, although few can have aspired to that; another was midwifery. Until the mid-seventeenth century in some areas, and until much later in most, childbirth was an exclusively female affair. Men (including the father) were rarely present, unless the wife was dying or needed medical attention from male physicians. Many midwives, especially in rural areas, also doubled as healers. Although without formal medical education, they were often skilled in herbal remedies and practical solutions. Increasingly, however, medicine was being dominated by men, to the exclusion of women. These men were either barber-surgeons who performed crude and often fatal surgery (or blood-letting, the most common medical procedure), or university-trained physicians who dealt in ointments, potions, and the like. Women practitioners of medicine were increasingly marginalized, especially in cities, where male physicians and barber-surgeons were much more plentiful than in the country. Even midwifery ceased to be an exclusively female occupation: over the course of the seventeenth century, especially in the cities, male midwives and physicians began to infringe on what had previously been the domain of women alone.

One of the striking features of the sixteenth and seventeenth centuries is a dramatic growth in education and literacy, as will be discussed in Chapter 4. Here too we see an increasing divergence between the fortunes of men and of women. Previously, only very few people had received any kind of formal education. Largely as a result of religious impulses, a great many schools were founded in the sixteenth and seventeenth centuries. It is clear that most of these schools catered to boys only. In most of them, the education was very rudimentary: the catechism, or basic religious instruction, and basic literacy and numeracy. Not only did far fewer girls attend any sort of school, but their education was very different. The goal was to prepare them for their careers as godly wives and mothers. Their studies also included the catechism but also covered practical pursuits such as sewing. While sons of the elite attended grammar schools where they learned Latin in order to prepare for university, their daughters concentrated on "womanly" skills such as music, dancing, needlepoint, and other domestic pursuits. Very few women entered the ranks of the educated elite (universities were restricted to men only), and many of those were daughters of highly educated men who valued education for their daughters as well as their sons.

Witchcraft and Witch Hunts

One of the most striking phenomena that characterized sixteenth- and seventeenth-century Europe was the widespread witch hunts and witch trials that took place over large parts of the continent. Informed, though speculative, estimates place the number of trials at about 110,000 and the number of executions at about 60,000.[5] This was a uniquely early modern phenomenon. Although people in the Middle Ages had certainly believed in witches and witchcraft, trials for witchcraft were rare. Beginning in about 1450 and continuing for almost three centuries, these witch hunts were a basic fact of life over much of Europe, particularly in Germany and the surrounding areas: eastern France, Switzerland, the Low Countries, and Poland, as well as in England and Scotland. How can this be explained?

It is very clear to historians who have studied early modern witch hunts that there is no single explanation that suffices, whether class conflict or a woman-hating and woman-fearing patriarchal society. Rather, its origins and development lie in a number of different but related developments in the intellectual conception of witchcraft, the evolution of law and legal procedure, religious dissension and conflict, and social and economic tension.

Around the middle of the fifteenth century, intellectual and religious authorities underwent a shift in their conception of witchcraft. Previously, witchcraft was thought of as an isolated crime. It was the act of causing harm through supernatural means, or *maleficium*, which was prosecuted. By the sixteenth century, however, this had changed, and over most of Europe the very act of being a witch had become a crime, rather than the specific act of witchcraft or *maleficium*. Why this change should have come about at this time is unclear, but it likely has to do with the medieval elaborations of the figure of the devil, and the concern that all magic, whether overtly harmful or not (so-called "white magic") was inherently diabolical. In 1484, Pope Innocent VIII issued the bull *Summis Desiderantes*, lending papal authority to the developing conception of witchcraft. In 1486, two Dominican theologians and inquisitors named Heinrich Kramer (often called by his Latin name, Institorus) and Jakob Sprenger published a manual for witch hunters called the *Malleus Maleficarum*, or *Hammer of Witches*. Although influential and popular (it was reprinted fourteen times by 1520), it was neither the first, nor only, nor even the most comprehensive, such work. Nor did it set off an immediate witch-craze.

The *Malleus* was, however, only one albeit very influential brick in the developing edifice of witchcraft and witch hunting. By the mid to late sixteenth century, European religious and lay elites had developed a set of beliefs about witchcraft that ran roughly as follows: a witch was not simply a person (usually a woman, given women's weakness to temptation) who used supernatural means to gain her or his desired ends. Rather, a witch was a member of a satanic religion, one who had made a pact with the devil himself, usually sealed with a blasphemous act of sexual intercourse, called *succubus* for women and *incubus* for men.

As a sign of their pact with the devil, Satan imprinted the body of witches with a "Devil's Mark" or physical sign, usually in a concealed place. A witch was therefore not just a criminal, but also a heretic. Witches assembled periodically in gatherings known as Black Sabbaths, where they participated in a blasphemous and satanic parody of Christian worship, often accompanied by acts of ritual cannibalism and sexual orgies. Witches not only possessed the power to harm others (*maleficium*), but also to fly, enabling their attendance at the Black Sabbaths.

Although this conception of witchcraft was largely in place by the later fifteenth century, prosecutions for witchcraft would not really accelerate until after the middle of the sixteenth century, likely because the upheaval of the Protestant Reformation occupied the minds of many in positions of authority. It must also be emphasized that this conception of witchcraft was entirely the product of the learned elite. Ordinary people certainly believed in the possibility of witches and *maleficium*, and certainly acted as accusers of witches and as witnesses against them, but in the popular mind there was no connection to a diabolical and heretical conspiracy. But it was not enough for the learned elites to have developed a diabolic conception of witchcraft; there also needed to be a means to put this conception to work. This was provided by a series of developments in law and legal procedures across much of Europe. For although it was church officials and inquisitors who helped to formulate this conception of witchcraft, prosecuting and punishing witches fell overwhelmingly into the hands of secular governments.

In most of continental Europe the later Middle Ages saw a revival in the study and implementation of Roman law. Part of this revival involved a shift in the way criminal charges were brought and cases were prosecuted. In the accusatorial system that had prevailed previously, charges were brought by the aggrieved party, who was also responsible for the prosecution of the case and who faced legal retaliation if the accused were acquitted. Increasingly, European countries were adopting an inquisitorial system in which judicial officials not only weighed evidence and imposed punishment, but also played an active role in the proceedings. Evidence regarding guilt or innocence also underwent a transformation. In the earlier Middle Ages, trial by ordeal or by combat was the norm. That is, the accused would be compelled to undergo some sort of test, such as carrying a hot coal for a prescribed distance. If the wound healed quickly and cleanly, it was obviously a sign of God's favour and the accused was acquitted. Or physical combat might be prescribed, with God obviously granting victory to the innocent party. Now, however, judicial proof was increasingly seen in rational terms. As humans are fallible, it was thought that proof of guilt had to be ironclad before someone could be convicted. The standard that was adopted was drawn from the Roman law of treason: proof of guilt consisted of evidence from two eyewitnesses and the confession of the accused; nothing else sufficed. Obviously, eyewitness evidence of witchcraft, either of simple *maleficium* or of diabolism, was exceedingly rare. Therefore a premium was placed on extracting confessions from suspected witches. Hence, torture came to be used in trials for witchcraft.

In theory, the conditions in which torture could be used were tightly limited, as were its severity and duration. Before torture could be applied, there was supposed to be solid evidence that a crime had indeed been committed and that the person accused was reasonably suspected of having committed it. Inquisitors were theoretically forbidden to ask leading questions, in the understanding that someone in severe pain might make a false confession. Moreover, confessions extracted under torture were not in themselves admissible evidence. The confession had to be repeated outside the torture chamber within twenty-four hours. In practice, given the severity and diabolical nature of the crime of witchcraft, virtually all of these restrictions were loosened or ignored altogether. Inquisitors asked questions designed to uncover the "reality" of the diabolical conception of witchcraft. Of course, in severe distress, many unfortunates did indeed confess that they had cast spells on their neighbour's children, flown to Black Sabbaths, and indulged in orgiastic sex with demons. They were also frequently pressed to name accomplices and fellow witches, which again many did simply to stop the pain.

Although witchcraft was in its essence a spiritual crime, and although clergymen took the lead in developing the diabolic conception of witchcraft, prosecution and punishment of witches fell overwhelmingly into the hands of secular authorities, who claimed jurisdiction over the *maleficia* committed by witches, and also because witchcraft was equated with rebellion. In 1532 in the Holy Roman Empire, the legal code known as the *Carolina* contained a law against witchcraft. Statutes against witchcraft were passed by the English Parliament in 1542, 1563, and 1604, and in Scotland in 1563. Virtually every jurisdiction in Europe passed laws against witchcraft in the later sixteenth century.

The contribution to the witch hunts of the upheaval caused by the Protestant Reformation is difficult to assess. However, it is surely not coincidental that many of the areas in which witch hunting was most intense were also the areas in which Protestants and Catholics confronted each other most vigorously. These included Switzerland, eastern France (including the Duchy of Lorraine), southern and western Germany, Poland, and Scotland. It is likely that general religious instability made people and governments more fearful of subversion in their midst and hence more alert to the dangers of witchcraft. Conversely, in areas that were more religiously homogeneous, witch hunts were rarer and less intense, although certainly they still occurred. These areas included Spain and Italy, which remained solidly Catholic, and Scandinavia, which was thoroughly Lutheran.

It is likewise impossible to draw direct causal correlations between the social and economic turbulence of the age and the witch hunts. As with religious dissent, it is probable that social instability and economic insecurity produced tensions that might lead to accusations of witchcraft within a community; these in turn would set the official machinery in motion. It is clear, however, that religious dissent, social tensions, or economic instability in and of themselves were not sufficient to ignite a witch hunt. This is where the intellectual and legal developments examined above become crucial. An accusation of witchcraft against an individual could, in the right circumstances, set off a cascading reaction of torture, further accusations, and executions which ended only when the allegations struck too close to home, that is, when they began to implicate the political and religious elite who themselves took the lead in prosecuting witches.

Yet another variable in the equation seems to be the degree of political and judicial centralization in a given area. Generally speaking, witch hunts were more intense where there was a greater degree of local autonomy. At the higher levels, judicial, religious, and political authorities proved more sceptical in their attitudes. Therefore, highly decentralized areas, such as southern and western Germany, Poland, Switzerland, and the borderlands between France and the Holy Roman Empire, saw the most intense activity. In Spain, on the other hand, the authority of the Spanish Inquisition, somewhat paradoxically perhaps, proved to be a moderating influence, with its strict controls on the use of torture.

England deserves special attention in any treatment of the European witch hunts. Although, as we have seen, there was wide variation in the intensity and nature of continental witch hunts, England does seem different enough to constitute a special case. For one thing, England was highly centralized both politically and judicially, which tended, as we saw above, to act as a brake on witch hunting. England's legal system also differed from the continent. Roman law had virtually no impact in England, so the inquisitorial system was not adopted, and torture was strictly reserved for cases of high treason, depriving England of the chief mechanism by which an accusation of witchcraft was transmuted into an intense witch hunt. Moreover, for several reasons, England proved resistant to the conspiratorial and diabolical conceptions of witchcraft that dominated on the continent; in England individual acts of *maleficium* were prosecuted, but being a witch was not illegal in and of itself. For all these reasons, prosecutions for witchcraft in England remained endemic at a relatively low level. England experienced nothing like the mass panics and hysteria that spread across parts of continental Europe.

Over the course of the European witch hunts, an overwhelming majority of those accused of witchcraft were women. There was nothing specific in the diabolic conception of witchcraft to preclude male witches, but women were most frequent targets for several reasons. As we have seen, women were considered to be morally weaker than men and to be more enslaved to their sexual instincts. On both counts, therefore, women were thought to be especially susceptible to the temptation of the devil. In addition, women were generally in a position of social and economic weakness and were therefore thought to be more likely to use supernatural means to attain their goals. Indeed, it is likely that at least some of the accused were in fact witches, or at least believed that they were. That is, they did attempt to use supernatural means to manipulate the natural world. They were thus perhaps guilty of performing *maleficia*, but not of conforming to the conspiratorial and diabolical view of witchcraft, which was entirely a concoction of the learned elite.

Moreover, many women's occupations made them targets of accusations. For example, a cook could easily be suspected of using her knowledge of herbs and plants to concoct potions. Likewise, folk-healers, or "wise women" as they were known, were often suspected of using their knowledge and powers for evil ends. Midwives too came under suspicion. They were often blamed for the death of the infant and/or the mother, an all too common occurrence. It was also believed that unbaptized infants were sacrificed to the devil, and their flesh eaten at Black Sabbaths; midwives were therefore thought to be ideally placed to procure such infants. So while misogyny played a key role in who was accused of witchcraft, it is clearly a mistake to characterize the European witch hunts as a concerted and deliberate effort to further marginalize and subjugate women.

The heyday of European witch hunts was in the late sixteenth and early seventeenth centuries, with some variation by region. The number of trials tapered off toward the end of the seventeenth century, and by the mid-eighteenth century the great age of European witch hunts was past. The reasons for the decline and end of the witch hunts are just as varied and intertwined as the reasons for their rise in the first place. Certainly the abating of violent religious passions after the mid-seventeenth century played a role in decreasing the sense of crisis and instability that contributed to mass panics. More importantly, however, the attitudes of the civil and religious authorities toward the diabolic and conspiratorial conceptions of witchcraft changed drastically. Some of this is certainly attributable to the advancement of rationalism among European elites as a consequence of developments in science and philosophy. What had previously been seen as real and present danger was increasingly dismissed as superstition and humbug. Apart from a changing mental outlook on the parts of the elites who had prosecuted the witches, several legal or judicial developments helped to end the witch hunts. As governments continued to centralize their power, overzealous local officials were often restrained in their prosecution of witches. Moreover, the use of torture was increasingly restrained and regulated, with the result that there were fewer chain-reaction panics. Most ordinary people certainly continued to believe in the possibility of *maleficium*, and continued to level accusations of witchcraft, but these accusations rarely resulted in prosecution, and even if they did, witch trials had been shorn of the diabolical superstructure that had helped to produce the mass witch hunts of the sixteenth and seventeenth centuries. There were no witch trials or executions in England after 1682, although of course the famous Salem witch trials occurred in New England in the 1690s. In Scotland, the last execution for witchcraft was in 1722, and in Prussia in 1728. In France, the last execution for witchcraft occurred in 1745, but this was the first in a long time and was an isolated occurrence. There were other isolated trials and executions as late as 1793, but these are notable as being relics of a bygone era.

NOTES

1 There were some exceptions. In some parts of France, primarily in the south, the tax-exempt status belonged to the land, and not the person. Thus if a noble acquired non-noble land, he would still pay the *taille* on that portion.

2 Emmanuel Le Roy Ladurie, *The Peasants of Languedoc*, trans. John Day (Urban: University of Illinois Press, 1974).

3 The word "Cockaigne" is probably derived from a Middle French word for "cake." It was the subject of a thirteenth-century English poem satirizing monastic life and also of a famous painting by Pieter Brueghel the Elder (1525/30–69).

4 For the most complete examination, see Emmanuel Le Roy Ladurie, *Carnival in Romans*, trans. Mary Feeney (New York: George Braziller, 1979).

5 Brian P. Levack, *The Witch-Hunt in Early Modern Europe* (London and and New York: Longman, 1987) 19–22.

CHAPTER THREE

The Economy of Early Modern Europe

Seen in the very broadest terms, the period from 1559 to 1715 is divided between two major economic trends: until about 1600, there was a period of economic growth, rising prices, and rising population; after this time there was a period of stagnation, recession, and decline. But because so much economic activity was purely local in nature, it is difficult to generalize across Europe as a whole. Almost as important as the ups and downs of the European economy is the fact that it was changing at all: people believed in a static economic order, and they did not know how to deal with cycles of boom and bust.

The Price Revolution

One of the most important economic changes in early modern Europe is what historians have called the Price Revolution. That is, between 1500 and 1600, most prices doubled in real terms, although there was enormous regional variation in the commodities that were sold. For example, between 1500 and 1600, the price of wheat rose over fourfold in England, well over sixfold in France, and by similar amounts elsewhere. The prices of manufactured goods rose less, but still substantially. However, even if one assumes on average a doubling in most prices over the sixteenth century, this still works out to an annual inflation rate of less than 1 per cent, hardly striking by modern standards. As important as the economic effects of this "revolution" were, equally important was the fact that contemporary society was not equipped to deal with change of this order.

What lay behind the Price Revolution? In the 1930s the American historian Earl Hamilton asserted that the chief cause of this inflation was the influx of gold and especially silver from the mines of Bolivia and Mexico. From 1521 to 1660, Spanish ships brought to Europe from the New World approximately 18,000 tons of silver. The consequence was that there was now more money to buy the same number of goods, which produced higher prices. While no one would deny that such a huge infusion of precious metal would inflate prices, it is apparent that this can not be the only, or even the most important, factor at work. For one thing, New World gold and silver did not flow into Europe in amounts large enough to make a difference until after the middle of the sixteenth century, and there is clear evidence that prices started their upward trend in the late fifteenth century. Moreover, bullion shipments reached their peak in the first third of the seventeenth century, well after the general rise in prices had ceased.

The current consensus among historians is that while bullion imports may have had a role to play, the most important explanation for the Price Revolution is a demographic one. The population recovery after the demographic catastrophe of the fourteenth century meant that more people were now in the market for the same number of goods. This in part helps to explain why prices for agricultural products rose faster than those for manufactured goods. Population growth, especially in cities, produced a demand for food greater than agriculture's ability to expand production to meet it.

Contemporaries struggled to explain the Price Revolution, and they struggled even more in trying to deal with it. Many people blamed rising prices on the greed of speculators who would hoard goods in order to sell them after their prices had increased. But this of course confuses symptoms and causes. It makes no sense to hoard anything in the first place unless prices are already rising. Certain writers such as Jean Bodin in France and the Spaniard Martin de Azpilcueta saw the impact of American silver on prices. But the fact remains that whatever causes they assigned to it, contemporary society was ill equipped to deal with inflation on this scale. Wages failed to keep up with prices. Even if workers and peasants were able to secure nominal increases in their wages, these invariably failed to match the rise in prices; as a result real wages, that is wages measured in terms of purchasing power, declined over the course of the sixteenth century. In fact, a study of the wages of construction workers in England, Austria, and Spain shows that although nominal wages increased, their real wages were cut in half between the late fifteenth and the late sixteenth centuries. Or, to take another example, between 1480 and 1500 a stonemason in the southern French city of Montpellier earned about 4 *sous* per day, enough for about 15 kilograms of bread, enough to comfortably feed, clothe, and house his family. Thirty to forty years later, the same stonemason (or more likely his son or grandson) made 5 *sous* a day, a nominal increase of 25 per cent. Yet this higher wage would purchase only enough grain for about 9 kilograms of bread, down 40 per cent from the earlier period.

Governments were perplexed by this inflation no less than workers and consumers. In an age when endemic warfare was already driving up taxation, governments found that they needed to collect even more revenue. One of the chief means of doing this was devaluation of the currency. Governments would recall coinage, melt it down, and then reissue new coins with a lower content of precious metal, usually silver, while keeping the face value the same. Although such manipulations may have worked in the very short term, ultimately they only worsened inflation. Everyone knew that the new coins were inherently less valuable than the old ones, so merchants and craftsmen started demanding more of them for their products. After about 1600, prices levelled off over the long term, but as with the general rise in prices, there were enormous variations according to region and commodities.

Agriculture

As we have seen, the overwhelming majority of people were rural peasants, and agriculture was clearly the most important economic pursuit in early modern Europe. Superficially, European agriculture changed very little between the middle of the sixteenth century and the beginning of the eighteenth. Beneath the surface, however, important changes had taken place. Most of these changes have to do with the increasing influence of the market on agricultural production. By the early eighteenth century, it was much more common to grow food for sale on the open market than ever before. The increasing prevalence of market relations changed the way that wealth was extracted from the land, and also who benefitted, and in what form. As in any time of turmoil and transition, there were both winners and losers.

We are dealing here with the transition from a traditional subsistence agricultural system to one of agrarian capitalism, where food is produced for sale on the market. While the beginnings of this transition go back to the Middle Ages, and its completion is in the nineteenth century, it is probably safe to say that a crucial turning point was reached in the course of the sixteenth and seventeenth centuries. This transition, however, was not uniform or complete. We can distinguish three general patterns in different parts of Europe according to the level of transformation and its impact on rural society. First, in England and the Netherlands, the transition was most complete. Here we see the elimination of serfdom and the replacement of the traditional manorial agricultural system by agrarian capitalism. Second, in western Europe, primarily France and western Germany, and to a lesser extent Spain and Italy, we see increasing market relations in agriculture, but the transition to agrarian capitalism was less complete than in England and the Netherlands. Serfdom was eliminated, but the manorial system of agriculture remained largely intact, and large numbers of peasants still lived a life of subsistence agriculture. Finally, in eastern Europe we see the opposite of the two other patterns. Here we see the triumph of agrarian capitalism coupled with the imposition, or reimposition, of serfdom.

Immediately following the most devastating periods of the Black Death, those peasants who survived were in a relatively advantageous position; there was a scarcity of labour, so peasants were in a better position to extract concessions from landlords. Lords found themselves having to grant peasants more favourable deals in order to keep workers on their land. In western Europe, peasants used this power to eliminate serfdom, that is, the restrictions on their personal freedom, and the labour services they owed the lord. In many cases these were commuted to cash payments. Therefore, they still had to pay rents and dues of various kinds to the lord, but the relationship was less personal and more commercial than earlier in the Middle Ages. If one were lucky enough to survive wars and pestilence, the late fifteenth and early sixteenth centuries were a good time to be a peasant: wages were high because of the general scarcity of labour, and average landholdings were larger because there were fewer people. But a tremendous demographic expansion occurred, beginning in the mid-fifteenth century and lasting throughout the sixteenth. For a while, this was good for ordinary peasants. More people, especially in cities, meant greater demand for food, which led to higher prices and higher incomes for peasants who were able to sell their produce in urban markets. But ultimately, population came up against the ceiling on agricultural production. The inescapable fact was that European agriculture was inefficient and inflexible; without significant technological developments, there was a definite upper limit to the number of people it could support. And over most of Europe, this limit was reached in the later sixteenth century. As a result, the size of peasant holdings declined, as did real wages (since there was no longer a scarcity of labour), and prices went up, since more people were in the market for the same number of goods. Now the ordinary peasant was caught in a vicious scissors effect. Landlords wanted to maximize the return on their land by selling produce on the open market (where prices were rising), and they attempted to adjust to the new circumstances in several different ways. On their demesne lands they could raise rents, since land was now in greater demand than labour, or they could shorten the terms of leases, or practice sharecropping. They could cultivate their estates as commercial enterprises, which required the elimination of manorial and feudal restrictions on property. This process was known as enclosure, which essentially involved the lord asserting his property rights at the expense of those of the peasants and "enclosing" the open fields and common lands. These enclosures had the effect of turning peasants into agricultural wage-labourers, since they no longer had land of their own. Whereas ordinary peasants had earlier been the beneficiaries of changed demographic and economic circumstances, and had drawn their benefits in the form of higher wages, now other people benefitted, and in other forms.

In England, the main beneficiaries were the nobility and gentry, since they had been the most successful in asserting their property rights. Their benefits came in the form of profits: they either increased rents or decreased wages (or both), and then they sold the produce of their lands on the open market. In western Europe, lords were not as successful in asserting their property rights at the expense of the peasants. As we will see, the nobility and gentry had a much larger voice in the government in England than they did in western Europe where, in general, the profits found their way into different hands: a class of relatively wealthy peasants, known as *laboureurs* in France. They were able to rent or buy additional lands to increase their marketable surplus, and hire labourers to do the actual work. Thus, in contrast to England, where the top benefitted the most, in western Europe the top and bottom were squeezed, but the middle benefitted.

In eastern Europe the pattern was reversed. Before the Black Death, eastern European peasants had been better off than their counterparts in the west. Lords and rulers of sparsely populated lands granted peasants concessions to settle on and farm their lands. In the aftermath of the Black Death, lords responded to the labour shortage by attempting to restrict peasant freedom, to turn them into serfs. Royal governments were generally weaker in the east and could not stop this trend, and indeed hastened it and capitalized on it. The trend toward selling on the open market and higher sixteenth-century prices accelerated this trend, for huge profits were to be made by selling eastern European grain to the populous cities of the west, and serfdom guaranteed a cheap labour force.

When prices stopped rising around 1600, agricultural economics changed yet again. In the east, lords simply clamped down harder on their serfs in order to lower their labour costs and increase their profit margin. In the west, we see a more complicated picture. Population was now relatively stable, as were prices; the days of huge and rising profits gained from selling on the open market were over. On the other hand, population had stabilized at a relatively high level, and average landholdings had shrunk in size. Therefore, peasants needed somehow to find more land to farm. This drove up rents, thus favouring the landlord, as opposed, in earlier times, to the wage earner or the successful farmer. On top of this, in the seventeenth century taxation reached new heights; this tended to hit the peasants rather than the landlords, who were largely noble and therefore exempt. This would more or less remain the case throughout the rest of the seventeenth century, until in the eighteenth century a series of changes in the way land was cultivated would transform European agriculture in an unprecedented way.

Industry

In overall terms, industry played a small role in the early modern economy, at least when compared to modern industrialized economies. Most goods continued to be made on a handicraft basis, that is, in small shops for local consumption, and closely regulated by guilds. There were a few exceptions, such as mining and shipbuilding, where some large-scale enterprises employed up to several hundred people. Far and away the most important manufacturing sector was textiles, primarily woollens, but even this was conducted primarily on a small-scale craft basis. There were some rather large-scale textile enterprises in the cities of the Low Countries and Northern Italy, but they increasingly lost market share. They were hampered by inflexible and outdated guild regulations and were unable to respond to changing customer demand. They produced cloth that was of very high quality but that was also expensive and therefore had a limited market. Increasingly, textile production was shifting to rural areas in the form of cottage industry, also known as the "putting-out system," or proto-industry. Entrepreneurs would typically supply one peasant household with the raw wool to be spun into thread and then deliver the thread to another household where it would be woven into cloth. This cottage industry supplemented peasant incomes, since it could be performed during the slower periods of the agricultural cycle. The work could also be performed by women, who may have been limited to working in the house by their responsibilities for caring for children, and indeed could be performed by children themselves. From the entrepreneur's perspective, this system also had a number of advantages: because it took place outside of the towns, production was unencumbered by restrictive guild regulations; and since the work was being done to supplement peasant incomes, rather than as the main livelihood, lower wages could be paid. Nevertheless, as important as cottage industry was, practicality limited it almost exclusively to textiles. The raw material was light and easy to transport, it did not require expensive or complex equipment (just a spinning wheel or a hand-loom), and the basic skills were already widespread. It also required no power source other than human muscle power. These advantages were not easily transferable to other industries. Because these entrepreneurs were more flexible and their fixed costs were lower, they could afford to undercut established urban textile manufacturers. In any case, however, they catered largely to different markets. What these merchants discovered was that a lot of money could be made selling cheaper articles to lots of people, rather than more expensive items to fewer.

Despite the proliferation of cottage industry (which was, after all, simply a matter of exercising traditional methods in a different form), it is fair to say that, overall, industry took no great leaps forward in this period, certainly nothing that remotely compared with the Industrial Revolution that would come in the late eighteenth and nineteenth centuries. There were a number of barriers to the development of industry in early modern Europe. For one thing, there was a lack of markets: there was simply not enough purchasing power in enough hands to provide incentive for widespread innovation. Second, there was a lack of capital available for investment in industry. Or, more accurately, whatever capital was available was directed elsewhere. As soon as people made enough money, they retired from business and invested their capital in relatively unproductive investments such as government bonds, land, or royal offices. As a corollary of this, governments soaked up an increasingly greater portion of output to finance their continual wars.

There was also a lack of power and fuel. Most industrial power was rather primitive in nature—human, animal, wind, or water—and most fuel was wood or peat moss. As forests were cut down, wood became scarcer and more expensive, further limiting the possibility of industrial growth. Peat moss was cheap but bulky and expensive to transport. Coal came into more general use, but it was also bulky and expensive to transport. Besides, at this stage coal was used primarily as a fuel for heating. Most coal simply could not be used for industrial purposes such as refining iron because of the impurities it imparted to the end product. All of these things would begin to change in the course of the eighteenth century, but by 1715 little of what was to come was apparent.

Trade and Commerce

We need to distinguish among at least three different levels of commerce: 1) local or regional; 2) inter-regional, or European; and 3) overseas. The first, local or regional trade, is hard to assess, although certainly it increased in this period, if only because of the growth in cities. Nevertheless, few records have been left behind to enable historians to develop a complete understanding of local and regional trade. There were several important obstacles to trade on anything more than a purely local basis. Poor roads made overland transport difficult, slow, and expensive. Most roads were little more than glorified dirt paths that in winter would become impassable to wheeled vehicles. It is telling that until the eighteenth century many of the best roads in Europe had been constructed by the Romans more than a thousand years earlier.

Transport by water was of course more efficient. However, it was not without its own difficulties. Navigable rivers did not reach everywhere, and although there were some canals, the great age of canal building was still to come, although certainly the northern part of the Netherlands, or the Dutch Republic was more advanced in this respect than anywhere else in Europe. Moreover, rivers and canals were still subject to seasonal variations. Spring runoff might make navigation too difficult or dangerous, while a dry summer might reduce flow to the point where navigation became uneconomical. And even where rivers and canals were available, goods were subject to many kinds of tolls and customs, even within one state. For example, in 1567 on the River Loire and its tributaries (which were completely within the Kingdom of France), there were 200 different tolls levied in 120 different places. Transport on waterways that traversed multiple political jurisdictions, such as the Rhine, Meuse, or Danube, was of course even more cumbersome.

Adding to the difficulty of transporting goods was the lack of uniformity in currency and weights and measures. Even within one political jurisdiction, currency varied enormously. There would be numerous different coins in circulation, with values varying according to their precious metal content. There were also fictional "monies of account," which were used for accounting purposes, but their value in real coins varied from time to time and place to place. Different regions also had their own systems of weights and measures. The *setier* of Paris (a measure of volume used typically for grain) was not the same as the *setier* or Lyon or Rouen. All of this of course complicated commerce enormously and added to its expense.

In large part because of these barriers, the great expansion in trade that took place in the sixteenth and seventeenth centuries took place along the seacoasts, primarily in the Baltic Sea, the North Sea, and the Atlantic Ocean. A number of factors contributed to the growth of sea-borne trade. First of all, it was not subject to nearly as many obstacles as inland trade, whether by land or water. In addition, new mechanisms for advancing credit allowed merchants to keep their operations going while they had shipments in transit. They no longer had to wait until their last shipment was sold before financing a new venture. The development of maritime insurance spread the risk among many parties, so that one shipwreck, or the capture of a ship by enemies or pirates did not spell immediate and total ruin. Furthermore, developments in shipbuilding such as the Dutch *fluytschip* (see below) allowed cargo to be shipped more cheaply and efficiently. Finally, in this era we see the formation of ongoing joint-stock companies, such as the Dutch East India Company (also see below). Previously, merchants had usually made partnerships for a specific enterprise or voyage; when it was complete, the profits or losses were shared according to their investments. Now, however, these partnerships were kept on an ongoing basis, with their own stock of capital, and eventually shares came to be traded in them on a market.

The Supremacy of the Dutch Republic

In all these developments, the merchants of the Dutch Republic led the way. This was in large part a matter of survival. As a small country with a dense and highly urbanized population, the Dutch Republic could not feed itself, nor did it have impressive natural resources with which to purchase the food and other raw materials it required. The Dutch needed to import to survive, and if they could not export their own commodities to pay for their imports, they could at least act as middlemen and finishers of others' products. So the merchants and bankers of Amsterdam led the way in pioneering new means of advancing credit and providing banking and exchange services. Merchants from all over Europe could count on finding there everything they needed in the way of facilities and expertise. The Dutch also led the way in maritime insurance. Merchants pooled their risk by buying shares in each other's ships; thus if one went down or were captured, one merchant did not lose all. In shipbuilding, they developed the *fluytschip* as a single-purpose freighter. Most ships had previously been built to function both as cargo ships and as warships when needed. The *fluytschip*'s hull was longer and shallower than normal, and a flatter bottom allowed more room for cargo. It was made of fir and pine, rather than oak, and was cheaper to build. Rigged more simply, it required about half the crew of other ships of comparable size. As a result, the Dutch could ship goods anywhere more cheaply than anybody else. In the first half of the seventeenth century roughly half the tonnage of European merchants' ships was Dutch. Because they could ship so cheaply, Dutch merchants made sure that their ships never sailed empty. Their staple trade was in the North Sea and the Baltic. Dutch ships would bring from Scandinavia, Poland, Russia, and other areas commodities such as fish, grain, and lumber. On the return trip, they would take with them wine, textiles, and other manufactured goods. As a result, Amsterdam became the financial and commercial capital of Europe for the first half of the seventeenth century.

More dramatic and spectacular, but ultimately less important than this European trade, was overseas or colonial commerce. The European pioneers of colonial trade were the Spaniards and Portuguese, whose colonial empires dated from the late fifteenth century, but their colonial trade remained rather primitive and exploitive. Gold, silver, spices, and other luxury goods came to Spain or Portugal but were soon spread throughout Europe. Overseas trade remained strictly controlled by the government, and the mother country had little to ship back that the colonists needed or wanted.

Once more, it was the Dutch who changed the rules of the game, primarily in the formation of joint-stock companies. The most famous is the East India Company (Verenigde Oostindische Compagnie, or VOC), but there were others, such as the West India Company and more besides. These were private companies, with an ongoing existence, with a monopoly granted by the government. They also had an ongoing existence; that is, the enterprise was not dissolved after the voyage for which it had been formed, as happened previously. Founded in 1602 as a cooperative venture among Dutch merchants already involved in Asian trade, the Dutch East India Company was a private company that had been granted a government monopoly over Asian trade as well as the power to possess and govern territory. Very quickly the VOC came to dominate trade with Asia. Soldiers and sailors in the company's service soon expelled the Portuguese from the fabled Spice Islands and established complete control over the spice trade. The company gained a monopoly on trade with Japan, which had recently shut itself off from all other outsiders, and established an outpost in the city of Nagasaki. In order to facilitate the years-long voyage to Asia and to supply and replenish their ships, the VOC established a settlement near the Cape of Good Hope at the southern tip of Africa, as well as outposts scattered throughout the Indian Ocean and the East Indies. Although the VOC was not the first such company, it was unquestionably the most successful and powerful and provided a model for others to imitate. An English East India Company was founded at about the same time as the Dutch, and a French version in 1664. Even the minor powers of Sweden, Denmark, and Brandenburg founded their own East India Companies to try to establish a presence in this lucrative commerce.

The Dutch brought to overseas trade the same advantages as they did to European trade, and soon dominated there as well. In particular, the main problem in Asian trade was that Europeans had nothing the Asians wanted, except gold and silver. However, the Dutch used their efficiency and economic muscle to break into the inter-Asian trade, which effectively paid for the Asian goods brought back to Europe. This Asian trade consisted primarily of spices and luxury goods such as silk and lacquerware. Through the foundation of the West India Company in 1621, the Dutch also established a presence in Atlantic trade, although they never dominated here as they did in Asia, largely because of the entrenched position of the Spanish and Portuguese and fierce competition from the English and French. The ships of the Dutch and others engaged in a triangular system that took European manufactured goods to the New World and Africa, slaves from Africa to the New World, and raw materials such as gold, silver, sugar, timber, furs, and later on grain, from the New World back to Europe.

The Dutch Republic was the commercial and financial superpower of the late sixteenth and early seventeenth centuries, allowing the Dutch to play a major role in European affairs, as well as paying for the flowering of Dutch culture, as discussed in Chapter 12. By the end of the seventeenth century, however, the Dutch found their commercial dominance on the decline. Their very success made them the target of other powers, who, according to prevailing economic thought, believed that the only way to become richer was to make someone else poorer. Their methods were imitated by others, primarily the French and the English, both of whom had resources and populations that the Dutch could not match. England and the Dutch Republic fought a series of three naval wars in the later seventeenth century, and the English Navigation Acts were explicitly intended to break Dutch dominance in European commerce. French commercial and military policy under Louis XIV (1643–1715) was avowedly and explicitly directed against the Dutch. In terms of overseas and colonial trade, the eighteenth century was largely a commercial duel between the French and the English, with the Dutch, Spanish, and Portuguese as bit players.

But for all its dominance, Dutch commercial capitalism was essentially traditional in nature. They enhanced and developed traditional practices better than anyone, but they really did not change the nature or content of international trade. Greater quantities and a greater variety of goods were shipped to and from more different places in 1715 than in 1559, but the basic patterns and methods of trade remained very much the same.

Mercantilism

The characteristic economic assumptions of the age have been given the name "mercantilism," although this term was a later invention and was not used in the sixteenth and seventeenth centuries. Mercantilism was not an overt or conscious economic system or philosophy, but rather a set of assumptions about economic life shared more or less by everyone. One of its chief assumptions was that the purpose of economic activity was to strengthen the state and its ruler, in contrast with the modern notion that the purpose of government is to provide the conditions for a flourishing economy. Another of its assumptions was that precious metals, primarily gold and silver, were the best measure of wealth. Wealth, therefore, was finite and limited. Short of discovering fabulous new gold or silver mines, as the Spanish had done, the only way to become wealthier was to take wealth away from someone else, to make them poorer. International trade thus became a zero-sum game.

In practice, these assumptions meant a number of things. Governments encouraged domestic self-sufficiency by promoting exports and discouraging imports. If you imported more than you exported, wealth, in the form of precious metal, was leaving your country. If, on the other hand, you could export more than you imported, you would maintain a favourable balance of trade, and there would be a net inflow of bullion. This in turn led to intense government regulation of the economy. Although ownership of enterprises remained in private hands (this was not socialism), governments sought to direct economic development in the channels they thought would best enhance their power. So, for example, governments set up and subsidized industries to replace imported goods with those produced domestically. Heavy tariffs were imposed on imported goods to discourage consumption. Rulers sought to acquire colonial empires to supply raw materials for industry. International trade therefore became a kind of war by other means.

The great exception to these mercantilist policies was of course the Dutch. This was not, however, because of any abstract devotion to the principles of free trade, but only because they were forced into it. For one thing, the Dutch Republic had no effective central government capable of regulating the economy. Nor did it have the population or resources to support a vast overseas empire. Nor could the Dutch possibly be self-sufficient, least of all in food. So, making a virtue of necessity, Dutch merchants decided that instead of controlling all of something, they would rather have a little piece of everything. Even so, when they had the upper hand, they acted like mercantilists. Thus, Dutch merchants insisted on free navigation through the Danish sounds that connected the North Sea to the Baltic, but the East India Company was capable of acting with brutal swiftness to enforce its monopoly against interlopers in the Asian trade.

Mercantilist principles were first consistently applied beginning around the middle of the seventeenth century. This was not because they were new then, but because of several external factors. Up until then, central governments lacked the power to impose them against the will of all kinds of vested interests, such as guilds, cities, and provinces. By the later seventeenth century the process of centralization had proceeded far enough at least to make the attempt to impose mercantilist policies. The most famous example is France under Louis XIV and the policies of his finance minister Jean-Baptiste Colbert, but the same principles were acted on elsewhere as well.

CHAPTER FOUR

Religion and the People

By the middle of the sixteenth century, the first great wave of the Protestant Reformation had largely played itself out. This was the series of events set off by Martin Luther's protest beginning in 1517 against certain dogmas and practices of the Roman Church. By 1559, however, Luther's version of reformed Christianity (or Protestantism as the various branches of western European non-Catholic churches are called) was no longer a growing or dynamic movement. Within Germany, Catholic and Lutheran princes had fought each other to stalemate, as recognized in the Peace of Augsburg in 1555. This treaty brought religious peace to Germany according to the Latin principle *cuius regio, eius religio*: literally, "who rules, his religion." The religion of the territory and its inhabitants was determined by the religion of the ruler. A Catholic ruler had Catholic subjects and a Lutheran ruler had Lutheran subjects; no other creeds were permitted by the treaty. Martin Luther himself had died in 1546, and in subsequent years Lutherans became bitterly divided over theological questions. As a result, Lutheranism after the mid-sixteenth century was largely static and stagnant, confined to northern Germany, Scandinavia, and pockets of territory along the Baltic coast. Lutheran churches were organized territorially; there was no international Lutheran organization, so the churches tended to be dominated by the ruler and functioned essentially as a department of the government.

Besides the various Lutheran churches, on the non-Catholic or Protestant side, there were also scattered groups of Anabaptists, who tended to withdraw and live isolated in their own communities, trying to escape persecutions of both Catholics and other Protestants. After their catastrophic takeover of the northern German city of Münster in 1534–35, which was brutally suppressed by allied Lutheran and Catholic forces, Anabaptists were concerned first and foremost with living according to their interpretation of God's will and escaping the notice of hostile authorities. Among the more notable groups were the Mennonites (followers of a Dutch former priest named Menno Simon), and the Hutterites (named after their founder Jakob Hutter). These groups and others often emigrated to central and eastern Europe, where landowners were keen to populate their sparsely peopled territories and were prepared to overlook their "heresy" in exchange for a hard-working and peaceful workforce.

The dynamic and expanding Protestant movement was now the one founded and led by John Calvin (1509–64). French by birth and brought up as Catholic, Calvin experienced a religious conversion at some point in the early 1530s while a law student and renounced the Catholic Church. A series of circumstances forced him into exile in the city of Geneva, where with just one two-year hiatus he spent the rest of his life. By 1559, Calvinism, or Calvin's version of Protestant Christianity, had emerged as an international Protestant movement. Both Calvin and his successor Theodore Beza (1519–1605) consciously fostered the international character of the movement. They welcomed refugees from all over Europe and set up the Genevan Academy as a theological training school. They sent missionaries and preachers out to various areas, but especially to France. (Like Calvin, Beza was French by birth, and both remained intensely interested in and concerned with their homeland.) Ultimately, a number of jurisdictions became officially Calvinist: Geneva and parts of Switzerland, various cities of southern and western Germany, Scotland, the Dutch Republic, and the western German territory of the Palatinate. In addition, there were significant Calvinist movements and minorities in many other places: France, the Netherlands, England, Germany, Bohemia, and Hungary.

At the same time that Calvinism was coming into being and expanding internationally, and after several false starts and much debate and hesitation, the Catholic Church had managed to put its house back in order, a process known as the Counter-Reformation or the Catholic Reformation. This resurgence and revival was most evident in the Council of Trent, which, after three sessions meeting on and off for twenty years, finally concluded in 1563. The reformed Catholic Church is often referred to as the Tridentine Church, and reformed Catholicism as Tridentine Catholicism, after the Latin name for Trent, Tridentum. Although the Catholic or Counter-Reformation is seen most evidently in the reforms decreed by the Council of Trent, it is also evident in a number of other ways: the formation of the Society of Jesus or Jesuits in 1540, the revived Roman Inquisition, the Index of Prohibited Books, and the dramatic and emotional style of art known as Baroque.

At the risk of over-simplification, the religious conflicts that dominated Europe between 1559 and 1715 could be seen as a clash of these two dynamic and confident movements, international Calvinism and Tridentine or reformed Catholicism, each absolutely convinced of the divine justice of its cause and of the pernicious error and heresy of the other. In a world where people believed in one truth alone, and where rulers derived their right to rule from a divine mandate, religion was in the very nature of things a political issue. Religious unity was seen as an essential precondition for peace and stability; conversely, religious dissent was seen as a certain recipe for civil disorder and civil war. Accordingly, large numbers of people were willing to kill and be killed in the struggle for truth, however they defined it. On the other hand, much recent research has pointed out that probably the majority of people were in fact not so disposed: that, left on their

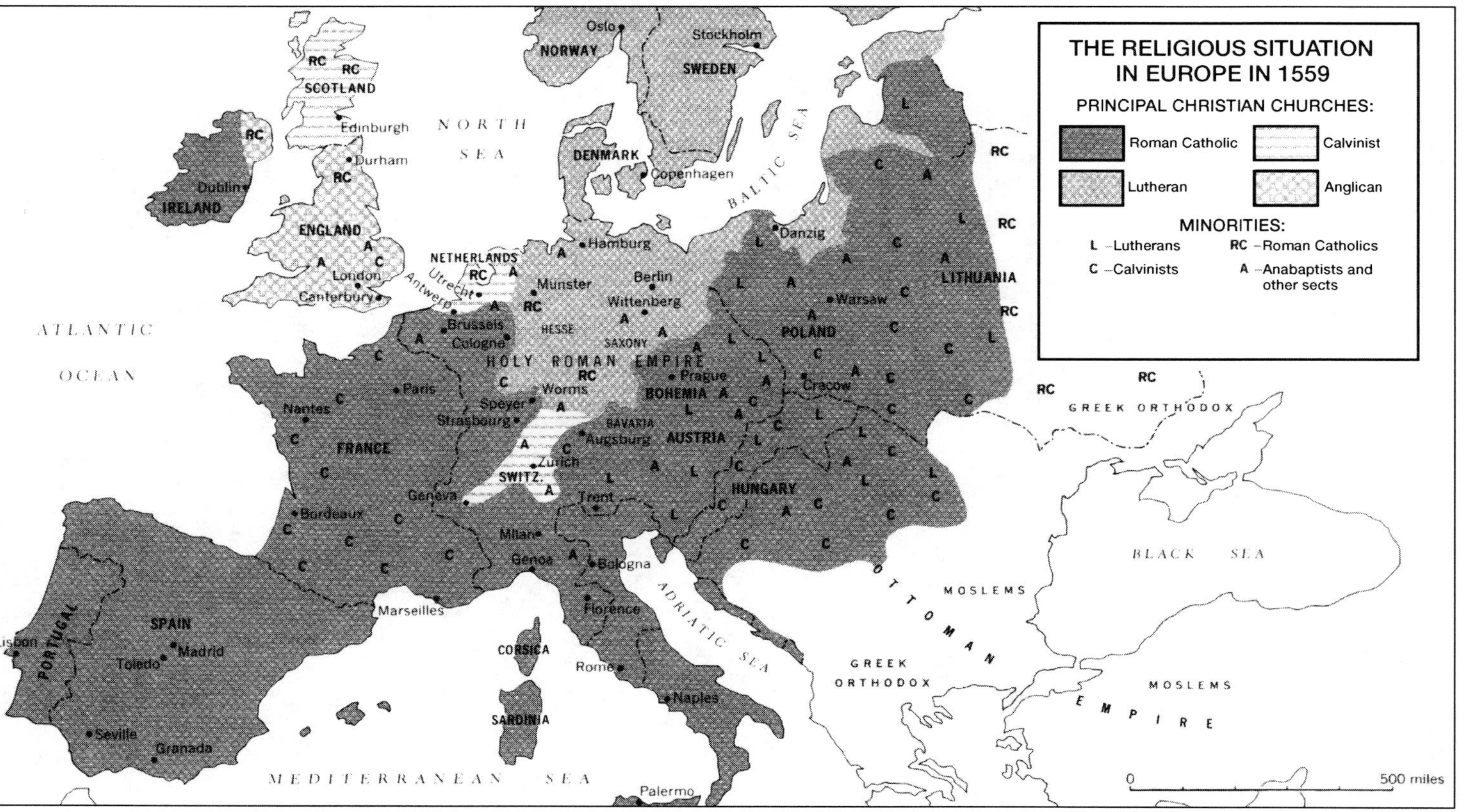

MAP 4.1 ⇸ RELIGIOUS DIVISIONS OF EUROPE, CA. 1559

own, most people would prefer peace and social harmony over religious struggle, even while they condemned the heresy they saw around them. The fact remains, however, that enough people were of the contrary opinion that religious violence was a basic fact of life in sixteenth- and seventeenth-century Europe.

Theology and Organization

The Catholic Church

Over the centuries since the Reformation, there has been a vigorous debate over the nature and origins of Catholic Reform. This debate is reflected in the names applied to the movement. "Counter-Reformation" was a term coined by nineteenth-century German Protestant historians to convey the idea that had it been left on its own, the Roman Church would have done nothing to reform itself. Only the shock of the Protestant Reformation and the threat of extinction roused corrupt church authorities into action, and even then they were purely reactive and negative, able only to reject Protestant positions rather than doing anything creative or original of their own. Catholic historians, on the other hand, pointed out that there were genuine sources of Catholic reform and religious revival prior to and independent of Luther and the other Protestant reformers. Today, most historians would agree that although there was a genuine Catholic reform and revival before the outbreak of the Protestant Reformation, religious schism inevitably influenced the shape and outcome of that reform, that it assumed forms it probably would not otherwise have taken.

This is evident most clearly in the area of theology and doctrine. The Council of Trent had responded to the challenge of the Protestant Reformation by reaffirming the sanctity and necessity of traditional Catholic doctrines and practices. In defining Catholic theology, the Council consciously and deliberately chose the path of confrontation over that of compromise. At every point, the decrees of the Council of Trent decisively and emphatically rejected key Protestant positions. Thus, the necessity of good works for salvation was reaffirmed, as was the necessity of all seven sacraments. The Council also reaffirmed the doctrine of transubstantiation: during the sacrament of Mass or Eucharist, when the priest pronounced the words *"hoc est corpus meum"* ("this is my body"), the bread and wine of the sacrament were physically and miraculously transformed into the body and blood of Christ. In the terms of medieval philosophy, the elements of the Mass retained their outward "accidents" (taste, smell, appearance), but their inner substance was transformed. The council also reaffirmed the divine inspiration of the Vulgate Bible translated into Latin more than a millennium earlier by St. Jerome. This was the official and truly inspired Word of God, to the exclusion of all others. Furthermore, while Catholics were not forbidden to read the Bible themselves, interpretation of its meaning was the exclusive monopoly of the Church and its clergy, who were guided by the Holy Spirit. In contrast to Protestants who maintained Scripture alone as the source of religious authority, the Council of Trent affirmed the equal authority of church law and tradition, both written and unwritten. Theologically, the decrees and canons of the Council of Trent were designed to make it crystal clear what one had to accept and what one had to reject in order to be a Catholic. There was to be no more confusion or ambiguity on points of doctrine such as had caused the Protestant Reformation, at least in the eyes of many Catholic leaders.

At the same time, the worst abuses and corruption that had made the Protestant Reformation appealing to many people were cleaned up: along with the theological confrontation, the Tridentine Church undertook a thoroughgoing moral and institutional reform. To remedy an insufficient and haphazard education for priests (indeed, a non-existent education for most), the Council ordered every bishop to establish a seminary in his diocese to educate parish clergy in the basics of their faith. It is not clear how widely or consistently this decree was followed, but it was certainly an important step forward. Bishops were given greater control over the clergy in their jurisdictions, especially over the regular clergy or monks, many of whom had previously claimed exemption from the authority of their local bishops. At the same time, the authority of the Pope over the whole church was reasserted, and the Church was declared to be a papal monarchy, with the Pope, the "Vicar of Christ," holding his office directly from God. Bishops and other important clergymen were declared to hold their office from the Pope and not directly from God. Thus, bishops were firmly subordinated to the power of the Pope, even while they were given greater authority in terms of governing their dioceses. These measures were meant to reinforce the hierarchical nature of church authority, to remedy what was seen as one of the major causes of the Protestant Reformation: that the lines of authority were unclear and murky, that no one was able to take effective action against Luther and the other reformers at the very beginning, when the whole thing could have been nipped in the bud. Although the doctrine of papal infallibility was not declared at this time (it was not formally proclaimed until 1870), it was certainly implicit in the decrees of the Council of Trent.

Although the Council of Trent set the Roman Catholic Church on the path to reform, it was only a beginning. As with any large and complex institution it took some time before reform made it off the drawing board and into the real world. For one thing, tensions between many Catholic rulers and the Church made implementation of the Tridentine reforms problematic. Only Philip II of Spain and the kings of Poland and Portugal formally accepted the decrees of the council in its immediate aftermath. Although they were adopted by the French clergy in 1615, they were never formally accepted by the kings of France. These kings, along with much of the French clergy and laity, claimed that the Catholic Church in France was semi-autonomous in issues of administration, finance, and personnel, and that the decrees of the Council of Trent violated these "Gallican Liberties." Even in Spain, the "Catholic Kings" as they were known possessed a great deal of authority over the Catholic Church. Even where such arrangements were not formally spelled out, such as in most of Catholic Germany, rulers were extremely reluctant to be seen to be putting themselves under the Church's authority. We see the weight of political issues as well in the case of the Roman Inquisition.

Not to be confused with the Spanish Inquisition, which was founded by a papal grant of 1478 but was independent of papal control and entirely under the control of the Spanish monarchs, the Roman Inquisition was established in 1542 at the urging of Cardinal Caraffa, later Pope Paul IV (1555–59). It was intended to operate everywhere in Catholic Europe as the primary means of enforcing discipline and orthodoxy. Most Catholic rulers, however, refused to let it operate in their territories, for fear of enhancing or reviving medieval claims of papal supremacy over secular rulers. Indeed, King Henry II of France (1547–59) established his own religious court, the *Chambre Ardente*, or Burning Chamber, to hunt down heretics but refused to let the Roman Inquisition operate in his kingdom. In practice, the Roman Inquisition was operative only in the parts of Italy over which the Pope had some influence or control.

It also took some time for the reforms proclaimed by the Council of Trent to be implemented. For example, even apart from political issues, it was no easy matter for bishops to set up seminaries for the training of priests. Where was the money to come from? Who was to staff these schools? How much, if anything, could be charged for tuition? What would the curriculum be? As a result, the establishment of such seminaries was neither immediate nor universal. And so it was with many other reforms proclaimed by the Council of Trent.

Furthermore, as with any large institution faced with turmoil and change, there was a great deal of resistance from within. Many of the important men within the Church liked things just as they were. They were respected, wealthy, and powerful, so why should they tolerate changes that threatened their status, power, and wealth? As a result of all these factors, the Catholic Counter-Reformation was by no means fully implemented during the sixteenth century. Indeed, the Catholic Church would show signs of real change in most areas only during the seventeenth century. In fact, it is probably not too much to say that Tridentine reforms were only fully implemented during the eighteenth century, just in time for the secular and anti-clerical movements of the Enlightenment and the French Revolution.

Probably the most powerful force in the Tridentine Church was the Society of Jesus, or the Jesuits as they are more commonly known. Founded by Ignatius Loyola (1491–1556), a former Spanish soldier, the order received papal recognition in 1540 and quickly established itself as a pillar of the Catholic Counter-Reformation. Unlike most monastic orders of the time, Loyola and the Jesuits stressed activism and engagement with the world, rather than withdrawal from it. Not confined to a cloister, or bound by the ritual observances of worship, the Society was the most effective vehicle for the implementation of the Counter-Reformation. If they were to make a real difference, Loyola and the other leaders of the Society believed, they needed a disciplined and educated body of followers. Jesuits therefore underwent an extensive and rigorous education, preparing them for their careers. From the very beginning, the Society was international in its outlook: among Ignatius's earliest followers were four Spaniards, one Portuguese, two Savoyards, and two Frenchmen. The goals of the Society were manifold: to aid the faithful in their religious devotions, to educate the young, but also to propagate the faith through foreign missions and to win back converts to Protestantism. In education, the Jesuits were spectacularly successful, founding and running many schools, universities, and seminaries throughout Europe. Very quickly, Jesuit missionaries found their way around the world: from St. Francis Xavier in India, China, and Japan, to the Spanish colonies in the New World, to the French Jesuits who proselytized among North American natives in the seventeenth century. Within Europe as well, Jesuits led in turning back the Protestant tide that threatened the survival of the Roman Church. St. Peter Canisius (1521–97) was instrumental in the preservation of Catholicism in Germany through his teaching, his foundation of Jesuit colleges, and especially through his writing of catechisms. When priests were needed in England to succour Catholics there under Elizabeth I, three Jesuits were sent at very real risk to their lives. In Poland, Bohemia, Austria, and everywhere that Protestantism threatened the Catholic Church, Jesuits were active in promoting the Catholic cause.

The Society of Jesus also sought to influence rulers and aristocrats. They acted as personal confessors to many Catholic rulers: all the kings of France from Henry III to Louis XV, that is from 1574 to 1774; all the Holy Roman Emperors after Ferdinand II (1619–37); as well as almost all the kings of Portugal and Poland. Jesuits, and those trained and influenced by them, were essential in the reconversion of much of the nobility of Austria, Hungary, and Poland.

Calvinism

Both theologically and organizationally, Calvinism was very different from the Roman Catholic Church. Protestants in general, and Calvinists in particular, denied the role of good works in salvation, while emphasizing human depravity and sinfulness. On its own, mankind is incapable of anything pleasing to God; salvation, therefore, is entirely God's work. He chooses whom he wishes for salvation, the Elect, and condemns whom he wishes to damnation. This is the doctrine of predestination or election. Most Protestant theologians, while they acknowledged the doctrine in theory, shied away from its more disturbing implications, stating, for example, that it was vain to try to understand God's power and majesty, and that in practical terms people should probably assume they were one of the Elect. Not so with Calvin. Calvin insisted on predestination in its harshest and most strident form. Before the creation of the world, God chose some for salvation and condemned others to an eternity of torment in Hell. This was entirely at God's pleasure: human merit had nothing to do with it. Calvin explicitly denied that predestination was the result of God's foreknowledge: that since God was outside of time, he knew who was going to be good, and who was not, and then chose the good for salvation and condemned the bad. Moreover, Calvin insisted, there was no way of knowing for sure in this life whether or not one was one of the Elect, and there was certainly nothing one could do to change one's eternal destiny.

It has often been asserted that predestination or election was the core concept of Calvin's theology. In fact, however, it was a result, not a cause. The core of Calvin's theology that produced the emphasis on predestination was his conception of God's utter majesty and sovereignty. For Calvin, to allow humans any role in their own salvation, to admit that, on their own, humans were capable of anything good, was to diminish the role and power of God. As he wrote in his major theological work, *The Institutes of the Christian Religion*,

> We shall never be clearly persuaded, as we ought to be, that our salvation flows from the wellspring of God's free mercy until we come to know his eternal election, which illumines God's grace by this contrast: that he does not indiscriminately adopt all into the hope of salvation but gives to some what he denies to others....

Protestant theology in general, and Calvinist theology in particular, also denied the intermediary role of the Church. The Catholic position was that the institution of the Roman Church had been founded by Christ Himself and had been guided by the Holy Spirit through the centuries. The Catholic Church (catholic means universal), therefore, was incapable of error and was the indispensable intermediary between God and humanity. The Church was the custodian of the sacraments, the vehicles of divine grace, without which no one could be saved. Its clergy stood in a special position before God, having a unique relationship with and access to the divine unavailable to laypeople. As a mark of this special status, Catholic clergy were in theory celibate, not only not allowed to marry, but also required to reject sex altogether.

Calvin, following Luther and other Protestant reformers, denied this role of the Church. It was still crucial as the fellowship of Christians, but it was no longer the intermediary between God and mankind. Thus, the Church lost its exclusive right to interpret the Bible, and the clergy lost their special status. As a mark of this denial of the elevated status of the clergy, Protestant pastors were allowed, and even encouraged, to marry. Luther himself had married a former nun, had a number of children, and wrote very tenderly about family life. Calvin also married, but he was never as forthcoming about his family life. Individual Christians, then, all stood in the same relationship to God as Catholic priests—they all had equal access, and none had a special status in God's eyes. This is the doctrine of "the priesthood of all believers."

In contrast once more to the Catholic Church, where Scripture and church law and tradition were equal sources of authority, for Protestants and Calvinists, Scripture alone was the source of religious authority. In conjunction with the "priesthood of all believers," this meant that Protestants, including Calvinists, emphasized the importance of individual reading of the Bible. This in turn led to an emphasis on education, not only for the basics of literacy, but also to teach people the "proper" interpretation of Scripture. Calvinism, it has been observed, is a "religion of the book," placing great value on individual Bible study.

For Calvinists, in common with other Protestants, there were only two sacraments: baptism and the Lord's Supper or communion. The sacraments, moreover, lost their essential role in salvation as the vehicles of divine grace. In particular, Protestants denied the Catholic doctrine of transubstantiation, although what exactly happened during the sacrament of the Lord's Supper was the single most divisive issue among Protestants. Luther, while he rejected transubstantiation, tried desperately to maintain some physical divine presence in the bread and wine of the sacrament. In his view, while the bread and wine were not miraculously transformed by the priest, Christ was still somehow physically present. This view has been called consubstantiation, or "Real Presence." Other Protestants followed the view first put forward by the Swiss reformer Ulrich Zwingli (1484–1531), who maintained that nothing happened to the bread and wine. They were simply symbols representing the body and blood of Christ. The only benefit to participants was in the reflection on Christ's suffering and death caused by the sacrament. Calvin denied that anything happened to the elements, but neither were they mere symbols. Although Christ was not physically present in the bread and wine, He was spiritually present. Believers received a real spiritual benefit from the sacrament over and above mere reflection on Christ's crucifixion and death.

In institutional terms, Calvinism was also very different from the Catholic Church. Although of course Calvin and later Beza had a good deal of influence on Calvinists throughout Europe, in common with other Protestant churches Calvinism had no international structure. Calvinist churches were organized territorially, by political jurisdiction. Unlike Catholicism, which was organized hierarchically, and Lutheranism, where the ruler was basically in charge, Calvinism was more "democratic," organized in a presbyterian system, with local, regional, and national assemblies or synods. Local churches would send delegates, usually both clergy and laypeople, to regional or provincial synods. These regional bodies would then send delegates to a national synod. This system allowed for significant lay participation in church government, for it was not monopolized by the clergy. It also allowed for a degree of popular participation and consultation. These things had several consequences. For one thing, it meant that throughout the organization a number of people, both clergy and laity, had significant experience in church organization and governance. It also meant that it was highly unlikely that the national church would come up with policies unacceptable to the local congregations, since the national synod itself was made up of people who had started out in local congregations. This organization also helped Calvinism to survive in a hostile environment. Even if the national synod could be eliminated by hostile authorities, the regional synods and local congregations would continue. A Calvinist church could not be killed by cutting off its head. In this way, it was somewhat similar to a modern terrorist organization with its separate and self-contained cells. Although the comparison may seem far-fetched, this probably reflects fairly accurately the feelings of Catholic authorities faced with Calvinist movements.

When it came to relations with secular rulers, the two movements had in theory very different attitudes, but in practice faced many of the same problems. Catholic theology and tradition put the Church and the Pope above merely secular rulers. In theory (restated by the Council of Trent) the Church had the right to depose wicked, tyrannical, or heretical rulers. In fact it did not have this power, and had not for a long time, if ever. So, in practice, the Church and Catholic rulers cooperated uneasily but were continually suspicious of each other. In reality, whatever Catholic theology said in theory, Catholic rulers continued to gain considerable power over the Church in their territories. We have already discussed the "Gallican Liberties" of the Catholic Church in France. In the Spanish kingdoms as well, rulers had significant power over church revenues and personnel. Even where these powers were not formally enshrined or spelled out, Catholic rulers had significant control over the Church in their lands, and continued to gain more. There was, as might be imagined, continual unresolved tension between the Catholic Church and secular rulers over such questions. Indeed, the Catholic Counter-Reformation produced somewhat of a revival in political theories that placed Church above Crown. Two Jesuits, the Spaniard Juan de Mariana (1536–1624) and the Italian Robert Bellarmine (1542–1621), justified tyrannicide and defended the Pope's power to depose secular rulers. Such theories could only further complicate church-state relations.

Calvin, like Luther and almost everyone else, emphasized the divine origin of political power. It was therefore sinful to rebel against or resist a lawful ruler. If a ruler was evil, tyrannical, or a heretic, the subject had three choices: conformity, exile, or martyrdom. In no case was resistance or rebellion justified. But, having slammed the door shut on any possibility of lawful resistance, Calvin proceeded to open it just a crack. He left several theoretical loopholes for political action against rulers. There were some states, he theorized, whose constitutions provided for "lesser magistrates" whose job it was to correct and guide rulers. So, in fact, resistance or rebellion might not be sinful if sanctioned or led by these "lesser magistrates." After all, they were only doing their job. This was how one might justify Luther's revolt against the Holy Roman Emperor: yes, he was rebelling against the Emperor, but he had the support of his own ruler, the Elector of Saxony. In Calvin's case, there is strong evidence that he considered French nobles to be just such "lesser magistrates," and that if the Calvinist movement was supported by the nobles, resistance to the king might be permissible. As we shall see, this had enormous consequences in France in the later sixteenth century.

Calvin also had before him the experience of Israel as portrayed in the Old Testament, where on several occasions prophets had led rebellions against wicked kings. Calvin therefore theorized that on occasion God might raise up "open avengers" to punish wicked rulers. He never discussed, however, how one might distinguish such an "open avenger" from a garden-variety rebel. The obvious implication was that if the rebel succeeded, he must have had God's blessing. So, despite emphasizing the divine nature of political authority and the sinfulness of resistance, Calvin left several theoretical loopholes that Calvinists exploited to justify political action.

Wherever the official church was Calvinist, there was continual tension between it and the government. Government is often a messy business, and rulers often have to make practical decisions and reach compromises, regardless of their impact on religious purity. (In the nineteenth century, the unifier of Germany, the "iron chancellor" Otto von Bismarck, noted that "politics is like sausage: if you want to enjoy the end result, you shouldn't watch it being made.") Many Calvinist ministers and zealous lay people were not interested in practicalities; they were interested in purity. The Dutch Republic, for instance, was officially Calvinist but actually had a majority Catholic population until around 1600. Zealous Calvinists were continually pressing the government to take a harder line toward the Catholics, something governments continually resisted for pragmatic political purposes. Likewise in Scotland, the government clashed repeatedly with the Presbyterian Church (the "kirk") over issues of moral discipline, education, and church governance. Even in Calvinist Geneva, Calvin himself became embroiled in jurisdictional disputes with the city government.

Religion and the People

It is no doubt ironic or paradoxical that although the differences between them were vast in some respects, in practice Calvinism and Tridentine Catholicism were in some ways very alike, certainly to a degree that would have shocked sixteenth-century Calvinists and Catholics. Both movements produced a core of committed followers who believed in the absolute truth and rightness of their cause and were willing to kill and be killed in its service. Among Catholics the best example of this elite is the Society of Jesus, or Jesuits. Among Calvinists, we might expect predestination to produce apathy and fatalism, but for sixteenth-century Calvinists it had the opposite result. According to Calvin's theology, the purpose of life was not salvation, but rather serving and glorifying God on earth. If you turned out to be one of the Elect, you praised God for His mercy and grace. If you turned out to be one of the damned, it was only what you deserved, and you praised God for His justice. In either case, believers were freed from anxiety about their salvation so they could get on with their real task: doing God's will on earth. In both cases, we see a disciplined, ascetic lifestyle in which all else is subordinate.

Early in the twentieth century, the German sociologist Max Weber published an influential book called *The Protestant Ethic and the Spirit of Capitalism.* In it, he proposed what has come to be known as the Weber thesis: that Calvinist theology uniquely produced the mental conditions necessary for the rise and triumph of the modern capitalist ethic. This ethic consisted of qualities such as frugality, moderation, discipline, hard work, and sobriety. It also encompassed a disposition to value hard work simply for its own sake, rather than for the rewards it brings. Thus, despite material success, people will not rest on their laurels and enjoy the fruits of their work. They reinvest their profits in their business, rather than retire to a country estate to live a life of cultivated leisure.

Weber located the connection between Calvinist theology and the Protestant ethic in the doctrine of predestination. According to Weber, the uncertainties of the doctrine and of one's salvation, and the powerlessness to affect one's eternal destiny, produced in Calvinists an "inner loneliness" that caused them to reassure themselves that they were one of the Elect. Thus, the thesis goes, Calvinist businessmen, craftsmen, and merchants worked especially hard to convince themselves of their own salvation. And of course it became a self-fulfilling prophecy: the harder they worked, the more they denied themselves the enjoyment of the rewards of that work, the more convinced they became of their own salvation. After all, why would God favour with worldly success those whom he condemned to Hell, especially if they were leading moral, upright lives, which they knew was possible only with God's grace?

Over the last century, there have been a number of objections to Weber's thesis. Probably the most effective counter-argument is that Weber imagined what predestination would have felt like to a secular, modern German like himself, rather than investigating what it meant to sixteenth-century Calvinists. In fact, far from producing "inner loneliness," as we have seen, the doctrine of predestination produced in the sixteenth century a body of confident activists who were set free from anxiety about their salvation precisely because it was out of their hands. They did not have to worry if they had confessed all their sins, or if their confession was sincere, or if their faith was strong enough. In addition, there is absolutely no evidence that Calvin, Beza, or any Calvinist theologian connected economic success with God's blessing. Moreover, it is unclear why God's blessing should appear in the form of economic success rather than other, more overtly religious areas such as missionary activity, charitable works, personal morality, and so on. For every example of a successful Calvinist businessman who seems to embody the "Protestant" ethic, one can find many more Catholic examples, both before and after the Reformation, who also embody these "Protestant" values.

Yet however many arguments can be amassed against the Weber thesis, and while few historians would now wholeheartedly agree with it, it simply will not go away. It is probably beyond the scope of historians ever to establish definitively, but perhaps we could say that Weber's idea of a capitalist ethic arising in this period had much to recommend it, but that he identified it too closely with Calvinism. In other words, this ethic could be, and indeed was, accommodated within a variety of religious milieux; it was not specifically Protestant or Calvinist.

Both Calvinism and Reformed Catholicism also attempted to internalize their beliefs in their adherents. Pre-Reformation popular religion was based largely on practice and observance rather than on belief. That is, one was a Christian not so much because one understood and assented to a certain creed or confession or statement of beliefs, but because of what one did and the community to which one belonged. Over the centuries of the Middle Ages, popular religion had developed in ways that were suitable to a world made up largely of uneducated and illiterate peasants. The medieval church had developed a series of ceremonies and practices to shepherd its flock through life. The sacraments, for example, whatever their theological significance, also acted as rites of passage and mechanisms of social reconciliation. Baptism not only wiped away the effect of original sin, but was also a rite of initiation into human society. The social significance of marriage hardly needs comment. The sacrament of penance functioned as a means of resolving communal tensions. Mass was a very tangible demonstration of the organic and religious unity of the community. Besides the sacraments, many other ceremonies and rituals—quasi-sacraments—also were incorporated into people's lives. There were ceremonies for blessing fields and animals, for example, as well as many others.

Traditional popular religion was also largely corporate or collective rather than individual. The individual stood before God primarily as a member of a community. Salvation was very much a communal concern, and religious life consisted mostly of communal events: processions and feasts on saints' days, the great feast days of the Church, and the weekly assembly of the community to witness the miracle of Mass. In general, medieval popular religion made few demands on ordinary people. They were expected to confess and receive Mass once a year, usually at Easter, although it is very unclear how many did even this. In large part, this collective sense of religion helps to explain much of the religious violence of the period. People believed not only that heretics were going to hell, but that they also threatened the salvation of the entire community.

Protestants, on the other hand, rejected the effectiveness of ceremonies altogether. The individual Christian stood alone before God, without an intermediary church to intercede for him. This was "the priesthood of all believers." If this were so, then the individual alone was responsible for himself or herself. There was no longer a professional priesthood that could intercede on the individual's behalf. People had to be able to read the Bible for themselves and be conversant with the fundamental elements of their faith. Education was therefore essential, and Protestant authorities everywhere took great pains to make education more widely available. Pastors were instructed to conduct classes for both children and adults, and visitation commissions were regularly sent out into the country to gauge the extent of the progress in this area.

The Catholic Church, too, in the Counter-Reformation, sought to internalize and individualize Christianity in its adherents. Like Protestants, Catholics emphasized the importance of religious education or catechism for laypeople, although of course the content was very different. In the Counter-Reformation, confession became a much more interior and individual act. Prior to the Reformation, the sacrament of confession was usually a communal or semi-public event, conducted typically in a corner of the church. It is surely significant that the Catholic Counter-Reformation saw the invention of the confessional as separate enclosed space to reinforce the interior and individual nature of the sacrament. Thus, the physical layout of churches reflected changing religious ideas. During the Catholic Counter-Reformation, religious reformers also urged people to confess much more frequently, and also to take Mass more regularly. The annual confession and Mass were increasingly regarded as a bare minimum, rather than as the fulfilment of one's duties.

Medieval popular religion had also infused the material world with sacred significance. Priests and others performed ceremonies designed to influence the physical world, to ensure the fertility of fields and animals, to drive out demons and witches, to bless newlyweds, and so on. The saints were believed to have the power to intercede on behalf of individuals and communities, and might be persuaded to do so with appropriate rituals, vows, or offerings. Thus communities and trades had their patron saints, whom they venerated. St. Anne was the patron saint of miners, St. Elizabeth of bakers, St. Matthew of accountants, St. Joseph of carpenters, and so on. Certain saints also had their own specialties: St. Roch protected against plague, St. Christopher protected travellers, and St. Vitus against snakebites, to name only a few. Nations, cities, and villages also had their own patron saints to whom they would appeal for protection. St. James (Santiago) was the patron saint of Spain, St. George of England, and St. Stephen of Hungary. In times of turmoil, Parisians looked for help to St. Genevieve and St. Denis, while in Florence they appealed to St. John the Baptist, and in Venice to St. Mark.

There were also holy places. There were the great pilgrimage sites such as Chartres or Santiago de Compostela, as well as more humble local sites like shrines, wells, and groves. Certain times of year were also holier than others. Easter and Lent, which preceded it, were the holiest, but there were others as well. Indeed, people's lives consisted largely of a procession of saints' days and religious feasts that made up the liturgical calendar of the church year.

Protestants did away with this religious superstructure completely. No place or time of year was holier than another. The saints had no special merit or powers, and in fact were poor sinners like everyone else. If they lived holier lives than anyone else, this was due entirely to God's grace and no special merit of their own. It went without saying, then, that saints had no special power to intercede with God, and certainly none to affect the course of events in this world. Venerating saints was at best irrelevant superstition, and at worst a survival or remnant of pre-Christian pagan religions that had to be rooted out.

The Tridentine Catholic Church followed suit, at least part of the way. Catholic reformers, too, recognized that many of these things were pagan vestiges and that many people only vaguely understood the essentials of Christianity. In many places people worshipped the saints as gods, for example, or expected automatic results from their rituals as from a magical spell. Catholic reformers tried to prune away some of this religious undergrowth, to emphasize the separateness of the sacred and the material worlds. Along the same lines, the Church more strictly controlled and interpreted the role of the saints, more carefully laying down the criteria for sainthood and pruning away many of the more fanciful or legendary saints.

There is a significant amount of debate among historians on the impact of the Protestant and Catholic Reformations on women. In general, most historians would agree that in late medieval religion, women played an important but subordinate role. The Church itself was of course an exclusively male hierarchy, but in a number of ways late medieval popular religion allowed women their own sphere of devotion. There were of course the convents where nuns lived communally under the authority of the abbess. There were also female religious communities, known as *béguinages*, where women lived communally without taking formal vows. There were female saints to whom women could look for support and inspiration. Foremost among these was of course the Virgin Mary, whose cult underwent a significant expansion and elaboration throughout the Middle Ages. For example, St. Anne (according to tradition Mary's mother) was widely appealed to by pregnant women and women in labour.

According to some historians, the Protestant Reformation was a significant benefit for women.[1] The "priesthood of all believers" included women as well as men, and women had equal access to God. No longer did women depend on a celibate male clergy. Women were allowed, and even expected, to read the Bible for themselves. The elimination of clerical celibacy no longer devalued women's roles as wives and mothers. No longer was virginity to be prized as superior to marriage. Protestant pastors were allowed and even encouraged to marry. In Protestant theology, marriage was no longer a sacrament. This brought with it significant changes in laws governing marriage: divorce became permissible, and in theory either the husband or the wife could initiate it. Critics of this positive view point out that women's supposed spiritual equality did not translate into meaningful participation in church governance. Women were still expected to be subordinate to men. When some women did actively preach or write on religious matters, they were almost universally condemned by church authorities. Moreover, these critics point out, the elimination of female monasticism removed the one sphere where women could truly express their devotion in a uniquely female environment. In addition, the elimination of women saints and of the veneration of Mary took away women's role models and inspiration.

On the Catholic side, the reforms of the Catholic Reformation sought to subordinate women (and men too) to the hierarchical authority of the Church. Women may have retained the veneration of Mary and female saints and female monasticism, but efforts were made to more tightly control and regulate these uniquely female spheres of spirituality. The practice of enclosure was to be strictly enforced; that is, nuns were to be completely isolated from the outside world in order both to preserve their purity from the corruption in the secular world, and also to preserve the outside world from the threat posed by a community of unmarried women. There were some attempts to establish women's orders modelled after the Jesuits in order to pursue educational and charitable works in the secular world, but these were eventually condemned and suppressed. Some women's organizations did pursue these aims, but they succeeded by carefully subverting the strictures of the male-dominated hierarchy of the Church, not by overtly challenging them. For example, the Daughters of Charity, established by St. Vincent de Paul in seventeenth-century France, managed to carry out their activist agenda only by maintaining that they were not a religious community. They took no vows, wore no distinctive habit, and were careful to work only in areas where they had the approval of a bishop or priest.

In religious life, then, women remained firmly subordinated to men in both Protestant and Catholic Europe, but in somewhat different ways. In Protestant areas, women were spiritually equal to men, but this spiritual equality did not translate into equal participation. Women shared with men a single sphere of religious devotion, but remained firmly subordinated to male authority. Catholic women, on the other hand, were granted (or carved out for themselves) a uniquely female sphere of spirituality, even while this sphere was subordinate to male authority in both theory and practice.

We see yet another similarity between Protestant and Catholic churches in attempts at moral reform and the reform of popular culture. To an extent that is difficult to appreciate today, governments and churches had always claimed the right to regulate and punish the moral conduct of their people. As a result of the Protestant and Catholic Reformations, governments, with the support of their respective churches, attempted this moral regulation with greater rigour than before. Protestant reformers thought that their new theology would and should be reflected by a moral regeneration. This would be the surest way of demonstrating the truth of their faith when compared to the moral laxity of the old church. Catholics, by the same token, believed that a moral revival was the way to turn the tide against the Protestants. Thus governments and clergymen of all churches tried to regulate moral conduct, although there were of course differences in details and execution.

In Lutheran areas, where churches were under tight government control, church and state cooperated, but the rulers had the final say, and enforcement of morals was carried out largely through the legal system. In Calvinist areas, where the churches and clergy were more independent; enforcement of morals was conducted through the Consistory, a committee of pastors and laymen. The powers of the Consistory were more purely religious than legal. Among Catholics, the most important means of moral control were the confessional and the watchful eye of the priest.

Indeed, the Catholic Counter-Reformation produced a new type of priest, one who was better suited to the role of educating and reforming his flock. Previously, a typical village parish priest was virtually indistinguishable from his congregation in terms of education and culture. His education, haphazard as it was, did not set him above his flock. He was probably illiterate, having learned by rote the appropriate words to celebrate the sacraments. He baptized the babies, married the young, and buried the dead. He was a full participant in the communal life of the village, its festivals and celebrations. He provided the villagers with the appropriate rituals and ceremonies to lead them through this life and into the next, and to ensure the fertility of their fields, animals, and marriages. The new priest, the ideal priest of the Counter-Reformation, was very different. He was formally educated and literate. He was better paid. In many ways, he was a cultural foreigner in the village. He was in the community, but not of it. He was expected to maintain a dignified distance from his flock. He disapproved of peasant celebrations with their excesses and overtones of paganism. Even his dress differed: it was during the Counter-Reformation that we see the first widespread effort to enforce the wearing of a cassock to distinguish priests from laymen. The new ideal of the priest was a remote and stern figure, ready to reprove his flock's ignorance and moral shortcomings.

Part and parcel of this general moral reform was an attempt to clean up popular culture. Elites of all churches agreed that certain elements of popular culture were immoral and needed reform. Among the objectionable elements in popular culture were many practices and beliefs that reformers saw as remnants of a pre-Christian pagan past. They took issue with such traditional practices as dancing around a maypole to celebrate the arrival of spring or lighting bonfires to celebrate midsummer. This is in addition to some of the reforms discussed above, when for example the Catholic Church adopted a more rigorous approach to sainthood and deleted a number traditional saints who were in fact Christianized versions of pagan mythical figures. Other elements of popular culture were targeted because of the immoral conduct that went along with them. Indeed, the two prongs of moral reform often went together. We see this most clearly in the celebration of Carnival or Mardi Gras. This celebration ushered in Lent, the forty days preceding Easter. Because Lent was supposed to be a time of self-denial and sober reflection, Carnival evolved as a huge party, one last chance to indulge before the privations of Lent. Carnival was thus characterized in much of Europe by feasting, drinking, and dancing. There were festivals, games, and races, such as the famous *palio* of Siena. It was a time when "the world turned upside down" was much in evidence. Youth groups elected "abbots of misrule" to preside over the festivities. It was a time of "carnal" license (note the similarity of the words).

Religious reformers objected to Carnival on a number of fronts. Morally, such licentiousness was hardly a fitting prelude to sombre reflection on Christ's crucifixion and death. It was simply an excuse for people to eat and drink too much and to indulge their lusts in immoral ways. Theologically, reformers saw in Carnival celebrations vestiges of pagan culture, specifically of the *bacchanalia* of antiquity. In some ways Protestants had an easier task than Catholics in this regard, because they simply outlawed the festival. Therefore, although the change was more traumatic and drastic, Protestants were able to simply condemn the whole apparatus as immoral and diabolical. Catholics, on the other hand, wanted to keep the observance, but purify it, to make it a genuinely religious occasion rather than an excuse for getting drunk and eating too much.

Although Carnival is the most dramatic example of this attempted reform of popular culture, it extended far beyond this one celebration. Most other kinds of popular festivals came under similar kinds of attack. More prosaically, it was reflected in efforts to close down taverns and alehouses during church and to prohibit dancing on Sundays. Some Protestants, most notably the Puritans in England, took this campaign of moral reform even further. So, when the Puritans seized control of England during the 1650s (see Chapter 10), theatres and alehouses were closed down, dancing and games of chance were prohibited, and even Christmas was abolished. Puritans objected to celebrations of Christmas because, in their eyes, it was not a commemoration of Christ's birth (there is no evidence that He was born on December 25), but rather a thinly veiled continuation of the Roman mid-winter festival of Saturnalia. Christmas was also a time of excessive eating and drinking, which was hardly a fitting commemoration of Christ's birth.

There is no doubt that there was in these efforts to reform and clean up popular culture a desire on the part of political and religious elites to control the unruly masses. It would, however, be a mistake to see this campaign as simply a naked attempt at social control. Although it may seem invasive and paternalistic to us today, much of this was genuinely well intentioned. If religious and political leaders took their duties seriously, then it was incumbent on them to improve the moral character of their people.

But of course it did not work. In fact, not only did it not work, it was counterproductive. Rather than purifying the culture of ordinary people, religious reformers simply alienated them, driving them away from official religion. In the short term, state and church power may have forced people to conform, but nothing could make them like it. A cultural wedge had been driven between European elites and ordinary people: whereas all had previously participated in the same culture, but elites had also shared a literate, educated culture, now elites existed in a different cultural universe than ordinary people, whom they increasingly saw as uncouth and unrefined.

As part of the campaigns to internalize and unify religious belief and to reform popular culture, both Catholics and Protestants attempted to improve people's education, especially their religious education. All churches tried to impose a catechism upon their members, which would teach them the essentials of their faith. In general, church officials despaired of the state of ordinary people's religious knowledge, especially in rural areas. For example, a French priest wrote in 1637 of the state of religious knowledge in his parish: "they are ignorant of even the commonest things that have to be known before one can receive the sacraments and be saved." In the late seventeenth century, a French bishop would write to the Pope that the people in his diocese were "quite uneducated, hardly initiated in even the rudiments of the faith; [they live] in crass and deeply-rooted ignorance." Things were no better among Protestants. In 1583 an inspector in Lutheran Brandenburg asked villagers about their religious knowledge:

> We asked them how they understood each of the Ten Commandments, but we found many who could give no answer at all, who could not even say against which commandment a given sin offended. Moreover, none of them thought it a sin to get dead drunk and to curse, using the name of God.

Just as there were efforts to produce a better-educated clergy, so there were efforts to produce a better-educated (and in theory consequently more Christian) laity.

There was a huge expansion of schools and educational materials in sixteenth- and seventeenth-century Europe. In Protestant areas especially, we see increased literacy, largely because Protestants stressed individual Bible-reading to a much greater extent than Catholics.

Tracking the rise of literacy is a very difficult undertaking. It is usually done through analysing the proportion of people who can sign their names to important documents as opposed to making a mark. However, certainly many people painstakingly learned to form the letters of their name, but were otherwise illiterate. Furthermore, since reading was taught before writing (as it is now), many people could likely read a bit, but could not sign their name. However, even if this research cannot tell us the exact proportion of people who were literate, it does tell us a great deal about trends. Based on this research, the following general statements can be made with a fair degree of certainty: a higher proportion of people were literate in 1715 than in 1559; more men were literate than women, more city-dwellers than peasants, and more Protestants than Catholics; literacy also varied with wealth and social status, with the bourgeoisie and aristocracy more literate than urban workers or peasants.

Higher levels of literacy, however, like the reform of popular culture, did not work quite as reformers had thought it would. Their primary goal in promoting literacy was to improve religious knowledge and thereby construct a more moral and Christian society. Once people have been taught to read, however, it is impossible to control what they read, or what they write for that matter. Religious reformers and educators thought people would read the Bible and other pious works. Although these continued to be very important, there was a vast market for secular works. For entertainment there were adventure stories, works of chivalry, and romantic derring-do. There were also practical books like almanacs, and eventually magazines and newspapers.

Literacy allowed people access to new worlds of thought, which were often at variance with official religion. Such was the case of Domenico Scandella, known as Menocchio, a miller in the northeastern Italian region of Friuli. Thanks to the existence of inquisitorial records, historian Carlo Ginzburg has given us a unique look into an early modern mind. In his book *The Cheese and the Worms*, Ginzburg recreates the mental universe of a sixteenth-century miller. A respected member of his community, Menocchio had had some schooling and was able to read and write. Over many years, he read whatever he could lay his hands on and expressed a number of opinions that went against the teaching of the Catholic Church. He had no use for priests or monks, thought that the sacraments were invented to make money, and expressed a generally pantheist view of God and the universe. Although his views were certainly out of the mainstream, Menocchio lived undisturbed in his village for many years and was generally well liked and respected despite his strange ideas and argumentative nature. The only reason we know about him was that he was denounced anonymously to the Inquisition in 1583. After being imprisoned and interrogated, he was released, the inquisitors apparently being satisfied that he had abandoned his heretical ideas. He resumed his place in the community before being denounced again in 1598. This time, as a lapsed heretic, he was sentenced to death, and the sentence was carried out in 1599.

Through careful research, Ginzburg was able to identify a number of the books that Menocchio had read, and he shows how the semi-educated miller filtered the ideas he found there through the peasant consciousness of the time. What is unusual about the case of Menocchio, then, is twofold. First, he was unusually inquisitive and argumentative, not willing to dissemble his beliefs. Second, the only reason we know about him is that he came to the attention of the Inquisition. How many others must there have been who had similar ideas, but not the access to the world of books and ideas to help form them?

Another similarity among churches was that to some extent they were all rent by internal dissension or schisms. Following Luther's death, Lutherans were divided over the role of works in salvation and compromises with Catholic theology. One group, followers of Luther's right-hand man Philip Melanchthon (hence known as the Philipists), believed that people in some way cooperated with God's grace in salvation, and that there was room for reconciliation with the Catholic Church. Their opponents, who called themselves "genuine" Lutherans, or "gnesio-Lutherans," believed that the Philipists compromised the very essence of the Reformation. After several decades of bitter acrimony, the two sides managed to hammer out a Formula of Concord in 1580.

The Church of England, while Protestant in theology, was divided over the proper form of church government. Because of the political origins of the English Reformation, the government of the Church remained firmly in the hands of the monarch and was exercised through bishops. To many Protestant English people, this was an unacceptable "Popish remnant." These people, known generally as Puritans (because they wanted to purify the Church of England of such Catholic vestiges), wanted a more Calvinistic form of government, allowing for more lay participation. So, the Church of England remained an episcopal church (after the Latin word for bishop, *episcopus*), while the Puritans wanted a presbyterian church (after the lay elders or presbyters who would play a large role in such a church). Generally speaking, the ruler and those who supported the Church of England as it was constituted tended to support more lavish and ritualistic church services, while Puritans favoured simplicity and purity, with greater emphasis on the spoken word in the sermon than on elaborate worship. Therefore, in England, the dispute was not so much about basic theology as it was about liturgy and governance.

In many ways, the divisions among Calvinists and Catholics are mirror images of each other, having to do primarily with predestination and the role of human effort in salvation. The dominant forces in both movements had staked out extreme positions on these issues. On the Catholic side, the Jesuits emphasized the importance of human effort in salvation, to the point where they seemed to many to minimize or dismiss human sinfulness. In 1588, the Jesuit theologian Luis de Molina published a book entitled *Concordance of Free Will with the Gifts of Grace*. In it, he argued that while man's nature was sinful, free will still had a large role to play in attaining salvation. Although Molina's views were not universally accepted, and several popes attempted to calm down the controversy without condemning either Molina or his opponents, his views were popular among many seventeenth-century Jesuits. And, as we have seen, Calvin had upheld an unusually strict view of predestination. What happened in the seventeenth century was a kind of reversion to the mean. In both churches there were significant movements that tried to moderate these extremes.

Interestingly, the key theologians in both movements were from the Netherlands. Cornelius Jansen (1585–1638) was a Dutch Catholic theologian, Bishop of Ypres, and professor at the Catholic University of Louvain in the Spanish Netherlands. Based on his reading of the Bible and St. Augustine, Jansen concluded that the Jesuits' positive view of human nature and potential had gone too far, that in fact they verged on Pelagianism, the ancient heresy that people could attain salvation unaided by divine grace. In particular, Jansen stressed human sinfulness and depravity and the all-important role of divine grace in salvation. Theologically, Jansenism (as his views came to be called) is a kind of Catholic Calvinism, with its emphasis on human sinfulness and predestination, leading one historian to characterize Jansenism as "perdition for the unfortunate many, and ascetic gloom for the fortunate few." Jansen's major work *Augustinus* was published only in 1640, two years after his death. Although Jansen's ideas found a following throughout Catholic Europe, his followers in France were especially prominent and powerful.

Within France, the epicentre of Jansenism was the convent of Port-Royal, just outside Paris. There, the Mother Superior Marie-Angélique Arnaud and her spiritual advisor the Abbé de St-Cyran made Jansenism fashionable among certain segments of the French elite. The Arnaud family was especially prominent in the upper reaches of the legal system. The Mother Superior's father was a judge in the Parlement of Paris, the most important court in France. One of her brothers, Antoine, was a leading Jansenist writer and theologian. In addition, the famous playwright Jean Racine was attracted to the movement, as was the painter Philippe de Champaigne. The most famous Jansenist, however, was the scientist and mathematician Blaise Pascal (1623–62). Having experienced a mystical conversion experience in 1654, which he called his "Night of Fire," he devoted the rest of his short life to religious meditation and writing, particularly defending the Jansenists against their archenemies, the Jesuits. His *Provincial Letters* (1657) is a withering attack on Jesuit moral casuistry.

Jansenism also assumed political dimensions in France, where it was repeatedly attacked by the Pope and Cardinal Richelieu, and later by King Louis XIV. It was formally condemned by the University of Paris, and a papal bull of 1653 decreed heretical five propositions that it claimed were characteristic of Jansenism. Jansenists agreed that these propositions were indeed heretical, but that they were not to be found in Jansen's works. Jansenism remained a divisive force throughout the seventeenth century and beyond. Even the physical destruction of Port-Royal in 1711 and a definitive papal condemnation in the bull *Unigenitus* of 1713 could not destroy the movement, which lived on through the eighteenth century among influential segments of French society.

On the Calvinist side, the revisionist theologian was a Protestant Dutch professor at the Protestant University of Leiden, Jacob Arminius (1560–1609). Arminius came to believe, contrary to strict Calvinism, that humans can choose to accept or reject salvation. He attracted a group of followers within the Dutch Republic who became known as the Remonstrants because they remonstrated or protested against the official theology of the Dutch Reformed Church. Like Jansenism, Arminianism assumed political dimensions. It was especially popular among the group of people known as regents: the wealthy bourgeois who dominated the world of commerce and the urban political scene. Politically, they tended to favour the continued decentralization of the Dutch Republic, peace with Spain, and practical toleration for Catholics. They were opposed by the Counter-Remonstrants, or Gomarists, after their leader Francis Gomarus (1563–1641). Religiously, the Gomarists upheld Calvin's view of predestination in all its strictness. Politically, they made common cause with the supporters of the House of Orange, which was trying to centralize power in the Dutch Republic in their hands, and supported continued war against Spain. Although the Gomarists won the day in the Synod of Dort in 1618, Arminianism remained a divisive force in the Dutch Republic. (See Chapter 12.)

These schisms and divisions had much the same effect as many of the other issues examined above. If professional theologians and churchmen could not agree on something as basic as salvation, what hope was there for ordinary laypeople? Many devout people were confused by these interminable wranglings. In all churches, there was an increasing tendency in the late seventeenth and early eighteenth centuries toward Quietism or Pietism—an emphasis on the love of God and fellow humans, and practical, interior religion, as opposed to external official religion or theology.

In much the same way that many ordinary people were alienated from official churches by their emphasis on conformity and coercion, many educated people were alienated by these theological and jurisdictional disputes. Together with the legacy of a century and a half of religious warfare, and developments in science, this alienation would help to produce the secular frame of mind of the eighteenth century known as the Enlightenment. Voltaire, the most prominent figure in this movement, would write,

> I know to be sure that the Church is infallible; but is it the Greek Church or the Latin Church, or the Church of England, or that of Denmark and Sweden? In short, would it not be better not to lose ourselves in these labyrinths and simply preach virtue? When God judges us, I doubt very much if he will ask whether grace is versatile or concomitant. Shall I not render a service to men in announcing to them nothing but morality? This morality is so pure, so holy, so universal, so clear, so ancient that it seems to come direct from God, like the light of day which we consider his first cre-

ation. Did he not give men self-love to insure their preservation; sympathy, beneficence and virtue to control self-love; mutual needs for the formation of society; pleasure in the satisfaction of them; pain which causes us to enjoy with moderation; passions which lead us on to great things, and wisdom to curb passions?

NOTE

1 See for example, Steven Ozment, *When Fathers Ruled: Family Life in Reformation Europe* (Cambridge, MA: Harvard University Press, 1983). For an example of the opposite view, see Lyndal Roper, *The Holy Household: Women and Morals in Reformation Augsburg* (Oxford: Oxford University Press, 1989).

PART TWO

Wars of Religion, 1559–1648

In 1559, Philip II of Spain and Henry II of France signed the Treaty of Cateau-Cambrésis, bringing to an end 65 years of war. These wars had begun over control of Italy, but they evolved into a duel for European hegemony between the Valois dynasty of France and the Habsburgs, who governed the Spanish kingdoms, the Netherlands, Hungary, Bohemia, and Austria, and possessed the title of Holy Roman Emperor. Technically, Spain was the victor, since the treaty conferred control of Milan and Naples on Philip, and France renounced all claims in Italy, but both sides were exhausted by generations of warfare. Peace would allow them time to recover, to put their finances in order. An additional incentive for peace was that both kings were concerned about heresy among their subjects: Henry II in France itself, and Philip II in the Netherlands. Concluding peace with each other would allow them to deal with the threat of heresy at home. Thus, according to the historian J.H. Elliott, "the Europe of Cateau-Cambrésis was born beneath the double sign of bankruptcy and heresy...."[1] The peace established between the two greatest rulers in Europe in 1559, was destined to be short-lived, since for the next century Europe was to be convulsed by one religious war after another: in France from 1562 to 1598, in the Netherlands from the 1560s to 1609 and again from 1621 to 1648, and in Germany, the Thirty Years' War from 1618 to 1648. England managed to escape religious strife largely through the shrewd politics of Elizabeth I, but it would experience a bitter civil war in the seventeenth century in which religious differences played a large role.

In the past, many historians discounted the religious element of these wars. My approach here is that while there were certainly other issues at stake—political, economic, diplomatic or social—religion was the most important factor in these wars. That is, while there were certainly other causes for warfare, without the religious element one simply cannot explain the brutality, duration, or course of these wars. Without the passions engendered by religious division, European history of the sixteenth and seventeenth centuries would have been very different indeed.

NOTE

1 J.H. Elliott, *Europe Divided, 1559–1598* (Ithaca: Cornell University Press, 1968), 11.

CHAPTER FIVE

The Wars of Religion in France

From the early 1560s until 1598, France was torn apart by a series of civil and religious wars. Officially there were eight wars in all, but in some senses this is a purely arbitrary division; the distinction between one war and the next is often quite meaningless. Historians of France used to downplay the importance of religion in these conflicts. Religion was seen purely as a cloak, a pretext for the real motives of the participants. For example, the nobles used religion as a pretext to justify their rebellion against the king; or, in various Marxist or semi-Marxist interpretations, the middle class justified its social and economic aspirations on the basis of religion. More recent generations of historians, however, have tended to put religion back into the Wars of Religion. In keeping with the approach outlined above, my central approach here will be that the French Wars of Religion were not exclusively religious (or exclusively anything else). Rather, the wars were the result of a confluence of crises. As these crises converged, they reacted with each other, making them more serious *en masse* than they would have been on their own. Three major crises combined to produce decades of civil and religious strife in France: religious, political, and socio-economic. In this chapter we will examine the religious and political crises, while the socio-economic crisis in France was part of the larger European crisis examined in Chapters 2 and 3.

The Religious Crisis: the growth of Calvinism

After about 1555, Calvinism became the dominant Protestant movement in France for several reasons. Calvin himself, and later Beza, always remained concerned with the land of their birth. Calvin's works and other Protestant literature were translated into French and smuggled into France, or were printed surreptitiously within France. Geneva's geographical proximity to France, and the fact that it was a French-speaking city, made it a natural destination for French religious refugees, such as Calvin himself had been. After about 1555, many of these refugees went back into France as missionaries and pastors and imposed a

Calvinist framework on what had been an unorganized and inchoate French Protestant movement. Between 1555 and 1562, 88 missionaries were sent from Geneva into France, a tendency that intensified after the founding of the Genevan Academy in 1559 as a training school for pastors and missionaries. About 80 per cent of the Academy's students were French; even so, Geneva could not supply all the requests for pastors. As a result many French Calvinist churches were without regular full-time pastors.

French Calvinists became known as Huguenots,[1] and by 1559 the Huguenot movement had organized itself in a way that was well suited to surviving in a hostile environment. In that year, the first national synod of the French Reformed Church met under the King's nose in Paris, writing a constitution and confession of faith. By the early 1560s, Calvinism had reached its high-water mark in France. About 10 per cent of the population were Huguenots (about 2 million out of about 20 million), organized in about 1,000 churches throughout France. In fact, French Calvinism was more powerful than this figure would indicate, because Huguenots were concentrated both socially and geographically, that is within certain groups in French society and in certain areas of the kingdom.

By the early 1560s, about half of the French nobility was Huguenot. Calvin was especially interested in converting the nobility as a way to convert France from above. Moreover, the nobles corresponded with his "lesser magistrates," whose support might lend legitimacy to opposition to the royal government. King Henry II (1547–59) had seen heresy primarily as a problem of the lower classes, and although he set up a special court, the *Chambre Ardente* or Burning Chamber, to deal with heretics, noble Huguenots were relatively unmolested, while middle- and lower-class Huguenots were persecuted. There is no doubt that many noble conversions were cynical and political in nature. Many less powerful nobles converted because their patrons did; many others converted as a way to legitimize rebellion. Many other conversions, however, were undoubtedly sincere, while the motives of many others were mixed or unclear even to themselves. They may have sincerely believed that theirs was a genuine and sincere religious conversion, but at the same time it may have benefitted their political or social standing. The "real" motive for many conversions remains unclear.

Huguenots were especially noticeable at the very highest levels of the nobility, among the clans who were politically significant on a national level and who were a powerful presence at the royal court. A good example is the Bourbon family, the closest relatives of the ruling Valois dynasty, descended from a younger son of King Louis IX (1226–70) and tied to the royal family through a series of marriages. In 1527, Marguerite of Angoulême, sister of King Francis I (1515–47), married Henri d'Albret, ruler of the tiny Kingdom of Navarre in the Pyrenees between France and Spain. In 1548 their daughter, Jeanne d'Albret, Queen of Navarre, married Antoine de Bourbon, leader of the Bourbon family. Jeanne herself was a sincere and committed Huguenot, and for a time her husband flirted with the new religion. Their eldest surviving son, Henry of Navarre, would much later become King Henry IV of France. More immediately, Antoine's younger brother Louis, prince of Condé, also converted to the new faith and would become the military leader of the Huguenots in the early stages of the religious wars.

Another important noble clan was the Montmorency family. The chief of the family was Anne (often a man's name in sixteenth-century France), a war hero and close confidant of King Henry II, as well as Constable of France (a sort of commander-in-chief of the army). The Constable remained Catholic, but other members of the family became Huguenot. Most notable among the Montmorency Huguenots were the three Châtillon brothers, nephews of the Constable. They were Odet de Châtillon, successively archbishop of Toulouse and bishop of Beauvais, and a cardinal of the Catholic Church, who tried to hang onto these positions despite his conversion to Calvinism; François d'Andelot, who became an important Huguenot military figure; and, the most prominent of the three, Gaspard de Coligny, Admiral of France (sort of a commander-in-chief of the navy). Coligny would play a very prominent role in the Huguenot movement, succeeding Louis de Condé as chief military leader of the Huguenot forces.

The prominence of the nobility had several important consequences for French Calvinism. It did give the Huguenots powerful political and military protection, without which its survival would have been very doubtful. It was, however, a mixed blessing. The prominence of powerful nobles within the movement meant that the French Reformed Church was inevitably caught up in the nobility's political struggles. Noble concerns and methods came to dominate the movement, with the result that religion was often used as a cloak for other goals.

Calvinism also held a special appeal for large sections of the bourgeoisie and urban working classes. The "priesthood of all believers" assured them that they were no longer subordinate to the clergy, and lay participation in the administration of Huguenot churches allowed a previously unheard-of input. Calvin's doctrine of the "calling," in which all vocations were honourable in God's eyes, sanctified their livelihood. Since so many of them were educated and literate, Calvin's emphasis on personal Bible study was music to their ears. Accordingly, large segments of the judicial and financial bureaucracy converted, as did many professionals and merchants. Among the working classes, skilled craftsmen were much more likely to convert than unskilled. Printers, who were literate by the very nature of their trade, were especially prone to conversion. On the other hand, those in trades that were more closely linked with the rural world, such as vintners and butchers, were less likely to convert.

French Calvinism was a distinctly urban phenomenon, and it made very few inroads among peasants, with a few exceptions. Most peasant villages were isolated from the major currents of intellectual life, and peasants were notorious for their conservative and suspicious nature. They were not likely to welcome "foreigners" preaching new doctrines, especially since their religion was so very closely integrated into a rural, agricultural world, as we saw in Chapter 4. Moreover, the vast majority of peasants were illiterate, a reality that made personal Bible study, a hallmark of Calvinism, impossible. One of the very few exceptions to the low incidence of Calvinist conversions in rural areas was in the mountainous region of the Cevennes in south-central France. But this was a very rare exception to the general picture.[2]

French Calvinism was also concentrated geographically: first, as we have seen, in the cities, and second in the cities of the south and west. These latter regions were farther from Paris and the centres of power—the king, the Sorbonne, and the chief law court of the kingdom, the Parlement of Paris. They were subject to regional *parlements*, which could be more tolerant than that of Paris. They were also distinct from much of northern France in their history, culture, language, and institutions. In particular, these regions were characterized by greater noble and municipal autonomy, which allowed greater scope for religious dissent.

So by the early 1560s there was a powerful and widespread Huguenot movement with powerful political and military potential. This was an alarming situation for many Catholics, made much more troublesome by the political crisis that broke out in the country in the late 1550s and early 1560s.

The Political Crisis

As part of the peace settlement of Cateau-Cambrésis, Henry II had arranged for the marriage of his daughter Elisabeth to Philip II of Spain. As part of the wedding celebrations on June 30, 1559, King Henry, then in vigorous middle age and an experienced and hardy warrior, took part in a tournament. Unfortunately, his opponent's lance splintered, pierced the King's eye, and went into his brain. It appeared at first that he might recover; however, several days later Henry II died at the age of forty.

The King's unforeseen and accidental death ushered in an extended political crisis that combined with the religious crisis in very explosive manner. He left behind an Italian widow, Catherine de Medici, and four young sons, the three eldest of whom would reign as king. It was completely unforeseeable at the time that none of his sons would have legitimate sons of their own, which in three decades would produce a constitutional and dynastic crisis. The eldest of these sons became King Francis II, technically an adult, but in fact a sickly and dim-witted teenager, incapable of ruling on his own. In this situation, the new king's in-laws seized control of the royal government. Francis was married to Mary Stuart, who besides being the daughter of King James V of Scotland, was also a member of the French noble family of the Guises.

The Guise family was descended from the younger son of a previous duke of Lorraine, then an independent duchy within the Holy Roman Empire. In 1559, the family was led by François, duke of Guise, and his brother Charles, a Catholic cardinal known as the Cardinal of Lorraine. The Guises were, along with the Bourbons and the Montmorencys, one of the most powerful noble factions within France. Previously, kings Francis I and Henry II had ruled with the help of these great noble clans and their supporters and clients in the provinces. When one faction looked like it was becoming too powerful or too arrogant or too complacent, the king would favour another in a delicate balancing act. With the accession of the young and weak Francis II, this balance was destroyed. In other words, there was no strong, controlling hand at the top to keep the noble factions in rough equilibrium. The new king was entirely dependent on the Guises, for the Duke of Guise was his wife's uncle. Upon Francis II's accession in 1559, there was a palace coup in which the Guises seized control of the young king's person and of the government. This of course aroused the hostility and resentment of the Montmorencys and also of the Bourbons. The factional fighting was intensified by religious considerations: as we have seen, Huguenots were well represented in both the Bourbon and Montmorency clans, while the Guises were thoroughly Catholic.

The Guises used their new power to intensify the persecution of the Huguenots. In reaction, in March 1560 a number of Huguenot nobles plotted to kidnap the King, to rescue him from his "evil advisors" and eliminate Guise power. This was the Tumult, or Conspiracy, of Amboise. Guise was forewarned of the plot, and the conspirators were ambushed and many were killed or captured. Several hundred were summarily executed. Louis de Condé, a Bourbon, was heavily implicated, although his exact role, if any, is unclear. In any case, he was arrested, imprisoned, and sentenced to death, but before the sentence could be carried out the young king died and was succeeded by his younger brother, who became King Charles IX.

In the meantime, the religious situation continued to grow more tense. All over France, Huguenots and Catholics became embroiled in violent conflict. Anne du Bourg, a judge in the Parlement of Paris, was executed for heresy in 1559. That same year in Paris, there was a riot outside the Church of St. Medard, where an illegal assembly of Huguenots was rumoured to be taking place. In many other cities throughout France, relations between Huguenots and Catholics became more strained and more violent. This can be explained in part by the collective or corporate nature of traditional religion, as discussed in Chapter 4. Among many people there was a strong sense that failure to exterminate the heretics in their midst threatened the fortunes and salvation of the entire community.

The accession of the new king completely transformed the political situation. Unlike his elder brother, at ten years of age Charles was not even technically an adult, and so a formal regency became necessary. The Queen Mother, Catherine de Medici, became regent, and the Bourbons, as the closest relatives of the ruling dynasty, assumed a more important role. The power of the Guises was overthrown, but Catherine, being only regent (and a foreigner and a woman to boot), had to rely on the other factions, for she did not possess the authority or power to disregard them. Above all, she wanted to calm things down. Accordingly, in 1561, she sponsored the Colloquy of Poissy, a theological conference whose goal was to try to reach compromise on religion. The conference was doomed to failure, as the gulf between the two sides was far too great to be papered over. In 1560 and 1561 as well, there were meetings of the Estates-General. These were notable particularly for the reform proposals of the Chancellor, Michel de l'Hôpital. Catherine and l'Hôpital hoped that the project of reforming the government would take some of the sting out of the religious conflicts, a hope that was proven utterly futile.

As a means of mollifying the Huguenots as well as the Montmorencys and Bourbons, the Edict of St-Germain in January 1562 (or the Edict of January as it became known) granted the Huguenots a limited degree of practical toleration. This only made the situation worse, however, as the Huguenots were emboldened by their progress, and many Catholics grew increasingly fearful and hostile.

The First Three Wars, 1562–70

One incident in particular is usually taken as the beginning of the Wars of Religion. This is the Massacre of Vassy in March 1562. Accounts of the incident vary, but a group of armed men with the Duke of Guise disrupted a Huguenot worship service in the eastern French town of Vassy (or Wassy, as it is now known). In the ensuing melee, a number of Huguenots were killed. Similar massacres in several other towns led the Huguenots to take up arms in their own defence, under the leadership of Louis de Condé. In the spring of 1562, a number of important towns were seized by the Huguenots, and after some minor skirmishing the war was ended in 1563 with the Peace of Amboise. This treaty recognized freedom of conscience for the Huguenots and extended their rights of worship as they had been granted in the Edict of January. It proved completely unenforceable, however, for Huguenots ignored its restrictions and zealous Catholics ignored the limited toleration it granted. This first war set the pattern for the subsequent wars: some outrage prompts one side or the other to take up arms, a few battles are fought, a few towns change hands, and then a peace is declared. The peace treaties experimented with varying degrees of freedom for the Huguenots, but it was always too much for the ultra-Catholics, led by the Guises, and always too little for the Huguenots. Catherine and her sons were trying desperately to find a middle ground where none existed.

Indeed, the young king and the Queen Mother were in a very difficult position. Above all, Catherine wanted to maintain royal authority. The two main obstacles in her path were the Huguenot rebels and the Guises, as religious and factional conflict threatened royal authority throughout the kingdom. She wanted to defeat the Huguenots, but not deliver the royal government into the Guises' power in the process.

One other incident during this first war of religion deserves mention. In February 1563, the Duke of Guise was assassinated by a Huguenot nobleman. Under torture, the assassin implicated Admiral Coligny, who vigorously denied the charge. Guise's son and successor as duke, Henri, however, bore Coligny a bitter grudge over the death of his father, a grudge that would go on to have fatal consequences in the St. Bartholomew's Massacres of 1572.

The second and third wars of 1567 to 1570 were for all practical purposes one war, punctuated by a brief truce because both sides had run out of money.

The second war began with another attempt, led by Condé, to seize the King and the Queen Mother at Meaux in 1567. The plot failed as Charles and Catherine were taken to Paris under a heavy escort. Once again, the war was inconclusive in a military sense: the royalist and Catholic forces won some important victories, but they could never deal the Huguenots a crushing blow. At the battle of Jarnac in 1569, Condé was killed, leaving Coligny as the chief Huguenot commander. The rising star in the Huguenot movement, however, was young Henry of Navarre, the son of Antoine de Bourbon and Jeanne d'Albret. A member of the House of Bourbon, he was also King of Navarre in his own right. Should the unthinkable happen (as it eventually did) and none of the four sons of Henry II have legitimate sons of their own, Henry of Navarre stood in line to inherit the French throne as well.

The third war ended with the Peace of St. Germain in 1570. For the Huguenots, this was a significant advance over the Peace of Amboise in terms of the freedom they gained to practise their religion. But this only further inflamed the Guises and their zealous Catholic supporters.

St. Bartholomew's and its Aftermath

The St. Bartholomew's Massacre of 1572 is without a doubt the most famous (or notorious) incident of the wars. Its origins lie equally in domestic and foreign politics; in fact the two were very closely linked. On the domestic side, Catherine was concerned as always to preserve royal freedom from either the Huguenots or the Guises. But she also wanted to reconcile the Huguenots as part of a longer-term strategy to restore civil peace to France. One element of this strategy was a marriage alliance between her daughter Marguerite and Henry of Navarre, the heir apparent to the leadership of the Huguenots. The wedding took place in Paris amid much fanfare in August of 1572. On the foreign policy side, the major question was relations with Spain, specifically whether or not to assist rebels in the Netherlands against the King of Spain (see Chapter 6). Coligny and the Huguenots favoured support of the Dutch rebels, even if that meant war with Spain, which after all was France's traditional enemy. Many Catholics, led by the Guises opposed such intervention. They felt that weakened by almost a decade of civil war, France was in no condition to fight the strongest power in Europe. Besides, it was deeply repugnant to many Catholics to support heretic rebels against their legitimate Catholic ruler, Philip II of Spain.

Leading up to the marriage, many Catholics feared that Coligny was gaining influence with the young king, which caused a great deal of fear and resentment. The marriage took place on August 18, and four days later there was an attempt on Coligny's life. The assassin was posted in a window and had a clear shot at the Admiral, but just as he shot, Coligny either turned his head to spit, or bent to tie a shoelace, and so was only wounded. The Duke of Guise was heavily implicated in this attempt (remember that he blamed Coligny for his father's death in 1563).

Most of the important Huguenot nobility was in Paris for the wedding and were outraged by this attack on their leader. Faced with a tense and explosive situation, on the night of August 23, Guise apparently convinced the King and Catherine that the only thing to do was to wipe out the Huguenot leadership. If they failed to act decisively, Guise argued, there was a very real danger from the angry and heavily armed Huguenot nobles. They would never get another opportunity like this to destroy the Huguenot leadership in one fell swoop. Catherine and Charles were won over by Guise's arguments and assented to a surgical and pre-emptive strike against a handful of leading Huguenots. On August 24, the eve of St. Bartholomew's Day, Coligny was murdered in his bed, Navarre and his cousin the young prince of Condé were taken into custody, and a number of other prominent Huguenots murdered.

What Catherine and the King had seen as a quick and limited pre-emptive strike soon became much more. The Catholic mob of Paris, urged on by many priests, and in many cases led by members of the civic militia, began to massacre anyone suspected of being a Huguenot. Exact responsibility for this general massacre is impossible to pinpoint. Many of the rioters sincerely believed that they had royal permission to kill the heretics, and certainly there were contradictory signals from the government. Many also believed that Guise desired such a bloodbath, but there is no evidence for this, and in fact Guise sheltered Huguenots from the mob. In any case, the massacre in Paris went on for the better part of a week. The city gates were closed to prevent escape, and known and suspected Huguenots were systematically hunted down and killed. Through September and October, a number of other cities also experienced their own massacres as news of events in Paris filtered out to the provinces. All told, probably about 5,000 people were murdered in the various massacres throughout France.

These massacres of course prompted the Huguenots to take up arms once again to defend themselves. Officially there were three wars in the 1570s, but for all practical purposes, there was really only one continuous war, coming to an end in 1576. The massacres also changed the basic nature of the wars. Up until this point, the Huguenots had maintained that they were not rebels against the King; they were simply trying to "rescue" him from his "evil advisors" (the Guises). Now, however, the King and the Queen Mother had instigated a massacre of Huguenots. It was therefore no longer possible for the Huguenots to maintain their loyalty to the King. Several writers and theorists came forward to justify Huguenot resistance against royal authority. François Hotman's *Francogallia* was an examination of French history that maintained the elective and contractual nature of the French monarchy. From its origins, the power of French kings had always been limited by the power of the people, expressed in the Estates-General. That the monarchy had in practice been hereditary for many centuries and that the Estates-General had ceased to play their limiting role in no way invalidated the principles. So the Huguenots were fighting not just for freedom to practise their religion, but to restore the original and true character of the French monarchy. Theodore Beza's *Right of Magistrates*, and the *Vindicae contra tyrannos* (probably by the Huguenot nobleman Philippe Duplessis-Mornay), based their arguments not on history, but on natural rights. That is, by his actions Charles IX had shown himself to be a tyrant who forfeited the allegiance of his subjects, according to universally acknowledged principles of natural law.

Following the massacres, Huguenot nobles and towns of the south and west established their own federation, to all intents and purposes an independent state complete with a constitution and a fiscal and military structure. Some historians have even referred to it as the "United Provinces of the Midi," an echo of the United Provinces of the Netherlands then in revolt against Philip II. (The Midi is a term often applied to the south of France.) It was based primarily on fortified towns, most notably the great Atlantic seaport and stronghold of La Rochelle.

The 1570s also saw several other notable developments. One was the death of Charles IX in 1574 and the succession of his younger brother as King Henry III (r. 1574–89). He had just been elected king of Poland and arrived in his new kingdom when his brother died and he rushed back to France (see Chapter 13). The other development was the emergence of the last of the royal brothers as a political actor: François duke of Alençon (later Anjou). As heir presumptive to the throne, he was an important political player. Anjou had great plans and ambitions, but he was neither very smart nor constant in his tactics. In order to enhance his own power, he allied himself with the Huguenots and moderate Catholic enemies of the Guises. Here we see the origins of a group that would later be called *politiques*: those who, while Catholic, preferred limited toleration of the Huguenots to continued civil strife. Faced with a powerful Huguenot opposition, in 1576 Henry III signed the Edict of Beaulieu, or Peace of Monsieur. (The king's brother was called simply "Monsieur," and the treaty was thus called because of the support that Anjou gave the Huguenot cause.) This was the most generous treatment accorded the Huguenots thus far in the wars, and it inevitably aroused the indignation of many Catholics, who once again looked to Guise for leadership of the zealous Catholic cause.

The Catholic League, 1576–89

Throughout France following the Peace of Monsieur, Catholics upset with the favourable treatment of the Huguenots formed associations to defend the Catholic faith. Such local leagues were not new: there had been such organizations on a local level as early as the 1560s. What was new now, however, was the scale and national scope of the movement. This Catholic League of 1576 was in fact made up of numerous regional associations and was given overall leadership by the Duke of Guise, although he mostly encouraged and capitalized on what was already going on. In the Estates-General that met at Blois in 1576, delegates who supported the Catholic League dominated and imposed their agenda on the King. Henry III, for his part, promised to wage war against the Huguenots if the Estates granted him the money to do it. But the Estates refused to grant the money, and Henry was now committed to a war without the means to fight it. Two more inconclusive wars followed, ended by two inconclusive treaties. At the same time, Henry sought to co-opt the Catholic League by declaring himself its head.

Henry III was a very interesting character. He was clearly the smartest of the four sons of Henry II and Catherine de Medici, but he was also undisciplined, lazy, and sexually ambiguous. He aroused the opposition of many because of his extravagant lifestyle and his numerous boyfriends or *mignons*. Pierre de Lestoile, a Parisian who wrote massive memoirs of the period, described them:

> There is now much talk about the *mignons*, who are greatly loathed and despised by the people, as much for their haughty ways as for their effeminate and immodest appearance, but most of all for the excessive liberality of the king towards them.... These nice *mignons* wear their hair long, curled and recurled, and surmounted by little velvet caps like those of the women of the streets. Their collars are wide and loose so that their heads resemble St. John's upon the platter.... Their pursuits are gambling, blasphemy, leaping, dancing, quarrelling, seducing, and attending the king everywhere. They do everything to please him, giving no thought to honour God, contenting themselves with the grace of their master.

The King's behaviour oscillated between wild parties and extravagant displays of piety and repentance, alienating many devout Catholics, who contrasted his conduct unfavourably with that of their hero, the irreproachable and manly Duke of Guise. Politically, Henry was inclined to be reactive rather than proactive: he would wait and see what happened and then respond to it. As a younger prince he had led royal armies against the Huguenots and had gained a reputation as a zealous defender of the Catholic Church. When he became king, however, he was faced with the same difficulties as his brothers and his mother. That is, he was trapped between the Guises and the Huguenots. Unable to find a compromise satisfactory to both, he struggled desperately to maintain royal authority.

The Catholic League of 1576 had petered out by about 1580. For one thing, it was primarily a noble undertaking, and many towns and bourgeois suspected nobles of dressing up their selfish concerns in the language of defending the faith. Very few civic governments gave it anything more than lukewarm support, and many refused to endorse it altogether. In addition, the League's goals were amorphous and ill defined. What did it mean in practical terms to defend the Catholic faith? How would they know when they were successful? Eventually, Henry III declared all such associations illegal, no doubt thinking that he had put the final nail in the coffin.

Everything changed, however, in 1584, when the King's younger brother, the Duke of Anjou, died. Anjou had been heir-presumptive, since Henry III had no legitimate heir. According to the rules of succession, the young Huguenot prince and commander Henry of Navarre stood in line to inherit the French throne. In

1572 he had been held prisoner at court in the aftermath of St. Bartholomew's and had abjured his Protestant faith. In 1576 he had escaped and declared his abjuration invalid, since it had been coerced, and he resumed his position of leadership in the Huguenot movement. The prospect of a heretic king revived the Catholic League, even among more moderate Catholics. In other words, many Catholics who would not have fought for the Guises, or to exterminate the Huguenots, would fight to keep Navarre off the throne. This revived League was much more effective than its predecessor. For one thing, it had a concrete motive: to keep Navarre off the throne. Leaguers argued that Navarre's heresy disqualified him from the succession and that the throne should pass to the next candidate in line, Navarre's uncle, the elderly Cardinal de Bourbon. This renewed League also found much greater support among the towns, especially in Paris. In the capital, from the early to mid-1580s there was a clandestine League movement known as the *Seize* or the Sixteen, after its delegates from the sixteen districts or *quartiers* of the city. The Sixteen recruited members in positions of influence and sponsored preachers and the printing of literature and pamphlets advocating their cause.

Meanwhile, in 1585 the Guises signed the Treaty of Joinville with Spain, by which Philip II subsidized the Catholic League. Faced with this opposition, Henry III signed the Treaty of Nemours, caving in to the League's demands. As soon as he signed it, however, Henry III looked for ways to free himself from the influence of Guise and the League. In the war that followed, Henry sent one of his favourite *mignons*, Joyeuse, to fight Navarre and the Huguenots, and sent Guise to fight a force of Swiss/German mercenaries coming to the aid of the Huguenots. The King secretly hoped that Joyeuse would defeat Navarre and that Guise would lose, thereby weakening both his opponents. Instead, the exact opposite happened: Joyeuse was defeated and killed at Coutras, while Guise was victorious at Auneau. Afraid of Guise's power and popularity, Henry forbade him to come to Paris. But in May 1588, Guise defied Henry and came to Paris after all, where he was welcomed as a hero, and the King had no choice but to acquiesce and welcome Guise. But on the night of May 11, Henry posted Swiss mercenaries around Paris, probably to arrest and execute Guise's key supporters. There were riots in the streets whipped up by the Sixteen and their organization in the neighbourhoods of Paris. The King's Swiss guards were saved from a massacre only by Guise's intervention. On May 13, the King managed to escape from Paris, leaving it in the control of Guise and the Sixteen. This series of events is known as the Day of Barricades because of the barricades that rioters erected in the narrow streets to prevent the movement of troops around the city. Once again, faced with the overwhelming power of the Catholic League, Henry gave in and in July signed an Edict of Union with the League, giving in to the League's demands.

Among the League's demands was a meeting of the Estates-General. So, in October 1588, the Estates-General met at Blois and was completely dominated by the League. Having run out of room to manoeuvre, Henry then decided on a desperate course of action. On December 23 he summoned Guise to his chamber, where the duke was murdered by royal bodyguards. At the same time, the duke's brother, the Cardinal of Guise, was arrested and then murdered in his cell the next day. Other prominent Leaguers were arrested and imprisoned, including the Cardinal of Bourbon and the leaders of the Sixteen. Henry had hoped to cripple the League by cutting off its head. In this, however, he badly miscalculated. Instead of crippling the League, he only riled up greater opposition. The Sorbonne declared that by his actions, Henry had made himself a tyrant and therefore his subjects were released from their loyalty. He was excommunicated by the Pope. The League declared Guise's younger brother, the Duke of Mayenne, lieutenant-general of the kingdom, in essence delegating royal power to him until a new king could take charge.

The murders at Blois also led to a turnabout in the propaganda wars. Since 1584, the Huguenots had been on the side of legitimacy since their man, Navarre, was in line to become the next king. Now the League was challenging rather than defending royal authority, and the murders at Blois completed this process. Now League writers adopted the political theories previously advanced by the Huguenots. In particular, League theorists claimed that the fundamental laws of France dictated that the king be Catholic.

Having hopelessly alienated Catholic opinion by his actions, the King now had no choice but to make common cause with Navarre and the Huguenots. As the two were besieging Paris, in August 1589 Henry III was assassinated, making the Huguenot Henry of Navarre King Henry IV of France and the first king of the Bourbon dynasty.

Henry IV, Pacification, and the Edict of Nantes 1589–98

Henry of Navarre had become king, but large numbers of his subjects refused to acknowledge him: the League and the Sixteen of course, but also many moderate Catholics. His strategy was to cultivate the moderate Catholics, the *politiques.* Navarre had likely known for some time that he would have to convert if he wanted to be truly accepted as king. The trick was to do it on his terms, out of strength rather than weakness—he could not be seen to be giving in. He won several important military victories at Arques in 1589 and at Ivry in 1591, but every time he began to press his advantage, a Spanish army from the Netherlands invaded under the Duke of Parma.

Meanwhile the League itself was having its own problems. There was increasing tension between Mayenne and the Sixteen, and between its noble and middle-class components. When the Sixteen executed several more moderate members of the Parlement for their lack of zeal, Mayenne had those responsible arrested and executed. The Cardinal of Bourbon had died in 1590, leaving the League without a candidate for king. Under Spanish pressure Mayenne called a meeting of the Estates-General in 1593 to consider the claim of a Spanish princess. There was almost unanimous hostility to this, since French law prevented a woman from inheriting the throne. At this moment, Henry announced his intention to convert.

This took the wind out of the League's sails. Once the King became a Catholic, there was now no longer any religious reason to oppose him. Only a few diehards maintained either that his conversion was insincere, or that since he had been a heretic when he claimed the throne, he continued to be ineligible whatever his current religious stance. Regardless, enough Catholics were either exhausted by decades of war, or satisfied that they now had a Catholic king (which was, after all, the whole point of the League), or both, that Henry was able to pacify the country and make good his claim to rule France. One by one, Henry defeated or bought off his opponents, giving rise to the aphorism "pas rendu, mais vendu" ("not surrendered, but sold"). In this process Henry showed himself not only to be a gracious victor, but also an extremely shrewd politician. Instead of punishing those who only recently had rejected him as a condemned heretic, the King agreed to let bygones be bygones. For example, towns that agreed to submit themselves to his authority found that all their privileges and liberties were confirmed, and that all but a few of the King's most inveterate and irreconcilable opponents were amnestied and confirmed in their positions in town governments and/or the royal bureaucracy.

By mid-1594 Henry had been crowned and had taken control of Paris. By 1598, all his opponents had been brought over, and Spanish armies expelled from France. Meanwhile, relations with the Huguenots had deteriorated badly, as they felt betrayed by their former champion, and by 1597, it looked as if Henry might have to fight them to compel their obedience.

Accordingly, in 1598 he issued the Edict of Nantes, yet another in the long line of edicts and treaties of pacification. Like its predecessors, its terms were still less than the Huguenots wanted and more than most Catholics wanted to give, but the Edict of Nantes was more successful, largely because everyone recognized that the only alternative was continued war, instability, and foreign invasion. The Edict allowed the Huguenots full freedom of conscience even as it limited their freedom to practise their religion. Huguenot worship was allowed only in towns where it had existed in August 1597, in places where it had been authorized by previous treaties, and in the households of Huguenot nobles. Catholic worship, on the other hand, was to be permitted everywhere, even in Huguenot areas where it had been absent for decades. Huguenots were granted full civil rights and were not to suffer discrimination in French society because of their religion. Thus, they were able to serve in the royal bureaucracy, go to university, practise law, and so on. To judge cases involving Huguenots and Catholics, bipartisan chambers were set up in the *parlements*, with judges of both faiths. In a series of secret articles and royal *brevets*,[3] the Huguenots gained other advantages. The King agreed to pay the salaries of Huguenot pastors. More importantly, the Huguenots retained approximately 200 walled and armed towns as a guarantee of the terms of the Edict. The towns were to be garrisoned with Huguenot soldiers paid for by the royal government.

It is clear that the Edict of Nantes was not a recognition of the ideal of religious liberty, nor a conscious decision to subordinate religion to the interests of the secular state. Rather, it was a messy and unwieldy compromise, accepted by both sides as a last resort, in the recognition that the only alternative was continued civil war and instability. Recent interpretations have emphasized the idea that from the beginning the limited toleration it granted was intended to be only temporary, pending the re-establishment of religious unity in France. While this may be true, the very terms of the compromise meant that the possibility of restoring religious unity was extremely remote. Although the royal *brevet* granting the Huguenots their political and military autonomy ("a state within the state," according to some historians) was limited in time to eight years, after which it expired, could anyone reasonably expect the Huguenots to give these powers up without a fight? There was therefore a fundamental discrepancy between the avowed eventual goal and the terms granted to ensure peace. This more or less guaranteed that the conflict was not yet over, for no king who desired truly to rule France would tolerate a large number of subjects having their own government, towns, and army effectively beyond royal power.

NOTES

1 Several different explanations for the term "Huguenot"have been advanced. The most compelling has to do with the origins of Calvinism in the Swiss city of Geneva. The German name for the Swiss Confederation was the *Eidgenossenschaft*, literally, "those united by the oath." In France, those influenced by the new faith became known, in French, as Eidguenots, and eventually, Huguenots.

2 Historians disagree as to why the peasants of the Cevennes proved so amenable to the Calvinist message. It likely has to do with the presence of a large number of rural artisans in the area. In addition, it is possible that the inhabitants of this remote and mountainous area saw Calvinism as a means of reinforcing and demonstrating their distinctiveness from their neighbours.

3 A *brevet* was a special order that, unlike other laws (such as the Edict of Nantes), did not have to be formally registered by a *parlement* in order to become effective. Judges in the *parlement* could resist registering royal edicts if in their minds the edict conflicted with the fundamental laws of the kingdom or subverted the interests of justice. By enacting these controversial measures through *brevets*, the king was avoiding what was sure to be a long and messy confrontation with the *parlement*. Even so, *parlements* throughout France resisted registering the Edict of Nantes. The last to do so was the Parlement of Rouen, which registered the Edict only in 1609.

CHAPTER SIX

Spain and the Netherlands

The Castilian Empire of Philip II

When Holy Roman Emperor Charles V abdicated his various titles in 1555–56, he divided his huge dynastic empire into two parts, a recognition that it was too vast and too diverse for one man to rule. His younger brother Ferdinand became Holy Roman Emperor Ferdinand I and took over the Austrian territories, Hungary, and Bohemia, inaugurating the Austrian branch of the Habsburg dynasty. His eldest son Philip got the Spanish kingdoms of Castile and Aragon, the Italian possessions of Naples, Sicily, and Milan, the Franche-Comté or Free County of Burgundy, and the Netherlands, as well as the Castilian empire in the New World.

Philip's possessions formed a purely dynastic and personal empire, for each of the territories retained its own government, laws, and customs. Thus Philip II was not King of Spain, but rather King of Castile and King of Aragon. Likewise he was King of Naples, Duke of Milan, Count of Burgundy, Count of Holland, Duke of Brabant, Count of Flanders, and so on. His rights and powers varied according to the territory, as did the liberties and privileges of his subjects. Clearly, Castile was the most important of his territories and increasingly became the core of his empire. It was the most populous, the most firmly under royal control, and with its possessions in the Americas the most lucrative. Whereas Charles V had been a Fleming (or native of Flanders) by birth and international in outlook, and had travelled widely among his possessions, Philip was Castilian and after 1559 never left the Iberian peninsula.

Philip was an extremely serious ruler and took his duties just as seriously, locking himself up in his office for days at a time, going over reports from his possessions, making notes in the margins, checking the arithmetic in long columns of numbers, and even correcting the grammar in the documents that came across his desk. He also took his religious duties very seriously and saw himself as the leader of the Catholic crusade against the Turks and the heretics. Philip did not, or could not, distinguish among what was good for the Catholic Church, what was good for Castile, and what was good for the Habsburg dynasty, for they were all part and parcel of the same thing.

Over the centuries, Philip's reputation has suffered at the hands of historians, especially Protestant English and American historians who saw in Philip and his reign all that was repugnant to them about royal absolutism and the Roman Catholic Church. John Lothrop Motley, the nineteenth-century American historian of the Dutch Revolt, wrote of Philip, "If there are vices ... from which he was exempt, it is because it is not permitted to human nature to attain perfection even in evil." Caricatures aside, Philip was an intriguing character. For the most part unappealing as a personality, he was not, however, entirely unsympathetic. Severe and reserved in his personal style, he nevertheless inspired an impressive loyalty among his closest associates. He was suspicious by nature and was inclined to keep information to himself, which only complicated the machinery of government. For the most part, he was strictly legalistic in his approach to government, but he was not beyond acting duplicitously and high-handedly when he saw the need.

Governing such a far-flung and diverse empire posed very serious difficulties for a ruler. Charles V had tried to deal with these problems by personally visiting his territories. He was constantly on the move between Spain, Germany, the Netherlands, and the rest of his empire. Philip, however, chose to stay in Spain for the last three decades of his life, and although he did travel within Spain, increasingly Madrid became his permanent capital. In 1563, he began construction of a new royal palace at El Escorial, northwest of Madrid, which was completed in 1584. The palace itself is a telling reflection of the ruler: rigid and severe in its plan, it also incorporated a monastery and royal mausoleum.

Immediately under the king, at least on paper, there was the Council of State. This was made up largely of Castilian noblemen and remained an almost purely ceremonial body with little real power. Indeed, the King himself never attended its meetings. Matters of policy were decided by the King alone, with advice from a small group of hand-picked advisors. Philip governed his empire through a system of viceroys and councils. In the more distant territories, such as the Netherlands, Naples, Sicily, Milan, and New Spain, royal power was exercised by a governor or viceroy, usually a Castilian nobleman. He reported to a council that supervised his activities and reported to the King. Therefore, there was a council for Castile, one for Aragon (and eventually after 1580 one for Portugal), one for Italy, one for the Netherlands, and one for the Indies. The only link between the various councils was Philip himself. The whole system was cumbersome and inefficient, given the state of communications and Philip's own cautious character. It would often take months (sometimes years, in the case of the Indies) to communicate and relay orders.

Another difficulty faced by Philip, perhaps the most serious one, was financial. Although gold and silver were pouring in from Mexico and Peru, he was always short of money. This was partly due to the unbalanced nature of the Castilian economy. For example, Castilian industry and merchants were unable to supply the needs of the colonists in the Americas, so these had to be imported from elsewhere and paid for with gold and silver. In reality, the bullion passed through Castile on its way elsewhere, most importantly through Antwerp, the greatest commercial centre of the early sixteenth century. Because Philip's power was greatest in Castile, Castile bore the financial burden of the Habsburg Empire, which further depressed economic activity. Because of the bullion pouring in, it was easier to import food to feed a growing population than to reform agriculture in Castile. As a result, Castilian landowners tended to concentrate on raising sheep, an activity with the promise of more immediate profits. Raw wool would be exported to the Netherlands and elsewhere, where it would be spun, woven, and dyed and then sent back to Spain or re-exported throughout Europe. An organization called the *Mesta* was extremely important in directing the Castlian economy toward sheep raising rather than agriculture. The *Mesta* was an association of sheep raisers that had gained enormous privileges and power in exchange for financial contributions to the government. It was a noble organization whose power was directed toward protecting the interests of sheep raisers at the expense of farmers, further handicapping the development of Castilian agriculture.

On top of all this, of course, were Philip's enormous military commitments and obligations. There was war with the Turks in North Africa and the Mediterranean. There was the revolt in the Netherlands. There were raiders and pirates to be dealt with in the Caribbean. Although France was largely neutered by internal conflict, Philip took an active interest in French affairs, and the Catholic League was financed by Spanish gold. Then there was war with England, culminating in the Spanish Armada.

Historians are still debating the nature of Philip's foreign policy. Specifically, some historians have argued that Philip's foreign policy was primarily an improvised and *ad hoc* affair, responding to events rather than anticipating or dictating them. Others, specifically Geoffrey Parker, have argued that Philip did possess a "Grand Strategy."[1] They suggest that Philip's policies were essentially defensive in nature and were driven by two overarching principles: preservation of the Catholic Church against the heretics and Turks, and preservation of his dynastic empire. Within these guiding principles, the interests of his various possessions were arranged hierarchically, with the Spanish kingdoms at the top, followed by Italy and the Mediterranean, and then the Netherlands and the North Sea. Executing such a "grand strategy" proved extremely problematic, however, for the real world kept getting in the way. For example, the revolt in the Netherlands required suppression on the basis of both overarching principles, but it tied up money and resources that could otherwise have been used in Italy and the Mediterranean against the Ottoman Turks. Philip's "grand strategy" was also hindered by his limited understanding of finance. Although immense, his revenues were never able to keep up with his expenses, and as a result he had to borrow extensively. The main creditors were Genoese bankers, who charged exorbitant rates of interest but supplied ready cash against the revenue of future years. By 1575 the total debt was equal to 5 years' revenue, and the entire revenue for any year was consumed in repaying loans. Even so, his government defaulted on loans, essentially declaring bankruptcy, three times during his reign.

The Spanish Kingdoms

During the long reign of Philip II (1556–98), Spain continued to develop along the same lines as under his predecessors, his father Emperor Charles V (Charles I of Spain) and his great-grandparents Ferdinand of Aragon and Isabella of Castile. Since there was no such entity as "Spain," Philip was not "King of Spain" but rather King of Castile and King of Aragon, two separate kingdoms that had become united, in a personal sense only, in the late fifteenth century with the marriage of Ferdinand and Isabella. Each of the two kingdoms retained its own laws, institutions, and governments. Increasingly Castile was the senior partner in this personal and dynastic union of kingdoms; for one thing, it was the more populous and prosperous of the two. Moreover, whereas the process of expelling the Muslim Arabs or *Reconquista* had been accomplished centuries earlier in Aragon, in Castile the crusading spirit was still fresh and vital, with the last Muslim outpost of Granada conquered only in 1492. Economically and commercially, Aragon's interests were directed toward the Mediterranean and Italy, and were in decline, whereas Castile was more oriented to the rising Atlantic economy, spurred by its new and very lucrative colonies in the New World.

Royal power was also greater in Castile than in Aragon. The "Crown of Aragon," as it was known, comprised three distinct territories: Aragon itself, Catalonia, and Valencia, each with its laws and administration. Within the "Crown of Aragon" the rights and liberties of subjects (or *fueros*) were extensive and explicit. The ruler meddled with these *fueros* only at his peril. Castile, on the other hand, was much more pliable and submissive to royal authority, with local institutions of self-government not nearly so extensive, well defined or jealously guarded. The representative assemblies, or *cortes*, in the components of the Crown of Aragon were powerful institutions, meeting regularly as an integral part of the government. In Castile, on the other hand, the *cortes* met only at the discretion of the monarch, and no one had the right to representation. As a result, the Castilian *cortes* hindered royal authority not at all. On the other hand, the nobility in Castile was very powerful, especially the great nobles or grandees. Although they remained at the pinnacle of Castilian society and economy, by Philip's time they had essentially been cut off from real policy-making power within the royal government. They were by and large content with their wealth and prestige, their military commands, their positions as viceroys and governors, and their positions at the royal court. As a result, not only in his empire as a whole, but even within Spain, Philip's rule was essentially Castilian, a fact bitterly resented by others.

Philip's reign was also notable for continuing and intensifying the emphasis on religious and racial purity, or *limpieza de sangre* (literally, "purity of blood"). Medieval Spain had been not only politically fragmented, but also religiously and

MAP 6.1 ⇚ THE SPANISH KINGDOMS UNDER PHILIP II

culturally diverse and cosmopolitan. There were large Jewish and Muslim populations, even within territories that had been conquered during the *Reconquista*. For the most part, Christians, Jews, and Muslims lived and worked together relatively harmoniously. In the late fourteenth and early fifteenth centuries, however, growing anti-Semitism had led a number of Jews to convert to Christianity. These converted Jews were known as New Christians, *conversos*, or *marranos*.[2] Many *conversos* rose to positions of great wealth and influence in fifteenth-century Spain. Yet many Old Christians were suspicious that their conversions were insincere, and they were resentful and jealous of the power and wealth achieved by some *conversos*. Indeed, some *conversos* were suspected of secretly practising their old faith. While there is no evidence of a widespread or organized secret practice of Judaism among the *conversos*, many of them did continue to practise some Jewish customs, such as maintaining traditional dress and names, which only strengthened suspicions of secret Judaism. In order to allay these fears, Ferdinand and Isabella had received permission from the Pope in 1480 to establish a specifically Spanish Inquisition to investigate such allegations and punish offenders. The Spanish Inquisition was therefore created, not to deal with Christian heresy, or with Jews or Muslims as such, but rather with *conversos* suspected of secretly practising their old religion. Still, its very creation was a harbinger of later persecutions of "heretics," Jews, and Muslims.

In 1492, Ferdinand and Isabella had completed the *Reconquista* with the conquest of Granada, the last outpost of Muslim Arab rule in Spain. In the atmosphere of religious triumph that followed, the King and Queen decided to expel all Jews from Spain. Since the Inquisition had obviously been unsuccessful in eliminating the secret Jews from the ranks of the *conversos*, it was thought that expelling Jews would remove a source of temptation. As had been the case with the establishment of the Inquisition, many *conversos* pressed for the expulsion of Jews in order to demonstrate their unimpeachable Christianity. Of the 200,000 Jews still living in Spain, probably between 120,000 and 150,000 chose exile over conversion. Ironically, however, the expulsion only exacerbated the problem with which the Inquisition had been created to deal. Now, there was a whole new group whose sincerity of conversion was open to question. Thus, the expulsion of the Jews did not diminish but rather increased the importance and role of the Inquisition.

Although many *conversos*—most notably Antonio Perez, Philip II's personal secretary—continued to occupy important positions in the Church and government, increasingly they found themselves on the outside of the Spanish elite, looking in. More and more, being able to prove a pure Old Christian ancestry became necessary for attaining high office in church and state. Philip himself contributed to this identification of Christian purity with ancestry, remarking that "all the heresies in Germany, France, and Spain have been sown by descendants of Jews." Because of the prominence of many *conversos*, and because there had previously been no stigma attached to intermarriage, many prominent families had at least some Jewish or *converso* heritage. Great pains were taken to cover up such "impure" ancestry. From Philip's time on in Spain, there was, therefore, great concern with ancestry and purity, and power was exercised more and more by men whose unimpeachable religious orthodoxy was demonstrated in the purity of their descent.

The conquest of Granada had produced yet another problem, that of the Muslim Arabs, or Moors. There had been Muslim minorities in Spain, a relic of the *Reconquista*, but they were small, scattered, and poor. The conquest of Granada brought the question of the Moors to a whole new level. Government policy oscillated between practical toleration and official repression. The treaty that had ended the war with Granada guaranteed the Moors the right to practise their religion and customs, but very quickly they came under pressure to convert. Technically they were given the choice of conversion or exile, but most of those who were able to leave already had done so. Those who stayed behind had no choice but to accept conversion. Although they were now officially Christian, no effort was made to educate them in their new faith, and as a result these *moriscos*, as they were known, continued to practise their old religion to a much greater extent than the *conversos* ever had. Since they were not nearly as wealthy or prominent as the *conversos*, the Inquisition did not immediately see them as a priority. Moreover, since they were a majority in Granada, it was feared that efforts to crack down would produce rebellion. In effect, therefore, the *moriscos* of Granada continued to practise their old religion and customs through the first half of the sixteenth century.

By the mid-sixteenth century, however, this had begun to change. For one thing, Spain was involved in a bitter conflict with the Muslim Ottoman Empire, and the *moriscos* came under suspicion as a potential fifth column within Spain. At the same time, the Inquisition stepped up its activity in Granada, in accordance with the spirit of the Counter-Reformation then beginning to take shape. The *morisco* population was also expanding more quickly than that of Spain as a whole, a fact that did not go unnoticed. Therefore in early 1567, an edict came into effect imposing various restrictions on the *moriscos*. The use of Arabic was prohibited, the *moriscos* were ordered to adopt Castilian dress, they were to abandon their customs and ceremonies, and Moorish surnames were prohibited. There was nothing particularly new in these restrictions; they had mostly been decreed before, but their enforcement had been mitigated by considerations of finance and pragmatism. What was new this time was the insistence on enforcement. This was largely due to Philip's desire for real religious uniformity in his kingdoms (this was at the same time as he sent an army to the Netherlands to punish his opponents there—see below), and his fear of collaboration between the *moriscos* and the Turks. After a year of attempting to moderate the decree, the *moriscos* of Granada realized the futility of their efforts to compromise, and their resentment erupted into rebellion in 1568. The core of the rebellion was the mountainous region of Alpujarras, and its repression was long and difficult, but by 1570 the rebels had been defeated. Philip and his government decided on a drastic solution to the *morisco* problem. They were to be expelled from Granada and forcibly resettled throughout Castile. Although some *moriscos* managed to remain in Granada, most were dispersed throughout Castile. The threat in Granada may have been mitigated, but a new and even more difficult *morisco* problem was created as a result, a problem that was only solved in 1609 with the decision to expel them from Spain entirely. (See Chapter 11.)

With the growth of Protestantism throughout Europe, the Inquisition turned its attention to Christian heresy in addition to the *conversos* and *moriscos*. Thanks to an earlier series of reforms, the Catholic Church in Spain was largely free of the kinds of corruption that elsewhere attracted many people to the new churches. The Inquisition, ever vigilant however, still found "heretics" to persecute. It is highly doubtful that there was any organized Protestant movement in Spain, but many people were intrigued by humanist writings and other "advanced" religious ideas and literature. In the new climate of intolerance and repression, they became fair game for the Inquisition, especially during the tenure of Grand Inquisitor Hernando de Valdés (1547–66). Valdés was also responsible for the arrest and imprisonment of the Archbishop of Toledo, the primate of Spain, although in this case theological issues disguised an intense personal and professional rivalry. The Spanish Inquisition also issued its own Index of Prohibited Books, since the

Roman Index was not accepted in Spain. Censorship was tightened up. All books required a licence from the Inquisition before they could be published, and all bookshops and libraries were subject to being searched; importing of books without a licence was punishable by death. In 1559, so that they would not be exposed to unorthodox or undesirable ideas, Spanish students were forbidden to attend foreign universities.

At the same time, however, Spain under Philip II became a stronghold of the Counter-Reformation. Spanish churchmen and theologians played an integral role in the Council of Trent. Even if Spain did not accept the papalism of Trent, insisting on the autonomy of the Spanish Church, and even if political and diplomatic relations between Philip and the Pope remained problematic, if not hostile, nevertheless Spain proved fertile ground for many of the devotional aspects of the Counter-Reformation. Ignatius Loyola was a Spaniard, and sixteenth-century Spain gave birth to an impressive roster of religious and devotional figures: the mystics and monastic reformers St. Teresa of Avila (d. 1582) and St. John of the Cross (d. 1591), and the ecclesiastical reformer Archbishop Gaspar de Quiroga of Toledo (d. 1594), among others. It is important to note that these different currents did not always coexist harmoniously. St. Teresa came under suspicion by the Inquisition, as had Loyola himself. St. John of the Cross was actually kidnapped and imprisoned by his enemies. Jesuits and Dominicans were frequently at each other's throats. The Counter-Reformation in Spain was therefore not a monolithic or homogeneous movement. There were stresses and strains, but they help to explain the religious and devotional vitality of sixteenth-century Spain. Under Philip II, then, Spanish society developed its own religious culture, which shared some elements of Counter-Reformation Catholic culture, but was also distinct in some respects. This was a society obsessed with orthodoxy, with purity, with status, distrustful of all things foreign. At the same time, the very nature of Philip's empire necessitated his involvement in the wider world of European culture and diplomacy.

In terms of foreign policy, as discussed above, Philip's great preoccupation was with the threat posed by the Ottoman Turkish empire and their allies, the so-called Barbary Pirates who controlled much of the North African coast. Turkish naval power in the Mediterranean posed a threat not only to Spain itself, but also to Philip's territories in Italy, as well as to the extremely important commercial and financial connections between Spain and Italy. Once peace was made with France in 1559, Philip was free to pursue his goals in the Mediterranean. An early attempt to take the stronghold of Tripoli ended in disaster in 1560, but later ventures were more successful. Spanish forces took the pirate haven of Peñon de Vélez in 1564, and in 1565 a Spanish fleet defeated an Ottoman assault on the island of Malta. Yet Philip was largely unable to follow up this victory because of developing problems in the Netherlands that required his attention. Nor had the Ottoman threat receded. Although the great sultan Suleiman the Magnificent had died in 1566, power was being exercised by the very able grand vizier Mehmed Sököli. Strangely, the Ottomans neglected the opportunity granted them by the rebellion of the *moriscos* in 1568–70. By 1570, with the situation in the

Netherlands seemingly under control, Philip was able to turn his attention back to the Mediterranean. He agreed to an alliance with Venice and the Pope against the Turks, who were threatening the important Venetian possession of Cyprus. In May 1570, the Turks launched their attack on the island and the combined Spanish, Venetian, and papal fleet set sail to repulse it under Don John, Philip's bastard half-brother who had played a very important role in the repression of the revolt in Granada. Cyprus, however, fell before the Spanish fleet arrived. Don John then resolved to seek out the Turkish fleet and engage it in battle. The two fleets of comparable size—about 300 ships and 80,000 men—met in battle at Lepanto off the Greek coast on October 7, 1571, in the greatest naval engagement up to that time. The result was a resounding defeat for the Turks, who lost 117 ships and some 30,000 men, while the Christian forces lost only fifteen or twenty ships and about 8,000 men. It was the greatest victory in the war against Islam since the conquest of Granada in 1492 and was widely celebrated throughout Europe.

Yet the victory at Lepanto was not followed up to any great degree. It was late in the season, and the coming of winter storms made continued naval operations impractical. Disagreements among the allies also precluded decisive action, and once again Philip found his attention being drawn to affairs in the Netherlands and northern Europe. Moreover, the Turkish fleet was able to quickly rebuild itself. The importance of Lepanto, therefore, is twofold: first, even though the Turkish fleet remained powerful and the Turks continued to dominate the eastern Mediterranean (Cyprus remained in Turkish hands), the threat to the western Mediterranean was vastly reduced, in conjunction with the defeat of the revolt in Granada, and continued Spanish progress in the war against the Barbary Pirates. Second, Lepanto was a very significant moral boost, not only for Spain, but for all of Christian Europe. The Muslim Ottoman Turks had been a terrifying spectre since the mid-fifteenth century when they had conquered Constantinople. Since then, they had posed a significant threat, not only in the Mediterranean, but also on land in central and southern Europe. In 1526, Turkish armies had defeated and killed in battle the King of Hungary and occupied most of that country. On several occasions they had besieged Vienna. Now the tide seemed to be turning. The Ottoman Empire remained very powerful, and continued to pose a real threat, but there was a sense that the tide had turned, as indeed it had, and that the Turks were not invincible.

Philip was also able to fulfill a longstanding ambition of the rulers of Castile: the unification of all the Iberian peninsula under one ruler. In 1578, King Sebastian of Portugal had been killed in an ill-advised military operation in Africa, leaving his elderly uncle Henry, a Catholic cardinal, as heir to the throne. Philip himself was the most plausible heir to Henry, as there were longstanding marital connections between the ruling families of Castile and Portugal. Philip's mother had been a Portuguese princess, his sister had married King John of Portugal and was the mother of the unlucky Sebastian, and Philip's first wife was Portuguese. Through careful plotting and judicious bribery of influential Portuguese aristocrats, Philip gained recognition as Cardinal Henry's heir. When Henry died in early 1580,

Spanish armies crossed the border to make good Philip's claim. With only token resistance, Portugal was quickly incorporated into Philip's dominions. To conciliate his new subjects, who were notoriously and bitterly anti-Castilian, Philip swore to uphold all the laws and customs of Portugal and to maintain its identity separate from Castile.

The annexation of Portugal was mutually beneficial, at least for a time. Portugal, like Castile, possessed a vast overseas empire, in Brazil, Africa, and Asia. But, unlike Peru or Mexico, Portuguese possessions had no vast deposits of gold or silver, so Portuguese merchants needed Spanish silver to pay for their Asian imports. Since they now shared the same ruler, the Portuguese felt that Spanish arms could be employed to protect their empire. On the other hand, Philip gained access to the wealth of the Portuguese empire and its maritime expertise. Lisbon was a more convenient Atlantic port than Seville, and Philip's foreign policy became more oriented toward the Atlantic and northern Europe than to the Mediterranean, Italy, and the Ottoman Empire.

Yet Philip's own sense of obligation and the need to reconcile his new subjects meant that Portugal's benefit to Philip and Castile was not as great as it might have been. In addition to swearing that he would uphold Portugal's laws and customs and maintain its separate identity, Philip agreed to appoint only Portuguese to positions in Portugal itself and in its empire. Portugal was to maintain its own coinage, and trade with its overseas empire was to remain exclusively in the hands of the Portuguese themselves. When, in the seventeenth century, Spain proved unable to protect the Portuguese empire, and when Philip's grandson attempted to alter the relationship between Castile and Portugal, the Portuguese were able to reassert their independence. Despite the initial promise, therefore, the union lasted for only sixty years.

Despite these successes, Philip's reign in Spain also had its share of personal setbacks. For a long time Philip had been plagued by the lack of a suitable male heir. His first wife, Princess Maria of Portugal, had died giving birth to his eldest son Don Carlos in 1545. He subsequently married Mary Tudor, Queen of England from 1553 to 1558, purely as a diplomatic arrangement between two traditional allies against France. Mary was 11 years older than Philip, and the marriage remained childless, and loveless, at least as far as Philip was concerned. In 1559, as part of the peace settlement of Cateau-Cambrésis, he married Elisabeth of Valois, daughter of Henry II of France. Although he grew to love her very much, they managed to have only two children together, both daughters. Meanwhile, Don Carlos was showing himself utterly unfit to succeed his father. Physically and mentally handicapped, he showed disturbing signs of sadism and sexual deviance. Reluctantly, Philip felt forced to exclude him from positions of responsibility, which only further estranged father and son. When Carlos began to collude with the Dutch rebels against Philip, and conspired to escape to the Netherlands, Philip felt he had no choice but to imprison his son. On the night of January 18, 1568, shortly after the outbreak of the revolt in Granada, Philip and a number of his closest advisors broke into the prince's bedroom. After Don Carlos was disarmed,

Philip informed his son that for his own good he was being taken into custody. This was the last time that the King saw his son. Philip justified his actions on the basis of the welfare of the state and of his son:

> since ... it has been God's will that the prince should have such great and numerous defects, partly mental, partly due to his physical condition, utterly lacking as he is in the qualifications necessary for ruling, I saw the grave risks which would arise were he to be given the succession and the obvious dangers which would accrue; and therefore, after long and careful consideration and having tried every alternative in vain, it was clear that there was little or no prospect of his condition improving in time to prevent the evils which could reasonably be foreseen. In short, my decision was necessary.

Don Carlos died in his cell on July 25, 1568, giving rise to rumours that Philip had ordered his death. There is no evidence for this. Although we will forever remain ignorant of what really happened, the prince did talk of suicide. More likely, however, his health, never robust, was adversely affected by alternating hunger strikes and bouts of gluttony. Philip was married again in 1570 to his fourth and last wife, Anne of Austria, the daughter of his cousin Emperor Maximilian II. Together they had four sons and one daughter, but only one of the sons survived childhood. He would eventually succeed his father as King Philip III (1598–1621). Without a doubt, however, the greatest setback of Philip's reign was his inability to contain or reconcile the dissatisfaction of his Dutch subjects.

The Dutch Revolt

The Origins of the Dutch Revolt

Part of Philip's inheritance from his father was the Low Countries, or Netherlands, roughly the modern kingdoms of the Netherlands and Belgium. Now, of course, we know what would happen in this area: an independent Protestant state in the north, with the south remaining Catholic and under Spanish rule. There was, however, nothing inevitable or natural about this split: there were not more Protestants in the north (in fact there were fewer), or more Catholics in the south. This split was purely historical, almost accidental in nature, a product of the sixteenth century rather than of any historical necessity.

In the sixteenth century, there was no such thing as the "Netherlands," just as there was no such thing as "Spain." The Low Countries consisted of seventeen different provinces.[3] Philip was therefore not ruler of the Netherlands, but rather Count of Flanders, Duke of Brabant, Count of Holland, and so on. The Low Countries were part of Philip's Burgundian inheritance from his great-great-grandmother, Mary of Burgundy. These territories had come under Burgundian rule at different times and in different ways and Philip's powers and rights varied in each

MAP 6.2 ⥼ THE PROVINCES OF THE NETHERLANDS IN THE 16TH CENTURY

one. Even within each province, there was little effective authority; in fact, the provinces themselves were collections of semi-autonomous towns and cities. They were also very diverse within themselves. They were mostly Dutch or Flemish in language and culture, but there was a French-speaking population in the south, known as Walloons, and German speakers in the north and east. Generally speaking, the southern provinces were more populated, more urbanized, and wealthier. Here we see the great medieval industrial cities of Ghent and Bruges, and the financial and commercial centre of Antwerp. This had been the industrial and commercial heartland of northern Europe in the Middle Ages. Along the coast there were fishing villages, and inland there were agricultural districts.

Each province, and each town within each province, was jealous of its own identity and rights and privileges. Each province had its own assembly, known as Estates or States, and the ruler was represented in each by a governor or *stadtholder*, usually hereditary among the great noble families. To counter this deeply ingrained provincialism, Charles V had set up a rudimentary central government in Brussels, with a regent and several councils for advice. There was also an assembly for all the provinces, the States-General, made up of delegates from the provincial States. But all its decisions had to be unanimous, and voting had to be unanimous within each delegation. Therefore, the States-General was more like the United Nations than an effective legislature.

When Philip became ruler, the regent was his half-sister Margaret of Parma, an illegitimate daughter of Charles V. She was advised in her council of state by the greatest nobles of the Netherlands, but the real power was her chancellor, Antoine de Perrenot, Cardinal Granvelle. To the Netherlanders, Philip was a foreigner, unlike his father, who had been born in Flanders and whose mother tongue was Flemish. Philip did not understand the people or the language, and he had no desire to understand.

The roots of the Dutch Revolt stem from two sources: Philip's financial needs, and his desire to combat heresy. In fact, Philip's policies provoked three revolts: in 1565–68, 1569–76, and 1576–81. After 1581 the seven northern provinces agreed to closer cooperation and renounced their allegiance to Philip. From 1581 to 1609 the Spanish attempted unsuccessfully to reconquer the north; likewise, in the north, they wished to "liberate" the southern provinces, but could not. The split between the north and the south reflects a military stalemate, rather than any inherent differences between the two.

The First Revolt, 1565–68

In the early years of his reign, Philip became increasingly alarmed by the growth of Calvinism in the Netherlands, especially in the commercial and industrial centres of the south, which were crucial to his plans. In general, the Netherlands were relatively tolerant about religion, what might be considered a "don't ask, don't tell" attitude. Philip considered this a personal affront, for it ran counter to all he held most deeply. Accordingly, he proposed a reorganization of the church in the Low

Countries, which was just about as chaotic as the political situation. Specifically, he wanted to increase the number of bishops from 4 to 18 in order to make episcopal oversight more effective in the fight against heresy. This of course antagonized the Calvinists, but for the most part they had little power; more importantly, it alienated many powerful nobles. This plan had been drawn up without their consent, and therefore it violated their powers and privileges. Moreover, it threatened their control over the church and its wealth and power. For the most part, it was not Calvinists but Catholics who objected on administrative and political, rather than religious, grounds.

Among the opposition were a number of very powerful nobles. Foremost among them was William, Count of Nassau, Prince of Orange, *stadtholder* of Holland, Zeeland, and Utrecht, the wealthiest and most powerful nobleman in the Low Countries. He was also a sovereign prince in his own right, ruler of the small enclave of Orange in southern France. Known as William the Silent for his ability to keep his own counsel, he had been a confidant of Charles V and knew Philip II well, having spent a good deal of time in Spain during his youth. However, he had alienated Philip through his marriage to a German Lutheran princess. Orange would eventually emerge as the single most important leader in the opposition to Philip II. Among the King's other prominent opponents were Count Egmont, *stadtholder* in Flanders, and Count Hoorn. Orange, Egmont, and Hoorn demanded Granvelle's dismissal, and when it was not forthcoming they resigned from the Council of State. With no army in the Netherlands, and trying to fight the Turks in the Mediterranean, Philip gave in and Granvelle was dismissed in 1564; William, Egmont, and Hoorn returned to the Council of State. But Philip insisted on carrying out his campaign against the Protestants, insisting that nothing had changed. While most of the high nobility remained Catholic, a good many lower nobles had become Calvinist, and they formed an association called the Compromise. Although religiously mixed in composition, its members shared the same goal: to defeat Philip's rigorous religious policies. In 1566 several hundred of them rode into Brussels to deliver a petition to the regent requesting a relaxation in the heresy laws and the persecution of Protestants. This was when the rebels acquired the nickname "Beggars." Berlaymont, one of Philip's supporters in the Council of State, observing the procession of the Compromise through the streets of Brussels, remarked to Margaret of Parma that there was no need to fear "these beggars" ("*ces gueux*"). The label was quickly seized upon by the protesters and their supporters as a badge of honour.

Besides the protests of the Compromise of the Nobility, the summer of 1566 saw considerable religious unrest as self-appointed preachers held open-air meetings and incited the crowds to invade Catholic churches and destroy the images they found. The fury of these riots scared Margaret and most of the nobles of the Compromise into cooperation. Nobody wanted all-out war, and certainly not the kind of social revolution that they feared in the riots. Most nobles, including Egmont and Hoorn, made their peace with Margaret and Philip. William of Orange, however, sat on the fence. He did not want to throw his lot in with the

Calvinists, nor could he make his peace with Philip, so he went into exile in Germany, where he tried to arrange support from the Lutheran princes of Germany, without much success. Margaret was able to mop up the few rebels who remained, and also requested troops from Spain to help her maintain control.

Religion played a very incidental role in this first revolt. Philip's opponents, both Catholics and Calvinists, objected to the King's plans to reorganize the Church and to his policy of harsh persecution of heretics. The Calvinists, however, piggy-backed their revolt onto a noble revolt that had essentially political causes. Religion also divided the rebels, however, for most nobles were scared and alienated by the iconoclasm and radicalism of 1566. Had Philip capitalized on these divisions, and adopted a policy of moderation to reconcile the nobles to his rule, it is likely the revolt would have ended there. But he did not. On the contrary, he decided on a policy of firm punishment and repression of those implicated in the troubles, to be implemented by his military commander, the Duke of Alba.

The Duke of Alba and the Second Revolt, 1567–76

Philip responded to Margaret's request for assistance by sending to the Netherlands a Spanish army of 10,000 men under the command of the Duke of Alba, a leading Castilian nobleman. Arriving in the Netherlands in August of 1567, Alba acted quickly and decisively to punish the rebels. Overruling Margaret of Parma, he garrisoned his troops even in towns that had remained loyal. He established a secret tribunal to hunt down and punish rebels, the Council of Troubles, known also as the "Council of Blood." The council tried more than 12,000 people for their roles in the revolts of 1566 and 1567. Of these, 9,000 had their property confiscated, and another 1,000 were executed. Egmont and Hoorn were arrested and subsequently executed.

Beyond this policy of repression and punishment, Alba also had orders to "make all the states into one kingdom, with Brussels as its capital." He pushed ahead with the plans to re-organize the church, but what aroused the greatest opposition was his attempt to impose a 10-per-cent sales tax, the "Tenth Penny," in order to pay for the occupation and to contribute to Philip's war effort. In fact, this tax proved so unpopular and aroused so much resistance that it was impossible to collect.

With Egmont and Hoorn dead, William of Orange was now the undisputed leader of the opposition to Philip and Alba. From his exile in Germany, he attempted without much success to enlist German Lutheran support for his cause. In 1568, he and his brother Louis of Nassau attempted an invasion of the Netherlands, but it was a complete failure. In addition, in his capacity as sovereign Prince of Orange, he had authorized a group of pirates to prey on Spanish shipping in the English Channel and the North Sea. These pirates were known as the Sea Beggars. In 1572, afraid of further antagonizing Philip, Queen Elizabeth I of England denied the Sea Beggars permission to operate out of Dover. In search of a port to put into, on April 1, 1572, a force of about 600 Sea Beggars captured the port town of Brill in Zeeland. Three weeks later, another force of Sea Beggars, reinforced by English and Huguenot supporters, seized the more important port of Flushing, which controlled the estuary of the Scheldt River and hence threatened the commerce of Antwerp. The Sea Beggars were fanatical Calvinists and imposed their rule on about fifty towns throughout Zeeland and Holland. William of Orange tried to capitalize on this revolt in the north by invading the south, but once again he failed to have any real impact. He had hoped for support from Gaspard de Coligny and the Huguenots, hopes that were dashed by the St. Bartholomew's massacre (see Chapter 5). He then decided to throw his lot in with the Calvinists and Sea Beggars. In 1573 he joined the Calvinist church, as a means of bolstering his support among the most zealous of the King's opponents rather than out of any religious conviction.

The seizure of parts of Holland and Zeeland was enormously important. It gave the rebels a territorial base largely out of reach of Spanish power, since the Sea Beggars controlled the sea and access from land was difficult because it was a landscape of rivers, islands, and swamps. The events of 1572 also marked a change in the basic nature of the revolt. Up to that time, religion had been a minor factor. The Calvinists had participated in it, but they were hardly the driving force. Now, through the Sea Beggars' seizure of parts of Holland and Zeeland, the Calvinists had shown themselves to be the most, if not the only, successful rebels. Whereas previously the Calvinists had piggybacked on the general opposition to the King, they now hijacked it. Even though they comprised no more than ten per cent of the population, they became crucial to the revolt's success. Yet they could not do it on their own; they needed the support of moderate Catholics, especially the nobles.

Meanwhile, the St. Bartholomew's massacre in France freed Alba to attack the rebels in the north. Several massacres in conquered towns only enhanced resistance and the will to fight. Clearly, the policy of repression had failed, and in late 1573 Alba was recalled and replaced by the more moderate Don Luis de Requesens. He quickly abolished the Tenth Penny and the Council of Troubles and issued a general pardon, but Philip absolutely refused to compromise on religion. He wrote in 1573, "I would rather lose the Low Countries than reign over them if they ceased to be Catholic." In the absence of any compromise on religion, the rebels continued to hold out in Holland and Zeeland. Ultimately, Requesens concluded that force would have to be used, as the two sides were fundamentally divided over religion. This never came to pass, however, for two major reasons. First, Requesens died in 1576 and was not immediately replaced. Second, and more important, were the fiscal troubles of Philip II. The Spanish army in the Netherlands was very expensive to maintain and was only one of Philip's commitments. Most notably, there was also the naval war against the Turks. The pay of the Spanish soldiers was continually in arrears, leading to mutiny and pillaging. Spanish troops in the Netherlands mutinied annually between 1573 and 1576. In particular, it was the mutiny of 1576 and the sack of Antwerp that lay behind the third revolt.

The Third Revolt, 1576–81

By November 1576, the pay of the soldiers was two years in arrears. In their rage and frustration, they sacked the city of Antwerp, killing 8,000 inhabitants and levelling about a third of the city. This "Spanish Fury" provoked the States-General into making common cause with Holland and Zeeland and the Calvinists. In an agreement known as the Pacification of Ghent, all 17 provinces agreed to cooperate in expelling Spanish troops, and to put the religious issue aside for the time being. Meanwhile, Calvinists had seized control of a number of towns in the south (where they were quite numerous): Brussels, Ghent, and Antwerp to name only the most important. The new governor, Don John (Philip II's half-brother and hero of Lepanto), tactically accepted the Pacification of Ghent but immediately began to work at dividing the rebels—and there was plenty to divide them. Despite the Pacification of Ghent, Calvinists and Catholics still distrusted each other. The nobility and civic elites feared the urban working classes in the industrial cities of the south, among whom were to be found the most militant and zealous Catholics. Don John died, however, in 1578, before he could have any real impact. He was replaced by Philip's nephew, Alexander Farnese, Duke of Parma, son of the former regent, a brilliant commander and very able politician. Parma was able to play on the divisions among the King's opponents, and in 1579 he signed the Treaty of Arras with the Walloon provinces of the south. In it, Parma agreed to recognize and maintain their privileges and withdraw Spanish troops in return for their deserting the rebel cause. In response, the three northern provinces of Holland, Zeeland, and Utrecht, and a handful of southern cities, formed the Union of Utrecht. Neither side, however, foresaw a permanent split. William of Orange and the Union of Utrecht still believed that the south could be "liberated," while Philip and Parma still believed that the north could be reconquered.

Independence and Survival, 1581–1609

In 1581 William persuaded 13 of the 17 provinces to renounce their allegiance to Philip II. But he realized that he was too identified with the Calvinists to lead the rebel provinces himself. Still clinging to his vision of a religiously tolerant state, he wanted someone who could appeal to the majority of Catholics while not offending the Calvinists. The man they turned to was François of Anjou, brother of Henry III of France, who was recognized as hereditary ruler of all the various provinces except Holland and Zeeland, of which Orange himself became ruler. Anjou, however, proved to be an unfortunate choice. He had no real commitment to anything except himself, did not listen to the States-General, and was generally angry and frustrated by the lack of obedience and respect he perceived among his new subjects. In 1583 he tried to seize the city of Antwerp but was ignominiously rebuffed by Catholics and Calvinists alike. Having lost all credibility, Anjou returned to France where he died unexpectedly in 1584, setting off the crisis of the Catholic League in that country. Now, rid of the embarrassment of Anjou,

William was faced with a difficult problem. How were the newly independent provinces to be governed? It seemed likely that William had resigned himself to the necessity of assuming some sort of royal title, but he was assassinated in 1584 by a Spanish agent.

Meanwhile Parma went from strength to strength. By 1585 he had reconquered the cities of Brussels, Ghent, and Antwerp, as well as the province of Brabant and most of Flanders. As a result, Calvinist refugees continued streaming from these areas into the northern provinces, enhancing their numbers and ensuring that the rebel provinces became more and more Calvinist in nature. In 1585, faced with Parma's success and the absence of William of Orange, the remaining rebel provinces asked Elizabeth I of England for aid, and she sent an army under the Earl of Leicester, who was named governor-general of the provinces. He was no more successful than Anjou at imposing his authority, and by 1588 he had resigned his position and gone home. Had Parma been able to concentrate on the remaining rebel provinces now, he might have been able to conquer them. Philip, however, had other ideas. First, he was putting together a fleet to invade England—the Spanish Armada—to punish Elizabeth for her assistance to the Dutch rebels. Parma and his army were to rendezvous with the fleet and be carried across the Channel. This never happened, but it was a distraction from the campaign against the rebel provinces. Following this, with the civil war in France, Parma was diverted into France to aid the Catholic League, and he then died in 1592 before he could turn his attention to the Netherlands again. Command of the army of the rebel provinces fell to William of Orange's son Maurice, who managed to assert control of the seven northern provinces. Thereafter, the two sides established a military stalemate. In 1609, a truce for 12 years was signed. This was a *de facto* Spanish recognition of the seven northern provinces as an independent state. Both sides still hoped for eventual reunion, but religion was the chief stumbling block. The southern provinces insisted on toleration of Catholics in the north, which Calvinist control of the north made unlikely. Moreover, the merchants of the north, many of whom had fled from the south, did not want to see the recovery of southern commerce; having established themselves in Amsterdam, they did not care to see the commercial revival of Antwerp.

The new state of the seven northern provinces, known variously as the United Provinces or the Dutch Republic, was economically prosperous but politically divided and unstable. It was a republic by default, having tried unsuccessfully to replace Philip II with a ruler of their choice. It remained highly decentralized, with each province retaining its own customs and liberties, and within each province each town remaining highly autonomous. Increasingly, however, the province of Holland, and the city of Amsterdam within it, were emerging as the dominant forces. Had William of Orange lived, it is likely he would have been named ruler of the provinces, but his son, Maurice of Nassau (who was a young boy when his father was killed), simply did not have the prestige. There was enormous tension between Maurice and his successors, who continued as commanders-in-chief and *stadtholders*, and the merchants elites of the towns. The supporters of the princes of Orange favoured continued war with Spain, while the merchant elites of the towns, known as regents, favoured peace, but on their conditions. These included that they be allowed to continue trading with the Spanish, which the war party saw as treason. In addition, they wanted to continue the blockade of the Scheldt River and Antwerp, in order to benefit the commerce of Amsterdam. The Orangists favoured political centralization under the leadership of the princes of Orange, while the regents favoured the status quo of decentralization. These tensions were also complicated by religious factors. The rigid Calvinists favoured Orange and the war party, while the regents favoured Arminianism and peace. The rigid Calvinists also wanted to crack down on the Catholics, who were a majority in the north even as late as 1600, but the regents feared further unrest and were inclined to be more tolerant. As a result, even at the height of Dutch prosperity, as Dutch merchants and shipping came to dominate European and Asian commerce, the Dutch Republic was riven by bitter political and religious division.

NOTES

1 Geoffrey Parker, *The Grand Strategy of Philip II* (New Haven, CT: Yale University Press, 1998).
2 *Marranos* was a pejorative term for Jewish converts, derived from the word for swine.
3 Seventeen is the traditional number assigned to the Dutch provinces, although in reality the number varied a bit over time as several provinces were at times merged and then separated.

CHAPTER SEVEN

Elizabethan England

In 1558, when Elizabeth I became queen of England, no one could have guessed that she would have a long and glorious reign. In fact, there were more reasons to be pessimistic than optimistic about the future. For one thing, she was a female ruler in an age that considered women irrational, emotional, and unfit to rule. England's only previous experiences with female rule had been disasters, most recently her older half-sister Mary, known somewhat unfairly as "Bloody Mary." Elizabeth, however, proved to be an extremely shrewd politician, able to bamboozle and manipulate friends and foes alike. She was able to turn being an unmarried woman into an advantage. Diplomatically, she held out the prospect of her marriage as bait in order to achieve her goals. She knew how to play the weak and naive woman when that suited her purposes. She also knew when to go against the stereotype and confound people's expectations by assuming traditionally male modes of speech and behaviour. For example, in a famous speech at Tilbury in 1588, threatened with the arrival of the Spanish Armada, she addressed her troops thus:

> Let tyrants fear, I have always so behaved myself that, under God, I have placed my chiefest strength and safeguard in the loyal hearts and goodwill of my subjects; and therefore I am come amongst you, as you see, at this time, not for my recreation and disport, but being resolved, in the midst and heat of the battle, to live and die amongst you all; to lay down for my God, and for my kingdom, and my people, my honour and my blood, even in the dust. I know I have the body but of a weak and feeble woman; but I have the heart and stomach of a king, and of a king of England too ...

At the same time, she was determined not to share power with any husband. Her advisors were continually urging her to marry, since without a direct heir England faced the prospect of a renewal of the Wars of the Roses of a century earlier. Yet Elizabeth understood that if she were to marry either a foreign prince or an English nobleman, her husband would necessarily assume the more powerful role. Elizabeth also knew how to pick able advisors and ministers and let them do their jobs. In politics, she relied heavily on Sir William Cecil (later Earl of Burghley), and after his death in 1598 on his son Robert, and on Sir Francis Walsingham (d. 1590). In the Church, she made able use of Matthew Parker, Archbishop of Canterbury until 1575, then of Edmund Grindal (d. 1583), and then of John Whitgift.

The kingdom that Elizabeth inherited in 1558 was far from stable. In the north, the Scots were continually stirring up trouble, usually in connection with the French, their traditional ally against their mutual English enemy. When Elizabeth became queen, Scotland was being ruled by a regent on behalf of its underaged queen, Mary Stuart. The regent was the widow of the late James V, Mary of Guise, Queen Mother, and sister to the Duke of Guise. Mary Stuart was married to Francis II, the young king of France, making her queen of two kingdoms. In addition, she also had a claim on the English throne, since her paternal grandmother was a sister of Henry VIII. Should Elizabeth die without heir, Mary Stuart had the strongest claim on the English throne. Domestically, England had been through tremendous turmoil in the previous thirty years. Elizabeth's father, Henry VIII (1509–47), had broken away from the Roman Catholic Church for political and dynastic reasons. He wanted to get rid of his first wife, Catharine of Aragon, who had produced only one daughter, the princess Mary (later "Bloody" Mary). The Pope refused to grant him an annulment, so he removed England from the Roman Catholic Church and established an independent English Church, with himself at the head, which then granted him an annulment. This break was accomplished through a series of acts of Parliament in the 1530s, not because it had to be done this way, but to demonstrate the support of his subjects for his actions. Using Parliament in this way strengthened his position. As a Spanish ambassador wrote, the King "fortified himself by the consent of Parliament." Henry then proceeded to marry his mistress Anne Boleyn, who gave birth to Elizabeth in 1533. Under Henry, who had no sympathy for Protestants, the newly independent Church of England remained essentially Catholic in doctrine, but without the Pope. Henry also dissolved the monasteries and confiscated their property, which he sold or gave away to his supporters. Meanwhile, Jane Seymour (the third of Henry's six wives) finally produced the long-awaited son and heir, who upon his father's death in 1547 became King Edward VI.

As a boy of nine years of age, he obviously could not govern England. During his short reign (never healthy, he died in 1553 at the age of fifteen), the Church of England became a Protestant church. He had been raised as a Protestant and educated by Protestants, and the two men who successively governed England in his name, the Duke of Somerset and the Duke of Northumberland, were Protestants. When he died, his older half-sister Mary became queen. As the daughter of Catharine of Aragon, Mary was a Catholic. Indeed, even apart from her own personal convictions, she had to be Catholic for political reasons if for no other. If not, she was illegitimate, her father and mother's marriage having been annulled, with no right to the throne. Immediately upon her accession, she began the process of reversing her father's Reformation. The acts of Parliament that had separated England from the Roman Church were repealed by Parliament. The only thing she could not do was to reverse the dissolution of the monasteries and the confiscation of their property. In 1554, she married the much younger Prince Philip of Spain (soon to become King Philip II), who thereby became King of England. The marriage was enormously unpopular, and Philip and his English subjects took an immediate and intense dislike to each other. At first, Mary was relatively lenient toward the Protestants, giving them ample opportunity to return to the Roman Church, or if not to go into exile. By the time several years had passed, however, her policy of leniency seemed not to be working, so the Queen and her chief advisors—her chancellor Stephen Gardiner, Bishop of Winchester, and Cardinal Reginald Pole—decided on a firmer policy. Accordingly, about 300 people were burned for heresy during Mary's reign, earning her the epithet "Bloody Mary." Among those executed were Thomas Cranmer, former Archbishop of Canterbury, Nicholas Ridley, former Bishop of London, and Hugh Latimer, former Bishop of Winchester. Yet by sixteenth-century standards this was not exceptionally brutal: during the reign of Charles V, some 6,000 people in the Netherlands were burned for heresy. Part of Mary's problem was that she was too principled. Rebels she could and did pardon, but her Catholic convictions left her no room for compromise on religion. Yet the persecutions did not work: rather than bringing people back to the Roman church, the courage and example of many of the Marian martyrs inspired further resistance. Mary had nothing else to threaten people with after burning them failed to have its desired effect. In any case, Mary died, largely unmourned and childless in 1558, making her younger half-sister, Princess Elizabeth, queen of England.

The Elizabethan Religious Settlement

Elizabeth's most pressing problem upon becoming queen was settling the religious issue. To begin with, there was no question that England would once again be removed from the Roman Catholic Church. According to Rome, her mother and father's marriage was bigamous, so she was a bastard with no right to rule. This was clearly recognized at the time, for as soon as Mary died English Protestant refugees made their way home from Geneva, Frankfurt, and other Protestant centres. In 1559, Parliament passed a Supremacy Act, once again making the Church of England independent of Rome. Institutionally, then, Elizabeth had returned to the situation established by Henry VIII in the 1530s: an independent Church of England. But what about doctrine? In theory, she could have maintained a largely Catholic theology within an independent Church of England, as her father had done. Her own religious beliefs she kept well hidden. Probably, if she had been free to choose any creed she liked, she would have been a Lutheran. She liked the more ornate churches and richer liturgy of the Lutherans more than the austerity of worship seen among Calvinists. Lutheran churches were also much more under the control of the ruler than Calvinist ones. But above all she wanted peace and unity, and she was faced with a hard core of militant Protestants, many of whom had been in exile under Mary, many of them in Geneva. Politically, Elizabeth was dependent on them; they were the ones who supported most strongly the re-removal of England from the Roman Catholic Church. They were not likely to be happy with a half-hearted reform. The Queen was thus faced with a difficult balancing act. How could she keep this hard core of militant Protestants happy while at the same time arriving at a religious solution that would restore peace and unity to England after thirty years of religious and political turmoil? We have already seen that in France, there was no solution that could keep both sides in the religious conflict happy. Was there one in England? And could Elizabeth make it work?

The solution was this: a church that was largely Catholic in structure, with the monarch rather than the Pope at the head, governed by bishops firmly subservient to the Crown, but broadly Protestant in doctrine without being militantly so. Elizabeth managed to find the right mixture, one that would not offend the majority of Protestants, or most of those who would rather have remained Catholic but who were not willing to give their lives for the powers of the Pope or the sacrament of the Mass. On certain key points, the Elizabethan church was an ingenious compromise. Rather than the title "Supreme Head" with which Henry VIII had adorned himself, Elizabeth adopted the less provocative "Supreme Governor." As for worship, Elizabeth wanted to adopt the Prayer Book of 1549, which while largely Protestant in doctrine was a compromise on Catholic forms of worship, especially when it came to the sacrament of the Mass. Instead, however, Elizabeth was forced to adopt the more uncompromisingly Protestant Prayer Book of 1552, with several modifications. The 39 Articles adopted by the Church of England in 1563, while Protestant in theology, deliberately left key areas ambiguous, susceptible to various interpretations, most notably on precisely what happened to the bread and wine during the sacrament of the Eucharist.

Extremists on both sides were unhappy with this compromise settlement, or middle way (*via media*) as it has been called. Mary's Catholic bishops resigned rather than go along with it, and they were promptly replaced by Protestant supporters of Elizabeth. On the other side, zealous Protestant preachers railed against "popish vestiges" in the Church. But Elizabeth was able to make the compromise work. For one thing, although many (perhaps most) English people remained committed to their traditional Catholic faith, most were able to accept the new arrangement. Very few were willing to fight and die for the old faith, whereas Protestants had already demonstrated their willingness to become martyrs. In sixteenth-century England, Catholics were better losers than Protestants. In addition, by sixteenth-century standards, Elizabeth was quite lenient when it came to matters of conscience. Thus, Catholic bishops and priests who were unwilling to go along with the new order may have been forced to resign their positions, but they were not punished for their beliefs *per se*. Under Elizabeth, people were punished for treason, rather than heresy. That is, you could believe what you wanted, but you would be punished only if those beliefs led to actions against the church or state. In a famous excerpt from one of her proclamations on religion, Elizabeth stated, "We do not wish to make windows into men's souls."

All but the most militant and zealous Protestants also accepted this compromise. Many were of the opinion that this settlement was to be temporary, that in time the Queen would eliminate the "popish vestiges" in the Church and establish a truly Protestant Church of England in form and doctrine. As the years and decades went by, however, it began to dawn on many that Elizabeth intended this compromise to be permanent. Dissatisfaction over this would eventually lead to the formation of a powerful Puritan movement in Elizabethan England.

Religion and Foreign Policy

Elizabeth's religious settlement also had diplomatic ramifications. With France descending into civil war and chaos, England and Spain no longer had a common enemy to tie them together. Yet Philip II's approach to England was cautious at first. He was occupied elsewhere, and a small and relatively poor kingdom on Europe's northwest fringe was well down his list of priorities. He also waited to see what Elizabeth would do. He certainly understood that Elizabeth could not be a Roman Catholic, but she could have set up an English Catholic church, as her father had done. He also toyed with the idea of marrying his former sister-in-law to cement an anti-French coalition. Moreover, the only conceivable alternative to Elizabeth was Mary Stuart, and at this point Philip preferred a Protestant Elizabeth to a Catholic but French Mary Stuart. Throughout the 1560s, therefore, relations between Spain and England remained cautiously neutral.

Elizabeth's immediate priority was Scotland. Scotland, it will be remembered, was ruled by the Regent Queen Mother and widow of King James V, Mary of Guise. Her daughter, Mary Stuart, or Mary Queen of Scots, inherited the Scottish throne as a young child and had been sent off to France for her education. She had been married to the dauphin or heir to the French throne, who became King Francis II in 1559. Thus, Mary was at the same time queen of France and Scotland, besides being heir presumptive to the English throne. Upon her husband's death, she returned to a Scotland divided in politics and religion. The Protestant Reformation had made significant inroads there, largely through the preaching of John Knox, a militantly Calvinist preacher who had returned from exile in 1559 and become the most vociferous opponent of both Mary of Guise and her daughter. He found a ready audience among the nobles and clan chiefs who still had a great deal of power and who resented royal efforts to diminish that power. Upon her return to her kingdom, Mary Stuart managed to pour gasoline on both fires, both with her policies and with her personal life. Young, beautiful, and flirtatious, Mary apparently believed that her feminine charms were sufficient to attain her goals.

Elizabeth's problem was that Mary was next in line for the English throne, should Elizabeth die without heir. Mary also sought to strengthen her claim to the

English crown by marrying her cousin Henry Stuart, Lord Darnley, like herself a descendant of Henry VIII's sister. England and Elizabeth could hardly be disinterested spectators of events in Scotland. Mary, meanwhile, was doing her very best to alienate what meagre support she had. Dissatisfied with her marriage to Darnley, she had an affair with her private secretary David Rizzio. Darnley had Rizzio murdered in a jealous rage, while the unfortunate secretary clung to Mary's skirt. Darnley was himself murdered in circumstances that strongly suggested Mary's knowledge if not her complicity. Mary then ran away with and married Darnley's suspected murderer, the Earl of Bothwell. By 1567 her conduct had made it impossible for her to rule effectively, and she was forced to abdicate in favour of her infant son, who became King James VI, and who would later inherit Elizabeth's throne as James I of England. Mary herself was imprisoned in Scotland, but she managed to escape to England where she was granted refuge by her cousin Elizabeth. For the next nineteen years, Mary would remain a "guest" of her cousin, under a very comfortable kind of house arrest.

Mary's conduct here again betrays her fundamental political stupidity. As a Catholic and as heir to the English throne, her very existence was a threat to Elizabeth. There were numerous plots to kill Elizabeth and put Mary on the throne. Mary was ignorant of some of these; in others, however, she was a willing conspirator. Elizabeth's advisors continually urged her to take care of this problem by arranging Mary's demise, but for two decades the Queen resisted. Murdering lawful sovereigns, whatever their religion and personal conduct, was a precedent that Elizabeth was very reluctant to set. She also likely had some personal sympathy for her captive, based on her own experiences during the reign of her sister Mary when her own life had hung by a thread but her sister had steadfastly refused to have her killed.

An example of Mary Stuart's threat to Elizabeth may be seen in the Northern Rebellion in 1569. Royal authority along the Scottish border had always been weak, and this was the preserve of several of England's most powerful and independent noble families, the Percys and the Nevilles, earls of Northumberland and Westmorland respectively. The origins of the revolt lie in dissatisfaction with Elizabeth's religious policies and her increasingly anti-Spanish foreign policy. The core of the revolt was to have Mary marry Thomas Howard, Duke of Norfolk, depose and possibly kill Elizabeth, and put Mary and Norfolk on the throne while restoring England to the Roman Catholic Church. Elizabeth forbade the marriage, which Norfolk meekly accepted, but the northern earls rose in rebellion anyway. The rebellion was inept and poorly timed, and was easily put down by royal forces, with some 800 peasants put to death for their roles.

Meanwhile, relations with Spain were deteriorating from cautious neutrality into cold war. Without the mutual threat of France to bring them together, religious differences and other irritants came to the fore. English incursions into the Spanish colonies in the Caribbean caused a great deal of friction. The English captains John Hawkins and Francis Drake, among others, caused no end of trouble in the Spanish Main. Elizabeth also tried to aid Philip's Dutch rebels as inconspicuously and indirectly as possible. Elizabeth was in a difficult position: she wanted and needed to oppose Philip, but not so overtly as to provoke open war against the most powerful ruler in Europe. Therefore, for a time she allowed the Sea Beggars to put into English ports, and in 1568 she seized a ship full of Spanish gold bound for the Netherlands to pay the Spanish army there. By 1585, Elizabeth had become alarmed by Parma's progress against the Dutch rebels, and she gave in to her advisors, sending an army of 6,000 men to assist the Dutch under the Earl of Leicester, who was named governor-general of the rebellious provinces. It became apparent to Philip that the pacification of the Netherlands depended on neutralizing England, so plans were set in motion to punish England and Elizabeth for their opposition. These were the origins of the "enterprise of England," or, as it is better known, the Spanish Armada.

The Spanish Armada

For more than two years, all of Philip's energies and resources were directed toward the invasion of England. After much debate and indecision, Philip and the Armada's commander, the marquis of Santa Cruz, decided on a final plan. A massive fleet would set sail from Lisbon, carrying a large army. This fleet would sail up the English Channel, where it would rendezvous with the Duke of Parma and his Army of Flanders. Loaded onto small ships and barges, Parma and his army would cross the Channel and land in England, protected by the Armada. The supposed aim of the invasion was to put Mary Stuart on the throne and restore England to the Roman Catholic Church. Mary, however, had finally worn out Elizabeth's patience with her plotting. The Queen gave in to her advisors' pleas, and Mary went to the scaffold on February 18, 1587. Without an obvious candidate to put on the throne, a number of alternative aims for the Armada were considered. Eventually, it was decided that Philip would nominate a candidate for the English throne, to be approved by the Pope. Philip likely intended his daughter Isabella for the honour.

The Armada was originally intended for the summer of 1587 but was delayed by several factors. One was the sheer magnitude of the undertaking. Another was a raid by Sir Francis Drake on Cadiz during which he destroyed many of the supplies being stockpiled for the fleet. These included a number of seasoned barrel staves. Since there was not enough time to produce and season new staves, unseasoned staves were eventually used, with the result that the soldiers and sailors of the Armada suffered from putrid food and water. In addition, in early 1588 the marquis of Santa Cruz died and was replaced as commander by the Duke of Medina Sidonia, who was not only less experienced, but who had doubted the Armada's potential for success all along.

By the next summer, however, all the preparations had been made, the ships and men assembled, and on May 28, 1588, the Armada set sail, although a gale forced it to put into the northern Spanish port of Corunna for nearly a month before it could set out again. Boasting 130 ships and 30,000 men, 19,000 of them soldiers, it represented the largest amphibious assault force ever assembled. In hindsight, we can identify several problems with the plan. The most glaring of these flaws was the difficulty of the rendezvous with Parma and his army. Without anything like radio communication, the two forces were ignorant of each other's position and the timing of the rendezvous was very tricky. Moreover, the Spanish Netherlands lacked a good deep-water port. This meant that the Armada could not come close enough to land to provide an escort for the small ships and barges that were to carry Parma's army. In addition, the advantage of surprise had been completely lost through a series of leaks and informers. The English knew precisely what the Spanish intended, and that they did not have to destroy the Armada or Parma's army. On the contrary, all they needed was to disrupt the rendezvous between them, whose success was very doubtful in the first place.

The fate of the "Invincible Armada" is of course well known. Appearing at the mouth of the Channel in late July, the Spanish ships sailed up the Channel in a tight, crescent-shaped formation, harassed by an English fleet that was about the same size, but more mobile and better armed. The Armada was prepared to fight a land battle at sea, such as Lepanto had been, with ships at close quarters being grappled and soldiers boarding the enemy ships. The Armada's artillery was therefore powerful, but of limited range. The English guns, on the other hand, had greater range but were unable to penetrate the Armada's hulls.

The fleet arrived off the coast of the Spanish Netherlands on August 6, but could not approach land close enough to protect Parma's army, while Parma dared not expose himself to the English fleet. On the night of August 7, the English set a number of fireships adrift on the current, into the midst of the Armada. In the panic that ensued, the Spanish ships dispersed to avoid catching fire. The next day, having disrupted the Armada's defensive formation, the English moved in for the kill. They were, however, unable to destroy the Armada, which had largely managed to reconstitute its formation. Technically, the battle of August 8 may have been a draw, but in fact it was something of Spanish victory, since the Armada remained largely intact and there was still hope that the invasion could be carried out as planned. However, strong winds pushed the Armada into the North Sea and made a return to the Channel impossible. Medina Sidonia then decided to make the best of a difficult situation and, keeping the fleet together, decided to return to Spain by sailing north around Scotland into the Atlantic, keeping well clear of the dangerous Irish coast. Yet his plan was thrown into disarray by unusually horrible weather. Throughout the fall of 1588, what was left of the Armada straggled back to Spain. All told, only about 80 of the 130 ships made it back to Spain, with tremendous loss of life.

The significance of the failure of the "enterprise of England" has been vastly exaggerated. It did not represent the "beginning of the end" of Spanish power, even of Spanish sea power. Philip managed to assemble two even larger armadas in the 1590s, and in general the Spanish navy was stronger after the Armada than before it. Nor did it represent the beginning of an English empire, or the beginning of English naval domination. In fact, quite the contrary: the voyage of the Armada demonstrated that England was vulnerable to invasion, which led Philip to assemble the two armadas of the 1590s, both of which were stymied, like their predecessor, by foul weather. Spain remained the hegemonic power in Europe for decades yet, while England remained a bit player in European diplomacy. Spain and England remained at war until 1604, but there were no further confrontations on the order of 1588.

England did, however, derive a significant moral boost from the failure of the Armada. Indeed, there is something to be said for the idea that the joy and relief that followed the failure of the Armada helped to produce the sense of confidence and vitality for which we remember the Elizabethan age: the age of Shakespeare, Marlowe, Raleigh, Jonson, Spenser, and Bacon. In *Richard II*, Shakespeare captures well the sense of English peculiarity and divine favour that seemed to animate the age:

> This royal throne of kings, this scepter'd isle,
> This earth of majesty, this seat of Mars,
> This other Eden, demi-paradise,
> This fortress built by Nature for herself
> Against infection and the hand of war,
> This happy breed of men, this little world,
> This precious stone set in the silver sea,
> Which serves it in the office of a wall,
> Or as a moat defensive to a house,
> Against the envy of less happier lands,
> This blessed plot, this earth, this realm, this England. (II.i.40–50)

Puritans and Parliament

The failure of the Armada, however, had a darker side as well. While under the threat of imminent invasion, Elizabeth had been able to defuse or deflect many of the political and religious tensions within England. Now, however, without an imminent threat from Spain, these tensions became more acute. In religion, as we have seen, there were many who were dissatisfied with the moderate nature of Elizabeth's settlement. Their basic complaint was that the Church of England was still too Catholic. They wanted to purify it of what they called "popish vestiges," and so they became known as Puritans, originally a term of derision applied by their opponents. They objected to the form of government of the Church of England: they did not want an episcopal church governed by bishops appointed by the ruler; rather, they wanted a presbyterian system such as had been established in Scotland, where the church was more independent of political control and governed by assemblies of ministers and laymen. They also objected to "popish vestiges" in both doctrine and practice. This division within the Church of

England first emerged in the 1570s when some protested the continued use of elaborate robes or vestments by clergy during worship. They also disliked the ambiguity in official doctrine, wanting it replaced by an explicitly Protestant doctrine that left no room for compromise. They also wanted the government to pursue a harder line against English Catholics, or recusants as they were known. They wanted an avowedly Protestant foreign policy, which would include overt support for the French Huguenots and the Dutch rebels against Philip II. In general, they also believed in the necessity of thorough moral reformation of society. They were opposed to taverns, dancing, and gambling, and it was Puritans who took the lead in the efforts to reform popular culture discussed in Chapter 4. Their basic attitude was that the duty of church was to serve God, not the Crown. At the very least they challenged the royal control over the church established by Henry VIII and so painstakingly preserved by Elizabeth.

At first, most Puritans bided their time. They thought that Elizabeth intended her religious compromise to be temporary, that they could nudge her in the right direction. As time went on, it began to dawn on them that this was intended to be permanent, and the opposition of the Puritans became more vocal and open. In the 1570s Elizabeth found herself having to give in to the Puritans on the persecution of Catholics. As relations with Spain worsened, Catholics came under suspicion as traitors, especially as there were numerous plots to kill Elizabeth and put Mary Stuart on the throne. Catholics therefore suffered a kind of guilt by association. Moreover, beginning in the 1570s, dozens of English Catholic missionaries, trained on the continent, were smuggled into England to succour English Catholics. Most prominent among these were the Jesuits Edmund Campion and Robert Parsons. Campion was caught, tortured, and executed in 1581. Scores of others met the same fate, and much more serious penalties were imposed on recusants.

However much the Puritans disliked the current form and doctrine of the Church of England, most still believed in the necessity of a single national official church. A minority among the Puritans, however, denied the need for a national church at all. These were the separatists or congregationalists, who believed that each local congregation should be left free to determine its own doctrine and form of worship, and to choose its own minister. Though a small fringe group under Elizabeth, the congregationalists would become very important in the Civil War of the seventeenth century.

Once the Spanish menace had been defeated, Elizabeth imposed a severe crackdown on Puritans through John Whitgift, her Archbishop of Canterbury. Whitgift imprisoned Puritan leaders, broke up their cells, uncovered and destroyed secret Puritan presses, and imposed severe penalties for not attending the services of the Church of England. Many Puritans would find their way into exile in the late sixteenth and early seventeenth centuries, in Germany or the Netherlands, and some in New England, where they would attempt to erect their ideal community, their "city on a hill," as a beacon and a light for sinful humanity.

From the Queen's point of view, the threat of the Puritans was rendered even more potent by their support in Parliament, especially in the House of Commons.

As was the case with the Puritans, tensions between Elizabeth and Parliament increased over the course of her reign, and reached their worst in the 1590s once the threat of foreign invasion had receded. The most significant development was the increasing power and self-awareness of the House of Commons. In the sixteenth century, the House of Commons was very far from the democratic body we think of today. In fact, only about five per cent of the population could vote for members of Parliament. It did not represent "the people" in any abstract sense; rather, it represented the wealthy and powerful. Parliament met only when the monarch called it, and for only as long as the monarch allowed it to meet. The Speaker was a royal appointee, and the agenda was entirely at the discretion of the monarch. Nor did the ruler have to legislate through Parliament; under previous rulers there were often decades between meetings of Parliament. On the other hand, the power of the rulers was enhanced if they could show that their policies had the support of their subjects. This is precisely why Henry VIII chose to break away from the Roman Catholic Church through a series of acts of Parliament. He did not have to, but it was to his advantage. It strengthened him in his confrontation with Rome. Parliament's one great strength was its power to approve new taxation. If the ruler needed more money than the ordinary revenues of the Crown brought in, for example to fight a war, and sought to impose a new tax, the approval of Parliament was considered necessary. Parliament after all represented those who would be paying the tax. This was especially true since, unlike in France, the salaried bureaucracy was very small, with only a few hundred people, mostly in London. For enforcing its laws and policies throughout England, the government relied on a network of several thousand locally important men, who served on a volunteer basis: Justices of the Peace, sheriffs, and so on—in other words, the very people who either sat in the House of Commons or elected those who did. Thus, the most effective way to govern England was to ensure that these people were on side beforehand, and Parliament was the arena for doing this.

Over the course of the sixteenth century, the House of Commons became more and more the vehicle of the gentry. These were the people who benefited from the boom years of the sixteenth century and also from the confiscation and sale of monastic lands in the 1530s. Beginning with the nearly continual meetings of the "Reformation Parliament" in the 1530s, Members of Parliament (MPs) began to acquire a sense of common identity and purpose.

After the mid-1580s, with an English army in the Netherlands and war with Spain, Elizabeth needed more money and had to call Parliament more frequently in order to obtain it. Although she still had ultimate control over government policy, MPs begin to demand a larger voice, something Elizabeth was not willing to concede. There was a fundamental conflict here between two conceptions of what Parliament was and what it was for, about the basic nature of politics and government. However, no one at this time was thinking about limiting the ruler's power. Parliament simply believed that its members ought to be taken seriously, that they had an important contribution to make, especially since they were being asked to foot the bill.

There were many Puritans in Parliament, and several times Elizabeth had to intervene forcefully against Puritan bills. Probably even more significant was the fact that even the non-Puritans in Parliament had interests in common with the Puritans. For example, when Elizabeth crushed debate on Puritan bills, many non-Puritans saw in this a threat to free speech and their rights as MPs. One of the major clashes came in 1601 when the House of Commons began to criticize the Queen's right to grant monopolies and licences regulating economic life. Many of the merchants and gentry in the Commons objected to these restrictions on their economic freedom and began to say so. Elizabeth managed to avoid a major showdown only by promising a complete inquiry into abuses, but the issue of who was ultimately responsible for government policy had been raised and would not go away.

Elizabeth died in 1603 after a long and glorious reign, without having had a major confrontation with either the Puritans or Parliament. Her most significant accomplishment was restoring order and stability to the troubled and divided kingdom she had inherited nearly half a century earlier. The centrepiece of this achievement was her moderate religious settlement, which proved acceptable to the majority of English men and women, as it was intended to do. Though the settlement was opposed by zealous Catholics and, more importantly, by the Puritans, Elizabeth was a shrewd enough politician to deflect most such opposition. Almost uniquely among sixteenth-century rulers, she was able to find the religious formula that satisfied the broad majority while not forcing dissenters into rebellion. England was thus spared both the fratricidal religious warfare then ravaging France and the insular intolerance of Spain under Philip II. Still, Elizabeth left unresolved some serious problems for her successor, the now-adult son of Mary Queen of Scots who became King James I of England, the first ruler of the Stuart dynasty. There was the ongoing war with Spain and its attendant expenses and reliance on Parliament for money, not to mention unresolved tensions with both Puritans and Parliament. The major question on the threshold of a new century, a new reign, and a new ruling dynasty, was whether or not Elizabeth's successors would be as adroit in handling these tensions as she had been.

CHAPTER EIGHT

Germany and the Thirty Years' War

THE HOLY ROMAN EMPIRE, 1555–1618

The area of Europe that we know as Germany was in 1559 subsumed within the entity known as the Holy Roman Empire. Stemming from Charlemagne's revival of the Roman Empire in the west in the ninth century, the Holy Roman Emperors had earlier been the most powerful rulers in medieval Europe. Successive dynasties of emperors, however, had never succeeded in establishing the hereditary principle. Aspiring emperors therefore had bargained away to individual German princes and nobles the powers of the imperial government in exchange for their support. Moreover, the powerful emperors of the Middle Ages had clashed repeatedly with successive popes over political supremacy in Europe. The result was that while emperors were fighting with popes, individual German territories and rulers were largely able to go their own way. By the middle of the fifteenth century, then, imperial power in Germany had reached its low point. There was still an emperor, but he was virtually powerless except in his own hereditary domains. There was no imperial army, fiscal system, judicial system, or currency. For most of the fifteenth century, the emperors were drawn from the Habsburg dynasty, whose own hereditary possessions were primarily in Austria. Real power, however, was exercised by a series of regional princes, such as the Dukes of Saxony and Bavaria, the Landgrave of Hesse, and so on. There was also a series of ecclesiastical territories, whose bishops not only were princes of the church, but also ruled substantial swaths of territory. In addition, there were about 150 imperial cities such as Augsburg, Frankfurt, and Nuremberg, in theory subordinate only to the emperor, which in reality meant that they were virtually independent. By the fourteenth century it had been established that the emperor was elected by seven of the most important territorial rulers in Germany. Three were ecclesiastical rulers (the Archbishops of Cologne, Mainz, and Trier), while four were secular (the Electors of Saxony, Brandenburg, the Elector Palatine, and the King of Bohemia).

In the early sixteenth century, the fortunes of the Habsburg emperors were revived in the person of Holy Roman Emperor Charles V (1519–55). Through a fortuitous series of dynastic marriages and untimely deaths, Charles inherited a vast, dynastic, multinational empire. This included not only the Austrian lands and the title of Holy Roman Emperor, but also the Spanish kingdoms of Castile and Aragon, where he ruled as King Charles I. As King of Castile, he also ruled its overseas territories in the New World, with their fabulous gold and silver mines. As King of Aragon, Charles ruled the Italian kingdom of Naples, and he was also successful in conquering the wealthy and important duchy of Milan in northern Italy. He was also heir to what was left of the territories of the medieval dukes of Burgundy. These consisted of the Free Country of Burgundy (Franche-Comté) and, more important, the various provinces comprising the Low Countries or the Netherlands. When in 1526 the King of Hungary and Bohemia was killed in battle with the Ottoman Turks, Charles's younger brother Ferdinand was elected king of those kingdoms, further adding to Habsburg possessions and power.

Charles's self-appointed mission was to bring the power and resources of his non-German possessions (particularly Castile) to bear on Germany and to restore real power to the title of Holy Roman Emperor. In this he was not successful. The Protestant Reformation launched by Martin Luther in 1517 was soon adopted by a number of German rulers who saw in the new religion a means of further resisting imperial power. In addition, the Empire's southeastern frontier was under continual threat from the Ottoman Empire.

The first round of religious war in Germany, the one provoked by Luther's Reformation, had ended in 1555 with a military stalemate recognized in the Peace of Augsburg, with its formula of *cuius regio, eius religio*. This left the religion of the territory up to its ruler. At the same time, Emperor Charles V abdicated, leaving to his brother Ferdinand both the title of emperor and the Austrian lands, which he added to his kingdoms of Bohemia and Hungary. He now became Emperor Ferdinand I (1556–64). He was succeeded by his son Maximilian II (1564–76), who was relatively tolerant and, left on his own, would likely have been a Lutheran. Ferdinand and Maximilian's principal concern was defence against the Ottoman Turks, for which they needed the cooperation of the German Lutheran princes. Thus, they were concerned primarily with not rocking the boat, rather than with restoring Catholicism. As a result, Protestantism flourished in the hereditary Habsburg lands. In the Austrian lands, the majority of the nobility were Lutheran, as were a large number of peasants and bourgeois. Maximilian confirmed several times the religious and political liberties of the Austrian nobility, for again he needed their cooperation against the Turks.

Bohemia was culturally, linguistically, and ethnically distinct from the Austrian lands. The people were Czech, with their own distinct churches derived from the Hussite movement of the later Middle Ages. The Bohemian nobles also had a great deal of political power, expressed in their assembly or Estates, and their power to elect the king. Since 1526, they had elected a Habsburg, but they did not have to. The Habsburgs were in a different constitutional position here than they were in the Austrian lands, where they were hereditary rulers. Habsburg control of Hungary was even more tenuous. Most of the country was under Turkish control; the nobility had extensive powers and were largely Protestant.

When Maximilian II died he was succeeded by his eldest son, Rudolf II (1576–1612), a committed Catholic who had been educated in Spain. He encouraged the activity of the Jesuits in Austria, beginning the Counter-Reformation in his territories. He could not tamper with the powerful nobility, but he was largely successful in stamping out Protestantism in the towns. A peasant revolt in the 1590s gave him an excuse to forcibly restore Catholicism in the countryside. He would have liked to reimpose Catholicism in Bohemia, too, but the Protestants were simply too well entrenched there, and his political position was too tenuous. In addition, he was increasingly caught up in a power struggle with his brother Matthias, his heir-apparent as emperor. Rudolf became increasingly depressed and acted strangely, eventually turning into a recluse in his palace in Prague, obsessed with alchemy and astrology. As a result, in 1609, he guaranteed the political and religious liberties of the Bohemian nobility in a document called the "Letter of Majesty" in order to solidify Bohemian support against Matthias.

Elsewhere in the Habsburg lands, much the same was taking place. Beginning in the 1580s, Archduke Charles (a younger son of Ferdinand I) re-Catholicized his territories of Styria, Carinthia, and Carniola. He withdrew guarantees previously granted to Protestants, encouraged the activity of the Jesuits, and founded a Jesuit-run university at Graz that became the epicentre of the Catholic revival in these lands. Upon Charles's death in 1590, his son Ferdinand (later King of Bohemia and Emperor Ferdinand II) continued and intensified the Counter-Reformation in these Austrian lands.

Within Germany as a whole, the Peace of Augsburg became subject to increasing strain toward the end of the sixteenth century. Several sources of tension arose from the Peace of Augsburg itself. The "ecclesiastical reservation" prohibited the further secularization of church land, most especially the territories of the prince/bishops. This was especially important because it preserved a Catholic majority among the seven electors, three of whom were prince/bishops: Cologne, Mainz, and Trier. Further secularization threatened the imperial future of the Habsburg dynasty. In Cologne, for example, in the late 1570s, a recently appointed archbishop converted to Lutheranism and granted freedom of worship to Protestants in his lands. Ultimately, he was forcibly removed from power and replaced by a brother of the very Catholic Duke of Bavaria. The Archbishopric of Magdeburg was governed by a Protestant administrator, whose right to sit in the Imperial assembly, or Diet, was hotly disputed by its Catholic members.

The Peace of Augsburg permitted only Catholicism and Lutheranism. No other faith, including Calvinism, was permitted. But in the years after 1555, Calvinism had become the growing and dynamic Protestant movement. Several German princes illegally became Calvinist, most importantly the Elector Palatine after 1584. Not only was he one of the seven electors, his lands included the Lower Palatinate, an extremely important territory along the river Rhine, and the

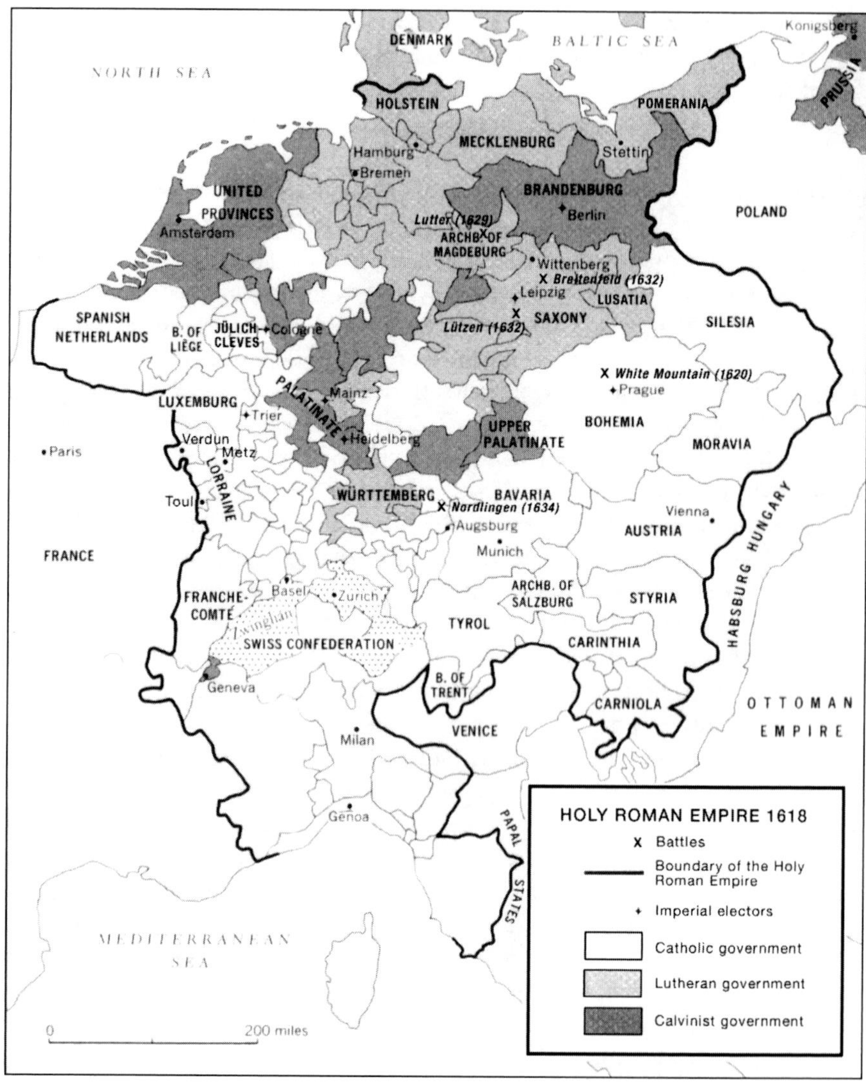

MAP 8.1 ⇶ THE HOLY ROMAN EMPIRE IN THE 17TH CENTURY

Upper Palatinate, which was adjacent to both Bohemia and Bavaria. Not only was the Elector illegally Calvinist, but he was an active and involved Calvinist, sending soldiers to fight in France and the Netherlands and establishing his capital of Heidelberg as one of the leading centres of Calvinism. Further, in 1613, the Elector of Brandenburg converted to Calvinism, but he continued to allow the practice of Lutheranism in his lands. The incursion of Calvinism was resented and feared by both Catholic and Lutheran princes. In fact, the Lutherans generally tended to side with the Catholics rather than the Calvinists. Nevertheless, three of the four secular electors were now either Lutheran or Calvinist: Palatine, Brandenburg, and Saxony; only the King of Bohemia was Catholic, and the tenuous Habsburg control of Bohemia was by no means secure.

On top of these tensions produced by the terms of the Peace of Augsburg and the growth of Calvinism was the revival of the Catholic cause with the Counter-Reformation. Not only were Habsburg rulers in Austria imposing Catholicism on their territories, but so too were other German Catholic princes. This is most clearly seen in the duchy of Bavaria, ruled by dukes of the Wittelsbach family, relatives of the Elector Palatine. In addition, in many imperial cities Catholics were able to take over, further disrupting the balance established by the Peace of Augsburg.

German Catholic princes found themselves in a somewhat awkward situation. While they wanted a Catholic Germany, they did not want it at the cost of an effective and powerful emperor. There was a divergence between their political and religious agendas, and as a result, relations between Catholic princes and the Habsburg emperors were often very delicate and ambivalent.

Complicating things even further was the fact that virtually every ruler in Europe had an interest in what happened in the Empire. The Spanish Habsburgs were tied to their Austrian cousins by blood and by religion. If the Emperor could enforce his authority in Germany, they could gang up on the Dutch rebels and encircle France. Of prime importance to the Spanish as well was the preservation of the "Spanish Road." This was a series of routes from northern Italy, through the Alps and western Germany. The Spanish Road was the main route by which Spanish men, money, and communications were transmitted from Spain to the Netherlands. The kings of France were embroiled in civil war until 1598, but afterwards, Henry IV's chief concern was to prevent the revival of Habsburg power in Germany, in order to prevent encirclement of France, and to disrupt the Spanish Road, which paralleled France's eastern boundary. The Dutch feared that a revival of Habsburg power in Germany would allow the two branches to cooperate in defeating them, giving the Spanish an additional front. So, whatever happened within Germany, it was highly unlikely that the Germans would be left alone to work things out for themselves.

These tensions increased dramatically in the early years of the seventeenth century, as illustrated by the formation of rival military alliances. The Protestant princes formed the Protestant Union in 1609, led by the Elector Palatine, and the Catholics responded with their own Catholic League, led by the Duke of Bavaria. Two incidents in particular illustrate the growing tensions in Germany: the Jülich-Cleves dispute; and the Bohemian dispute, which began the Thirty Years' War.

Jülich-Cleves was a small but strategically important territory in the Rhineland of northwestern Germany, near the Dutch frontier. In 1609, the Duke of Jülich-Cleves died, leaving as claimants to the territory his two Lutheran sons-in-law, who agreed to rule jointly pending the outcome of mediation. This was unacceptable to both Spanish and Austrian Habsburgs because of the territory's strategic position and proximity to the Netherlands. It was also a religiously mixed territory. Emperor Rudolf II sent a Habsburg cousin to occupy the territory, claim-

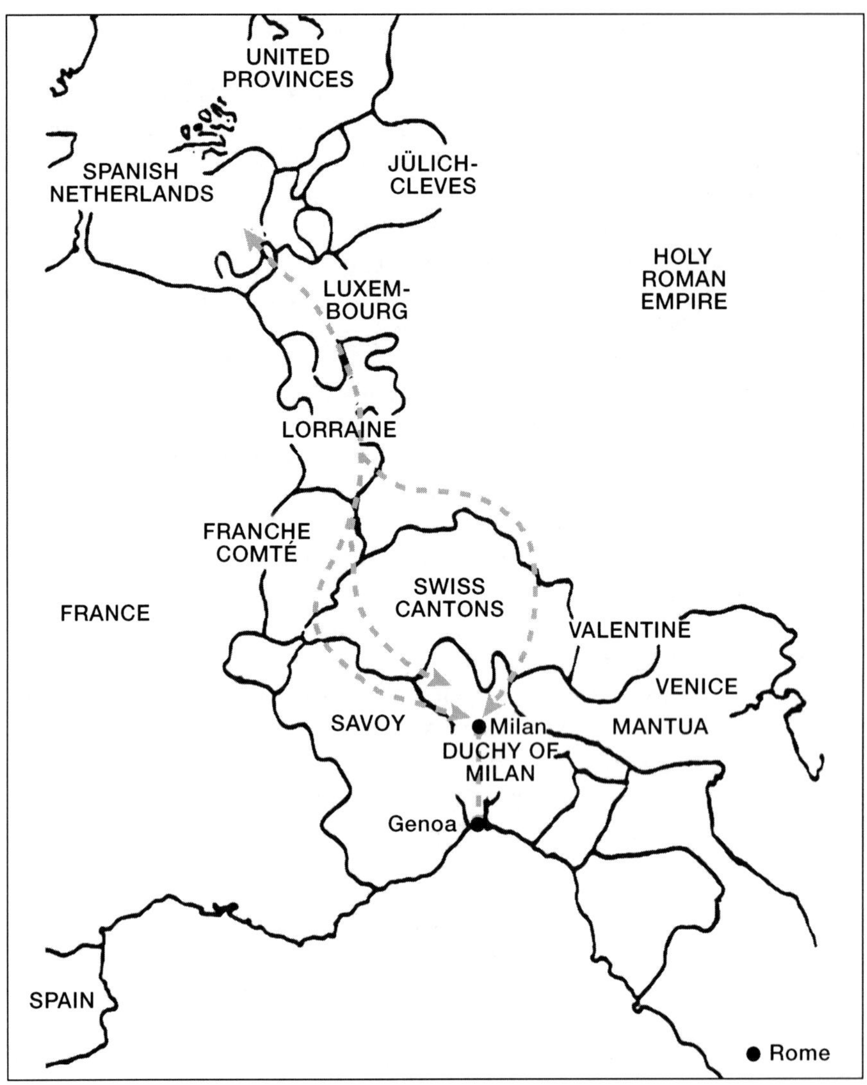

MAP 8.2 THE SPANISH ROAD

ing to be protecting the interests of the Catholics there, but he was opposed by a joint army of France, the Dutch Republic, and the Protestant Union. It looked very much like war would break out over this issue, but it was prevented by the assassination of Henry IV of France in 1610. Ultimately, in 1614, the territory was split, with part going to a Lutheran ruler and part to a Catholic. But the affair demonstrates several things: the militarization of religious tension in Germany, and the interest of outside states in German affairs. More serious was the Bohemian crisis, which actually led to the outbreak of the Thirty Years' War.

In 1612, Rudolf II died and was replaced as Holy Roman Emperor and king of Bohemia by his brother Matthias. Matthias, however, was elderly and childless and was clearly a caretaker king and emperor. Matthias and the rest of the Habsburgs decided that his heir would be Ferdinand of Styria. Ferdinand was, as we have seen, a committed and zealous Catholic, and had continued the work of his father Charles in re-Catholicizing the Austrian territories of Styria, Carinthia, and Carniola. The Czech and largely Protestant Bohemian nobility looked upon Ferdinand's impending succession with alarm, but they were assuaged by his promises to abide by the guarantees spelled out in the Letter of Majesty of 1609. Ferdinand was thus elected king of Bohemia in 1617.

Very quickly, however, the new king alienated his Protestant nobles by violating their religious and political liberties. He appointed Catholics to powerful positions in the government and harassed Protestants. On May 23, 1618, during a meeting of the Bohemian nobility in Prague, a group of upset Protestant nobles seized Ferdinand's two chief representatives in Bohemia and threw them out of a window in the royal palace; the two men (and their secretary, who was thrown out for good measure) survived this "Defenestration of Prague." Catholics attributed their survival to divine protection, while Protestants ascribed it to the pile of refuse and dung in the moat below, which cushioned their fifty-foot fall. While the nobles maintained that they were simply objecting to the King's policies, and not disputing his right to rule, in fact they were repudiating everything Ferdinand stood for, and everyone knew it. They set up their own government and actively canvassed support from Protestant rulers.

When the elderly Emperor Matthias died in March 1619, he was replaced by Ferdinand, who now added the title Holy Roman Emperor to his other distinctions. The Bohemians responded by deposing Ferdinand as their king and electing in place the young Elector Palatine, Frederick V, the leading Calvinist in Germany. War between Ferdinand and his rebellious Bohemian subjects was really now inevitable. Ferdinand could not let the Bohemians get away with this for any number of reasons. For one, it was a deliberate challenge to his religion and the Habsburg family. It also changed the electoral politics of the Empire: if Frederick were recognized as King of Bohemia, all the secular electors would be Protestant, thus jeopardizing the future of the Habsburg dynasty in Germany. Moreover, the Estates of Austria had joined the Bohemians in rebellion, and a Bohemian army had in fact laid siege to Ferdinand's capital of Vienna.

The Bohemian Phase, 1619–22

With the advantage of hindsight, we can see that the Bohemian rebellion was likely doomed from the start. The Bohemian nobles were themselves divided along religious lines and were hesitant to mount a widespread national resistance movement for fear of a social revolution. Frederick was young and inexperienced, and he proved to be an ineffective leader. The foreign support they had hoped for was not forthcoming. Most of the Protestant German princes remained neutral, and the Lutheran Elector of Saxony actually allied with the Emperor. The French were occupied with the Huguenots, the Dutch and Spanish were preparing for the end of their truce, which was to expire in 1621, and England also remained neutral despite the fact that James I was Frederick's father-in-law.

Ferdinand, however, had problems of his own. Most significantly, he did not have a sufficient army to punish the Bohemians, let alone restore order in the Austrian lands. This problem was soon rectified, thanks to three sources of help: Duke Maximilian of Bavaria, who put the army of the Catholic League under General Tilly at Ferdinand's disposal; the Spanish army in the Netherlands, which came to the Emperor's assistance; and the Lutheran Elector of Saxony, who supported Ferdinand by invading and occupying the Bohemian province of Lusatia. Maximilian wanted the Upper Palatinate, which was adjacent to Bavaria, and the Electoral title for his own branch of the Wittelsbach dynasty. The Spanish wanted control of the Lower Palatinate to guarantee communications with the Netherlands in preparation for the end of the truce. And the Elector of Saxony wanted the territory of Lusatia. Tilly's army invaded Austria, put down the rebellion there, and then turned toward Bohemia, where he crushed the Bohemians at White Mountain outside Prague in November 1620. Frederick fled into exile in the Netherlands, earning the derisive nickname of "the Winter King." Tilly's army proceeded to occupy the Lower Palatinate, and in 1623 Ferdinand formally transferred both it and the Electoral title to Maximilian of Bavaria. Spanish troops had occupied the west bank of the Rhine, and the Elector of Saxony occupied Lusatia with hardly a fight. In addition, in 1621 the Protestant Union was dissolved at the order of Ferdinand, having lost its leader and shown itself utterly incapable of action.

Meanwhile, Ferdinand was dealing very harshly with the Bohemian rebels. In June 1621, 27 of the leading noble rebels were executed. About half of the land in Bohemia was confiscated and redistributed to loyal nobles and army officers. All Protestant ministers were exiled, and in 1627 all Bohemians were ordered to convert to Catholicism or go into exile; in all, about 30,000 families chose exile. In 1628 the crown of Bohemia was declared hereditary in the Habsburg dynasty. Ferdinand also seized his moment of triumph and eliminated the last vestiges of Protestantism and autonomy from among the Austrian nobility. The Bohemian war thus resulted in greater Habsburg control of Austria and Bohemia, the strengthening of Maximilian of Bavaria and the Catholic League, and the dissolution of the Protestant Union. Ferdinand's position as Holy Roman Emperor was also greatly strengthened, as he had demonstrated his power to depose rebellious princes (Frederick) and transfer their territory and rights to others.

The Danish Phase and the Edict of Restitution, 1625–29

In 1625, King Christian IV of Denmark entered the war on behalf of the German Protestants. He had several reasons. He himself was a German prince, since part of his territories were within the Empire, so the expansion of Ferdinand's power threatened his own. In addition, Tilly's army had moved northward and occupied strategically important parts of northern Germany, thus threatening Denmark. Christian himself had designs on these same territories, so he persuaded the Protestant princes of northern Germany to form an alliance for the defence of their privileges, and sought and received diplomatic support from the English and Dutch. In 1626 the Danish army invaded northern Germany, only to be defeated at the Battle of Lutter in August. This effectively doomed Danish intervention, although some fighting went on for several years along the Baltic coast. Support was forthcoming from neither the Dutch nor the English. The Dutch were preoccupied (as always) with their war with Spain, while Charles I of England was having his own domestic problems that precluded intervention in Germany. In 1629, Christian was forced to give in and signed the Treaty of Lübeck, which, while allowing him to keep most of his German possessions, also forced him to renounce any further territorial ambitions in Germany.

Perhaps the major factor in Ferdinand's triumph over Christian of Denmark was that he now had an army at his disposal, freeing him from dependence on Maximilian of Bavaria and the Catholic League. This army was gained through the figure of Albrecht von Wallenstein (1583–1624). A Protestant Bohemian noble by birth, Wallenstein converted to Catholicism and was rewarded in the aftermath of the Bohemian rebellion when Ferdinand made him duke of Friedland. He managed to marry a wealthy widow and was able to use his wife's wealth to build his landholdings by speculating in the land confiscated from the Bohemian rebels. At one point it was estimated that Wallenstein personally owned about 25 per cent of Bohemia. In 1625, he agreed to recruit and lead an army for Ferdinand on a contractual basis. An organizational genius, Wallenstein took the money from Ferdinand but paid his soldiers primarily by allowing them to loot the areas they occupied.

There was nothing particularly new in such private military entrepreneurs providing armies to rulers. Indeed Tilly was a figure of this sort, as was Mansfeld, the commander of the Bohemian forces during their rebellion. Wallenstein, however, raised the practice to a whole new level. War was his business, and the maintenance of his position and wealth depended on its continuation. With Wallenstein we begin to see the tail wagging the dog. His army was a business proposition that required war for its ongoing function: it fought because it had to, not to achieve any particular aim. In the fight against the Danes and their German allies, Wallenstein's army occupied large parts of northern Germany.

After a decade of war, the Emperor's position was vastly strengthened. Rebellion and Protestantism had been defeated and extinguished in the hereditary territories of Bohemia and Austria. The leading Calvinist in Germany, the Elector

Palatine, had been defeated and humiliated, his lands and titles confiscated. Protestant princes had been defeated and cowed, and the King of Denmark sent home with his tail between his legs. Ferdinand now had an effective army at his disposal, and Catholic armies occupied large parts of primarily Protestant northern Germany. Ferdinand therefore felt free to impose his will upon the Holy Roman Empire as a whole. In March of 1629, therefore, he issued the Edict of Restitution, fundamentally altering the Empire's constitution and its balance of power.

The edict ordered the restitution of all church lands secularized since 1552. Two archbishoprics, twelve bishoprics, and more than a hundred convents and monasteries were to be restored to the Catholic Church. In a number of towns where confessional coexistence had been prescribed by the Peace of Augsburg, Protestant worship was outlawed. The prohibition against Calvinism was renewed. Lutheranism was to be the only permitted form of Protestant worship. Many of these territories and cities were occupied and forcibly re-Catholicized.

With the advantage of hindsight, however, we can see that in the Edict of Restitution, Ferdinand's reach exceeded his grasp. For one thing, the edict crystallized the religious conflict as it had not been before. His policies practically precluded any further cooperation with Protestant princes, as had been the case, for example, when the Lutheran Elector of Saxony had allied with the Emperor during the Bohemian rebellion. Moreover, the edict alienated the Catholic princes, most importantly the Duke of Bavaria, who feared—rightly—that Ferdinand was aiming at a really united Empire under firm Habsburg control. In addition, the manner in which the edict was proclaimed alienated even the Catholic princes of Germany. It was implemented through an imperial edict without the consultation or approval of the Imperial Diet. The edict also aroused the fear of foreign powers, who feared a united Germany under the Habsburgs. France, though a predominantly Catholic country and governed by Cardinal Richelieu, feared Habsburg encirclement more than anything else. The Dutch Republic also feared a united Empire under Habsburg control, for fear of its cooperation with its Spanish Habsburg enemies. Lutheran Sweden also had reason to be alarmed at the expansion of Catholic power in Germany. Sweden controlled not only Finland, but also a string of territories around the Baltic Sea, and Catholic Habsburg control of northern Germany necessarily threatened Swedish power.

That Ferdinand had overreached soon became apparent. He called the Diet of the Empire to meet in 1630 to endorse two proposals that were dear to his heart: to elect his son (the future Ferdinand III) King of Romans, recognizing his succession to the Imperial title; and to approve aid for the Spanish in the Netherlands. The Protestant princes had boycotted the Diet, but even the Catholics refused to endorse Ferdinand's program. To appease them, Ferdinand fired Wallenstein, whom the princes feared and hated as an upstart and a threat to themselves. Even so, Ferdinand was unsuccessful in his aims at the Diet. In the meantime, however, in June 1630, Gustavus Adolphus, the Lutheran king of Sweden, invaded northern Germany in order to protect both German Protestants and Swedish interests.

The Swedish Phase, 1630–35

At the age of 35, Gustavus Adolphus was already an experienced ruler and soldier. King of Sweden since 1611, he had conducted numerous campaigns against Sweden's traditional rivals in the Baltic, Denmark, and Poland. He was also an advanced military thinker and effective general. Through efficient organization and use of resources, Sweden, with a population of only 1.5 million, was able to fund and supply an impressively large army (see Chapter 13). He built on previous tactical developments, with the result that the Swedish army was an effective fighting force. Gustavus was also a sincere Lutheran and genuinely believed in the importance of protecting German Protestants. The Swedish invasion was also aided by the fact that with Wallenstein's dismissal and the alienation of Catholic princes, Ferdinand was in no position to strike back. In addition, in 1631, Gustavus signed the secret treaty of Bärwalde with King Louis XIII and Cardinal Richelieu of France. In this treaty, France agreed to subsidize the Swedish campaigns in Germany. In essence, France gained a proxy to fight the Habsburgs in Germany, while it confronted the Spanish Habsburgs directly in the Low Countries and northern Italy.

The Swedish invasion was immediately successful, as Gustavus and his army occupied large parts of northern Germany and made alliances with important Lutheran princes and cities, including the large and important city of Magdeburg. In May 1631, the city was stormed by Imperial troops, who massacred the garrison (as was common practice), murdered some 20,000 of its inhabitants, and burned down the greater part of the town. This atrocity not only further hardened Protestant attitudes toward Catholics and the Emperor, but also greatly aided Gustavus in enlisting allies.

In September 1631, the Swedes destroyed the Imperial army under Tilly at the battle of Breitenfeld. This was one of the major turning points in the war. At a stroke, all the Imperial gains in northern Germany through the 1620s were erased. Gustavus then took the battle into the heartland of Catholic and Habsburg power. The Swedish army overran Bavaria, while their Saxon allies occupied Bohemia and captured Prague. Faced with this new threat, and without an army to oppose Gustavus, Ferdinand recalled Wallenstein. On November 16, 1632, the two armies met at Lutzen in Saxony. A terribly hard-fought battle resulted in a Swedish victory, as Wallenstein was forced to retreat into Bohemia. But it was a costly victory, as the Swedes lost their king.

Since Gustavus's heir (his daughter, who would later become Queen Christina) was still underage, overall direction of the Swedish war effort was assumed by his chancellor and long-time collaborator, Axel Oxenstierna. But there is no doubt that some of the passion went out of the Swedish war effort after the death of the King. Essentially, a stalemate ensued in which neither side was strong enough to defeat the other, nor was anyone yet willing to give up.

Meanwhile Ferdinand was beginning to have doubts about Wallenstein's loyalty. Wallenstein saw himself as virtually a free agent and began to shop his services around to others, all the while doing the minimum he could for the Emperor. Accordingly, in early 1634 Ferdinand once again dismissed the general and ordered his apprehension dead or alive. Physically ill, Wallenstein fled but was ultimately caught and murdered by a group of his own officers who had been suborned by Ferdinand.

Imperial fortunes were dramatically revived in 1634, for in September, a combined Imperial-Spanish army annihilated the Swedes at Nördlingen. In essence, this victory was a Catholic Breitenfeld, restoring Habsburg and Catholic power in southern Germany, just as the earlier victory had done for the Protestants in the north. Most of Sweden's major German allies now made peace with the Emperor. Peace was concluded on the basis of the repeal of the Edict of Restitution, the reaffirmation of the Peace of Augsburg of 1555, and the restoration of the religious boundaries as they had been in 1627. Thus, this settlement recognized the catholicization of Bohemia, but it also restored most of northern Germany to Lutheran rule. Having lost their king, and now much of their army, the Swedes were sorely tempted to go home. However, having invested so much in the German war, they were reluctant to depart without any tangible benefit. Moreover, faced with the revival of Habsburg strength in Germany and with Swedish doubts about fighting on, France now felt compelled to enter the war openly, alongside Sweden, against the Emperor.

The Franco-Swedish Phase, 1635–48

The war dragged on for another thirteen years, but by now it had ceased completely to be a German religious war. The Germans had already largely arrived at a religious settlement that reflected the military stalemate, and left to their own devices the war would likely have ended here.

They were not, however, left to their own devices, for the war was kept going by the French and Swedes on one side, and the Spanish on the other, for their own distinctly secular purposes, for the German war had become inextricably linked with two other major conflicts. One was the war between Spain and the Dutch Republic, which had resumed in 1621 and was still going on. The Spanish wanted to preserve the "Spanish Road" through western Germany and, if possible, to open up another front. The other was the war between France and Spain that had broken out in the late 1620s. The French were concerned, as they had been for over a century, to prevent Habsburg encirclement. They were therefore concerned to keep the Spanish from defeating the Dutch and to disrupt Spanish communications and the Spanish Road. Louis XIII and Cardinal Richelieu also sought to break Spanish control of northern Italy and its important alpine passes. They also wanted to keep the war in Germany going to prevent Habsburg control in Germany, and as a further distraction for the Spaniards. The Swedes, as mentioned above, after having invested so much in the war, wanted to see some return for their efforts. Moreover, they now found that they had a tiger by the tail. The

Swedish army by this point was largely mercenary (as were all the others), and their pay was badly in arrears. Without the cash to pay the soldiers, the Swedish government had to keep the war going in order to allow the soldiers to pay themselves by pillaging the German countryside. Otherwise, they faced the distinct possibility that the army would invade Swedish territory to extort payment.

This was the most destructive—and pointless—phase of the Thirty Years' War, as armies marched back and forth across Germany, pillaging and sacking as they went. The pointless violence and brutality are well reflected in several contemporary works of art. One is *The Miseries of War*, a series of engravings by the Frenchman Jacques Callot, which followed a group of recruits from their enlistment. They displayed in uncompromising detail the horrors and brutality of war. The other is the semi-autobiographical *Adventures of a Simpleton* by Hans Jacob Christoffel von Grimmelshausen, one of the great works of German literature. In it, a naive and innocent young peasant boy, known as Simplicius, is wrenched from his isolated farm and his family and experiences at first-hand all the horrors of war that seventeenth-century Germany had to offer.

The Peace of Westphalia

After more than two decades of war, the major combatants were nearing exhaustion. A general sense of futility and war-weariness opened the way to peace negotiations by 1644. But since these negotiations were not accompanied by a truce or cease-fire, they tended only to intensify the fighting, as negotiators sought to exploit victories, or to stall for time after defeats. Ultimately, however, by 1648 the combatants signed the two peace treaties of Münster and Osnabrück, known collectively as the Peace of Westphalia. All the major combatants gained something in the Peace of Westphalia. Although Habsburg ambitions to control the Holy Roman Empire were decisively and permanently defeated, their increased control of their hereditary lands of Austria and Bohemia was formally recognized. Sweden gained important pockets of territory along the Baltic coast. These included western Pomerania with the important port city of Stettin and control of the mouth of the Oder River, as well as the secularized bishoprics of Bremen and Verden, which controlled the mouths of the Elbe and Weser rivers. Sweden thus stood to benefit from German control of Baltic commerce and also received a large subsidy with which to pay off its soldiers. France gained parts of Alsace and Lorraine, and some important fortresses along the Rhine, which strengthened its eastern frontier while hindering Spanish communications with the Netherlands. France also gained formal recognition of its possession of the important border fortresses of Metz, Toul, and Verdun, which it had occupied for nearly a century. France and Sweden were also named as guarantors of the terms of the treaties, or "protectors of German liberties." This gave them, especially France, virtual *carte blanche* to meddle in German affairs, since it was a simple matter to manufacture some violation of the treaties. The Duke of Bavaria kept the Upper Palatinate and the Electoral title, while Frederick V's son was restored to a reduced Lower Palatinate and was also given an Electoral title. Saxony kept Lusatia, which it had gained by its support of Ferdinand II against the Bohemian rebels at the beginning of the war. The Dutch Republic and Switzerland (previously technically part of the Empire) were legally recognized as independent of Imperial control, although in fact such control had been non-existent there for years (centuries in the case of Switzerland).

Within Germany, the German princes gained at the expense of the Emperor, now Ferdinand III (1637–57). They were recognized as virtually independent of the Emperor, finally defeating Habsburg ambitions in Germany. They were declared fully sovereign in their internal affairs and were allowed to conclude treaties and alliances with whomever they pleased, as long as they were not directed against the Emperor. Although the Empire continued to exist on paper, it was now reduced to little more than an empty shell. Although the Habsburg emperors continued to participate in German affairs through the rest of the seventeenth and into the nineteenth century, their main ambitions were now directed to the south and east at the expense of the declining Ottoman Empire.

In religion, the formula of Augsburg was reaffirmed, with the addition of Calvinism as a legal religion. The religious boundaries were frozen as they had been in 1624, undoing the Edict of Restitution, but keeping Bohemia and Austria Catholic. Rulers were henceforth free to change their own religion but not that of their subjects. Concessions were made to liberty of conscience, though not to freedom of worship, and relatively generous terms were granted to those who wished to emigrate for religious reasons. As a result, northern Germany remained solidly Lutheran, southern Germany was solidly Catholic, and there were enclaves of Calvinism along the Rhine. In the meantime, Spain, faced with its own internal problems, had finally given up on reconquering the Dutch Republic, and recognized its independence from Spanish control in 1648. On the other hand, the war between France and Spain continued for another decade, until the Peace of the Pyrenees in 1659.

The Thirty Years' War was simultaneously the last and the most destructive of the wars of religion. Historians are still debating the destructiveness of the Thirty Years' War, a task made more difficult by the complete lack of accurate statistics. While no one disputes that it was terribly damaging, historians have reevaluated the level of destruction. Earlier generations of historians saw the level of destruction as near total. In the 1930s, C.V. Wedgwood wrote, "Morally subversive, economically destructive, socially degrading, devious in its course, futile in its result, it is the outstanding example in European history of meaningless conflict."[1] More recent research has revealed a somewhat more nuanced view. Earlier estimates of population loss in the Holy Roman Empire ran as high as 40 per cent, but more recent estimates run in the range of 20 per cent. There were, however, very significant regional variations. Some areas, such as northwestern Germany and Austria, were relatively untouched, while others—Brandenburg, Pomerania, Alsace, and Bavaria, to name a few—suffered horribly. In general, larger cities suffered less than smaller towns and the countryside, though Magdeburg was a notable exception, as we have seen. The town of Nördlingen in south-central Germany lost between 50 and 70 per cent of its population, and the population of Augsburg sank from 48,000 in 1620 to 21,000 in 1650. Even among armies, actual battle was not the leading cause of death. Rather, famine, malnutrition, and disease were the real culprits. Armies, whether "friendly" or hostile, tended to wreak havoc in the countryside, even if they were well paid and well disciplined. If they were unpaid and mutinous, catastrophe could ensue. In the immediate aftermath of the war, however, there was in many areas a demographic boom as couples were finally able to marry and begin having children in relative peace and security.

It is equally difficult to generalize about the economic effects of the war. Certainly the actual conduct of the war, the fighting of battles, the passage of armies, and the sieges of cities had disastrous economic effects. Once again, the rural economy was especially heavily hit as the agricultural cycle was disrupted, livestock slaughtered or stolen, farm buildings destroyed, and peasant families killed or scattered. War, however, then as now, also produced economic winners. There were huge fortunes to be made in supplying armies with food, arms, and other supplies. Soldiers were usually paid better than unskilled craftsmen—when they were paid, that is. Some cities, such as Hamburg, which was relatively untouched by the fighting, benefited enormously from supplying armies.

Although one hates to think of a "good side" of mass destruction and slaughter, those peasants who survived the war were in a relatively advantageous position, just as those who survived the Black Death had been three centuries earlier. With fewer people to provide for, the less fertile lands were abandoned, and per-capita agricultural production probably increased. On the other hand, this "artificial" decline in population also eliminated the need to innovate. In other countries (such as England and the Dutch Republic), where the population did not decline, or at least did not decline so dramatically, fundamental changes were underway in the agricultural economy, as we saw in Chapter 3. In Germany, this was not necessary, with the result that in terms of economic development, Germany lagged behind the rest of western Europe until well into the nineteenth century. Whatever the extent of destruction and disruption, however, the Thirty Years' War was the most destructive war in European history until the conflagrations of the twentieth century.

Nationally minded German historians of the nineteenth and early twentieth centuries also condemned the Thirty Years' War and the Peace of Westphalia for their deleterious effects on the German nation. The recognition of each prince as sovereign in his own territories delayed the process of national unification, which was not achieved until 1871. These historians saw the Peace of Westphalia as a betrayal of the German nation and blamed it for all of Germany's ills in the coming centuries. This, however, is an entirely anachronistic view, imposing the values of nineteenth-century nationalism on a time when they did not exist. In practical terms, it is extremely difficult to see that there were any other options. At the same time, the provisions of Westphalia greatly aided the internal political development of the individual German states, as seen most notably in the subsequent dramatic rise of Brandenburg-Prussia (see Chapter 16).

The Thirty Years' War was also the last of the religious wars to stem from the fragmentation of the Catholic Church in the Reformation. After the Peace of Westphalia in 1648, religion really ceased to be the driving factor in international relations among European powers. Already during the war we see cross-confessional alliances, most notably between the Catholic king of France and his chief minister (a cardinal of the Catholic Church), and the Lutheran king of Sweden, all against the Catholic emperor. As we have seen, left to their own devices the Germans would likely have settled the religious issues in the 1630s. By the later stages of the war, religion was definitely in the background of the fighting. The Peace of Westphalia was an entirely secular affair. Pope Innocent X condemned the treaties as "null, void, invalid, iniquitous, unjust, damnable, reprobate, inane, empty of meaning and effect for all time," but his fulminations were ignored. After Westphalia, it was assumed that the religious boundaries, specifically in Germany and by implication throughout Europe, were now settled. Henceforth, rulers would no longer go to war for the "true faith," whatever that might be. This is one reason why the recognition of the sovereignty of each German prince was important: it transformed German religious affairs from domestic into foreign policy. Throughout the rest of the seventeenth and eighteenth centuries, wars would be fought for more limited and therefore attainable goals: territory, trade, resources, and so on. These, unlike the triumph of the true faith, are capable of rational calculation, of cost-benefit analysis. Not until the upheavals of the French Revolution and the Napoleonic era would ideological considerations once again drive international relations. So, ironically, while developments in weapons, tactics, and logistics were making warfare more deadly on the battlefield, warfare was becoming more restrained and "civilized," not least in its impact on civilian populations. At the same time, however, all rulers and all governments still believed in the importance of religious uniformity within the state: that is, while religion no longer drove diplomacy, it remained a vital matter in domestic politics.

NOTE

1 C.V. Wedgwood, *The Thirty Years War* (New York: Anchor Books, 1961) 506.

PART THREE

The General Crisis of the Seventeenth Century

Although in this book I have chosen to deal with the Thirty Years' War as part of the era of religious war that began in 1559, it also forms part of what some historians of the seventeenth century have called "the general crisis of the seventeenth century." Beginning in the 1950s, historians started looking across national boundaries and compared a series of upheavals that wreaked havoc across Europe in the several decades around the middle of the seventeenth century. For the last, most pointless, and most destructive phase of the Thirty Years' War was complemented by equally serious developments elsewhere. In England, we have the Civil War and Puritan Revolution, which saw the trial and execution of King Charles I, the abolition of the monarchy, and the establishment of a republic. In France, there was the series of revolts known as the Fronde, which challenged the previous several centuries of political development and growth in monarchical power. In Spain, there were simultaneous revolts against the central government: one in Catalonia (which was unsuccessful), and one in Portugal (which was). The Dutch Republic, as we have seen, was caught up in a struggle between the forces of centralization and those of particularism. Sweden was embroiled in an admittedly non-violent power struggle between the Crown and the high nobility. In Denmark, following the death of King Christian IV (r. 1577–1648), a coup gave the nobles control of the government.

Beyond the realm of politics and government, historians have also seen evidence of a "general crisis" in other realms of human activity. In economics and demographics, the great boom of the sixteenth century petered out over most of Europe around 1600, as we saw in Chapter 3. At the same time, the European population had largely recovered its pre-Black Death levels. So the economy was stagnating or declining just as there were more mouths to feed. Moreover, rising population meant that the landholdings of peasant farmers (who were the vast majority of the population) were declining in size. They were thus forced to look for subsistence to the general economy at the very time that it was least able to provide it. The economic pie therefore remained the same, or shrank, just when more people were wanting a piece of it. In many cases there was a crisis of expectations, when ordinary people understood that things had been better in the past. This brought in its wake increased tensions in social relations.

At the same time, the European religious crisis set off by the Protestant Reformation continued, producing the religious warfare examined in the preceding chapters. During the century from 1560 to 1660, there was almost continual warfare. This was of course very expensive, and the expense was compounded by the changing nature of warfare: larger armies, increased firepower, improved fortifications, and other developments led to very expensive and time-consuming siege warfare. Governments were increasingly hard pressed to finance this warfare and resorted increasingly to higher taxation of their subjects. On top of this were the longer-term trends of centralization and absolutism, which involved chipping away at the society of orders—the entrenched rights and privileges of various social and geographic groups. Faced with a declining or stagnant economy and the fiscal demands of war, governments sped up their attacks on the privileges of the society of orders. What had previously been incremental and evolutionary change now became revolutionary, wholesale change, driven by the fiscal needs of the "warfare state." The various groups and institutions whose rights and privileges were being attacked naturally fought back. The details of these confrontations varied, according to the needs and capacities of the central government, which group was under attack, the relative strength of the parties, and so on. Mostly, the society of orders was defeated, or at least had to strike a compromise that was very favourable to rulers. Thus, most of Europe saw the triumph of royal absolutism in the later seventeenth century, most notably in France, but also (with variations) in the Habsburg lands, Brandenburg-Prussia, and Russia. In a few countries, the society of orders fought back more successfully, resulting in political systems where the power of the central government was tempered very much by the rights and privileges of the society of orders. The primary example of this was England, but we see it also in the Dutch Republic and Poland.

Absolutist and Limited Governments

As mentioned above, absolute monarchy, or royal absolutism, became the dominant form of government in seventeenth-century Europe. We must, however, be extremely careful about definitions when discussing absolute monarchy. The experience of totalitarian regimes in the modern world often leads us into misunderstandings of seventeenth-century absolute monarchy. First, it might be helpful to mention several things that absolutism was not. It was not totalitarianism, where the government attempts to control all of life and thought in its territory. Nor was it tyranny: the theorists of monarchy were always very careful to distinguish between tyranny and legitimate absolute monarchy. Nor were the monarch's subjects his slaves, with their lives and property at his disposal. Once more, theorists were careful to distinguish between despotism and absolute monarchy. Despotism they somewhat ignorantly assigned to Russia and eastern states such as the Ottoman Empire or Persia.

What, then, *is* absolute monarchy? Historians of the period have spilled oceans of ink in debating this question, even whether or not the term can be usefully employed to describe monarchical government of the period. I think it can, as long as we are careful to describe and define the term precisely. To this end, there are several contexts in which the term can be used to describe the evolution of monarchical government in this period.

First, we can say that in an absolute monarchy, all legitimate political power is in the hands of the ruler. That is, he does not share it with any other person, group, or institution: not Estates, Parliament, judges, church, nobility, and so on. This is in fact the original meaning of the word "absolute," that is, pure or unmixed. Throughout the Middle Ages, there had been varying and sometimes contradictory conceptions of monarchy. Sometimes when people thought of royal power, they thought of the king as chief feudal lord, whose vassals were tied to him by a personal contractual arrangement. At other times, they thought of him as the chief warrior whose main function was to lead his soldiers in battle. At yet other times, they conceived of him as the chief judge of the kingdom. Increasingly, however, in the late Middle Ages, lawyers and bureaucrats working for kings expounded the theory that the king was really the successor of the Roman emperors of antiquity. They found numerous principles in Roman law that seemed to exalt the power of the ruler, such as "What pleases the prince has the force of law." Increasingly the refrain of royal theorists was *rex in suo regno imperator est* ("the king is emperor in his kingdom"). That is, he was subject to no earthly authority. As rulers consolidated their power through the fifteenth and sixteenth centuries, this concept of kingship increasingly crowded out the others. By the seventeenth century, for reasons that are discussed below, I believe we are justified in talking about absolute monarchy as being noticeably different from earlier forms.

In an absolute monarchy the ruler possessed a monopoly of *legitimate* political power. That is, rulers did not in theory have *carte blanche* to do anything they pleased. No ruler could legitimately cry "Off with his head" for no reason at all. Subjects did have rights and privileges, which rulers swore to honour and preserve. Theorists were unanimous, for example, in stating that a king was still subject to divine and natural law, and to the fundamental laws of the kingdom. For example, he could not alter the succession to the throne. Nor could he deprive a subject of his property or his life without due cause and process. That these things did of course happen no more invalidates the existence of absolute monarchy so defined than their occurrence in the western world today invalidates the existence of democracy.

Absolute monarchy therefore does not preclude the existence of subjects' rights and liberties. Indeed, much of the confusion surrounding the concept of absolute monarchy stems from the continuing existence of the rights and liberties of subjects, inherent in the society of orders. Many have assumed that absolute monarchy was incompatible with subjects' rights and liberties. Therefore, the thinking goes, any monarch who did not attempt to override or eliminate his subjects' rights and liberties could not, by definition, be an absolute monarch. If this is the test applied, then absolute monarchy cannot be said to have existed in seventeenth-century Europe, for all monarchs were bound to some extent by their subjects' rights. Much of this confusion can be cleared up, however, if we think of royal power as existing in two spheres. One sphere consisted of the powers that were generally agreed to be entirely within the royal prerogative, that is, within the king's power alone. These usually included such things as the royal household, the choice of ministers and advisors, and conduct of war and diplomacy. In the other sphere were the areas where the king's power was constrained by the rights and liberties of his subjects and whose exercise required the consent of the subjects in one form or another. These included justice and especially property rights, which of course bears directly on the area of taxation. Therefore, in the one sphere the king's power could be said to be absolute (that is, pure or unmixed), but not arbitrary, while in the other it was limited by the rights of his subjects. A difficulty, of course, arises from the fact that these two spheres were not self-contained, and from the fact that there was continual debate and conflict about the contents and boundaries of the two spheres of royal power. To take one very important example: while warfare and the command of armies was completely within the royal prerogative, raising the tax revenue required to pay for these things required the consent of those paying the taxes. Taxation was therefore the chief arena where differing interpretations of royal power collided.

The overwhelming justification given for absolute monarchy was divine right. That is, not only did rulers derive their mandate to rule from God, but royal power was also comparable to divine power in its scope and extent. For example, Bishop Jacques Bénigne Bossuet, tutor to Louis XIV's eldest son and one of the most important contemporary theorists of royal power, wrote, "Princes act as minister of God, and as his lieutenants on earth. It is by them that he exercises his rule.... The royal throne is not the throne of a man but the throne of God himself ... God has had them anointed by his prophets with a sacred unction as he has his pontiffs and his altars anointed." And King James I of England, who fancied himself a scholar, echoed these sentiments:

> The state of monarchy is the supremest thing upon earth; for kings are not only God's lieutenants upon earth and sit upon God's throne, but even by God himself they are called gods.... [kings] make and unmake subjects; they have the power of raising and casting down; of life and of death; judges over all their subjects and in all causes and yet accomptable to none but God only.

No doubt part of the reason for this emphasis on the divine origins of monarchy and royal power stems from the fact this was a very dangerous era in which to be a monarch. Two kings of France (Henri III in 1589 and Henry IV in 1610) were felled by assassins. There were numerous plots against the life of Elizabeth I and her successor James I, most notably the Gunpowder Plot of 1605. Stressing the divine nature of kingship can therefore be seen as a means of elevating the status of the monarch, making it harder to contemplate killing him (or her).

There were, however, advocates of absolute monarchy who stressed its secular origins and justification. One of these was the French lawyer Jean Bodin, whose *Six Books of the Republic* was published in 1576, in the middle of the French religious wars. Bodin argued that in order to avoid chaos, there had to be a single authority in the state. This authority he termed the sovereign. Much of the work is therefore an exploration of the attributes of sovereignty. According to Bodin, sovereign power must be perpetual and thus irrevocable, for anyone who could revoke it would then be sovereign. It must also be absolute: not subject to any other authority on earth, since that authority would then be sovereign. Thus the ruler must be above the laws of both himself and his predecessors, for if he were not, he would be subject to another and therefore not sovereign. Bodin was careful, however, to insist that kings are subject to divine and natural law, as well as certain fundamental laws of the kingdom:

> ... all princes of the earth are subject to the laws of God and of nature, and even to certain human laws common to all nations.... All princes of the earth are subject [to divine and natural laws], and cannot contravene them without treason and rebellion against God. His yoke is upon them, and they must bow their heads in fear and reverence before His divine majesty. The absolute power of princes and sovereign lords does not extend to the laws of God and of nature.... The constitutional laws of the realm, especially those that concern the king's estate ... cannot be infringed by the prince. Should he do so, his successor can always annul any act prejudicial to the traditional form of the monarchy, since on this is founded and sustained his very claim to sovereign majesty....

Bodin also distinguished between laws, which cannot bind the ruler, and covenants or agreements with his subjects, which are binding:

> A law and a covenant must therefore not be confused. A law proceeds from him who has sovereign power, and by it he binds the subject to obedience, but cannot bind himself. A covenant is a mutual undertaking between a prince and his subjects, equally binding on both parties, and neither can contravene it to the prejudice of the other, without his consent.

In addition, Bodin delineated three types of monarchy: despotic, royal, and tyrannical. In a despotic monarchy, "the prince is lord and master of both the possessions and the persons of his subjects by right of conquest in a just war; he governs his subjects as absolutely as the head of a household governs his slaves." In a royal (or legitimate) monarchy, "the subject obeys the laws of the prince, the prince in his turn obeys the laws of God and natural liberty and the natural right to property is secured to all." In a tyrannical monarchy, "the laws of nature are set at nought, free subjects oppressed as if they were slaves, and their property treated as if it belonged to the tyrant." Bodin further distinguished between two types of tyrants. One was a usurper with no legitimate claim to the sovereign power; such a tyrant may be legitimately resisted and even killed. The other was the legitimate sovereign, whether despotic or royal, who may never be resisted no matter how tyrannical their conduct:

> I conclude then that the subject is never justified in any circumstances in attempting anything against his sovereign prince, however evil and tyrannical he may be. It is permissible to fail to obey him in any commands contrary to the laws of God and of nature, but one must then seek refuge in flight, go into hiding or suffer death rather than attempt anything against his life or his honour. What a great number of tyrants would be discovered if one might kill them.

Probably a more important justification for absolute power in the long run was given by the Englishman Thomas Hobbes (1588–1679) in his massive work *Leviathan, the Matter, Forme, and Power of a Commonwealth Ecclesiasticall and Civill* (1651). Like Bodin, Hobbes wrote in the midst of civil war and upheaval, in this case the English Civil War, and he too sought a way to restore peace and stability. He was greatly influenced by the scientific thought of the day, and he resolved to treat politics in as scientific a manner as possible. His views on the origins and exercise of power are entirely materialistic, without reference to God or divine right. Humans he considered simply as machines, governed by their passions and self-interest. In their natural state, therefore, without any form of government or authority, people exist in a state of "the war of every man against every man." According to Hobbes, "the laws of Nature, as 'justice,' 'equity,' 'modesty,' 'mercy,' and in sum 'doing to others as we would be done to,' of themselves, without the terror of some power, to cause them to be obeyed, are contrary to our natural passions, which carry us to partiality, pride, revenge, and the like." Life in this state of nature is, in his famous phrase, "solitary, poor, nasty, brutish, and short." This state of nature is so miserable that people will do anything to escape it. The solution, Hobbes wrote, is an agreement among everyone to give up all their natural liberty to a single authority, which, like Bodin, he termed the sovereign:

> This is more than consent or concord: it is a real unity of them all in one and the same person, made by covenant of every man with every man, in such manner as if every man should say to every man, "I authorize and give up my right of governing myself to this man, or to this assembly of men, on this condition, that you give up your right to him and authorize all his actions in like manner." ... This is the generation of that great "leviathan," or rather of that "mortal god," to which we owe under the "immortal God," our peace and defense.

The sovereign power may never be resisted, no matter how evil or tyrannical, since resistance defeats the purpose of the agreement in the first place, and because no matter how odious the sovereign may become, the state of nature is infinitely worse:

> And because, if the essential rights of sovereignty ... be taken away, the commonwealth is thereby dissolved and every man returns into the condition and calamity of a war with every other man, which is the greatest evil that can happen in this life.

Hobbes was much maligned in his day as an atheist, the "Monster of Malmesbury," and certainly his views were not widely accepted, even by proponents of absolute monarchy. Divine right continued as the primary justification of royal rule, and Hobbes's artificial origins of political power offended a deeply Christian society. In the long run, however, *Leviathan* was tremendously influential in stressing the secular and utilitarian origins of the state, and even the idea that the state existed to benefit the individual, rather than the other way around.

Historians of the nineteenth and early twentieth centuries believed that one element of seventeenth-century absolute monarchy was a revolution in the methods of government. That is, the personalized and haphazard administrative methods of the Middle Ages were replaced by a rationalized, impersonal, and bureaucratic system typical of modern western governments. Mountains of research into the actual practice of government, rather than its theory, have shown that this was not the case. Seventeenth-century absolute monarchies were not appreciably more rational or bureaucratic in their methods than their predecessors. It seems clear that historians who thought so were in fact searching for the origins of the nineteenth-century national bureaucratic states in which they lived, and that their views are tenable only through a very selective and misleading interpretation of the evidence.

Much recent research has concentrated on the actual exercise of royal power and emphasizes its limitations in a practical sense. The primitive state of transportation and communications limited very effectively the exercise of political power, no matter how absolute it might be in theory. This was, of course, an age without telephones, computers, and all the other tools of modern technology. The fastest information could travel was by a man on horseback. It was quite simply impossible for governments to exercise absolute power effectively at any great distance entirely unaided. Therefore, although monarchs were absolute in theory, in practice they had to contend with and appease numerous people and groups in order to maintain their authority throughout their territories. Absolute monarchies (and indeed all effective governments) operated by co-opting and appeasing local elites, by bringing them inside the system of absolute monarchy and sharing with them the spoils of political power. Absolute monarchies thus tamed the society of orders, but they did not and could not eliminate it. In a practical sense, therefore, the power of Louis XIV over his subjects' lives was far less than that of a modern city council over the city's residents.

All rulers aspired to more absolute rule, but not all were equally successful, and in some places they failed altogether. France under Louis XIV is the dominant example of absolute monarchy. Other varieties of absolute monarchy emerged in the Habsburg lands, in Brandenburg-Prussia, Russia, and a host of smaller states. England is the best example of a country where monarchs failed to impose a more absolute monarchy. Here after a civil war, the execution of the king and abolition of the monarchy, and the restoration of the monarchy, the aristocracy and the monarchy arrived at a balance of power in which the power of the monarch was restrained, but not eliminated, by the elite represented in Parliament. In the Dutch Republic, the House of Orange and mercantile elite of the towns, or regents, contended throughout the seventeenth century for control of the government. In Poland, the victory of a powerful nobility over the monarchy meant that that large kingdom evolved into a kind of noble republic with a figurehead king. These situations, however, remained the minority, and they came about not because of any *a priori* decision, but because rulers were prevented from imposing absolutism by the defence of the rights and liberties of the society of orders. For that reason, in writing about them, I prefer to use the term limited monarchy rather than constitutional monarchy. This latter term implies that the ruler's power was limited by some prior constitutional arrangement or provision. As we have seen, these governments emerged as the result of a failure to impose royal absolutism, not a prior decision to have a limited monarchy.

Though it may be confusing and seemingly oxymoronic, absolute monarchies were limited in important ways. In a theoretical sense their power was limited by divine and natural law and by the rights and privileges of their subjects as embodied in the society of orders, or, as Bodin put it, by covenants agreed upon between rulers and subjects. In practical terms, they were limited by primitive technology and the need to co-opt and appease the local elites who, after all, were the ones who had to enforce royal policies. Absolute monarchy and limited monarchy are therefore not different kinds of things, not different species; instead, they can be seen as different points along a spectrum. Toward one end of the spectrum, royal power is greater and the rights and liberties of subjects weaker; toward the other, the opposite is true. Where precisely along this spectrum the dividing point between absolute and limited monarchies lies is open to debate, but it is ultimately a moot issue of terminology and semantics.

CHAPTER NINE

The Construction of Royal Absolutism in France, 1598–1661

The Reign of Henry IV, 1598–1610

As we have seen, Henry IV brought peace to France in 1598 after a long period of foreign and civil war. It was therefore really only after 1598 that the work of reconstruction could begin, and in this Henry was spectacularly successful. He is viewed as one of the most popular kings in French history, and deservedly so, especially when one compares him with his immediate predecessors. His chief concern was to give France some breathing space to recover from years of turmoil, and so, for most of his reign, his foreign policy was cautious and non-aggressive. He was also concerned to restore royal authority after forty years of drift and weakness. In this, too, he was very successful. Certainly his attractive personality played a large part in this, but there was more to it than that. As a result, when he was assassinated in 1610, the royal authority that he had revived could survive a subsequent period of weakness and drift.

His most pressing concern was to restore royal finances, which were in a state of chaos following decades of civil war. The primary figure here was Henry's finance minister and closest advisor, the Protestant nobleman Maximilian de Bethune, the Duke of Sully. Sully and the King had been friends and comrades-in-arms for decades. Unlike his master, Sully had maintained his Huguenot religion but had risen to this powerful position. By 1610, the royal budget was running a surplus, the debt had been cut in half, and a large cash reserve had been accumulated. This was accomplished primarily through traditional means of raising revenue rather than any bold innovation. Sully was what we today would call a hands-on manager. He carefully supervised the system and dismissed or disciplined incompetent or corrupt officials. While important, these reforms had only a minor impact on the overall fiscal picture. Sully also managed to reduce payments on the debt by simply informing creditors that they would have to be satisfied with partial payments at lower rates of interest. But even with all this, new sources of revenue had to be found. Sully certainly understood that the major problem facing government finances was that nobles (and many commoners) were exempt from the *taille*, the most important direct tax and the source of the bulk of government revenues. As a result, a great deal of wealth was simply not taxed, and the burden of the *taille* fell overwhelmingly on those least able to cope with increased demands—the peasants. Sully recognized that such exemptions were a real problem, but even if he had wanted to, he could not challenge them without widespread resistance and revolt. Accordingly, he placed more emphasis on sources of revenues, such as sales taxes, which everyone, including nobles, paid. As a result, during Sully's tenure, the burden of the *taille* actually declined.

By far the most important and successful of the new methods of raising revenue was the *paulette*, introduced in 1604 and named after the official who came up with the idea. The *paulette* was a fee that guaranteed to venal office-holders the right to pass their posts on to their heirs. As we saw in Chapter 2, venal office-holding was the method preferred by socially ambitious bourgeois for advancing to noble status. Maintaining these positions in the same family was therefore an extremely important part of the strategy of upward social mobility. Prior to the introduction of the *paulette*, these offices could be passed on to one's heirs, but it was technically illegal, difficult, and uncertain. Now, for an annual fee of 1/60 of the office's assessed value, venal office-holders were granted full heritability of their offices. This had a number of important consequences. For instance, it helped to defray the costs of salaries by having the office-holders essentially subsidize their own salaries. It also assured a constant flow of revenue from these offices rather than having to create batches of new offices every few years as had previously been done. By tying the *paulette* to heritability, Sully and Henry attempted to ensure the loyalty of the office-holding class, for this was an essential element in the agenda of the society of orders. It did work in the short term, as these bureaucrats were tied more closely to the royal agenda. In the longer term, however, it created dynasties of noble office-holding families who could not be removed from office. It strengthened the order of the office-holders, whose interests were not always those of the king or his government.

The end of the wars had brought back a measure of economic prosperity to France, and a succession of bumper crops in the early seventeenth century added to the general air of well being and good fortune, especially when compared with the widespread famine and misery of the 1590s. Henry had a genuine interest in the welfare of common people and took an active interest in economic affairs and the welfare of ordinary people. At one point, he remarked that his goal was to enable every subject's family to have a chicken in its pot every Sunday. This led to his nickname of "le roi poule-au-pôt." As with the restoration of royal finances, Sully played a key role in the economic revival of the kingdom. In his capacity as *grand voyer* or superintendent of communications, he revitalized the kingdom's infrastructure by building and improving roads, bridges, and canals. He reduced or abolished many of the tolls and internal tariffs that could quadruple the price of goods transported overland. He established the Council of Commerce, which raised tariffs to discourage imports, removed taxes on goods destined for export, and encouraged industry. Following the example of the Dutch, he set up the

French East India Company to share in the wealthy trade from Asia, although it never really succeeded in breaking into the Asian trade. More successfully, he founded the Company of New France, which sponsored the explorations of Samuel de Champlain and others in the New World.

In foreign policy, Henry was very cautious, as indeed he needed to be, given his financial situation and his recently established hold on the kingdom. Like previous French rulers, Henry recognized that his chief threat came from Habsburg Spain, but he could not yet afford to confront Spain directly. Instead, he patiently built a series of alliances in Italy and Switzerland designed to isolate Spain, in particular to prevent communication between Spain and the Netherlands via the "Spanish Road" through northern Italy, the Alps, and along France's eastern border. In the spirit of alliance building, in 1600 he married Marie de Medici, a niece of the Grand Duke of Tuscany.[1] He also mediated a dispute between the Pope and Venice, increasing his standing with each. Venice was particularly important because of its control of some of the most important alpine passes. He pressured the Duke of Savoy into abandoning an alliance with Spain and into forging a French alliance instead.

By 1610, Henry felt strong enough to challenge Spain directly. The immediate occasion was the Jülich-Cleves dispute (see Chapter 8). In 1599, Henry had signed a treaty guaranteeing the security of the region, to keep it out of Spanish hands. When the Duke died childless in 1609, the Spanish army occupied the territory to keep it out of Protestant hands. In early 1610, Henry signed an alliance with the German Protestant princes to dislodge the Spanish from Jülich-Cleves. It is possible that invasion plans were mere sabre-rattling, but we will never know for certain: on May 14, 1610, while driving through Paris in a carriage, Henry was assassinated by a fanatical Catholic named François Ravaillac, who objected to the King's plans to make war on a fellow Catholic monarch. With the King's death, his nine-year-old son became King Louis XIII; his mother, Marie de Medici, acted as regent until the king turned 14, the age of legal majority.

Louis XIII: The Early Years, 1610–24

On paper, the powers of regent ruling in the name of a minor king practically equalled the authority of a reigning monarch. In practice, however, they rarely did. Everyone understood that one day the King would grow up and might change the policies of the regent. The inherent weakness of a regency was even more pronounced in the case of Marie de Medici. As a woman and a foreigner, her authority was doubly weakened, so she played things very cautiously. With the exception of Sully, she kept all of her late husband's ministers. She calmed Huguenot fears by periodically reaffirming her commitment to the Edict of Nantes. In foreign affairs she was cautious as well, but in a different way from her husband. While Henry IV had tried to isolate the Habsburgs, Marie wanted better relations with them. To this end, she arranged a marriage for her son the King with the Spanish Habsburg princess Anne of Austria.

As in past periods of royal weakness or minority, the great nobles seized the opportunity to cause trouble, and very quickly Marie depleted the surplus accumulated by Henry and Sully through trying to buy the loyalty of the great nobles. Noble resentment was heightened by Marie's reliance for advice and support on her Italian friend Leonore Galigaï and her husband, Concino Concini. Greedy, ambitious, arrogant, and corrupt, they used their influence with the Regent to enhance their wealth and political power. The great nobles resented the Regent's reliance on these upstart foreigners instead of on them, the King's "natural advisors." In 1614, a handful of great nobles left Paris for their military governorships in the provinces, where they could cause no end of trouble. Marie was eventually able to mollify the rebels with huge pensions and a promise to convene the Estates-General.

The Estates-General met in Paris beginning in October 1614, their last meeting for 175 years until the eve of the French Revolution in 1789. Ultimately, the three orders of clergy, nobility, and the third estate (consisting mostly of venal office-holders) were unable to make common cause, and the assembly was dissolved in February 1615 with no real accomplishments. At virtually the same time, Louis XIII celebrated his fourteenth birthday, and the regency formally came to an end. Marie, however, was extremely reluctant to relinquish power to her son, and over the next several years, tensions between mother and son grew as Louis chafed under his mother's restraints. The Queen Mother continued to rely on the Concinis, prompting ostentatious displays of displeasure from a handful of important nobles. In the meantime, Louis had found for himself a mentor and father figure in the person of the Duke of Luynes. In April 1617, Luynes and several accomplices murdered Concini in the courtyard of the Louvre. His wife was later executed. Marie was retired to the city of Blois, where she was kept under house arrest.

From 1617 until Luynes's death in 1621, Louis governed with Luynes and a handful of remaining ministers. From 1621 to 1624, Louis went through a succession of ministers and favourites without finding the ones he really needed. As a result, the royal council was plagued with factional infighting. In 1624 he reluctantly accepted into his council the man who would become his chief advisor and chief minister for the rest of his reign: Cardinal Richelieu.

France under Louis XIII and Richelieu, 1624–43

Armand Duplessis, Bishop of Luçon, Duke of Richelieu, was born in 1585 into a family of provincial nobility in the western province of Poitou. His father had been a commander of some importance during the religious wars and had fought for the Catholic League. The future cardinal first became prominent as a spokesman for the clergy at the Estates-General of 1614–15. Impressed by the young clergyman, Marie de Medici gave him a post in her household, and he became one of her inner circle of advisors. The fall of the Concinis sent Richelieu to Blois along with the Queen Mother, where he was eventually successful in reconciling mother and son. At Marie's urging, Louis appointed Richelieu to his council in 1624. Marie intended him as her stalking horse and spy in the council. But very quickly, Richelieu and the King discovered that they could work together in an effective partnership.

The relationship between king and cardinal has been the subject of much debate. Surely the most famous portrayal is that of Alexandre Dumas in *The Three Musketeers*: a weak and silly king manipulated like a puppet by an evil, grasping, and power-mad cardinal. This is completely literary licence, stemming in large part from Richelieu's enemies and rivals, of whom there were many. Clearly, king and cardinal worked together effectively. All the major policies pursued after 1624 have their roots prior to Richelieu's ascendancy. He did not impose his agenda on an unwilling king; he did, however, supply discipline, focus, and direction to a king who knew what he wanted to do but could not clearly conceive the means to his desired ends. Richelieu, as it turned out, was a brilliant political operator, ruthless and skilful in dividing and defeating his opponents and those who defied royal policy.

Over the next several years, the servant and master became friends, but Richelieu never took Louis's favour for granted and was always careful to obtain royal approval for his policies. But Richelieu had enemies who would attack him when they could not attack the King and his policies directly. Throughout his career, Richelieu was faced with numerous plots and conspiracies against his power. Many of these schemes revolved around the King's younger brother Gaston, until 1638 heir to the throne. Gaston, Duke of Orléans, was particularly dangerous as a focal point for opposition, because apart from familial affection, politically he was too important and dangerous to be killed or exiled. The policies of Richelieu and Louis attracted a great deal of opposition from a group of people who believed that royal policies ought to be more Catholic in their goals. These people were known as the "devout ones" or the *dévots*. In particular, the *dévots* were opposed to the government's anti-Habsburg foreign policy. They believed that the King of France ought to make common cause with his fellow Catholic monarchs. They also wanted the government to pursue a harder policy against the Huguenots. They believed that better relations with the Habsburgs, and the resulting peace, would allow for a general domestic reform, particularly of the fiscal and legal systems. Among the chief members of the *dévot* party (pressure group is probably a more accurate characterization) were the Chancellor, Michel de Marillac; the Queen Mother; and occasionally the Queen herself, Anne of Austria, with whom the King had a very tense relationship. Amid much bickering and recrimination, in 1630, Louis finally repudiated his mother and the *dévots*, committing himself firmly to Cardinal Richelieu. Marie and Gaston fled into exile. Gaston eventually made his peace with his royal brother, although he continued to make political mischief. However, Louis never saw his mother again, although they did communicate through letters.

By 1630, then, the future course of French policy was determined: opposition to Spain and the Habsburgs, and deferral of domestic reform. This was the triumph of Richelieu's version of *raison d'état*, the concept that "necessity knows no law." Moral or religious considerations do not impinge on government policy, and any measures required are therefore legitimate precisely because they are necessary. What would it profit the kingdom to have thoroughly reformed its administration, but to be subservient to the Habsburgs?

Toward the end of his life, in his memoirs or *Political Testament*, Richelieu wrote to the King about his major policy goals: "to ruin the Huguenot party, to abase the pride of the nobles, to bring all your subjects back to their duty, and to restore your reputation among foreign nations to the station it ought to occupy." Although this statement implies a unity and continuity to Richelieu's policies that did not always exist in practice, it is nevertheless a helpful summary to keep in mind. Roughly speaking, the first three are domestic policy goals, while the fourth concerns foreign policy, but they are intimately linked. In order for France to fight the Habsburgs, Louis needed effective control at home. He could not go off to war with dissatisfied nobles, restive Huguenots, and rebellious subjects causing trouble at home. At the root of this agenda were two fundamentally different views of society: was France a society of orders, each with its own rights, privileges, and powers, or was it a society equal in its subservience to the king? Implicit in the society of orders was the idea that the king was bound by the liberties and rights of each order. Or did the king's position as sovereign, as emperor in his own kingdom, take precedence? In the words of Louis XIII's biographer, "was French political society a hierarchy of overlapping authorities or an entity with one sovereign authority?"[2]

The Huguenots

After three decades of civil war, the Edict of Nantes gave the Huguenots legal recognition as an order within French society. Significantly, both Louis XIII and Richelieu were of a similar mind regarding the Huguenots: they wished them to convert but were not willing to use force to convert them, recognizing that the inevitable result would be renewed civil war and that the use of force in matters of conscience was futile. On the other hand, Huguenot military and political power stood in the way of royal power. How could the King truly claim to rule France when a large minority of his subjects had their own fortified towns, law courts, and army? This is what Richelieu meant when he wrote about "the ruin of the Huguenot party." Significantly, however, this policy predates Richelieu's ministry. Immediately upon his personal rule in 1617, Louis decreed that Catholic worship was to be allowed in Béarn, a heavily Huguenot region in southwest France. For three years, the Béarnais Huguenots defied this decree, but in 1620 Louis took an army to Béarn and enforced it. These actions led to severe suspicions among the

Huguenots and, coupled with the outbreak of war in Germany, induced them to take up arms. In 1621, in an illegal assembly in their great fortress town of La Rochelle, Huguenot leaders began to prepare for war. Faced with this direct challenge to his authority, Louis had no choice but to fight. In a series of campaigns through 1621 and 1622, Huguenot power was significantly reduced. The Peace of Montpellier of October 1622 allowed the Huguenots to keep their two major fortresses at Montpellier and La Rochelle and a few others; but they lost 80 towns and agreed not to hold assemblies without the King's permission.

In addition, Louis had built a fortress opposite La Rochelle in order to keep an eye on the Huguenot stronghold. In 1625 the Huguenots again rebelled, trying to make up what they had lost, and in 1626 they signed another unfavourable treaty. This was, of course, unpopular among the Huguenots, but also among the *dévots*, who saw it as a sell-out. In fact, however, it was just a truce, and when La Rochelle appealed to the English to protect them against the King, Louis felt he really had no alternative but to crush them. So, in September 1627, Louis began a year-long siege that resulted in La Rochelle's surrender and the loss of the great Huguenot fortress. Although the town's defences were levelled and it was put under direct royal control, Protestant worship was still permitted. Once La Rochelle had fallen, the Huguenot cause was doomed; the rest was only a mopping-up operation. In 1629, Louis imposed the Peace of Alais on his Huguenot subjects, on much the same terms as he had imposed on La Rochelle: destruction of fortifications, elimination of the state within the state, but preservation of Protestant worship. To their great credit, Louis and Richelieu resisted the *dévot* pressure to do away with Protestant worship, ensuring Huguenot loyalty for the rest of the reign and beyond.

The Nobles

With respect to the nobility, as with the Huguenots, Richelieu did not impose a program or policy on the King, but rather put into effect what Louis desired and had already begun. Once again, at stake here was a fundamental clash of visions: were the nobility the King's vassals, tied to him by personal and voluntary service? Or were they his subjects, just like everyone else, albeit with far greater status and prestige? The goal was not to ruin the nobility, but to "abase their pride," to transform them into loyal subjects rather than independent political players. There were at least three ways in which the nobility stood in the way of the royal agenda: their military potential, expressed in their own fortified castles; their rights of private justice expressed in duelling; and their political ambitions as expressed in periodic plots to "rescue" the King from his "evil advisor."

As long as nobles had their own fortified castles, they could defy the King with impunity. As had happened during the regency of Marie de Medici, when important nobles wanted to demonstrate their dissatisfaction, they ostentatiously left court for their estates, where, behind their walls and drawbridges, they remained a potential threat to royal authority. In 1626, the King decreed the destruction of all fortifications in the interior of France. (Along the frontiers, fortifications were needed in the case of invasion.) This edict of course was not immediately or universally obeyed, and periodically the army would have to physically besiege and destroy a nobleman's castle.

The noble practice of duelling was offensive because it expressed a right of private justice, outside the King's control, and also because it also posed a problem of public order. Since the mid-sixteenth century, many laws had been decreed against it, and all were ineffective. In 1626 yet another law was decreed, but it too was winked at in several cases. Indeed, Louis himself as the chief nobleman of France was slightly ambivalent about the subject, pardoning offenders on several occasions. There was one case however, where the violation was so flagrant, the challenge to royal authority so overt, that drastic action had to be taken. This was the case of the Count of Bouteville. This nobleman, a member of the powerful and prestigious Montmorency family, was an ace dueller who, it was said, had killed 27 men in duels. In defiance of the new law, in May 1627, Bouteville fought a duel in one of the most public places in Paris, the Place Royale (now the Place des Vosges). He and his opponent were arrested and sentenced to death. A stream of supplicants begged the King to spare Bouteville's life: his pregnant wife threw herself at the King's feet; the duke of Montmorency also pleaded for the life of his kinsman. All their appeals were to no avail, for Louis was deaf to their pleas. He is reported to have said, "I pity the woman [his wife], but I must defend my authority"; "It is necessary for a little blood to be shed in this instance to stop the stream that flows daily." In fact, however, duelling did not disappear, for it was too closely integrated into the noble warrior culture to be eliminated by the passing of a law. At the most, Louis XIII and Richelieu tried to make key examples of the worst violators, but they let others off with minor punishments, if they punished them at all.

Richelieu also had to contend with noble plots against his position and power, couched in terms of the King's "evil advisor," even when everyone knew that he had the King's confidence. These schemes usually involved, in one way or another, Gaston, Marie (until her exile), various noble schemers, and assorted *dévots*. Richelieu was successful in defending his position, and many of these plotters paid the price with their lives.

The Third Estate

When Richelieu wrote of bringing the King's subjects "back to their duty," he was concerned most of all about the payment of taxes. In particular, war and its tremendous expenses after 1635 forced tremendous increases in taxation. By 1640 the level of the *taille*, the major direct tax, was double what it had been in 1610. There were clearly limits to what could be collected this way, for attempts to raise taxation beyond a certain level sparked revolts that required suppression, which in turn cost more money. So the government resorted to other expedients. Tax collection was privatized in return for immediate cash. Certain taxes, such as the *gabelle* or salt tax, were extended to areas where they had never been collected before. Various sorts of loans and *rentes* were floated, often at very high rates of interest, up to 20 per cent. New blocks of offices were created simply to be sold. The amount that office-holders paid in the *paulette* was raised, or, alternatively, the government would threaten to abolish it as a means of extorting more money. All of these measures were tremendously unpopular and led to resistance, obstruction, and outright rebellion. Often the venal bureaucrats whose job it was to assess and collect the taxes, and to judge evaders and delinquents, simply refused, either out of fear for their own lives and property, or because they sympathized with the poor peasants on whom the weight of the tax burden fell.

It was to overcome this obstruction and resistance that a different type of royal official, called an *intendant*, was introduced. Some historians have seen in their introduction a master plan for revolutionizing the administration. This, however, was not the case. Rather, these innovations were brought about by an *ad hoc* response to circumstances, not by any preconceived master plan. The circumstances were foreign war and the need for vastly greater tax revenues, and the resulting resistance and evasion. Actually, *intendants* were not even completely new; officials like them had been used since the sixteenth century. What was new under Richelieu and Louis XIII, however, was the scope of their use. Although drawn from the same social milieu as the venal bureaucrats, *intendants* did not own their positions and therefore could be dismissed by the government without compensation. Their primary task was that of inspector or troubleshooter: to make sure that bureaucrats were carrying out the policies and instructions of the government. Failing that, they were empowered to do these things themselves. Thus, they acted as judges, administrators, and tax collectors. The *intendants* were an improvised solution to an extreme situation, not a pre-planned administrative revolution. In fact, *intendants* were later abolished, and they would not be not fully integrated into the administrative structure until the reign of Louis XIV later in the seventeenth century.

Foreign Policy

The overriding concern of Louis XIII and Cardinal Richelieu was to prevent encirclement by rulers of the Habsburg dynasty. This had been the cornerstone of French foreign policy for at least a century, but it was given a new urgency in the 1620s with the revival of Imperial fortunes in the early stages of the Thirty Years' War. War had also broken out between France and Spain in the late 1620s over the Italian duchy of Mantua. This was a strategically significant territory in that it adjoined the Habsburg duchy of Milan and controlled access to several important alpine passes along the Spanish Road. In 1627 the duke died without a male heir, leaving his territories to a distant cousin who was a French nobleman. In order to prevent French possession of the duchy, it was occupied by Spanish armies, except for several important alpine fortresses that were seized by French forces.

At the same time, now that the Huguenots had been defeated and Richelieu's political position cemented, greater attention could be paid to Germany. In 1631, France and Sweden concluded the Treaty of Bärwalde, by which France agreed to subsidize the Swedish army in Germany. Sweden was clearly being used as a French proxy; Richelieu and Louis XIII's primary goal was to keep the war in Germany going for as long as possible without actually committing French troops, so that they could concentrate on the war with Spain. With the Swedish defeat at Nördlingen in 1634, however, France was compelled to enter the Thirty Years' War as a combatant. At the same time, an alliance was concluded with the Dutch Republic and war was resumed with Spain. At first the war with Spain went very badly for France. Their initial three-pronged invasion of the Spanish Netherlands, Germany, and northern Italy was repulsed. In 1636, the Spanish launched an invasion of their own, and the Spanish army reached the town of Corbie, a mere 80 miles from Paris.

France, however, weathered the storm, and was in later years able to invade the Spanish Netherlands. The Dutch also won some important victories against Spain in the Netherlands. It was at this time as well that Portugal and Catalonia launched their revolts against Castilian rule, greatly hampering the Spanish war effort. In May 1643, at the Battle of Rocroi, the French army inflicted on the Spanish the worst defeat ever suffered by a Habsburg army. This battle, more than anything else, marked the end of Spanish military dominance in Europe. Neither Richelieu nor Louis XIII, however, lived to witness this triumph of French arms. The cardinal died in December 1642, followed by the King on May 14, 1643, just five days before the famous battle. In foreign policy, they left much unfinished business, specifically French involvement in the Thirty Years' War and the war against Habsburg Spain. But they had also transformed the government of France, a process completed during the reign of Louis's son, Louis XIV (b. 1638). After Richelieu's death, Louis XIII relied increasingly on his protégé, the Italian cardinal Giulio Mazarini, or Jules Mazarin as he was known as a naturalized French subject. Upon the death of Louis XIII, his widow Anne of Austria would act as regent for the young Louis XIV, with Cardinal Mazarin as her chief minister.

Louis XIV, the Regency, and the Fronde

Louis XIII and Richelieu had succeeded in challenging the society of orders, in scaling back the range of its rights and liberties. The decade after the deaths of the cardinal and his king, however, were to see a number of very serious challenges to this achievement, as the society of orders took advantage of a royal minority to fight back. During the regency of Anne of Austria and the first years after Louis XIV was declared an adult in 1651, there were a series of revolts that would shake the monarchy to its core, known collectively as the Fronde.[3] A number of factors gave rise to the Fronde. A royal minority is always a troubling period; although the regent was authorized to act in the name of the king, everyone understood that she did not act with an adult king's full authority. The long-term growth in royal power and the assault on the society of orders of the previous reign caused enormous resentments among those who were its victims. Specifically, the nobles and the venal bureaucrats felt the effects of this assault, as did the poor peasants who were subjected to much higher taxes. The wars in Germany and with Spain continued, as did the need for enormous amounts of money. There was to be no let-up in the demands for revenue nor in the extreme means used to get it. Perhaps a capable adult king could have managed these tensions better, but the king was a mere child and his regent was a woman and a foreigner.

Personalities also played a key role, especially those of Anne of Austria and her chief minister, Cardinal Mazarin. As a Spanish Habsburg princess, Anne was extremely proud of her illustrious lineage, could be haughty in her treatment of opponents and inferiors, and was inclined to lose her temper. Above all, she was determined to preserve royal power in all its fullness for her young son. Mazarin, Italian by birth, had been in the service of the Pope and had come to the attention of Richelieu during diplomatic negotiations. He subsequently became a naturalized French subject and would soon become Richelieu's protégé and eventual successor. A diplomat by training and inclination, he was certain he was always the smartest person in the room, and believed that all problems could be solved by trickery, manipulation, and bribery. He was concerned above all with foreign affairs, with bringing the wars in Germany and with Spain to successful conclusions. He did not understand domestic French matters, nor did he care to. Anne and Mazarin were almost certainly lovers and were rumoured to have been secretly married, for Mazarin, although a cardinal, was not an ordained priest. There were, therefore, two foreigners in charge of the government in what was already a very explosive situation.

Over the years, Mazarin and Anne and the other ministers took a number of very unpopular steps that eventually drove the Parlement of Paris to try to undo the achievements of Louis XIII and Richelieu. Under Anne and Mazarin the government continued and expanded the most unpopular policies of Richelieu and Louis XIII in terms of raising money and enforcing its wishes. All told, these various practices amounted to an assault on the dignity, prestige, and wealth of the venal office-holders. The last straw was an attempt to meddle with the *paulette*. In April of 1648 the government announced that it would renew the *paulette* in return for a "gift" of four years' salary. This was blatant extortion, and it galvanized and united the venal bureaucrats as nothing else could. In June, members of three of the most important law courts, led by the judges of the Parlement of Paris, drew up a list of grievances. Their demands included abolishing almost all the *intendants*, reducing the *taille*, and ceasing the creation of new offices to be sold. After having agreed to these demands, the government tried to arrest several of the leading judges; then, in January 1649, the government and the royal family secretly left Paris, and the army surrounded and besieged the city, attempting to intimidate the judges into submission. At the same time, a number of important and restive noblemen came to Paris to offer their support to the Parlement. These nobles cared nothing about the legal principles espoused by the judges. They simply wanted the power that in their view was being exercised irresponsibly by Anne and Mazarin. The next several years saw complex scheming in Paris between the nobles, the Parlement, and various opponents of Mazarin. In order to defuse the situation, Mazarin went into exile in Germany in early 1651. In the early part of 1652 there was serious fighting around Paris. In the meantime, the judges of the Parlement of Paris were horrified by the chaos that they had unleashed. (The execution of King Charles I of England by Parliament in 1649 no doubt was seen as a portent of what might happen in France.) As a result, Anne and Mazarin were able to drive a wedge between the judges and rebellious nobles, and by 1653 Mazarin was able to return permanently from exile. In the meantime as well, Louis XIV had attained the age of majority, which greatly strengthened Mazarin's position, since he was now acting in the name of a king who was technically an adult, rather than that of a regent.

As well as pointing out both the weaknesses and strengths of the royal government, the Fronde demonstrated above all that there was no practical alternative to strong royal rule. Its major weakness was the existence of separate centres of power: the Parlement, the nobles, the venal bureaucrats—in short, the society of orders, with each order jealous and protective of its own powers and rights. On the other hand—and this was the strength of the royal government—each of these power centres was narrowly concerned with its own interests. They were held together briefly during the Fronde by hatred of Mazarin, but ultimately the cooperation was fleeting. They were thus susceptible to divide-and-rule tactics. So when there was a determined and effective king, such as Louis XIV would turn out to be, to a very great extent the limitations imposed on royal power by the society of orders could be mitigated, but not entirely eliminated. On the other hand, the Fronde demonstrated that royal government could not run roughshod over the rights and privileges of the society of orders without dire consequences. In this case in particular, the Fronde showed that the venal office-holders needed to be treated very cautiously.

Mazarin would continue to govern France as Louis XIV's chief minister until his death in 1661, providing the young king with his political and practical education. In foreign affairs, Mazarin's chief accomplishments were the successful conclusion of the wars in Germany and with Spain, positioning France to be the dominant European power through the rest of the seventeenth and eighteenth centuries. In Germany, as we have seen, a series of French and Swedish victories finally convinced the Habsburg emperor to make peace, resulting in the Peace of Westphalia in 1648. Meanwhile, the war with Spain continued. Having made peace with the Dutch in 1648, Spain could now concentrate on France, and during the Fronde the French suffered some serious reversals. With the end of the Fronde, however, Mazarin could effectively fight back, aided by the entry of England into the war. The war ended in 1659 with Peace of the Pyrenees. This treaty was favourable to France, but not overwhelmingly so. France got minor territorial gains along the borders with Spain and the Spanish Netherlands. Its most important provision was for the marriage of Philip IV's daughter, Maria Theresa, to Louis XIV, along with a huge dowry. In exchange, Maria Theresa renounced her claims to Spanish possessions, conditional on full payment of the dowry, which was highly unlikely. In the coming years this would provide a pretext for Louis XIV to lay claim to Spanish possessions. The Peace of the Pyrenees thus marked the end of Habsburg Spanish predominance in European affairs, and the beginning of French dominance.

NOTES

1 Henry had previously been married to Marguerite de Valois, sister of three French kings (Francis II, Charles IX, and Henry III). It was their wedding that provided the occasion for the St. Bartholomew's Massacre of 1572. Never close, they both indulged in frequent adulterous relationships. Finally, in 1599, the marriage (which had produced no children) was annulled. They had not laid eyes on each other since 1582.

2 A. Lloyd Moote, *Louis XIII, the Just* (Berkeley and Los Angeles: University of California Press, 1989) 190.

3 A *fronde* was a slingshot used by the urchins of Paris to fling rocks and refuse at the carriages of the rich.

CHAPTER TEN

England, 1603–60: Rebellion and Revolution

When James VI of Scotland became King James I of England in 1603, no one could possibly have predicted that within fifty years his son would be executed as a traitor, the monarchy would be abolished, and England would be a republic. The series of events that brought this about has been the subject of enormous debate ever since. This debate, and the resulting lack of consensus among historians, is reflected in the fact that there is no single accepted name for these developments: depending on the author, these events are known alternatively as the English Civil War, the Great Rebellion, or the Puritan Revolution. As we saw when we looked at the reign of Elizabeth I, there were some very serious long-term tensions in the English political system and society, mostly concerning unsettled questions about the position and powers of Parliament and the proper form and doctrine of the Church of England. These problems might possibly have been muted or even resolved with astute or inspired leadership. But instead there was weak and often inept leadership, which only compounded the problems and made their ultimate explosion much more violent and disruptive than it might otherwise have been.

Events in England provide an instructive comparison with the growth of royal absolutism in France. In essence, the kings of England were trying to accomplish what Louis XIII and Cardinal Richelieu were doing in France: to impose royal absolutism. Ultimately, English kings failed in their ambitions, in the process provoking a much more serious crisis than the Fronde. Some of the causes of the conflict in England were the same as in France, especially questions of taxation and privilege and the proper role of representative institutions, while some were unique to England, most notably the religious division between Puritans and Anglicans. There were also important differences in the political context, primarily the powers of Parliament, the prominence of the gentry, and the nature of the civil service.

Long-Term Tensions and the Failure of Leadership, 1603–40

When he arrived in England to begin ruling his new kingdom, James I was already an experienced ruler, having been King of Scotland since the age of thirteen months and having actually ruled since the age of nineteen. In contrast to Elizabeth, James seemed distinctly unregal in character. Lazy and foul-mouthed, with a lack of attention to personal hygiene unusual even for that unhygienic era, he had a paranoid fear of assassins; he habitually wore a coat with extra padding as protection against a dagger, causing him to appear lumpish and ungainly. Whereas Elizabeth knew how to play the part of a monarch, James detested publicity. Upon being told that he ought to show himself more in public to his new subjects, he asked caustically if he should also "pull down his breeches and they shall also see my arse?" Very well educated, at least in term of formal learning, he fancied himself a scholar but often came across as a pedant instead. Indeed, Henry IV of France called his fellow monarch "the wisest fool in Christendom." In particular, he was firm believer in divine-right absolute monarchy, having written a book, entitled *The Trew Law of Free Monarchies*, to enlighten his Scottish subjects.

In recent years his reputation as a ruler has been somewhat rehabilitated by historians. He did seem to know how to work with Parliament in normal circumstances, and it is only with the benefit of historical hindsight that we can see the origins in his reign of civil war and revolution. Yet there was disagreement about the proper role and function of Parliament in transacting the business of government. Whereas Elizabeth had flattered, manipulated, bribed, and stroked Parliament to get what she wanted, James thought it sufficient to lecture MPs on his powers. In 1610, he lectured Parliament thus:

> The state Monarchy is the supremest thing upon earth; for kings are not only God's lieutenants upon earth and sit upon God's throne, but even by God himself they are called gods.... And the like power have kings; they make and unmake their subjects; they have power of raising and casting down; of life and death; judges over all their subjects and in all causes, and yet accomptable to none but God only. They have power to exalt low things and abase high things, and make of their subjects like men at the chess, a pawn to take a bishop or a knight, and to cry up or down any of their subjects as they do their money.

No issue brought these disagreements into sharper focus than that of money. Elizabeth had avoided calling Parliament as much as possible by economizing on expenses and selling crown land. The result was that James was in a weakened financial position. Refusing to economize on court expenses as unbefitting his royal majesty, and faced with a recalcitrant Parliament, he resorted to a number of unpopular practices. He continued and expanded the sale of monopolies, which greatly annoyed consumers and merchants alike. In 1611 he created the noble title of baronet precisely to be sold to socially ambitious gentry. In his reign the number of peers sitting in the House of Lords rose from 59 to 121, alienating a large part of the aristocracy by cheapening their status. He also continued to sell royal land, which only postponed the day of reckoning while further weakening the Crown's financial position.

At the same time he refused to economize on the expenses of the royal court, and there was a widespread perception, mostly true, of corruption and debauchery at the court. In particular, James proved himself a spectacularly inept judge of character. He was especially susceptible to the charms of pretty and ambitious young men. One of these was Robert Carr, whom James created Viscount Rochester and then Earl of Somerset. Carr came to desire the beautiful but unscrupulous Frances Howard, wife of the Earl of Essex. In a spectacular scandal, James colluded with Carr and Lady Howard to fabricate evidence permitting Howard to divorce her husband and marry Carr. It later emerged that Carr and Howard had conspired to first imprison and then poison Sir Thomas Overbury, a vociferous opponent of the divorce. Carr and Howard were arrested and imprisoned for murder. It was hard to say which was worse: that the King was tied up in the unseemly mess, or that he abandoned his erstwhile favourite because a new object of infatuation had replaced Carr. This was George Villiers, second son of an impoverished gentry family. James showered the tall, handsome, athletic, and graceful young man with titles, favours, and money, making him the Duke of Buckingham and providing him with an annual income of £80,000—all while the government was running an annual deficit of £90,000. In short, through his actions, personality, and lifestyle, James was depleting the traditional reservoir of loyalty and goodwill toward monarchs that had seen Elizabeth through the difficult last years of her reign.

In religion, James disappointed the Puritans, who had hoped that a Scottish king would be more sympathetic. Little did they know that James could hardly wait to escape the meddling ministers of the Kirk, the Presbyterian Scottish church. Instead, James found the Church of England exactly to his taste, with royal control established through the bishops, and the ritual and liturgy suitable to his royal dignity. In a conference in 1604, he told a group of Puritans, "I will have one doctrine, one discipline, one religion, both in substance and in ceremony … a Scottish Presbytery agreeth as well with a monarchy as with the devil … No bishops, no king." He further alienated Puritans with his foreign policy. In 1604 he made peace with Spain after two decades of war. This peace was more or less forced on him by a lack of cash to keep fighting, but peace with the Catholic king of Spain irritated Puritans nonetheless. In 1618, with the revolt in Bohemia that signalled the beginning of the Thirty Years' War, Puritans wanted James to go to the assistance of his son-in-law, Frederick of the Palatinate, the new king of Bohemia. James refused, largely because he had no money and did not want to go cap-in-hand to Parliament. In 1623, the King's eldest son, Prince Charles (later King Charles I), and Buckingham set off on a madcap trip to Spain to woo the daughter of King Philip III as a bride for the young prince. (Buckingham was resolutely pro-Spanish, yet another bone that stuck in Puritan throats.) The Spanish princess was unimpressed, and the two young men returned home to general rejoicing that the marriage to a Spanish Catholic princess had fallen through. Buckingham then turned anti-Spanish and persuaded the King to hastily and unadvisedly declare war on Spain. To cement an anti-Spanish alliance with France, James arranged a marriage for his son with the sister of Louis XIII. Yet it is possible to exaggerate the religious division in England, knowing as we do what eventually transpired. If James was not the new Constantine that Puritans had hoped for, at the very least he did not give them cause to desert the established national church.

James died in 1625, and despite worsening tensions, he had managed to avoid a major confrontation with both Parliament and the Puritans. His son, Charles I (1625–49), would not be as fortunate, however. Whereas James was trying to maintain an increasingly unpopular status quo in both politics and religion, Charles tried to change it in both areas, but in ways that deeply concerned both Parliament and Puritans. He tried to make royal authority more rather than less absolute, and to make the Church of England more rather than less Catholic. His reign is a story of an ever-increasing spiral of suspicion and mistrust, in which each side continually interpreted the actions of the other in the worst way possible. Stubborn, rigid, self-righteous, and taciturn (largely because of an embarrassing stutter), Charles had a passion for uniformity and rectitude that led him to impute the basest of motives to those who had opinions that were different from his.

His reign got off to a bad start and worsened from there. First of all, Charles insisted on keeping as his chief minister the hated Duke of Buckingham, who embarked on several ill-conceived and wasteful campaigns against Spain and France. Traditionally, at the beginning of each reign, Parliament granted the new king certain revenues from import duties for the duration of the reign. These were known as "Tunnage and Poundage." Still upset with the way James had handled these revenues, Parliament voted that they be provided to Charles for only one year. The new king, not unreasonably, interpreted this move as a deliberate affront, and he simply continued to collect the revenue after the year had expired without Parliamentary renewal. Moreover, he resorted to other fiscal expedients, most notably a controversial forced loan from his most prosperous subjects. When a number of prominent men, including some members of Parliament, refused to contribute, they were arrested and imprisoned. Five of them brought a suit against the government for illegal imprisonment. This "Five Knights Case" was judged in favour of the King, but while royal actions were deemed to be technically legal, these actions only further increased suspicion and hostility. At the same time, Charles was infuriating Puritans with his policies and advisors. His wife was a French princess and openly practised Catholicism at court. He appointed a renowned anti-Puritan, William Laud, as Bishop of London and later as Archbishop of Canterbury. Moreover, he relaxed the enforcement of the anti-Catholic laws that were on the books.

Charles's chief critics in the House of Commons were Sir John Eliot and John Pym. Eliot had been one of Buckingham's most persistent and vociferous critics, and had for a time been imprisoned in the Tower of London for his effrontery. In 1628, both houses of Parliament (the House of Commons and the House of Lords), led by Eliot and Pym, passed a resolution called the Petition of Right, a condemnation of royal actions and a statement of what they considered the limits of the royal prerogative. The petition declared that non-parliamentary taxes, such as Tunnage and Poundage and forced loans, were illegal. Further, there should be no imprisonment without just cause, such as had occurred in the Five Knights Case. Soldiers and sailors were not to be billeted upon civilians without their consent, a favourite means of intimidation and extortion of forced loans. Finally, martial law could not be applied to civilians. The Petition of Right was not an attempt to overthrow the monarchy, nor to assert the supremacy of Parliament. Rather, Parliament was objecting to what it saw as abuses of the royal prerogative. They were attempting to restore what they saw as a proper constitutional balance against an innovating king.

Charles agreed to the Petition, in order to obtain a subsidy from Parliament, which he then prorogued, or dismissed. Despite having agreed to the Petition of Right, Charles continued the unpopular measures that had provoked it. Meanwhile, Buckingham was murdered by a former naval officer, for which Charles blamed Eliot. When Parliament resumed in January 1629, therefore, tensions had only worsened. When Eliot proposed three resolutions extremely critical of royal conduct, the Speaker of the House of Commons (a royal appointee) attempted to rise and end the session. The weeping Speaker was physically held in his chair by two MPs while the debate continued and the resolutions passed unanimously. This verged on the revolutionary, since it was undoubtedly within the King's power to assemble and dissolve Parliament. What had emerged by 1629 was a constitutional stalemate: Parliament would not grant money for actions over which it had no control, and the King was not able to do anything without money.

Charles then decided to rule England without Parliament, and was able to do so for eleven years, from 1629 until 1640. Although there were important differences in the political and social context, stripped to basics, Charles and his ministers were trying to do the same thing as Richelieu and Louis XIII were doing in France: to make the will of the King the supreme and unrivalled authority throughout the kingdom: in short, to impose royal absolutism. To assist him, Charles relied on his two chief ministers, William Laud, made Archbishop of Canterbury in 1633, and Thomas Wentworth, Earl of Strafford. Laud, as we have seen, was a staunch anti-Puritan, and as leader of the Church of England he was determined to insist on uniformity of belief and practice. Wentworth, later the Earl of Strafford, had been a parliamentary opponent of Charles I in the 1620s but by 1628 had entered the King's service. In 1628 he was made president of the Council of the North, and in 1633 Lord Deputy of Ireland. In both posts he demonstrated what might happen in England if he ever got the chance. He ran roughshod over established interests in the name of his master's will. Laud, in the meantime, was using all the tools at his disposal to hound the Puritans into conformity. As a result, a number of Puritans chose to emigrate to New England, where they believed they could live as God willed. A famous case involved William Prynne, an outspoken critic of the regime. In 1639 he was convicted of seditious libel. As his cheek was being branded and his ears cropped, he cried out, "The more I am beat down, the more I am lift up ... they spare none of what society or calling soever. None are exempted that cross their own ends. Gentlemen, look to yourselves. You know not whose turn may be next."

What was perhaps worse was that the doctrine and practice of the Church of England were being changed in a way that made it seem more Catholic. Not only did the Queen openly practise her Catholic faith at court, but now it appeared to many that England might be returned to Rome. Laud, through the bishops, insisted on a rich and elaborate liturgy that smacked of "papist idolatry" to the Puritans. He ordered that communion rails, which separated the clergy from the laity, be put back into churches and suggested a Catholic doctrine of the mass. In theology, he tended toward Arminianism, downplaying Calvinist ideas of predestination, suggesting that human effort does play a key role in salvation.

The role played by religious differences in the prelude to the Civil War has been the subject of a huge debate among historians. In part, it is influenced by hindsight. That is, knowing that Puritans would later play a large role in events, it is tempting to assign them more significance than they really had at an earlier date. There is no doubt that Puritans were a distinct minority within the Church of England, and that most of the opposition to the King was based on other grounds. On the other hand, the Puritans supplied an ideological zeal to the opposition that tended to infuse the conflict with a certain ideological rigidity. Although, as we will see, the Civil War was precipitated by the King's religious policies, its real origins were political and fiscal rather than religious. Would the Civil War have happened without the Puritan opposition to the King? It is impossible to say, but certainly once the Civil War broke out, Puritans played a very large role in the unfolding of events.

To enforce their policies, Charles, Strafford, and Laud relied on a series of prerogative courts. These courts bypassed the normal common law courts and, as the name implies, were subject much more directly to the royal prerogative. The two most important were the Court of Star Chamber for criminal cases and the Court of High Commission for religious cases. In these courts, the judges were appointed directly by the King and served at his pleasure. The ordinary rules of legal procedure did not apply, such as the right of the accused to examine the evidence against them and the right to cross-examine witnesses. The courts were therefore excellent instruments for enforcing the royal will and punishing the King's opponents.

In order to rule without Parliament, expenses needed to be reduced and new sources of revenue found, ones not dependent on Parliament's grant. Charles therefore concluded a peace treaty with Spain and thereafter avoided entanglement in European diplomacy. Charles, unlike his father, was personally frugal and economized somewhat on court expenses. Still, more money needed to be found, and the government resorted to a number of shady and controversial expedients.

The sale of monopolies was continued and expanded, often simply to extort more money from current monopoly holders. Teams of lawyers and researchers scoured the royal archives to dig up old and forgotten fees and taxes. Thus £165,000 was collected from all the gentlemen who had not presented themselves to be knighted at Charles's coronation in 1626. Royal lands were resurveyed and property owners who had encroached on them were subject to heavy fines. Rockingham Forest, for example, grew from six to sixty square miles. The practice of wardship was also exploited as a source of revenue: when a property owner died with minor children, wardship of the child or children reverted to the Crown, which administered the property and provided for the child or children until they reached the age of majority. In the sixteenth century a special court had been established to administer these lands and supervise the provision for the wards. Often, however, the government would sell its rights of wardship to courtiers or government officials who would receive the revenue of the estates but leave the wards in penury. During Elizabeth's reign, revenue from Court of Wards averaged £15,000 a year; by 1640 it was £71,000.

By far the most unpopular and controversial measure resorted to was Ship Money. Traditionally this was a tax assessed on certain coastal communities in times of emergency to defray the costs of the navy and coastal defence. In 1634 Charles declared such an emergency, and in 1636 extended the assessment of Ship Money throughout the kingdom. The pretext was that since the whole kingdom benefited from the navy and coastal defence, the whole kingdom ought to help pay for it, but this was clearly an attempt to cover a fiscal manoeuvre. While it may have been strictly legal, it also aroused enormous resentment. In a famous case in 1637, a country gentleman named John Hampden refused to pay it; he was arrested, tried, and found guilty, but only by a vote of 7 to 5. While this was technically a victory for the King, the slimness of the margin indicated that he was in a vulnerable position.

It is possible that Charles could have ruled without Parliament for the indefinite future, had he not made a huge mistake. Still, this blunder was part and parcel of his personal style and political agenda. Throughout the 1630s, Charles and Laud had been attempting to bring the Presbyterian Scottish kirk more in line with the Church of England or, rather, to impose the same vision on the Scottish church that they had for the English. Though he was born in Scotland, and had a lifelong Scottish accent, Charles was fundamentally out of touch with his northern kingdom. James had succeeded in installing bishops in Scotland, but a great deal of power still rested with the Consistory, made up of pastors and lay elders. Charles and Laud attempted, with some success, to increase the power of the bishops. At the same time, Charles pushed through an Act of Revocations, which restored to the church all lands secularized since the Reformation, alienating many of the elite that had scooped up these lands.

The final straw, however, was the attempt to fundamentally alter the liturgy of the Scottish church through the introduction of a new Prayer Book in 1637. The reaction was immediate and furious. A vast majority of nobles, ministers, and other important people signed a National Covenant to resist these changes. Faced with open rebellion, Charles felt he had no choice but to punish such disobedience, but the cost of raising an army far outstripped the fiscal resources of the personal rule. He thus had no choice but to recall Parliament to supply the required funding. The so-called "Short Parliament" met in the spring of 1640, and all the accumulated tensions and resentments of the previous decade came to the fore. Led by John Pym, Parliament demanded redress of grievances before they would listen to requests for money. Charles quickly dissolved Parliament in anger and determined to punish the Scots, with or without parliamentary money. In this course he was urged on by Wentworth, who had been recalled from Ireland, granted the title Earl of Strafford, and had taken his place as one of Charles's most trusted advisors. Charles managed to scrape together an army and went to punish the Scots. The enraged Scots quickly turned the tables on the King's makeshift army and invaded England, demanding a huge subsidy before they would go home. Unable to raise the required sum, in 1640 Charles now had no choice but to call Parliament once again. This was the "Long Parliament," which would meet off and on for more than twelve years. Very quickly the Long Parliament acted to severely restrict royal power, putting a decisive end to Charles's absolutist ambitions.

Here a comparison with France is instructive. As mentioned above, with his political situation stripped to basics, Charles was attempting essentially the same thing in England as Richelieu and Louis XIII were doing in France. But why did he fail? Part of the fault must be laid with Charles himself. Rigid and self-righteous, he automatically aroused resentment in his opponents. More important, there were significant differences between England and France. Although, as we have seen, the venal bureaucracy in France was often unwieldy and inefficient, for the most part it was fairly effective at carrying out the day-to-day business of government. In France, the salaried bureaucracy totalled about 40,000 people spread throughout the country. In England, on the other hand, the salaried bureaucracy consisted of about 1,200 people and was limited mostly to the royal court. To enforce its wishes, the English government relied on the volunteer service of the local elite who functioned as justices of the peace or as sheriffs. But these were the very people whom the royal government was alienating through its religious and political policies. The royal government was thus without effective instruments of its will at the local level, for it required the cooperation of local elites. At the same time, the nature of these local elites was changing. This is the phenomenon in English history known as the "rise of the gentry." The economic conditions of the sixteenth and seventeenth centuries had benefited primarily not the great nobles of England, but the lesser country squires, the gentry. They were the ones who benefited disproportionately from confiscation of church land, and the sale of royal lands. As a result, the ruling elite of England was not limited to a handful of great nobles who were personally known to the King. It had expanded to about 2,000 country squires, much harder to control and influence. They also had a national political forum in the House of Commons, which they came to dominate. Throughout the sixteenth and early seventeenth centuries they had acquired a sense of common identity and interests, and had come to believe that they had (or ought to have) a legitimate voice in the government. The net result of royal policies in the 1630s was to drive these people into active opposition to the King.

France, on other hand, had no viable national representative assemblies such as Parliament. The Estates-General met infrequently and never became established as an integral part of the government. Some French provinces had their own assemblies, but they tended to act on the basis of their own provincial interests and therefore were susceptible to tactics of divide and rule. The French crown also had greater fiscal resources at its disposal, which greatly increased its freedom of action and decreased its reliance on representative assemblies. In contrast to England, the tensions that produced the Fronde in France had no religious component. While the Puritans were not instrumental in the opposition to Charles I that led to the Civil War, they did impart a zeal and ideological rigidity that were lacking in France, which made political tensions all the harder to resolve. Moreover, the eventual execution of Charles I in 1649 provided the Frondeurs with an instructive and horrible example of what could happen if they continued their challenge to royal power.

The Long Parliament and Civil War, 1640–49

In the early 1640s the Long Parliament passed a number of acts restricting royal power, largely under the leadership of John Pym. These restrictions were designed not to overthrow the monarchy or to eliminate the power of the king, but rather to prevent what Parliament saw as abuses of royal power stemming from the personal rule of the 1630s. The Triennial Act of 1641 declared that Parliament must meet at least every three years, even without the consent of the king. Further acts declared that Parliament could not be dismissed or dissolved without its own consent; all taxation not explicitly approved by Parliament was declared illegal; the prerogative courts of Star Chamber and High Commission were abolished. Finally, Archbishop Laud and Strafford were attainted (that is, tried in Parliament), convicted of treason, and sentenced to death. (Strafford was executed in 1641, Laud in 1645.) Gradually, a number of MPs began to feel that they had accomplished what they had set out to do, namely to redress the abuses of royal power and assure Parliament's role in the government. Nevertheless, Pym and his followers continued their attacks on royal power. More conservative members began to defend the King, and we see the beginnings of a royalist party in Parliament. Significantly, the majority by which legislation was approved began to decline, whereas the earlier legislation had been overwhelmingly approved. In September 1641, the "Root and Branch Bill" abolishing bishops alienated a good many of the less radical MPs. In November, Pym and his supporters presented Parliament with the Grand Remonstrance, a catalogue of royal sins since the beginning of the reign. It attributed the current troubles to the King's "popish" advisors, who had "a malignant and pernicious design of subverting the fundamental laws and principles of government, upon which the religion and justice of this kingdom are firmly established." It further stated that the King should "employ such counsellors, ambassadors and other ministers in managing his business at home and abroad as Parliament may have cause to confide in." The choice of ministers had previously been considered to be completely within the King's prerogative, and the Grand Remonstrance appeared to many to be going beyond the correction of abuses and into constitutional revolution. It was eventually passed, but by a narrow majority of eleven votes.

Meanwhile a rebellion of Catholic peasants had broken out in Ireland. This put Parliament in a very difficult situation, for an army was required to put down the rebellion, but they did not dare entrust this army to the King. They feared that he would turn around and use this army against them. But command of the armed forces was clearly within royal power; Parliament had never claimed power over this. Nevertheless, in February 1642, Parliament passed by just 23 votes the Militia Bill, which stripped the King of control over the armed forces. In the eyes of many MPs, Parliament had now gone too far. It had clearly gone beyond asserting its "ancient rights and privileges," and had begun to attack the unquestioned authority of the King. When Pym and the radicals deliberately goaded Charles, threatening to impeach the Queen, Charles decided it was time to strike back. In January 1642, with 400 soldiers, he invaded the House of Commons to arrest Pym and four others, who had slipped out of the House and evaded capture. Charles left London for the north of England to gather support and form his army. Parliament too formed its own army, set up its own government, and declared Charles the aggressor. The tensions and resentments accumulated throughout Charles's reign now erupted into civil war.

There has been much analysis of the composition of the two sides; that is, who fought for whom and why. Earlier generations of historians, especially those inspired by Marxist analysis, sought to explain the Civil War in terms of social class and socio-economic interests. For example, R.H. Tawney attempted to explain the allegiance of the gentry by examining their economic interests and attitudes. According to Tawney, those gentry who were more capitalistic in outlook, who cultivated their estates and ran their affairs as market-oriented businesses, tended to support Parliament. On the other hand, those who were more "feudal" and conservative in outlook and attitude tended to support the King. This interpretation has not been supported by research, however. The social groups who made up the political class of England—the titled nobility, the gentry, and the urban middle classes—in fact split just about down the middle. Thus far, there has been no really convincing explanation of the choice of side based on class interest. It appears to have been an agonizing personal decision, in which individuals had to weigh their traditional loyalty, personal beliefs, and political interest. But we do know that Puritans, whether noble, gentry, or middle-class, invariably supported Parliament. This had an enormous impact on subsequent events, for it gave the struggle a religious and ideological component: they were fighting not just an unjust king, but the forces of Satan himself and of his handmaid the Whore of

Babylon, the Roman Catholic Church. They had on their side not just the traditional rights and liberties of freeborn Englishmen, but God Himself. In essence, the ruling elite of England had split, with part supporting the King and part supporting Parliament. The "people" played no role in the origins of the Civil War. It was not the "outs" trying to overthrow the power of the "ins"; rather, it was some of the "ins" against other "ins." The Civil War itself was largely over by 1646, with Parliament as the victor. Charles himself had surrendered to the Scots, who turned him over to Parliament in 1647. Over the course of the war, Parliament had several advantages that gradually began to tell as time went on. It controlled the south and east of England, the wealthiest and most populous part, and most importantly, the city of London with its vast human and financial resources. (Ironically, the taxes assessed by Parliament in the areas it controlled in order to prosecute the Civil War were much heavier than the royal taxes that had helped to bring the war about.) The Royalists, on the other hand, controlled the north and west of England, less populated and poorer areas. Moreover, at the beginning of the war, Parliamentary forces had seized control of the Navy, limiting the freedom of movement of the Royalists and making their re-supply much more difficult. Over the course of the war, Parliament also developed a very effective army. At first, the Parliamentary army fared quite badly under aristocratic leadership, leading to suspicions of treason and incompetence. In 1644, Parliament created a new army, known as the New Model Army. Command was to be based solely on merit, rather than on family or political connections. It was to be staffed with men absolutely committed to the cause, and, as a result, Puritans came to dominate the army. We see this especially in the man who emerged as its most effective general, and eventually its commander-in-chief, Oliver Cromwell.

Cromwell (1599–1658) is a fascinating and enigmatic figure. An obscure country gentleman and Puritan MP, he had played a very minor role in the political conflict thus far. Deeply devout and convinced of his own sinfulness and unworthiness, he nevertheless came to believe that God had chosen him for a special destiny. In religion, he was more radical than many, believing that there should be no single authoritative national church, that each local congregation should be independent. Socially, he remained conservative and committed to the existing hierarchical order, despite his religious radicalism. With no previous military experience, Cromwell nevertheless proved himself an effective leader of men, and in fact the only Parliamentary general who could consistently win battles, making him indispensable to Parliament.

The Search for Stability and the Restoration, 1649–60

Once the war had been won, Parliament had to face the very tricky question of what to do next. This was complicated by the fact that Parliament was increasingly divided along social, political, and religious lines. Two basic parties formed in Parliament. The more conservative were men of higher social position,

Presbyterian in religion, who believed that they were fighting to restrain the King's excesses, to restore what they saw as the proper constitutional balance. The more radical became known as "Independents" because they tended to favour a congregational church, where each individual church was independent; that is, they wanted to do away with a single official church altogether. They tended to be men of lesser social standing, although still the elite, and in politics their views ranged from advocating Parliament's supremacy to republicanism and the abolition of the monarchy. It was these men, including Cromwell, who were in control of the army. The less radical in Parliament feared the power of the Independents and the New Model Army, and some began to conspire with Charles, who promised to reform the Church of England along Presbyterian lines. In December 1648, fed up with this "treason," Cromwell and the army forcibly purged Parliament of its more conservative members, leaving a more radical "Rump." The purged Rump declared Parliament the supreme power in England, and abolished the House of Lords and monarchy. Charles I was put on trial as a "traitor, tyrant and murderer, and a public and implacable enemy to the Commonwealth of England" by a special court set up by the Rump. The King refused to plead, denying the legitimacy and competence of the court to try him. He was found guilty and sentenced to death, but significantly, only 59 of the 135 members of the court voted for his execution. On January 30, 1649, Charles met his fate calmly and with dignity, maintaining that he had defended the liberty and interests of his people. In death, Charles provided a more compelling argument for monarchy than he ever had in life. The crowd that had assembled to witness the execution saw something unprecedented in European history: the execution of a king for treason. Certainly monarchs had been killed before, but never before had a king been put on trial, found guilty, and executed. Indeed, the very notion of a king committing treason was a contradiction in terms to most people. To whom was he a traitor? Himself? The novelty and enormity of this act were clearly felt by those who witnessed it. One observer recalled that as the axe fell, the crowd "let out such a groan as I never heard before, and I desire I may never hear again." Some in the crowd fainted, while others rushed forward to catch drops of the King's blood with their handkerchiefs.

The trial and execution of the King was due largely to the efforts of Oliver Cromwell, who believed it was absolutely necessary. In Cromwell's mind, Charles simply could not be trusted. He could not be imprisoned or exiled, since his very existence presented a continual threat. Nor could he simply be replaced on the throne; rather, the monarchy had to be abolished, or in Cromwell's expressive words, "We must cut off the King's head with the crown on it." Having abolished the monarchy, Cromwell and the Rump now had to deal with the question of how England would be governed. The next decade saw several attempts to set up a new system of government, all ultimately unsuccessful. By 1660, the men in charge did not know what else to do and, facing the prospect of anarchy, restored the monarchy, calling Charles I's eldest son back from exile in Holland as King Charles II.

In 1649, however, England was declared a Commonwealth, with the Rump Parliament supreme, and actual government entrusted to a Council of State. But it was obvious that real power was in the hands of Cromwell and the army. By 1653, they were entirely fed up with the Rump and in a military coup dispersed it at swordpoint. It was replaced by a carefully chosen assembly of the "godly," subsequently known as the Barebones Parliament after one of its members, the exquisitely named Puritan preacher Praisegod Barebones. By the end of 1653, however, Cromwell had come to despair of this body and it too was dissolved. In the Instrument of Government of December 1653, Cromwell was named Lord Protector of England, in essence an uncrowned king. The power of the Lord Protector was to be restrained by a Council of State composed of civilians and army officers. There was to be a single house of Parliament made up of men "of known integrity, fearing God, and of good conversation," with the Lord Protector having the power to exclude unsuitable members. Ironically, however, Cromwell ran into the same problems with his Parliaments that Charles had with his, and in 1655, Cromwell, like Charles, chose to rule alone. England was now in effect a military dictatorship, ruled by Cromwell, whose orders were enforced by the army. Taxation under the Protectorate was much heavier than it had been under the King, and Cromwell's rule was increasingly unpopular, with only military power to prop it up.

With the triumph of 1649, the zealous Puritans were now in charge, Cromwell chief among them, and they sought to remake England in their own image, to effect a genuine moral reformation. Moral transgressions were strictly punished; theatres and alehouses were closed. Customary practices and festivals were outlawed, either as pagan or popish vestiges, or as occasions of sin and debauchery. The English revolutionaries were not unique in these aspirations, as we saw in Chapter 4. What was unique was that in England the "godly" had seized power and were in a position to implement their program of moral and religious reform more thoroughly than elsewhere. These acts also made the various governments unpopular among ordinary people.

Cromwell also faced threats from the left as well as from the right. Various radical sects went even further than the independents in their calls for radical reform. The Levellers, for example, advocated a much more egalitarian political order than had been envisioned to that point. They proposed universal male suffrage, annual Parliaments, abolition of an official church, and radical legal reform. They were especially prominent in the army, and in 1647 Cromwell and the leadership of the army confronted the radical social ideas of the Levellers in a famous debate at Putney. Cromwell and the commanders were able to purge the army of such radicals, but they remained in society at large. More radical yet were the Diggers, who proposed the abolition of private property and a return to what they saw as a primitive golden age where property was held in common. In religion, too, there were many groups much more radical than even the Independents who controlled the army. The Fifth Monarchists and the Muggletonians both believed that the Last Judgement was drawing nigh. More important were the Quakers, who rejected outward forms of religion entirely, emphasizing instead the "inner light" of Christ's spirit. Quakers rejected all forms of social distinction and political authority as inimical to the workings of this inner light. The Ranters, though never an organized or coherent group, tended toward antinomianism, that is, the principle that believers could sin freely, since greater sin resulted in greater grace from God.

Although Cromwell and the army could not establish domestic political stability, in military and diplomatic affairs they were very successful. The revolt in Ireland that had triggered the Civil War continued to smoulder, and in 1649 Cromwell led the New Model Army to Ireland and forcibly repressed the Catholic and Royalist Irish. At Drogheda and Wexford, defending forces and civilian populations alike were massacred. By 1652, Ireland had been brutally "pacified." Two-thirds of the land was confiscated and granted to loyal Englishmen, and the bulk of the Irish population were forcibly transported to the far west. The goal was to repopulate Ireland with English and Scottish Protestants, and here we see the origins of the religious and political divisions that have caused so much trouble to the present day. Scotland, meanwhile, had recognized Charles I's son as king rather than submit to an English Parliament. Cromwell and the army invaded and conquered Scotland, subjecting it to the same military dictatorship as England.

With dynasticism removed as a motor of foreign policy, trade and religion came to dominate English diplomacy. In 1652, England declared war on the Dutch Republic, its major commercial and naval rival. Cromwell also hoped to "enlist" the Dutch in a Protestant crusade against Catholic Spain. By 1654, the Dutch had been soundly defeated and forced into commercial concessions to England. In 1655, Cromwell went to war against Spain alongside France, helping to turn the tide against Spain, which resulted in the Peace of the Pyrenees of 1659. England's chief acquisition in this war was Jamaica, launching an English colonial presence in the Caribbean.

But unfortunately for Cromwell, no amount of military or diplomatic success could cover up the essential lack of stability and legitimacy in the English government. Cromwell died in 1658. He had named his eldest son Richard as his successor as Lord Protector, but Richard did not command the loyalty of the army and did not have his father's prestige. The generals of the army forced Richard to abdicate and recalled the Rump Parliament, which had been disbanded in 1653, in essence turning the clock back to before the Protectorate, to the Commonwealth of 1649–53. The Rump proved no more effective then than it had been before, and for the next year and a half there was no effective government in England. The commanders of the army contended with each other and various constellations of assemblies and Parliaments. Without a strong hand in control, all the radical religious and political groups re-emerged, threatening the control of the elite. The country was drifting toward political and social anarchy. In early 1660, General Monck, one of the commanders of the army, took charge of the situation and led his army to London. There he restored the Long Parliament, which then voted to invite the eldest son of Charles I to come back to England from his exile in Holland as King Charles II.

The exact nature of the restoration of the monarchy will be examined more fully in Chapter 15. For now, suffice it to say that although the monarchy was technically restored with its powers unmodified, no one could forget the experience of the previous twenty years, now consigned to legal limbo as an "Interregnum." The restored Charles II knew what had happened to his father and, far from seeking revenge, was determined not to follow his example. Parliament, likewise, had seen what had happened when they challenged too strongly the powers and prerogative of the monarch. What emerged was a still-powerful monarchy whose powers were nevertheless restrained and limited by a Parliament that had become a permanent and necessary part of the government. This was a partnership between king and elite that would form the basis of the English government until well into the nineteenth century.

In essence, the political and social elite of England, which had fractured in the Civil War, came to the conclusion that there was no alternative to monarchy. The revolutionaries had tried for over a decade to come up with a substitute, and had failed. Moreover, political instability and general disorder threatened both the control of the elite and the very fabric of society. They had seen what happens when the existing political order is overturned, and did not like what they saw. To a much greater extent than the simultaneous disorders in France, the events in England in the 1640s and 1650s drove home to the political and social elite that the only alternative to the existing order was anarchy and revolution. That the two countries came out of their mid-century crises with somewhat different political solutions should not obscure the similarities of the crises. In both cases, a major cause of the disturbances was the unrelenting quest for tax money on the part of the royal government and the efforts of governments to expand the royal prerogative powers to get it. In both cases, this caused substantial segments of the ruling elite to question the precise powers of the monarch with respect to the rights and privileges of his subjects. We have already examined some of the reasons why the French monarchy emerged from these crises with enhanced power, while the English Crown found its powers limited by Parliament. These reasons include the nature of the civil service and the presence of a Parliament in England that functioned as an effective voice of the elite. To these must be added the nature of leadership. Had Charles I been less rigid, stubborn, and self-righteous, more willing to make tactical compromises, things might indeed have turned out differently. There was nothing inevitable that led England toward a more limited monarchy. One must also keep in mind that during the troubles of the Fronde in France, the example and warning of the English Civil War were evident to the French. The execution of Charles I shocked public opinion throughout Europe, France included. Clearly this helped to restrain some of the opponents of the French government. Yet another difference between the two countries was that throughout the Middle Ages, England had been a more coherent political unit than France. Since the Norman Conquest of 1066, England had functioned more or less as a political and legal unit, whereas the kingdom of France was a hodgepodge of different territories and jurisdictions, with different legal systems, rights, and privileges. This meant that French governments faced opposition that was widespread, but not united, and without effective means of national coordination, allowing monarchs to adopt tactics of divide and rule, as happened in the Fronde. By the seventeenth century, however, English monarchs faced opposition that was less divided by particularist interests. Charles I had much less room to manoeuvre than did Cardinal Richelieu, Louis XIII or Mazarin.

CHAPTER ELEVEN

Spain in Decline

As we have seen, Spain under its Habsburg kings had been the dominant power in Europe since at least the middle of the sixteenth century. By the time of the Peace of the Pyrenees in 1659, this was obviously no longer the case, as France under Louis XIV had eclipsed Spain in European diplomacy and warfare. With hindsight, it is tempting to place the beginning of this decline earlier than was actually the case. Spain remained extremely strong, as we have seen, even after the defeat of the Armada of 1588, which, viewed in the longer term was really no more than a hiccup in Spanish power. Spain remained the dominant military power in Europe throughout the first decades of the seventeenth century.

But beginning around 1640, Spain experienced a rather rapid relative decline. In 1640, there were simultaneous revolts against the royal government in Catalonia and Portugal. In 1643, Spanish armies suffered their worst defeat in 150 years at the Battle of Rocroi. In 1648, Spain finally recognized the independence of the Dutch Republic. And in 1659, the Peace of the Pyrenees marked France's ascendancy over Spain in European diplomacy. Yet this decline did not come out of nowhere. Although Spain had been able to continue to play a dominant role in European affairs, this was despite some serious long-term and deep-seated weaknesses in the Spanish economy, society, and political system. Indeed, the fact that Spain continued to play a dominant role in European affairs worsened these structural problems, or at the very least made their solution more difficult than it might have been if Spanish rulers had chosen to concentrate exclusively on domestic matters. Like France and England, Spain underwent a serious crisis around the middle of the seventeenth century. To what extent was it similar to the crises in other countries? How much was it a product of uniquely Spanish circumstances?

Spain was able to play a dominant role in Europe only because of the wealth provided by its empire in the New World. As we saw in Chapter 6, the Spanish empire was really a collection of separate territories united only by having the same ruler. Within this empire, the kingdom of Castile was pre-eminent, so the Spanish empire was financed by Castile and its possessions in the New World.

But the apparent wealth of Castile covered up some serious weaknesses. First of all, Castile had a relatively small population: approximately six million people, compared to about sixteen million in France. Much of Castile is arid, with poor soil. Agriculture, therefore, the basic foundation of all early modern economies, was relatively unproductive in Castile. Moreover, the peasants who actually tilled the land were heavily burdened by various exactions such as royal taxes, church tithes, and seigneurial dues. As a result, Castilian agriculture was increasingly carried out in the form of large noble estates worked by an overburdened and overtaxed peasantry.

After roughly a century of population growth and general—if relative—prosperity, as the seventeenth century began, Castile suffered from both an overall decline in population and from rural depopulation. Peasants were forced off the land by excessive taxes and seigneurial dues, and they either drifted into towns in search of work or charity, or sought their fortune in the New World. The plague struck with a vengeance between 1596 and 1602, resulting in perhaps 500,000 deaths. The expulsion of the *moriscos* in 1609 (see below) resulted in the loss of perhaps another 275,000 people. There were therefore significantly fewer people to bear the cost of the Spanish empire.

There was little manufacturing, and that was primarily in very high-quality luxury goods for the aristocratic market, rather than in basic goods that might improve productivity. More basic—and productive—goods needed to be imported and paid for with gold and silver. Meanwhile, the bullion that poured in from Mexico and Peru did not stay in Castile for long, as it was quickly passed along to creditors in order to pay the government's enormous debts. Given the government's enormous military commitments, it was always short of cash, and it frequently mortgaged future revenues for quick cash at high rates of interest. In essence, Castile endured the main disadvantage of the influx of gold and silver (inflation) without receiving any of its benefits (investment in agriculture and industry). Moreover, the volume of shipments of bullion levelled off or declined in the early seventeenth century. Estimating bullion shipments is fraught with difficulty, since there was widespread smuggling and graft, but at the very least we can arrive at an assessment of the overall trend. From their peak levels in the 1590s, royal receipts from New World bullion fell steadily, so that by 1660 they were at barely 10 per cent of their peak volume.

Officially, trade with the New World was a Castilian monopoly operated out of Seville. In fact, however, there was a good deal of illegal trade, as Spanish colonists would buy goods from English, French, and Dutch merchants at lower prices. Once a year, the Spanish treasure fleet would set out from the Caribbean to Spain, a tempting target for pirates and the navies of rival rulers. In 1628 a Dutch captain captured the entire fleet, while in 1656 an English captain captured it, and in the following year he sank it. This, of course, placed tremendous strains on government finances.

The lopsided nature of the Castilian economy also had an effect on the broader society, reinforcing its aristocratic character, which in turn made fundamental reform more difficult and less likely. As far as the elites of Spanish society were concerned, there seemed to be enough money in government bonds and sheep raising that Spanish nobles held agriculture and industry in contempt. As a result, the tax burden fell overwhelmingly on an unproductive and poor peasantry, and capital that might have been invested in industry and agriculture was instead spent on conspicuous noble consumption, government bonds or *juros*, and seeking positions and power at court. Meanwhile, the other territories were lightly taxed. In 1610 the total tax revenue produced in the Crown of Aragon (made up of Aragon proper, Catalonia, and Valencia) was 600,000 ducats, while in Castile, the two major sales taxes alone produced revenue of more than 5 million ducats. Granted, the population of Castile was much larger (the Crown of Aragon and Portugal together had a population of barely 1 million), but Castile still paid proportionately far more. The territories in Italy and the Netherlands provided no net revenue; indeed, the war in the Netherlands was a serious drain on royal finances.

These problems did not go entirely unrecognized within Castile. A group of economic reformers known as *arbitristas* proposed a whole range of solutions. They ranged from the plausible to the hopelessly utopian, but in general they focussed on three major problems: the imbalance in the fiscal system between Castile and the other territories; the disproportionate burden of taxes within Castile that fell on the poor peasantry; and the misdirection of capital, away from productive investment in agriculture and industry and toward conspicuous consumption, pursuit of political influence at court, and patronage of the arts and literature. To remedy these problems, *arbitristas* proposed a number of solutions. For instance, other territories should share the tax burden more equally. Within Castile, tax reform would distribute the burden more fairly. Aristocrats should be encouraged to invest in agriculture and industry. Wasteful spending at court and in aristocratic circles should be curtailed. Yet nothing happened. Castilian society remained dominated by the nobles, who disdained such projects as beneath their dignity. Moreover, for the first part of the seventeenth century, the political will to take such drastic action was lacking. When there was such political will, in the 1620s and 1630s under the Count-Duke of Olivares, the entrenched obstacles made sustained action practically impossible. As one of the most prominent of the *arbistristas*, Martín González de Cellorigo, wrote in 1600, "Those who have the means have not the will, while those who have the will have not the means."

One of the ironies of this situation was that aristocratic patronage of the arts helped to produce a golden age of Spanish culture, even as these problems were becoming more severe. This was the society that produced Miguel de Cervantes, whose *Don Quixote* is one of the great works, not only of Spanish or European literature, but of world literature. This golden age also gave us the very popular plays of Lope de Vega (1562–1635), a contemporary of William Shakespeare, as well as the aristocratic drama of Pedro Calderón (1600–81). In art, El Greco, though a native of Greece, lived and worked in Spain from 1570 until his death in 1614. Diego Rodriguez de Velazquez (1599–1660) was possibly the finest portrait painter in European history. Although it is dangerous to generalize about a nation or period based on its art and literature (it is far too easy to pick out the elements one wants and ignore the others), one can see in Spanish culture of this period a certain nostalgic melancholy, a sense that although great things had been done in the past, people were living on borrowed time. Like Don Quixote, who discovered that the giants he had been tilting at were in fact windmills, that his chivalric lady love Dulcinea was in fact an ordinary village woman, Spaniards of this era recognized the illusory nature of their glory and power, but they were helpless to do anything about it except recall the glories of the past and contrast them with the shortcomings of the present.

When Philip II died in 1598, he was succeeded by his son Philip III (r. 1598–1621). Lazy and fundamentally uninterested in ruling, he left the government in the hands of his favourite, the Duke of Lerma. Lerma used his power primarily to enrich himself, his family, and his friends. The King and Lerma rarely took action on Spain's problems, and what they did do typically made a bad situation worse. Yet had they chosen to pursue it, Philip and Lerma possessed a window of opportunity to effect real reform. Due primarily to a lack of funds, Spain had concluded peace with England in 1604 and signed the Twelve Years' Truce with the rebellious Dutch in 1609, thus providing an opportunity to focus on domestic reform. Unlike that of his frugal father, Philip III's court was a lavish and extravagant affair. The cost of maintaining it was more than 10 per cent of the total budget. Lerma was extremely generous in granting pensions and positions to important nobles in an effort to solidify his power. Rather than effect any real economic and fiscal reform, the government resorted to the harmful expedient of currency manipulation. In 1599, copper coinage was introduced, and over the next several decades it was recalled and debased several times, resulting in greater economic instability and inflation.

Ironically, the one action during the reign that was carried out with relative efficiency was also self-destructive. This was the expulsion of the *moriscos* in 1609. In Philip II's reign, the *moriscos* had been expelled from Granada and resettled throughout Castile, where they were a tiny and economically insignificant minority. In Aragon and Valencia, however, *moriscos* were a substantial portion of the population. In Valencia, they made up one-third of the population and were essential in the role of agricultural labourers on many large noble estates. Fears still lingered about the sincerity of many *moriscos*' conversion to Christianity, and also of a potential Ottoman invasion, but there was no apparent or logical reason to take this action at this time. Rather, it was done to placate popular opinion and to distract attention from the government's failure on other fronts, and the *moriscos* were a handy and defenceless scapegoat. It is surely no accident that the expulsion of the *moriscos* was decreed on the same day as the Spanish signed the Twelve Years' Truce with the Dutch. All told, perhaps 275,000 of the *moriscos* in Spain were forcibly expelled, most of them to North Africa, where many died of hunger and exhaustion. The impact of the expulsion varied across Spain. It was a severe blow to agriculture in Valencia and Aragon; however, this was at least partly compensated for by the arrival of Christian settlers to take their place. In

Castile, on the other hand, the *moriscos* were so few and scattered that their expulsion had no appreciable effect.

By about 1615, Lerma's hold on power was beginning to slip. His greed made him genuinely unpopular, and his failure to address even the most serious problems caused former associates and underlings to create some distance from him. The King, too, was wearying of his favourite, and in 1618 Lerma was dismissed from office. He was made to cough up some of the riches he had amassed over the years but was otherwise allowed to retire to his country estate, where he died in 1625. His successor as royal favourite and chief minister was his own son, the Duke of Uceda. This was, however, a palace coup rather than any real change in policy, and in any case Uceda's hold on power was never as secure as his father's.

Philip III died at the age of 43 in 1621 and was succeeded by his son Philip IV (r. 1621–65) then a boy of sixteen. He would, over the course of his long reign, prove himself a more capable and energetic ruler than his father. His chief minister was Gaspar de Guzman, Count-Duke of Olivares (1587–1645). Unlike Lerma, Olivares was an energetic and capable man, full of ideas and schemes to reform Spanish society and government. Indeed, Olivares attempted to implement many of the solutions proposed by the *arbitristas*. His overarching goal was to effect a real governmental union among the different Spanish kingdoms, or as he wrote in 1625 to Philip IV,

> The most important thing in Your Majesty's monarchy is for you to become King of Spain. By this I mean, sire, that Your Majesty should not be content with being King of Portugal, of Aragon, of Valencia, and Count of Barcelona, but should secretly plan and work to reduce these kingdoms of which Spain is composed to the style and laws of Castile, with no difference whatsoever.

The proposed trade-off for this union would be the end of the Castilian monopoly on positions of power in the government.

The first step in this proposed integration was the Union of Arms of 1626. This was a proposal for a common Spanish (rather than Castilian) army of 140,000 men. Castile would still provide the largest contingent, but the other kingdoms were to provide fixed contributions. Catalonia and Portugal, for example, were to supply 16,000 men each. Philip IV managed to gain the reluctant consent of the Cortes of Aragon and Valencia, but the Catalonian Cortes refused altogether.

Catalonia indeed posed a special problem. It was strategically important, situated as it was along the French frontier. It had contributed no taxes to the monarchy since 1599, no Catalan units fought in Spanish armies, and it did not even contribute to the defence of its own frontier with France. It was a kingdom dominated by its petty nobility, infested with lawlessness and bandits. Any attempt to reform the situation, however, ran up against Catalonian liberties, or *fueros*, which were closely guarded and defended by a standing committee of the

Catalonian *Cortes*. According to Olivares, Catalonia was "entirely separate from the rest of the monarchy, useless for service, and in a state little befitting the dignity and power of His Majesty."

Olivares also had a number of projects for fiscal reform in Castile. The expenses of the court were dramatically reduced, as were grants to nobles. He introduced sumptuary laws to reduce noble extravagance. Although this mostly failed, it did help to eliminate the elaborate and expensive ruffled collar that had been the height of fashion. He appointed a commission to investigate fraud and corruption in the bureaucracy, with mediocre results. In 1627, the government declared a partial bankruptcy, suspending and reducing payments to its creditors, converting much short-term debt to longer terms. He tried to distribute the burden of taxation within Castile more fairly, and to encourage investment in commerce and industry, but his plans were strongly resisted by the Cortes of Castile, which in fact acted mostly to defend the interests of the oligarchies who governed the towns represented in the Cortes.

It is possible that Olivares might have succeeded in dramatically reforming the Spanish monarchy and government, but for one thing: after more than a decade of peace, beginning in the early 1620s, Spain was involved in a series of wars more or less continually until the Peace of the Pyrenees in 1659. For Olivares, there was no contradiction between his reform agenda at home and his bellicose foreign policy. Indeed, they were part and parcel of the same thing: what was the good of a reformed state that was at the mercy of its foreign enemies? Therefore, Spain came to the assistance of the Emperor in crushing the Bohemian revolt. In 1621, with the expiration of the Twelve Years' Truce, war resumed against the Dutch and would continue until 1648, when Philip IV finally acknowledged the independence of the United Provinces. From 1627 until 1631, Spain fought against France to keep the Italian Duchy of Mantua out of the hands of a French nobleman. This Italian territory was a crucial link in the "Spanish Road," by which Spanish men and money were transported to the Netherlands. After the combined Spanish-Imperial victory at Nördlingen in 1634, France declared war on Spain, a war that would continue until the Peace of the Pyrenees in 1659. The fiscal pressures of war meant that Olivares had to resort to the usual but short-sighted, counter-productive, and harmful expedients of raising money: massive loans, debasing the currency, and arbitrary taxation.

War with France after 1635 once again brought Catalonia to the fore and ultimately resulted in Olivares's fall from power. To defend the territory, a Castilian army was stationed in Catalonia at the expense of the inhabitants. By May 1640, widespread resentment had given way to open rebellion. By early 1641, the Catalans had repudiated their allegiance to Philip IV and placed themselves under French rule, and a French army had occupied Catalonia. The example of an apparently successful rebellion in Catalonia also inspired rebellion in Portugal. Portuguese resentment of Castilian rule centred on its inability to defend Portuguese commercial and imperial interests in Brazil and the Far East, primarily from Dutch incursions. In December 1640, the Portuguese nobles declared the

Duke of Braganza King John IV of Portugal. Faced with these rebellions, for which a resentful nobility and unhappy population blamed Olivares, he asked Philip IV for permission to retire from his service. The Count-Duke lived in seclusion on his country estate, increasingly mentally unbalanced, until his death in 1645.

The life and career of Olivares present a number of interesting comparisons with those of Cardinal Richelieu. To contemporaries, they were the two great statesmen of Europe, locked in a mortal duel.[1] Indeed, their careers parallel each other's almost exactly. Richelieu was born in 1585, Olivares in 1587. Richelieu became chief minister in 1624, Olivares in 1623. Richelieu died in December 1642, while Olivares fell from power in January 1643. Both had grand plans for the reform of their governments and countries, plans that were ultimately thwarted by war and its exigencies. Their treatment by historians, however, has been very different. The usual view is that Richelieu succeeded where Olivares failed. France dominated European affairs after 1659, and the court of Louis XIV became the diplomatic and cultural centre of Europe, while Spain turned in on itself and ceased to play a major role in European diplomacy. Historians have often treated this outcome as inevitable: France was on the ascent, while Spain had passed its zenith. And certainly, there is something to warrant this view. A century and a half of military and diplomatic hegemony had exhausted Castile and drained it of its New World treasure. Yet the struggle was closer than it appears in retrospect. In 1636, a Spanish army had come within 80 miles of Paris before being defeated at Corbie. Had things turned out differently, we might be talking about Olivares's triumph and the renaissance of Spanish power.

Still, things happened for particular reasons, one of which was the nature of the men themselves. Although they were equal in most respects, Olivares was nevertheless more cautious than Richelieu, less willing to take the bold chance. Perhaps equal in vision, Richelieu seems to have had a clearer idea of the practical steps needed to achieve his goals, and he was more ruthless in their pursuit. It must also be said with hindsight that Richelieu had an easier task than Olivares. France had more than double the population of the Iberian peninsula, and greater physical and natural resources. France, despite its regional anomalies, was nevertheless a more unified and territorially compact state than the Spanish monarchy. Though provincial and regional identities remained strong in France, there was no sense of belonging to a different people, as there was in Catalonians or Portuguese in thinking about Castile and Castilians, let alone Netherlanders or Neapolitans. In an age that greatly feared and mistrusted innovation and novelty, Richelieu also benefitted from the fact that he was attempting to restore the greatness of France and its king after the disorders of the Wars of Religion and the drift of Marie de Medici's regency. Olivares, on the other hand, was attempting something new, something that had not existed before: the blending of separate territories and peoples into a single kingdom.

Although, from the standpoint of diplomacy, Richelieu and France emerged triumphant over Spain and Olivares, in domestic politics their legacy was very similar, at least in the short term. In both countries, fundamental reform was subordinated to the demands of war, with similar results. As J.H. Elliott writes,

> The France [Richelieu] left behind him was, like the Spain of Olivares, a country seething with revolt; a country crushed by high taxation and reduced to misery; a country in the hands of tax-collectors and war-profiteers, and of officials who filled their own pockets as they preached the virtues of obedience in the name of that mystical entity, the royal authority. The Fronde, as much as the France of Louis XIV, was the legacy of Richelieu.[2]

With hindsight, we see that Olivares's frantic efforts were a desperate last gasp at reforming and re-energizing a country that believed its greatest days were in the past. Following his fall from power, all his grand schemes and visions were abandoned. The royal government gave up on attempts to unify its component territories into one kingdom. The political power of the nobility forestalled any further attempts to reform the Castilian economy, fiscal system, or society. If they no longer could play the dominant role in Europe they once had, at least they could still dominate Castile.

Following Olivares's fall from power, Philip IV determined to rule on his own, without resort to a favourite or first minister. By 1647, however, he had wearied of the task and appointed as his first minister Luis de Haro, who, coincidentally, was Olivares's nephew. Haro's power never equalled that of his uncle, and he had no similar reforming ambitions. He mended fences with the nobles, who had been greatly resentful of Olivares's power and policies, and managed to resolve the worst of the crises facing the monarchy by abandoning any idea of constitutional reform.

In Catalonia, a combination of French weakness due to the Fronde and Spanish military victories led to the suppression of the revolt by 1652. Moreover, the Catalans had found French rule no more to their liking than Castilian. Philip IV prepared the way for peace when he swore to observe Catalonia's privileges and liberties, thus bringing to an end Olivares's attempt to create a Kingdom of Spain.

Portugal, however, was a different matter. The Portuguese were united as the Catalans had not been, and they had a native nobleman as king rather than appealing to a foreigner as ruler. With assistance from England (both under Cromwell and the restored Charles II after 1660) and the Dutch, the Portuguese successfully resisted Spanish invasions. Philip IV adamantly refused to acknowledge Portuguese independence, but after his death in 1665, his widow, acting as regent for her young son, finally relinquished the Spanish claim to Portugal.

When Philip IV died in 1665, he was replaced by his four-year-old son Charles II, the last Habsburg ruler of Spain. Generations of Habsburg intermarriage had their inevitable result in the unfortunate king. Sickly, physically deformed, and mentally deficient, he was incapable of producing an heir. All of Europe expected him to die quickly, but he defeated all expectations by living until 1700. This was a period of drift and uncertainty in Spanish politics, where the royal government became the football of noble factions. For a time the Queen Mother, Mariana of

Austria, governed with her Austrian Jesuit confessor John Nithard. In 1669, Nithard was overthrown and exiled in a coup engineered by Don John, Philip IV's illegitimate son. In the 1670s, an Andalusian adventurer and soldier named Fernando de Valenzuela gained the Queen Mother's favour, and they governed until Valenzuela was himself overthrown in 1677 by Don John, who governed Spain until his death in 1679. By 1685, the Count of Oropesa had emerged as the dominant voice in the government, until a group of dissatisfied nobles persuaded the King to dismiss him in 1691. Oropesa at least attempted to reform the fiscal system and streamline the government, but with very limited success. It is perfectly obvious in hindsight that no reform could be accomplished without enlightened and energetic leadership at the centre of the government, which the unfortunate Charles II had no way of supplying.

Spain under Charles II was a society and a government dominated more than ever by its privileged groups, most notably the Church and the aristocracy. They took advantage of the weakness of the monarchy and their privileged position to reinforce their control. Rather than reform their estates to become more productive, the nobles treated the royal treasury as their own personal piggy bank. Likewise, the Church (whose numbers grew remarkably, despite the overall decline in population) used its clout to defend its position and possessions. Not only did the royal government fall prey to the privileged orders, but so too did local government administration. Large parts of Spain were essentially feudal dominions where powers of administration and justice were in the hands of the Church or the nobility, where royal government was largely a legal fiction.

The rulers and courts of Europe held their breath, awaiting Charles's death. Though much attenuated by the events of the previous century, the Spanish realms were nevertheless a tempting prize for any ruler to acquire when Charles II would die without heirs. Indeed, the question of the Spanish succession was the chief preoccupation in international affairs of the later seventeenth century. We will return to these events in detail in Chapter 17.

NOTES

1 For a more detailed treatment, see J.H. Elliott, *Richelieu and Olivares* (Cambridge: Cambridge University Press, 1984).

2 Elliott, *Richelieu and Olivares* 171.

CHAPTER TWELVE

The Golden Age of the Dutch Republic

The Dutch Republic, or the United Provinces of the Netherlands, was an anomaly among the states of early modern Europe. As we saw in Chapter 6, it was composed of the seven northern provinces that had successfully cast off the authority of Philip II of Spain. (The ten southern provinces remained under Spanish rule and were known as the Spanish Netherlands.) Although officially a republic, the government was dominated for long stretches by the Princes of Orange, who exercised near-monarchical powers. Politically, the Dutch Republic was a highly decentralized federation of seven provinces, with the terms of their union defined by the Union of Utrecht of 1579. The first decades of the seventeenth century saw bitter political division between and within the provinces, as well as between the ruling urban oligarchies, or "regents," and the descendants of William of Orange as the leading nobleman in the country. Yet, despite this decentralization and division, the Dutch Republic was somehow able to effectively prosecute a resumed war with Spain from 1621 until 1648, to fight three naval wars with England in the middle decades of the century, and to defend its land against the mightiest army in Europe, that of Louis XIV of France in the 1670s. A small country with no significant natural resources, dependent on importing food to feed its dense and highly urbanized population, the Dutch Republic nevertheless managed to dominate European and overseas commerce, as we saw in Chapter 3. It was officially a Protestant state, and only a minority of its population belonged to the Calvinist official Reformed Church (itself riven by bitter divisions) until well into the seventeenth century. Throughout the century, there remained substantial numbers of people outside the Reformed Church, including large numbers of Catholics, Mennonites, and others, who lived in a state of practical, if unofficial, toleration that was unequalled anywhere else. In a nation with a small and not very powerful nobility, dominated by its merchant elite, the armies of the Dutch Republic were, as mentioned above, able to fight to a standstill the greatest military powers of the day.

The political organization of the Dutch Republic betrayed its origins and fundamental ambiguity arising out of the revolt against Spanish Habsburg rule in the

MAP 12.1 THE DUTCH REPUBLIC AND THE SPANISH NETHERLANDS

sixteenth century. Was the new state simply the outcome of a revolt against a ruler who violated the traditional rights of his subjects? Was the Republic therefore primarily a vehicle for the preservation of urban and provincial liberties, with the functions of the central government to be kept to a bare minimum, concerned only with the most basic matters of common interest, such as defence and diplomacy? Or was the Dutch Republic the expression of a nascent nationality, primarily Protestant in nature, born out the struggle against the popish Spanish tyrant with a providential mission and vision that transcended provincial particularism?

The central government of the Republic, such as it was, was the States-General, an assembly of delegates from each of the seven provinces which met in The Hague. Each province received a single vote, and, in theory, all its decisions had to be unanimous, although exceptions were sometimes made. The jurisdiction of the States-General was highly circumscribed: it covered military and naval affairs, diplomacy, and administration of the Generality Lands (lands that were part of the Republic but belonged to none of the seven provinces, essentially the northern fringes of the province of Brabant, most of which remained under Spanish rule). All of the other functions of government, such as justice, taxation, and economic regulation, were carried out at the provincial or local level. When the assembly was not formally in session, its business was carried out by a number of standing committees, made up of representatives from the various provinces.

The seven provinces were highly protective of their powers and rights, and they were also extremely varied in nature and often decentralized internally. The most basic cleavage was between the so-called "maritime" provinces of Holland and Zeeland, and the inland provinces. The maritime provinces, Holland especially, were far more developed economically and more urbanized, and were politically dominated by the merchant elites of the towns. The inland provinces were more agricultural in nature and the nobility played a more prominent role.

Although all the seven provinces were in theory equal partners in the Republic, the province of Holland necessarily assumed the leading role. It contained about 40 per cent of the population and controlled approximately 60 per cent of the wealth in the Republic. Given the limited power and resources of the central government, Holland and its representatives necessarily carried enormous weight. Nothing could be done without Holland's political and financial support; likewise, it was difficult, if not impossible, to carry out policies that clashed with Holland's priorities. Holland's leadership in the States-General was reflected in the fact that the province had at least one member on every committee, and, like all the other provinces, it had a veto over decisions of the assembly. Holland's delegation to the States-General took its direction from the States (or provincial assembly) of Holland. This in turn was made up of delegates from the 18 major towns of the province, and from the nobility, each of whom had a single vote. Among the towns, Amsterdam, with a population approaching 200,000, was by far the largest. The next two largest towns, Leiden and Rotterdam, were respectively one-third and one-quarter the size of Amsterdam. Amsterdam therefore occupied the same position in the States of Holland that Holland had in the States-General:

although formally equal to all the others, its size and wealth made it the dominant voice. In any case, these arrangements meant that real power in the Dutch Republic lay with the governing elites or "regents" of the towns of Holland, and those of Amsterdam most especially.

Holland's interests in the central government were typically represented by the chief executive of the province, whose official title varied somewhat over time. In the several periods of the Republic's history where there was not a powerful Prince of Orange to contend for leadership, this official became in effect the chief executive of the Dutch Republic. This was especially the case with Johan van Oldenbarnevelt from 1588 until 1618, and Johan de Witt from 1652 to 1672. Oldenbarnevelt's title was *Advocaat van den Lande* (advocate, or lawyer, of the States of Holland), while de Witt's was *raadpensionaris* (Grand Pensionary) of the States of Holland. The formal titles may have differed, but the net effect was the same. Although in theory subordinate to the States of Holland and hence to the regents of the towns, their experience and knowledge of Dutch politics and foreign affairs made them the unofficial heads of government.

The other salient feature of the political "system" of the Dutch Republic was the presence of the Princes of Orange, which introduced a quasi-monarchical element into what was an otherwise republican state. As we saw in Chapter 6, William the Silent was in many ways the leading figure in establishing the independence of the seven northern provinces, and his assassination left a tremendous void in the Revolt. When he died in 1584, his eldest son Maurice (Maurits) was a youth of seventeen, and the influence of the House of Orange waned as Holland and Oldenbarnevelt took control of the struggle against Parma and Spain. As Maurice grew to manhood, he became the military leader of the Republic, and indeed one of the leaders of the military "revolution" in early modern Europe, as discussed in Chapter 1. It was inevitable that he would challenge the dominance of the regents and Holland. The powers of Maurice and successive Princes of Orange were derived from a number of sources. One was the enormous wealth and prestige of the family as the leading noble house in the country, especially the prestige derived from the crucial role played by William the Silent, who was considered the father of the country and a martyr to the cause. In times of war (which included most of the seventeenth century), the Prince of Orange held the title of captain-general and admiral-general by grant of the States-General, making him in effect commander-in-chief of the army and navy. The Prince of Orange was also *stadtholder* of most of the seven provinces. The office of *stadtholder* was a vestige of the Habsburg regime, which nevertheless survived into the Republic, all republican logic to the contrary. Originally, they were the representatives of the sovereign in each of the provinces. When the Union of Utrecht deposed Philip II, there was no need to keep the position, but it was kept nevertheless. Maurice and subsequent Princes of Orange took William's title of *stadtholder* of Holland and Zeeland, to which they added similar titles in most of the other provinces. (The title of *stadtholder* in Friesland, and often Groningen and Drenthe was held by a relative from a different branch of the family.) In the Republic, their positions as *stadthold-*

ers of the various provinces gave the Princes of Orange added prestige and influence. In many cases, the *stadtholder* appointed judicial and civic officials, which gave him significant powers of patronage. More than anything else, the political powers of the House of Orange were based on the title and position of *stadtholder*.

Not only was the Dutch Republic decentralized and fractured by political tension between the regents and the Princes of Orange, but there was significant religious dissension as well. Although it was officially a Protestant state, with the Calvinist Reformed Church as the official church, there were significant religious minorities who enjoyed a degree of practical toleration unthinkable elsewhere in Europe, and the Reformed Church itself was far from united.

As late as 1600, Catholics were probably in the majority in the infant Dutch Republic, and by the mid-seventeenth century it was likely that they still made up 35-40 per cent of the population. Although Catholics and others were officially granted freedom of conscience, Catholic worship was in theory forbidden. Nevertheless, Catholics throughout the Republic managed to worship in "secret" churches (*schuilkerken*). Authorities were very likely aware of these churches, but they usually turned a blind eye, as the difficulties involved in suppressing them seemed to outweigh any possible benefit. Their most immediate concern was preservation of order and stability, not the imposition of religious uniformity.

There were also Protestant groups who were not part of the Reformed Church. For example, the Remonstrants, as we saw in Chapter 4, sought to moderate Calvin's emphasis on predestination. After the Synod of Dort of 1618, many Remonstrants set up their own church structure, which tended to draw from the more educated and wealthy segments of Dutch society. There were also the Mennonites, followers of the sixteenth-century Anabaptist leader Menno Simons (1496–1561). Mennonite numbers declined throughout the seventeenth century as members feuded among themselves over obscure points of theology and practice. There was also a Lutheran minority in the northern and eastern fringes bordering on Germany.

Jews also enjoyed a degree of practical toleration in the Dutch Republic that was unequalled elsewhere. Concentrated heavily in Amsterdam, Dutch Jews played an important role in the intellectual and cultural life of the Republic. As was the case with Catholicism, Jewish worship was officially forbidden, but a series of informal agreements allowed Amsterdam's Jews to build their own synagogues and organize their community, which was composed largely of Jews of Spanish and Portuguese origins.

The Ascendancy of the House of Orange, 1609–50

In 1609 the government of the Dutch Republic signed the Twelve Years' Truce with Philip III of Spain. In terms of domestic politics this was a clear victory for Oldenbarnevelt and the regents and a defeat for Maurice and the Orangists, who favoured continued war with Spain. Maurice found a group of somewhat surprising allies in the merchant elite of Amsterdam, who feared that their interests in Asian and American trade would be sacrificed in the name of achieving peace. Indeed, one of the Dutch concessions to the Spanish was abandoning a proposed West India Company (WIC), modelled after the very successful East India Company, to trade in the New World. The merchant elite also feared that peace with Spain would lead to the lifting of the blockade of the River Scheldt and the commercial resurgence of Antwerp.

The political conflict between regents and Orangists also became closely linked with the religious conflict within the Dutch Reformed Church between Arminians and strict Calvinists, or Remonstrants and Counter-Remonstrants respectively. (The strict Calvinists or Counter-Remonstrants were also known as Gomarists, after one of their leading theologians, Francis Gomarus.) The regents tended to be Arminian in theology and more tolerant in religious matters, recognizing the difficulties involved in enforcing a stricter religious discipline and uniformity. The Counter-Remonstrants tended to be of more humble origins and, like the Princes of Orange, favoured continuing war with Spain, although for somewhat different reasons. They also wanted a more rigorous enforcement of laws against Catholics and other religious minorities. With the signing of the Twelve Years' Truce in 1609, these tensions came to a head. In 1610, an influential group of Arminian ministers, supported and encouraged by Oldenbarnevelt, presented their "Remonstrance" to the States of Holland, which called for revision of the official creed of the Reformed Church, explicit recognition of the authority of the state over the church, and restatement of Arminius's position on predestination. The strict Calvinists presented a "Counter-Remonstrance" which rejected Arminius's views and maintained that the government had no place telling the church what its ministers could and could not preach. The Counter-Remonstrants called for the issue to be settled by a National Synod of the church, where they knew they would carry the day, because they were in a majority in the church. Though the controversy began and was most bitter in Holland, where the Remonstrants were strongest, it soon spread throughout the Republic dividing families, towns, churches, and universities.

The religious controversy also assumed political and social dimensions. More of political necessity than religious conviction, Prince Maurice used his power and influence in aid of the Counter-Remonstrants. Using his powers as *stadtholder*, he appointed Counter-Remonstrants to positions in the judicial system and civic governments. Wherever he could, he used his influence to have Arminian ministers dismissed and put strict Calvinists in their place. They had a common interest in opposition to the regents and Oldenbarnevelt and in further pursuing the war with Spain. In some places, such as Utrecht, the conflicts pitted the ruling elite against the urban working classes, who tended to be Counter-Remonstrant.

By 1617, the tension had reached the breaking point, and the very existence of the Dutch Republic seemed to be hanging in the balance. Oldenbarnevelt and his allies, who included the famous humanist, lawyer, and scholar Hugo Grotius, used their influence in the States of Holland to pass a resolution allowing city councils (which were mostly Remonstrant), to raise their own troops to keep order. Maurice, with the support of the solidly Counter-Remonstrant city council of Amsterdam, responded by leading his army into Holland, and deposed Remonstrant city councils and replaced them with reliable Counter-Remonstrants. In August 1618, Maurice marched into The Hague and arrested Oldenbarnevelt and several of his leading supporters, including Grotius.

Having asserted his control, Maurice purged city councils, militias, universities, and churches of Remonstrants, and replaced them with religiously and politically reliable, if less experienced, supporters of the House of Orange and strict Calvinist orthodoxy. Oldenbarnevelt's office of Advocate of the States of Holland was abolished and replaced by a less powerful Pensionary. Although Holland remained the dominant province, Maurice's triumph over Oldenbarnevelt greatly reduced the province's role in the Republic. Oldenbarnevelt and his colleagues were put on trial for treason. In May 1619, the 72-year-old Advocate was beheaded in The Hague. Grotius and the others were sentenced to life in prison. The great scholar managed to escape, however, in 1621, fleeing into exile first in Antwerp and then in Paris.

In religion, the National Synod that Counter-Remonstrants had long been pressing for finally met in Dordrecht (Dordt) in November 1618, made up not only of Dutch theologians and ministers, but also of representatives from Germany, Scotland, England, and Switzerland. In its final conclusions of 1619, the synod decisively rejected Arminius's teaching and formally deprived all Remonstrant ministers of their positions. In the years that followed, the strict Calvinists strove to achieve their vision of a true moral reform, in the same way that English Puritans would in the 1650s. They preached against dancing, taverns, and popular festivals that smacked of "popish vestiges" or pagan superstition. They also attempted, although with limited success, to restrict the freedom of worship accorded to Catholics, other Protestant churches, and Jews.

With the triumph of Maurice and the Counter-Remonstrants, there was no question that the war with Spain would resume when the truce expired in 1621, especially given the attitude of Philip IV and Olivares. The Dutch Republic also supported the Bohemian rebels against the Emperor, and aided the Protestant cause in Germany. Yet, although Maurice had assumed control of the leadership of the Republic, the previous tensions did not disappear. Remonstrants still chafed under their persecution and could cause trouble at the drop of a hat. Likewise, Holland resented its diminished political role, even while taxes were dramatically increased in order to pay for the army. The reliable Counter-Remonstrants installed in power by Maurice proved themselves by and large incapable of efficiently managing the state and economy.

Maurice died in 1625 and was succeeded by his younger half-brother Frederick Henry in his posts as captain-general, admiral-general, and *stadtholder*. Frederick Henry was less committed to the Counter-Remonstrants than Maurice had been and relaxed the persecution of the Remonstrants, while politically attempting to cool the temperature by striking a delicate balance between the religious and political factions. In this he was aided by some notable military successes against Spain in the late 1620s and 1630s. Spain at this point found its resources diverted by the war over Mantua. In addition, an alliance with France in 1634, the Swedish victories in Germany, and the entry of France into the Thirty Years' War after 1635 all helped reduce the military pressure on the Republic.

Domestically, Frederick Henry was able to walk this fine line for a time. He gradually restored some Arminian regents to influence, while still managing to mollify the Counter-Remonstrants. The net result of this policy of balance, however, was that he was increasingly mistrusted by all factions. Increasingly too, he began to cultivate a quasi-monarchical style. Like monarchs elsewhere, he built palaces, patronized the arts, and surrounded himself with the pomp and ceremony of courtly life. He arranged a marriage of his eldest son to a daughter of Charles I of England, the first time that a member of the House of Orange had married a member of a major royal dynasty. The States-General began to address him as "Highness" rather than "Excellency," as did the King of France. In the English Civil War, he supported the royalist cause. In short, he began to arouse fears that he was aiming at a fundamental constitutional shift within the Dutch Republic, one that would see the Princes of Orange as virtual monarchs, thus displacing the hybrid nature of the Republic that had evolved over the previous half-century. Toward the end of his life, his authority was increasingly challenged by the regents of Holland, who had managed to put their religious division behind them and were now prepared to act to restore Holland's dominant role in the government of the Republic after thirty years of eclipse by the Princes of Orange.

Frederick Henry died in 1647, succeeded by his son William II. Father and son had feuded during the last years of Frederick Henry's life, and, upon assuming his father's titles, William abandoned Frederick Henry's policy of moderation and balance, reverting to the more confrontational style of Maurice. Meanwhile, in 1648, Spain and the Dutch Republic had concluded the Treaty of Münster, by which Spain formally recognized the sovereignty of the Dutch Republic.

William and his supporters had opposed peace, but they were powerless to stop it. The years after 1648 were difficult ones for the Dutch Republic. Though it was no longer at war, the blessings of peace were slow to materialize. Military cuts and reductions in garrisons spread recession in areas that had formerly benefitted from military spending. Peace allowed the commercial revival of ports in the Spanish Netherlands at the expense of Holland and Zeeland. A series of poor harvests drove up the cost of living and increased unrest among the poor and working classes. Strict Calvinists attributed these misfortunes to God's wrath at the Dutch people for having forsaken His truth, for making peace with the Spanish Antichrist, and for allowing the resurgence of the Arminian regents. William, though anything but a Calvinist in his personal life, made common cause with these dissidents.

William and the Holland regents clashed over proposed reductions to the army, but the real issue was ultimate control of the state. Yet again, divergent visions of the Dutch Republic reared their head. William, the Orangists, and the strict Calvinists stood for a Republic in which the States-General were sovereign and in which the provincial towns and states, dominated by the regents, played a subordinated role. They stood also for a single official church, united in doctrine and discipline, with minimal toleration, if any, for Catholics, Jews, and other Protestants. The regents of Holland, on the other hand, saw the republic more as a confederation of sovereign provinces, along the lines of the Swiss Confederation. In this vision, supported by Grotius, who continued to write about Dutch politics from his exile, each province was sovereign, including in its religious affairs, and the role of the central government was to be strictly limited to defence and diplomacy. In this vision, of course, Holland and its regents would play the dominant role, given the province's economic and demographic weight.

William II did whatever he could to stir up discontent toward Holland and its regents among the working classes and the strict Calvinists. Indeed, they were often one and the same, since urban workers, especially in Amsterdam, tended to be Counter-Remonstrant in any case. When he judged that the time was right, William staged his coup. In July 1650, his agents seized and imprisoned the principal regents in The Hague. At the same time, an army of 12,000 men was sent to occupy Amsterdam. The city was alerted just in time and closed its gates; however, faced with dissent within and force without, the city government capitulated and purged the leading opponents of the *stadtholder*. Over the next several months, William began to assert his control over the government. Whatever his ultimate plans might have been, they were forestalled by his untimely death from smallpox in July 1650. With his death, the House of Orange and its supporters were cast into disarray, for William II was childless when he died. His wife, however, was pregnant and in December 1650 gave birth to the future *stadtholder* and king of England, William III. For the foreseeable future, the Orangists were leaderless and rudderless, and control of the Dutch Republic once again reverted to Holland and its regents.

The Dominance of the Regents and Johan de Witt, 1650–72

With the *stadtholder* dead, and his son and heir a newborn infant, the regents of Holland acted swiftly to ensure their re-emergence as the dominant force in the Dutch Republic. The titles of *stadtholder* and captain-general were declared indefinitely vacant, and the provincial States took over the *stadtholder*'s duties, such as appointing civic officials and rural magistrates. The army was drastically downsized, and Holland asserted its primacy in appointing officers. Increasingly, the dominant figure in the Dutch government was the young Pensionary of Holland, Johan de Witt (1625–72). De Witt and the regents of Holland were able to dominate the Republic for two decades by deftly playing on the divisions between and within the other provinces. They were also aided by the infancy of the Prince of Orange, and division within the House of Orange over how best to promote and restore the family's interests. Nevertheless, the inherent tensions in the Dutch Republic did not disappear; rather, they were temporarily in abeyance as the young William III matured and was increasingly looked to as the successor of his illustrious forbears. In religion, too, de Witt and the regents managed to assert their viewpoint: relative toleration for Catholics, Jews, and other Protestant churches, maintaining that the form of religion was ultimately under the control of each province rather than the Republic as a whole. Strict Calvinists, overwhelmingly Orangist in sympathy, were left leaderless and mostly conformed to the demands of the new regime. But they did not disappear, and they formed an important constituency for the revival of the fortunes of the House of Orange.

De Witt and the regents were aided by the general commercial prosperity of the 1650s and by their successful prosecution of two naval wars with England. The first war began when the English Parliament, having won the civil war, passed the Navigation Act in 1651. This act was aimed squarely at Dutch commerce and required that all imports to England be carried in English ships. Cromwell and Parliament also hoped to use a military victory over the Dutch to impose an English protectorate over the Republic, as a prelude to a general anti-Catholic alliance. After some initial reverses, the Dutch eventually managed to fight England to a standstill; eventually the Dutch advantage in shipbuilding and commerce began to prevail, and the two sides made peace in 1654.

Dutch defeats early in the war led to Orangist discontent, but with William III still a small child, there was no one to capitalize on this. Indeed, de Witt and the regents attempted to exclude the House of Orange from any political function in the Republic. Although the States-General refused to ratify this exclusion, Holland did, effectively abolishing the position of *stadtholder*.

The second Anglo-Dutch War (1664–67) was brought on by commercial and colonial tensions. In addition, the restored Stuart dynasty in England, in the person of Charles II, had close ties with the House of Orange. Charles's sister Mary was the mother of William III, and Charles himself had found refuge with the Prince of Orange during his exile from England. As in the first war, the fighting began badly for the Dutch, but during 1666 the tide began to turn. The Dutch felt themselves very much the underdog, and the resulting patriotic fervour resulted in a unity that had been lacking in the first war. In June 1666 the Dutch admiral de Ruyter sailed up the Thames, burning five English ships and towing away the *Royal Charles*, the English flagship. This was followed shortly by the great London plague and fire. In this atmosphere of English gloom and defeatism, peace was made in 1667, on terms very generous to the Dutch. De Witt and the regents were riding high.

The foreign policy of de Witt and the Holland regents was increasingly based on friendship and cooperation with France against Spain and, after 1648 especially England. To this end, Louis XIV aided the Dutch in the second Anglo-Dutch War. Increasingly throughout the 1660s, however, Franco-Dutch relations were strained by strategic and commercial conflicts. Louis XIV had designs on the Spanish Netherlands, based on the dynastic claims of his wife (see Chapter 17), which greatly alarmed the Dutch on the principle that France made a better ally than neighbour. Commercially, the mercantilist policies of Jean-Baptiste Colbert, Louis XIV's minister of industry and finance (see Chapter 14), inevitably brought commercial and maritime tensions.

In 1667 Louis launched his invasion of the Spanish Netherlands, beginning the so-called War of Devolution (see Chapter 17). In order to prevent the French overrunning the Spanish Netherlands, de Witt spearheaded a Triple Alliance of England, the Dutch Republic, and Sweden. Its aim was to persuade Louis to be satisfied with what he had already conquered and, should he refuse, to take military action against France. Louis agreed to stop fighting, but he was infuriated by what he saw as Dutch duplicity and betrayal. Egged on by Colbert, who schemed to enrich French trade and industry by beggaring the Dutch, Louis laid elaborate plans for revenge. He made alliances with the German states that surrounded the Republic, and most importantly he signed the secret Treaty of Dover with Charles II of England in 1670, which committed both rulers to a war against the Dutch.

De Witt's response was to try desperately to mollify Louis. In this, however, he was handicapped by several factors. First, Louis could not be appeased without total Dutch capitulation. Second, de Witt's political position was weakened by the withdrawal of support of many merchants who saw their commercial dominance being undermined by French hostility. Finally, William III was now nearing the age of majority, and, as he did, there was a revival in Orangist sentiment, especially given the increasing hostility with France. Despite de Witt's furious politicking, the young Prince of Orange was appointed captain-general and admiral-general in early 1672.

In the spring of 1672, the Dutch Republic was subjected to a furious onslaught. With his massive army outnumbering the Dutch four to one, Louis XIV launched an invasion across the Spanish Netherlands. At the same time, Louis's German allies invaded from the east, and England attacked Dutch shipping, beginning the third Anglo-Dutch War. The French army occupied large parts of the Dutch Republic virtually unopposed, amid an atmosphere of gloom and defeatism. Amsterdam was saved only by the desperate measure of opening the dykes and flooding much of the countryside. De Witt and his supporters made desperate offers of peace, which Louis contemptuously rejected.

In towns throughout the Republic, there were riots and demonstrations against the regents, whose seeming cowardice, if not overt treason, had laid the groundwork for the current disasters. Everywhere, people looked to the young Prince of Orange as the saviour of the Republic. In July he was made *stadtholder* of Holland and Zeeland. In August, de Witt resigned his office of Grand Pensionary of Holland and retired from public life. Nevertheless, later that month in The Hague, de Witt and his brother Cornelis were lynched by an angry mob. With the regents completely discredited and the Dutch Republic in desperate straits all around, William III took control of the Dutch Republic.

Dutch Culture in the Golden Age

The period of de Witt's and the regents' dominance also represented a golden age of culture in the Dutch Republic. In art, science, and literature, Dutch scholars and artists, or those living in the Dutch Republic, made impressive contributions to early modern European culture. The achievements of these scholars will be treated in more detail in the appropriate place, but it is worth considering the contribution of the Dutch environment to their work. While Dutch contributions to European culture reflected and contributed to the broader European culture, the nature of Dutch society and the Dutch political system gave them a distinctive stamp. In particular, the political and economic weakness of the nobility, and the economic prosperity of the bourgeoisie, meant that in terms of art and literature, Dutch cultural output catered to a primarily middle-class audience. For example, excepting the court of the Princes of Orange, Dutch artists lacked the noble patronage of their Italian or French counterparts. While a number of names have entered the canon of the "Old Masters," such as Rembrandt, Vermeer, and Hals, there were vast numbers of lesser artisans who toiled producing the paintings destined for the walls of middle-class homes. The subjects of these paintings reflected the taste and interest of this market: landscapes, seascapes, town scenes, and family portraits. The simplicity of Reformed churches and worship also removed from the scene one of the major patrons of art in Catholic Europe. Accordingly, religious scenes are notably absent from Dutch painting of the seventeenth century.

In intellectual affairs too, Dutch scholars shared in the general European trends of the age but often gave them a unique stamp. As in religious affairs, Dutch scholars benefitted from a relative openness that was lacking elsewhere. In part, this can be attributed to the flexible and tolerant outlook of urban elites, a continuity of an Erasmian humanist flexibility inherited from the later Middle Ages. It also resulted, however, from the decentralized nature of the Dutch Republic. There was simply no institution capable of enforcing a thoroughgoing censorship. There were plenty of voices supporting more stringent thought control, particularly outside Holland and in the Reformed Church, but they lacked the political muscle to enforce such policies. As a result, the intellectual atmosphere in the Republic, especially in Holland, was much freer than elsewhere in Europe, though there were still limits to what could be said and written. Dutch publishing houses flourished, in part because they could print works that could not be published elsewhere, even as scholars from throughout Europe found a home there. The French philosopher and mathematician René Descartes (1596–1650), fearful of the Catholic Church, settled in the Dutch Republic in 1628. Despite arousing the suspicions of the strict Calvinist theologians, Descartes suffered no official sanction, in large part because he enjoyed the protection of the *stadtholder* Frederick Henry. (Likewise, the works of Galileo were published freely in the Dutch Republic despite their censure by the Catholic Church.) When he succeeded his father in 1647, William II effected a reconciliation with the strict

Calvinists, causing Descartes to fear for his future in the Dutch Republic. In 1649 he left for Sweden, where he spent the last year of his life at the court of Queen Christina.

Nowhere are the relative freedom and the ultimate limits of Dutch intellectual freedom and openness more apparent than in the case of Benedict (or Baruch) Spinoza (1632–77), a powerful thinker whose complex and difficult philosophy challenged some of the most closely held orthodoxies of the day, including the divine inspiration of Scripture, the divine sanction of government, and the immortality of the soul. Born into the community of exiled Portuguese Jews in Amsterdam, Spinoza was expelled from the synagogue as a young man for his radical ideas. He declined teaching appointments at several universities in order to preserve his freedom of thought. He supported himself as a lens maker, and indeed played a role in the invention of the microscope. Even Spinoza, however, recognized the limits of toleration in the Dutch Republic. His major work, the *Tractatus Theologico-Politicus* (1670), was published anonymously in Amsterdam, but with the place of publication being falsely given as Hamburg. This was undoubtedly wise, as the work was tremendously controversial and caused an uproar. Several other works, including his *Ethics*, were published only after his death, and even then anonymously and again with false places of publication. Despite the condemnations and controversies, however, the very fact that Spinoza was able to live, work, and write in the Dutch Republic is a testament to its relative toleration. Almost everywhere else in Europe, he would have been arrested and imprisoned or executed as a heretic, atheist, or blasphemer.

Dutch scientists also made important contributions to the technical and scientific progress of the day. Christiaan Huygens (1629–95) was a mathematician in the tradition of Descartes, though he rejected the latter's metaphysical views. He was an important astronomer as well as a developer and improver of both the telescope and microscope. In 1656 he invented the pendulum clock and showed its superiority over the other clocks of the day. But his most important contribution was in the field of optics. In his *Treatise on Light* (1690), he formulated his wave theory of light, and expressed in mathematical form the laws of reflection, refraction, and double refraction. He was also a friend and correspondent of Spinoza, although there is no evidence that he shared the latter's controversial philosophy. Anthonie van Leeuwenhoek (1632–1723) greatly improved the microscopes that had earlier been developed by Huygens, Spinoza, and others. A self-taught scientist, he knew little Latin and was often treated with disdain by other scientists. Using his microscope, he investigated the structure of blood, and in 1676 he discovered bacteria. It is significant, however, that the Dutch Republic never established a national body for the promotion of scientific investigation, such as the English Royal Society or the French *Académie*. As a result, Huygens lived and worked for many years in Paris, while van Leeuwenhoek's work was sponsored and popularized by the Royal Society of England.

The Dutch War and the Stadtholderate of William III, 1672–1702

With the defeat of de Witt and the regents in 1672, William III acted quickly to cement his new political ascendancy. He purged city councils of their most anti-Orangist elements. The States of Holland and Zeeland confirmed his stadtholderate and furthermore made the positions hereditary in the Orange family. Meanwhile, the French invasion had stalled, and William proved himself adept at military command. A series of Dutch victories at sea prompted England to sign a peace treaty in 1674, and, not long afterwards, Louis XIV's German allies also made peace with the Republic. By the middle of 1674, the French had been expelled from the Dutch Republic, except for two border fortresses.

Despite the Orange ascendancy, however, the tensions in Dutch society and political system did not disappear, although they were definitely muted by the national emergency. When the tide turned against France, these tensions began to re-emerge. Suspicions of Orange political ambitions mounted, and the regents began to regain their positions in the towns of Holland. Moreover, now that the immediate threat from France had receded, many people—even among Orangist supporters—began to question the need for a continued large army and navy and the attendant high taxes. These resentments were compounded by William's sullen and confrontational style and the alleged corruption of those whom he put into power. The city council of Amsterdam was dominated by those opposed to the Prince, and in 1678 their agenda prevailed in the signing of the Treaty of Nijmegen with France, over the objections of William III.

Following the peace treaty, William attempted, with some success, to mend fences with regents and broaden his popular support, especially in Holland. He thus allowed the rehabilitation of many of the regents he had purged in 1672 and backed away somewhat from his support of the strict Calvinist faction in the Church. On foreign policy, however, there was little agreement, as William remained suspicious and hostile toward Louis XIV, while the regents believed, as had de Witt, that friendship with France was the best guarantee of Dutch security and prosperity. William attempted to draw closer to England in the hope that better relations would prevent a revival of the Anglo-French alliance of 1670. To that end, in 1677 he married Mary Stuart, daughter of James, Duke of York, brother of Charles II and the future James II.

Whatever tensions there were in the Dutch Republic, however, were shortly overshadowed by Louis XIV's aggressive diplomacy. In the 1680s Louis began his aggressive policy of reunions in Germany (see Chapter 17) and increasingly put pressure on Dutch industry and commerce. The threat to Dutch prosperity caused the regents to put aside their distrust of William, and the Dutch Republic joined a general alliance against France. William in turn tempered his support for the strict Calvinists, continuing to allow practical toleration of Catholics, Jews, and dissenting Protestants. As long as France remained a threat to the security and prosperity of the Dutch Republic, tensions between Orangists and regents would remain muted.

William's position, both in his struggle against Louis XIV and within Dutch politics, was strengthened in 1688 when he also became king of England as a result of the so-called "Glorious Revolution." James II, who had succeeded his brother Charles II in 1685, was becoming increasingly unpopular in England, mostly because he was openly Catholic (see Chapter 15). With war against France looming once again, William III decided on a gamble. He would launch an invasion of England, based on his wife's claim to the throne (she was the daughter of James II by an earlier, Protestant wife). His goal was not only to prevent a revival of an Anglo-French alliance, but also to bring England's might and resources to bear in the struggle against Louis XIV. The English opponents of James II supported him in his plans, but it was by no means clear that they could make a difference. There was a real possibility of an English civil war. Certainly, Louis XIV was counting on this and made no effort to prevent the Dutch invasion. In November 1688, a Dutch fleet of 500 vessels crossed the Channel. The English fleet was kept from meeting the invasion force by a contrary wind, later immortalized as a "Protestant wind," and the Dutch force landed unopposed in Devon, well away from the English army that was concentrated in the southeast. James dithered and prevaricated as the Dutch army marched toward London, and his support evaporated. By December, William had entered London unopposed, and James had fled into exile in France. In early 1689 the English Parliament installed William and Mary as joint monarchs of England. Until his death in 1702, then, William controlled the Dutch Republic and England, and orchestrated and led the opposition to French aggression in Europe. When William III died childless, the regents of Holland once again asserted their dominance in the Dutch Republic, leaving the position of *stadtholder* vacant. This was to remain the case until the middle of the eighteenth century, in effect a reversion to the period of de Witt's dominance from 1650–72.

By the early eighteenth century, the Dutch Republic had passed its zenith as a European power. A century of more-or-less continual warfare had taken its toll on Dutch finances and prosperity. The national debt mounted precipitously, and Dutch merchants around the world found themselves increasingly pressured by their English and French rivals, who stole more and more of the market share from Dutch merchants in Asia and the New World. Dutch industry was being steadily threatened by the revival of industry in the southern Netherlands (after 1713 the Austrian Netherlands) and by the industrial mercantilism prevalent in England, France, Prussia, Austria, Sweden, and Russia. Dutch commerce and industry underwent both relative and absolute declines.

At the same time, the urban merchant and industrial elites who had driven the Dutch economic miracle of the seventeenth century withdrew from active participation in commerce and industry. Increasingly, they were investors rather than entrepreneurs, content to live off the revenue from government bonds and their shares in the East India Company.

It is no doubt terribly ironic that the fate of the Dutch Republic should in some ways mirror that of Spain at the end of the seventeenth century. Like Spain, the Republic was weakened by interminable internal conflicts, though of somewhat different sorts. Like Spain, the Dutch for a long time played a greater role in European affairs than they could indefinitely support, and with much the same results. Dutch elites, like their Spanish counterparts, eventually turned their backs on productive economic activity and became a class of *rentiers*. Like Spain, England, and France, the Dutch Republic underwent its own version of the "general crisis" of the seventeenth century. Unlike England and France, however, which emerged stronger from their crises, the Dutch Republic, like Spain, was never able to recapture its former glory—nor was it even willing to try.

CHAPTER THIRTEEN

Northern and Eastern Europe

In the sixteenth and seventeenth centuries, northern and eastern Europe were dominated by a group of states that were themselves in a state of flux and development. In the north, Sweden, Denmark, and Poland all contended for control of the Baltic Sea and its lucrative trade routes. Control of Baltic commerce rested on two factors: first, control of the Danish Sound linking the Baltic and North Seas; and second, control of the river-mouth ports of northern Germany and Poland—primarily Danzig, Stettin, Königsberg, and Riga—through which flowed the grain destined for export to the west. In the later Middle Ages these had been in the control of two powers that would be on the wane by 1500. The first was the Hansa, or Hanseatic League, an association of merchants in the cities of northern Germany that virtually monopolized later medieval Baltic trade. The second was the Order of the Teutonic Knights, which governed most of the land around the southern and eastern shores of the Baltic. The decline of both these powers created a vacuum that the rulers of the lands around the Baltic attempted to fill. Internally, Sweden and Denmark developed in similar ways to the monarchies of western Europe. Poland, on the other hand, was steadily devolving into a noble republic with a figurehead king, developments that would ultimately result in its complete dismemberment and disappearance in the eighteenth century. Further east, while in the process of developing into Russia, Muscovy, which had for centuries been concerned with the threat of the Mongols from the east, was just beginning to become involved in European affairs in the late sixteenth century. Distinguished from the rest of Europe by religion, culture, social structure, and political culture, by the end of the seventeenth century Russia would nevertheless play an integral role in European affairs. To the south, the Ottoman Empire was even more alien to European culture. An Islamic state that occupied the Balkans, the Ottoman Empire reached its zenith in the middle decades of the sixteenth century, when its armies conquered Hungary, laid siege to Vienna several times, and threatened central Europe, and its navies regularly threatened Spanish and Italian shipping in the western Mediterranean. After the death of the great Sultan Suleyman the Magnificent in 1566, the Ottoman Empire entered a stage of long and slow decline that, by the end of the century, would see it expelled not only from Hungary, but from much of southeastern Europe as well.

The Baltic World: Denmark, Sweden, and Poland

Denmark and Sweden

The kingdoms of Denmark, Norway, and Sweden (which included Finland) had been united into a single kingdom under Danish rule by the Union of Kalmar in 1397. Increasingly throughout the fifteenth century, however, the regents of the Danish king in Sweden had been acting as virtually independent rulers. The efforts of King Christian II (1513–23) to enforce his authority in Sweden led ultimately to a noble rebellion, the election of the Swedish noble Gustav Vasa as king, and Swedish independence. Christian's erratic and autocratic policies also led to his overthrow and the election of his uncle as King Frederick I of Denmark (1523–33).

Compared to the monarchies of western Europe, the newly independent Kingdom of Sweden was backward and undeveloped. At the accession of Gustav Vasa, there were perhaps three quarters of a million inhabitants. Stockholm, by far the largest and most important town, had a population of around 7,000. The bourgeoisie was correspondingly small and weak, all the more so since most trade was in the hands of the German merchants of the Hanseatic League. Feudalism as a social system had never taken hold in Sweden, and Swedish peasants had never been subjected to serfdom. Indeed, they were freer than their contemporaries in western Europe and owned about 50 per cent of the arable land. They had their own chamber in the national assembly or *Riksdag*. Correspondingly, the nobility, although politically powerful, were not tremendously wealthy as a group. In terms of wealth and social structure, Sweden was certainly more egalitarian and "democratic" than most European societies of the time. Administratively, the government was quite primitive, certainly in comparison with France, England, or the Spanish kingdoms. A good deal of tax revenue was collected in produce rather than cash. There were, however, productive iron and copper mines.

By 1540, both Denmark and Sweden had officially become Lutheran states, although these conversions were very much top-down processes driven by the political needs of their respective kings. The process of converting ordinary people to the Lutheran faith was a drawn-out process and was not completed for many years. For Gustav Vasa, the major incentives to break with Rome were financial and political rather than religious. The Church in Sweden owned more than 20 per cent of the land, and some of the bishops had opposed Swedish independence. In the end, Sweden wound up with a church that was Lutheran in theology, but firmly under royal control, in much the same way as the Church of England ended up under the control of Henry VIII at about the same time.

Having achieved Swedish independence and fortified himself with the wealth and power of the church, Gustav Vasa sought to diminish the political power of the nobility and cement the position of his dynasty. For two centuries the Swedish nobility had dominated the government through their control of the royal council and their right to elect the king. The king was in essence the chief executive officer of a noble government. To break this pattern, Vasa cultivated the non-noble elements in the *Riksdag*. In 1544, he succeeded in having the *Riksdag* accept the principle of hereditary monarchy. Despite the sporadic hostility of Denmark, Poland, Muscovy, and the Hanseatic League, Vasa avoided costly warfare even as he built up the Swedish navy and founded a conscript army, the first national standing army in European history. When he died in 1560, he was succeeded without incident by his eldest son, Erik XIV (1560–69).

Nevertheless, Gustav Vasa's death ushered in a long period of political instability in Sweden. For one thing, although the nobles had acquiesced in making the monarchy hereditary, they remained resentful and jealous of their position and prestige. In addition, in his will Gustav had made provision for his three younger sons by a second marriage. In a practice reminiscent of medieval feudalism, he provided them with territories and revenues that made them semi-independent rulers and thus threats to the effective control of the king. John (later King John III) was made Duke of Finland, Charles (later King Charles IX) was made Duke of Södermanland, and Magnus was created Duke of Östergötland. (This last brother was prevented from playing a political role by his mental illness.) Gustav Vasa had, therefore, quite unintentionally laid the groundwork for the potential undoing of much of his achievement.

In Denmark, the death of Frederick I in 1533 combined with noble resentment, religious division, and foreign interference to produce a civil war that lasted until 1536 when Frederick's son firmly established himself as King Christian III (d. 1559). Like his contemporary Gustav Vasa in Sweden, Christian studiously avoided the expense and uncertainty of war. However, his son and successor, Frederick II (1559–88), adopted a much more aggressive policy faced with what he perceived as a Swedish threat to Danish pre-eminence in the Baltic. Denmark's great concern was to preserve its control over the sound that linked the Baltic and North Seas. Denmark controlled the land on both sides of the sound and the tolls levied there constituted the major portion of royal revenues. Erik XIV, the new king of Sweden, was continuing his father's policy of expanding Swedish naval power, but he also had plans to expand Swedish holdings in the eastern Baltic. In 1561 the Estonian port of Reval was incorporated into the Kingdom of Sweden, and in 1562 he announced his intention to wrest the port of Narva from Russian control. For his part, Frederick had ideas of restoring Danish rule over Sweden. In a deliberate provocation he incorporated the Swedish royal coat of arms into his own. The two kings went to war in 1563 in the so-called Seven Years' War of the North (1563–70). Sweden was prevented from pressing its naval advantage by internal division and the growing insanity of Erik XIV. The last years of Frederick's reign (he died in 1588) were spent in less military pursuits, including patronage of the great astronomer Tycho Brahe (see Chapter 18). He was succeeded by his son Christian IV (r. 1588–1648), who was a boy of eleven when his father died.

The long period of regency, which ended only in 1596, saw an aristocratic resurgence in the government. Christian and the Danish nobility arrived at a marriage of convenience that gave the nobles a great deal of power internally but left the King free to pursue his foreign-policy goals of territorial expansion, reunion of Sweden under the Danish crown, and protection of the Danish position in the Baltic against Sweden, Poland, and Russia.

The first hereditary king of Sweden, Erik XIV was educated and highly cultured, unlike his rough-and-ready father. His promise and potential were eventually defeated, however, by the mental instability that was to rear its head periodically in the Vasa dynasty. Egocentric and suspicious to the point of paranoia, he saw plots and enemies everywhere, especially among the nobility, whom he suspected of wishing to end Vasa rule of Sweden. Relations between the King and the leading nobles were already tense, since the nobles felt shut out of political power by the King's reliance on non-noble councillors and advisors, especially the King's chief advisor, Jöran Persson. As early as 1563, Erik faced rebellion from his younger half-brother John, the Duke of Finland. John had insisted on marrying the daughter of King Sigismund II Augustus of Poland, even as Poland and Sweden were on the brink of war. John and his wife were captured and imprisoned for the next four years. The King's growing insanity only worsened the situation. In 1568, he stabbed to death one of his leading noble opponents, which resulted in a noble rebellion and his deposition. The nobles chose as King Erik's successor his younger half-brother, who became King John III (1569–92). John quickly concluded the war with Denmark by the Treaty of Stettin (1570). Little had been settled by either the war or the peace. In theory, Sweden gave up quite a bit by agreeing to withdraw from Estonia, but in fact never did. In reality this was just the opening round in a protracted conflict for control of the Baltic and, by extension, of northern Europe.

The deposition of Erik, however, did little to quell internal political tension. Although he had agreed to John's elevation as king, his brother Charles, Duke of Södermanland, caused no end of trouble. Indeed, in order to buy Charles's acquiescence, John agreed to Charles's virtual independence in his duchy. Moreover, the deposition of Erik did much to call into question the hereditary nature of the monarchy so painstakingly established by Gustav Vasa. John attempted to remedy this by having his son Sigismund recognized as his heir, but this brought with it its own problems, which were connected with developments in religion.

John III was an accomplished theologian who genuinely desired an end to the schism of the Reformation. To this end, in 1577 he introduced a liturgy, known as the "Red Book," which attempted to combine Lutheran and Catholic elements. He also accepted emissaries from the Pope, hoping that Rome could be persuaded to compromise on several key issues such as clerical marriage, communion in both kinds, and celebration of the Mass in Swedish rather than Latin. The negotiations ultimately failed, and in 1580 the Roman envoys were expelled. They had, however, managed to convert Prince Sigismund to Catholicism. The reaction against these negotiations drove the Swedish church in a more positively

MAP 13.1 ⇝ THE BALTIC, 1560–1660

Protestant direction. The Red Book remained in force, however, and this increased the suspicion between king and subjects. It only served to aggravate the situation that Duke Charles cultivated and supported the more zealous Protestants against his older brother.

The continuing internal instability in Sweden, however, did nothing to disrupt Swedish efforts to establish a Baltic empire. By the time of John III's death in 1592, Sweden was firmly established as the leading power in the eastern Baltic. Danish ambitions in Estonia had been decisively defeated; meanwhile, Sweden had managed to seize the port of Narva from Ivan IV of Russia and had signed a treaty with the Tsar that recognized Swedish possessions in Estonia. Much of this was possible due to an informal alliance with Poland. Indeed, there were close ties between the two kingdoms. Both had an interest in weakening Denmark and the Hanseatic League, and both kept a watchful eye on the rising power of Muscovy. John III had married a daughter of the Polish King Sigismund II Augustus, the last Polish king of the Jagellionian dynasty. Therefore, it was not entirely unnatural that when King Stephen Bathory died in 1586, John III proposed that his son Sigismund be elected king of Poland, with the understanding that when Sigismund acceded to the Swedish throne, the two kingdoms would be united, in much the same way that Denmark and Sweden had formerly been united.

So, when John died in 1592, Sigismund became king of Sweden as well as of Poland. He faced severe difficulties in both his kingdoms. In Poland, he was suspect as a foreigner, and the Poles still remembered with bitterness the brief reign of the French prince Henri of Valois, who had deserted Poland to become King Henri III of France when his brother died. In Sweden, Sigismund was doubly suspect, first as a committed and devout Catholic, and then as an aspiring absolutist who sought to further diminish the political power of the nobility. This was especially true of his uncle Charles, who was committed to the support of the Lutheran church and who viewed with alarm any threat to his independence as Duke of Södermanland.

Sigismund spent a tense two years in Sweden before returning to Poland in 1594. When he left, he made arrangements that were almost certain to produce hostility, conflict, and instability. Formally, the government of Sweden was entrusted to a joint regency of Charles and a council of leading nobles. Given the mutual hostility between Charles and a number of these nobles, it was highly unlikely that this council could operate smoothly or efficiently. Moreover, Sigismund had deliberately handicapped this council in order to preserve his own power in Sweden. The regency council was forbidden to raise taxes or to make foreign-policy decisions without Sigismund's consent. Furthermore, key fortresses and strongholds throughout the kingdom were placed under the command of officers directly responsible to Sigismund; even members of the regency council were forbidden access without the King's consent. In addition, several of these commanders were either Catholic or Catholic sympathizers.

In Sigismund's absence, Charles and the noble council clashed repeatedly. In this conflict, Charles relied on the support of the middle class and the peasants in the *Riksdag*, which he summoned frequently. He portrayed himself as the supporter of liberty against a selfish clique of noble oligarchs. Soon, Charles and the nobles were on the brink of civil war. In 1597 Sigismund attempted to reclaim his authority over his northern kingdom. He landed in Sweden with a force of Polish cavalry and disaffected Swedish noblemen. Ultimately, he was unable to defeat Charles, and in 1598 he left for Poland, never to see Sweden again. Sigismund was deposed by the *Riksdag*, and the crown offered to Charles, although he would not formally accept the title until 1604. Charles quickly consolidated his hold on power through the judicial murder of his leading noble opponents, who, after all, had done nothing more than support Sigismund, the legitimate king of Sweden. Although he had come to power through currying the favour of ordinary people as expressed in the *Riksdag*, over the course of his reign Charles's high-handedness and brutality alienated the commoners without reconciling the nobles. By the time he died in 1611, Sweden was filled with tension, hostility and division.

In foreign affairs, too, Charles IX was something less than a stellar success. Given the hostility between the Swedish and Polish branches of the Vasa dynasty, he was compelled to draw closer to Russia. Russia, however, was currently absorbed in its own internal dissension (the "Time of Troubles"; see below) and was unable to provide much support for Sweden. With his intemperate aggression, Charles drove Denmark as well as Poland into open hostility. Ultimately, Charles IX was not able to preserve Swedish control of Estonia and Livonia against a hostile alliance of Poland and Denmark. Therefore, when Charles died in 1611, his sixteen-year-old son and successor Gustav Adolf (or Gustavus Adolphus) faced difficult situations, both internationally and domestically.

In order to guarantee his accession to throne, Gustavus was compelled to accept the re-admission of the nobility to the centres of power. On paper, then, much of the aristocratic nature of Swedish government was restored. Yet, over the years of his reign, the King was able to free himself from most of these restrictions with, it must be admitted, the cooperation of the nobles themselves. Unlike his father, Gustavus knew how to work with people to get what he wanted, and was more likely to persuade than to threaten or bully. A genuinely attractive figure and a devout but not overly doctrinaire Lutheran, he was more than ably assisted by his chancellor and chief advisor, Axel Oxenstierna. Oxenstierna (1583–1654) was a member of the high nobility and, ironically, had drafted the restrictions imposed on royal power at the young king's accession. Nevertheless, Gustavus and Oxenstierna worked together in a mutually beneficial and even affectionate partnership.

Gustavus quickly extricated Sweden from the war that his father had provoked with Denmark in the Treaty of Knäred in 1613, but peace came with a heavy price. The price to be paid was Danish occupation of Älvsborg, Sweden's only port on the North Sea, until an enormous ransom was paid. This amount was eventually paid, but only through an enormous national sacrifice and tremendous royal debt. In 1617, Sweden concluded the Treaty of Stolbova with Russia, by which it obtained further land around the eastern shores of the Baltic and cut Russia off from the Baltic until the reign of Peter the Great. Swedish policy regarding Russia was twofold: first, to keep a Polish prince off the Russian throne, for Sigismund was attempting to have his son elected tsar, and second, to weaken Russia as much as possible as protection for Finland's and Sweden's Baltic possessions. War with Poland continued, although by 1629 Gustavus had occupied Polish Livonia (including the important port of Riga) and was in almost complete control of the southern shore of the Baltic. Hostility continued, however, given the threat that the Polish Vasas posed to the Swedish branch of the dynasty.

By 1629, however, a new threat to Swedish security and interests in the Baltic had emerged in the form of Wallenstein's conquests and the revival of Habsburg power in Germany (see Chapter 8). Christian IV of Denmark had tried to stem the Habsburg tide and had failed. So, in 1630, Gustavus Adolphus took the momentous decision to launch an invasion of northern Germany, both to protect German Protestants and to preserve the security of Sweden's Baltic Empire.

Swedish intervention in the Thirty Years' War was made possible only by a series of developments that greatly enhanced the government's revenue and efficiency. Sweden's possession of seaports along the southern and eastern shores of the Baltic brought in a great deal of revenue in the form of tolls on commerce. More efficient exploitation of the country's mineral resources was equally lucrative, as was domestic administrative reform. Together, Gustavus and Oxenstierna instituted wide-ranging administrative reforms, which brought a measure of rationality and efficiency to what had previously been a haphazard "system" that had depended to a very great degree on the personal presence and ability of the King. Similar reforms were also applied to the army and navy, which quickly became among the best in Europe. Moreover, a more efficient domestic administration allowed Gustavus to build a conscript army that effectively balanced the needs of the army and the country.

Under Gustavus Adolphus, Sweden emerged as a European power, able to contend with the Habsburgs and France. Upon his accession, Sweden was still little more than a backwater, threatened by Denmark, Russia, and Poland. Its government was chaotic and haphazard and had been the object of decades of infighting and instability. It was Gustavus's achievement that even his untimely death at Lützen in 1632 and a period of regency and instability could not turn the clock back. For the rest of the seventeenth century, Sweden was the dominant power in the Baltic and, by extension, in northern Europe, a position it would lose to Peter the Great's Russia only in the early eighteenth century. Internally, his domestic reforms made Sweden the best-governed state in Europe. In fact, when Peter the Great of Russia sought a model for his modernization of that country's government, he adopted the Swedish system. Some have argued that the German adventure that led to Gustavus's death was a huge mistake, draining the country's resources and committing it to an empire whose maintenance exceeded its capabilities. From a Swedish perspective, however, the empire was a defensive necessity, to counter the threats posed by Denmark, Poland, Russia, and eventually the Habsburgs. But as other conquerors have discovered, even defensive conquests lead inexorably to further conquests to defend what has already been conquered. Swedish efforts were rewarded in the 1648 Peace of Westphalia, which gave the Swedes the northern German territories of western Pomerania, with its important ports of Stralsund and Stettin, as well as the bishoprics of Bremen and Verden. Michael Roberts, the greatest modern historian of Sweden and biographer of Gustavus Adolphus, has this to say about Sweden's greatest king:

> Though his reign was filled with wars, it would be wrong to think of him primarily as a great soldier: if he had never fought a battle or conquered a province, his domestic achievements should have secured him a great place in Swedish history. The years after 1617 are a period of extraordinary creative activity. He was always conscious of his responsibility to God for the welfare of his people; and if he demanded great sacrifices, and was rigorous in exacting them, he could feel compassion for those who had to bear the burden. ... By any standards, this was a wonderful reign; and if strength of character, devotion to duty, and success in enterprise are acceptable criteria of greatness, then he was assuredly a great ruler, as certainly as he was a great man.[1]

On Gustavus's death in 1632, he was succeeded by his young daughter Christina. Actual control of the government, however, remained in the hands of Oxenstierna, who continued his late master's policies in all important respects. By 1644, Christina had been declared an adult and Oxenstierna was in large part eclipsed. (He would die in 1654, having been chancellor since 1612.) Increasingly, the government's military commitments led to a shortage of money, which Christina handled by alienating crown land, that is by selling it, mostly to the nobility. This, however, only narrowed the government's revenue base, and the shortfall had to be made up by increased taxation; this fell disproportionately on the peasants, who were not reticent in expressing their anger and fear.

Internal tensions were complicated by Christina's personal life. She refused to marry, and indeed intended to abdicate as soon as she could, proposing her cousin Charles as her heir. This did not sit well with many nobles, who saw an opportunity to restore the elective monarchy, but Christina was able to play upon the divisions in Swedish society to attain her goals. In the *Riksdag* of 1650, she threatened the nobles with a "Reduction," that is, the resumption of Crown lands, rights, and revenues that had been previously alienated. This was the most important demand of the other three estates, especially of the peasants, who saw their livelihood and freedom increasingly threatened by the ascendance of the nobility. Faced with this threat, the nobles recognized Charles as her heir, and Christina dropped her support for the reforms demanded by the non-noble estates. In 1654, Christina abdicated her throne, announced her conversion to Roman Catholicism, and relocated to Rome.

The new king, Charles X (1654–60), rewarded the commoners with a partial Reduction, restoring to the Crown all lands alienated since 1632, but at the same time he reassured the nobles that this settlement was to be final. He also embarked on an ambitious foreign policy. In 1655 he launched a very successful invasion of Poland, occupying Warsaw and Cracow in short order. This very success, however, alarmed others who feared the expansion of Swedish power on the southern shores of the Baltic. The Elector of Brandenburg, the King of Denmark, and the Russian Tsar all combined against Sweden. Charles X quickly diverted his army from Poland to Denmark and imposed a series of peace treaties on the Danes. The treaties of Roskilde (1658) and Copenhagen (1660) finally confirmed Sweden's ascendancy over Denmark. Sweden annexed the provinces of Skåne, Halland, Blekinge, and Bohuslän on the southern end of the Swedish peninsula. At the same time, the Treaty of Oliva (1660) with Poland restored things to their prewar status, except that the Vasa king of Poland gave up his dynastic claim to the Swedish throne.

Charles X died unexpectedly in 1660, inaugurating another royal minority and period of political ascendancy for Swedish nobles, as had been the case in 1611 and 1632. The new king, Charles XI, was only four years old, and though the Queen Mother was named regent, real power lay in the hands of a noble council led by the chancellor and king's uncle, Magnus de la Gardie. When Charles XI assumed personal power in 1672, he fundamentally remade Sweden's government in a more absolutist mould. It was under his son, Charles XII (1697–1718), that Sweden would challenge for supremacy in northern Europe for the last time. His nemesis, however, was not Poland or Denmark, as it had been in the past, but rather a revived and transformed Russia under Peter the Great (see Chapter 17).

Poland

As is no doubt apparent from the foregoing discussion, Poland also had a direct interest in the Baltic. Since 1385, the Kingdom of Poland and the neighbouring Grand Duchy of Lithuania had been united in a personal union. That is, except for several brief periods, the same person was ruler of both states, much as Castile and Aragon shared the same ruler but otherwise remained separate kingdoms. Although vast in extent, with a population that was second only to that of France, it was poor in resources, mostly landlocked, and devoid of natural defences. During the later Middle Ages, Poland had been a prosperous cultural centre, especially under King Casimir the Great (1333–70). Nevertheless, Poland's late-medieval greatness was something of a mirage, made possible by the decay of the Order of the Teutonic Knights, the decline of Imperial power in Germany, the weakness of Russia, and the break-up of the Scandinavian Union of Kalmar.

In the early sixteenth century, Poland was ruled by kings of the Jagellion dynasty, who seemed, on the surface at any rate, to rival the Habsburgs for power and prestige in central and eastern Europe. A branch of the dynasty ruled the kingdoms of Bohemia and Hungary, at least until the defeat and death of Louis I at the hands of the Ottoman Empire at the Battle of Mohacs in 1526. Appearances were misleading, however, for even more than Sweden, Poland was dominated by its nobility, who comprised a full 10 per cent of the population. While in western Europe the restrictions of serfdom were rapidly being eliminated, in Poland they were being reimposed, to the great benefit of the nobility and the detriment of the Crown. Lured by the possibility of selling grain to the rapidly expanding cities of western Europe, Polish nobles cultivated their vast estates as large agricultural businesses. The imposition of serfdom was their way of guaranteeing themselves a plentiful and cheap source of labour (see Chapter 3). Towns were few and small, so unlike their royal counterparts in western Europe, Polish rulers could not rely on a prosperous and burgeoning middle class for financial and political support. Indeed, in 1565, the noble national assembly (the *Sejm*) passed a law forbidding the urban bourgeoisie to engage in foreign trade.

Politically, the king of Poland was hamstrung by the political power of the nobles or *szlachta* as expressed in the *Sejm*. On most matters, a unanimous vote was required, which meant that little meaningful business could be transacted. Each individual noble in the *Sejm* possessed a veto over the assembly's business; this was the famous *liberum veto*. After the middle of the seventeenth century, a single dissenting voice not only defeated the measure at hand, but was also sufficient to end the assembly itself and to render null and void all the business previously transacted. Foreign rulers, especially the Russian Tsar, were able to paralyse the Polish government simply by keeping a few noblemen on the payroll to exercise the *liberum veto*. Above all, the concern of the Polish nobility was to protect their pre-eminent social, economic, and political liberties in Polish society. At a time when rulers in other parts of Europe were enhancing their power, when the processes of centralization and absolutism were gathering momentum, in Poland just the opposite was taking place. Although there was a king, Poland in reality was more a noble republic than a monarchy like France, England, or Spain. The closest parallel might be with the convoluted and complex constitution of the Dutch Republic (see Chapter 12).

Poland was a religiously mixed state unlike any other in Europe. Officially Roman Catholic, there was a large Russian Orthodox minority in Lithuania, as well as a significant number of Jews. While Lutheranism made substantial gains in German-speaking areas of the north, its German connections made it suspect in the eyes of many Polish nobles. Calvinism made impressive gains after about 1550, for it was a creed more suited to the outlook of Polish nobles. Its presbyterian system of government allowed for significant lay input, which enhanced the control of nobles over their estates and serfs. Protestant nobles quickly became a majority in the *Sejm*. King Sigismund II (1548–72) did his best to restore religious uniformity, but the political power of the nobles made this practically impossible. Indeed, Poland became something of a haven for persecuted religious minorities from elsewhere. The Bohemian Brethren, the followers of the Czech reformer John Hus, found refuge in Poland after being driven out of Bohemia. Various Anabaptist groups settled on the estates of nobles who either were sympathetic or were inclined to overlook their religious beliefs in order to gain farmers and settlers. The Unitarian followers of Lelio and Fausto Sozzini, the Socinians, established their own community at Rakow in 1569.

The revived and reformed Catholic Church, however, soon had a significant impact in Poland. Although the *Sejm* refused to accept the decrees of the Council of Trent, Sigismund did so, and in 1565 the Society of Jesus received royal permission to begin work in Poland. The Jesuits established a number of schools and seminaries to train and educate laymen and priests alike; they also managed to convert a number of leading nobles. The threat of a Catholic revival in Poland soon caused Polish Protestants to put aside their differences. In the Consensus of Sendomir (1570), Lutherans, Calvinists, and the Bohemian Brethren formed a common front in which each group kept its own form of worship but agreed to hold common synods. Further, in the Compact of Warsaw (1573), Polish nobles vowed to protect their religious and political liberties against the actions of any future rulers:

> Whereas there is a great dissidence in the affairs of the Christian Religion in our country, and to prevent any sedition for this reason among the people, such as we clearly perceive in other realms—we swear to each other, on behalf of ourselves and our descendants, in perpetuity, under oath and pledging our faith, honour, and conscience, that we who differ in matters of religion will keep the peace among ourselves, and neither shed blood on account of differences of Faith, or kinds of church, nor punish one another by confiscation of goods, deprivation of honour, imprisonment, or exile ...

Not only were the King's hands tied by the powerful political privileges of the nobles, he also needed their aid against the rising power of Russia to the east (see below). In 1558, Tsar Ivan IV (the Terrible) launched an invasion of Livonia. In 1569 the previously separate states of Poland and Lithuania were united in a federal union. Sigismund died in 1572, leaving no heirs and with the struggle for Livonia still unresolved. The nobles seized this opportunity to reassert their right to elect the king. Many Catholic Polish nobles preferred the Habsburg Emperor Maximilian II, while many Lithuanian nobles sought to elect Ivan IV of Muscovy. A compromise was eventually arrived at in the form of Henri, Duke of Anjou, younger brother of King Charles IX of France (later King Henry III of France). Much to his dismay, he was forced to accept the Henrician Articles, which severely circumscribed royal power: the *Sejm* was to meet at least every two years; the king was not to marry or name a successor without the consent of the of *Sejm*, thus preserving the elective nature of the monarchy; the *Sejm* was to approve all taxation as well as declarations of war; the religious toleration enshrined in the Compact of Warsaw was to be preserved. The nobles not only had the right to resist a king who violated his oath, they had a positive duty to do so. Henry had hardly arrived in his new kingdom, however, before he received news of his brother's death and his accession as King of France (see Chapter 5). He abandoned his new subjects and rushed back to France, without formally abdicating the throne, leaving a political vacuum in Poland.

In 1575, the absent Henry was formally deposed by the *Sejm* and a new king was elected. He was Stephen Bathory, Prince of Transylvania. An effective and attractive ruler, Bathory, though a Catholic, was politically adept and he understood the need for toleration in his new kingdom. Together, he and his Chancellor, John Zamyoski, were able to encourage the expansion of the Catholic Reformation in Poland without causing too much resentment among the nobles.

Bathory was also able to pursue the war with Russia over Livonia to a successful conclusion. In the Treaty of Yam Zapolski (1582), Russia gave up all its claims to Livonia, thereby ending Ivan IV's quest for a Russian presence on the Baltic, a quest that would not be fulfilled until the reign of Peter the Great more than a century later. With Bathory's death in 1586, the nobles elected as their new king Sigismund III Vasa, the Catholic son of John III of Sweden and his wife Anna, sister of Sigismund II (see above). Both countries were wary of Russia, and both found themselves at odds with the Hanseatic League and Denmark, so from a diplomatic point of view the union of the kingdoms made some sense. When his father died in 1592, Sigismund became king of Sweden as well as Poland. But Sigismund's Catholic zeal and intolerance soon alienated him from his Swedish subjects, as we have seen. Nor did his religious intolerance and apparent desire to strengthen royal power at the expense of the nobles endear him to his Polish subjects. In 1605 he married a Habsburg princess without the *Sejm*'s consent. Further, he stated his desire to invade Sweden and restore his authority there, and, in order to do so, he proposed a standing army, permanent taxation, and majority voting in the *Sejm*. These measures provoked an armed rebellion of the nobility and the Protestants, and Sigismund was forced to back down and accept the principle that the *Sejm* could depose the king if he acted against the constitution, meaning the entrenched power of the nobles.

Sigismund III tried to build on the gains made against Russia by his predecessor and perhaps gain the Russian throne for himself or his son. In this he was aided by the instability of the "Time of Troubles" that followed the death of Ivan the Terrible. In 1610, Polish armies conquered Moscow and held it for a year. In 1618 they attacked the city again, this time unsuccessfully. Although Sigismund was able to conquer and hold Smolensk, the benefit to Poland was small, and it was a continual sore spot in relations with Russia. Sigismund's main concern, however, was recovering his Swedish kingdom and Estonia. As we saw above, he was successful in recovering Estonia from his uncle Charles IX, conquests that were later reversed by Gustavus Adolphus, who conquered Livonia besides.

By the time of his death in 1632, Sigismund had met with defeat on all fronts. Not only had he failed to enhance royal authority in Poland, his inflexibility and intolerance had in fact weakened that authority and instead strengthened the political control of the nobles. His almost obsessive desire to recover his Swedish lands (he never renounced his claim to the Swedish throne) resulted in the loss of Estonia and Livonia and the decline of Polish power on the shores of the Baltic. His attempts to meddle in Russia and the conquest of Smolensk incensed the Russians without fatally weakening them. The unhappy reign of Sigismund III confirmed and cemented Poland's decline, which ultimately led to the kingdom's disappearance in the eighteenth century.

Sigismund was followed on the throne by two of his sons: Ladislaus IV (1632–48) and Johan Casimir (1648–68). On the surface, the early seventeenth century appears to be something of a golden age. The Baltic grain trade was at its height, although the profits benefitted the great nobles more than the peasants, townsmen or king. Although the King was Catholic (Johan Casimir had been a Jesuit and became a cardinal), and the most important posts at court and in the government were reserved for Catholics, the various elements in Poland's religious landscape managed to coexist peacefully for the most part, and the country avoided the religious fratricide then raging in Germany. For twenty years, there was peace abroad and prosperity at home. Yet neither of the last two Vasa kings was able to stop the process of decentralization and the gradual dismemberment of the royal government. Wars with Sweden (1654–60) and Russia (1632–34 and 1654–67) proved disastrous and ended Poland's pretensions to compete for domination in the Baltic. Henceforth, supremacy in the Baltic and in northern Europe was contested between Sweden and Russia and would lead to the Great Northern War of 1700 to 1721.

Yet the greatest blow to Poland's fortunes came from within. In 1647, the *hetman* or chief of the Dnieper Cossacks, Bogdan Chmielnicki, launched a rebellion against the King. The reasons are not entirely clear, but they may have had to do with his feeling slighted over the loss of a military command against the Crimean Tartars. As the rebellion dragged on, both Sweden and Russia took advantage of Poland's troubles, themselves launching invasions. Chaos reigned, as the Swedes occupied Warsaw and Chmielnicki transferred his allegiance to Tsar Alexis of Russia. In order to fight the Cossack rebellion and the foreign invaders, Johan Casimir proposed majority voting in the *Sejm* and a central treasury. His plans were strongly resisted by the nobles, and this resistance resulted in civil war. In 1668, Johan Casimir abdicated his throne and retired to France.

By the middle of the seventeenth century, then, Poland was no longer able to function as an effective state. Its one partly effective king was John Sobieski (1674–96), who made a glorious name for himself fighting the Turks, especially in 1683 when he led a Polish army to lift the siege of Vienna (see Chapter 16). By sheer force of personality, he was able to put together and lead the fractious Polish nobles in battle. Yet, rather than attempt to revive the royal government (which was probably impossible anyway), he spent most of his reign fighting the Turks. The net result was the further weakening of Poland at the expense of its neighbours: Russia, Austria, and the rising power of Brandenburg-Prussia. In three partitions in the later eighteenth century, Poland would disappear from the map, gobbled up by its three powerful neighbours.

Muscovy and Russia

In the later Middle Ages, "Russia" was a geographic or cultural, rather than political, concept. The state that had dominated the Russian cultural sphere earlier in the Middle Ages was based in the city of Kiev, and it had been destroyed by the Mongol invasions of the thirteenth century. It was succeeded by a constellation of rulers and states that owed allegiance and tribute to the Mongol khans, or rulers, of the Golden Horde, one of the successor states of Genghis Khan's empire. These rulers were continually at each other's throats as they jostled for power and territory. One of these rulers, and by no means the most powerful, was the Grand Prince of Moscow.

Yet by the sixteenth century, Muscovy (as it was known) had become the pre-eminent Russian state. Its rise was facilitated by several factors. One was its geographic position in the midst of a network of rivers, which made it a natural entrepôt for trade and communication. It was also well north of the grasslands or steppe, which were dominated by Mongol cavalry. It was also fortunate in the longevity and consistency of its rulers, the Grand Princes. In the two centuries from 1389 to 1584, Muscovy had only five rulers. These rulers proved particularly adept at manipulating the khans of the Golden Horde at the expense of their Russian rivals.

There was also a religious aspect to Muscovy's rise to power. The Russians had been converted to Christianity by missionaries from the Greek Orthodox Byzantine Empire, rather than from Catholic Rome. At a fairly early date, the Grand Prince of Moscow had succeeded in establishing himself as the chief patron and protector of the Orthodox Church in the Russian lands. The church's chief official, or metropolitan, was appointed by the patriarch of Constantinople and was usually resident in Moscow. With the fall of Constantinople to the Ottoman Turks in 1453 and the end of the Byzantine Empire, the Orthodox Church in Russia became virtually independent, and Moscow began its career as the "Third Rome," greatly adding to the prestige of its rulers. In western Europe, political and cultural boundaries cut across allegiance to the Roman Catholic Church, and the Protestant Reformation further fragmented religious allegiance. In Russia, on the other hand, culture, nationality, and religion all combined in a potent mixture. To a great extent, to be Russian was to be Orthodox, and vice versa. This sense of Russia's holy national mission would take on an even greater significance when the metropolitan of Moscow was raised to the rank of patriarch in 1589. This conflation of politics and religion would also pose some very serious difficulties over the course of Russian history.

It was during the reigns of Ivan III (the Great, r. 1462–1505) and his successor Vasilii III (1505–33) that the point of no return was passed in Muscovy's domination of Russia. Perhaps the most dramatic evidence of this is the territorial expansion that took place. In 1533, the Grand Prince of Moscow ruled an area three times the size of what he had ruled in 1462. Most importantly, Ivan III annexed the wealthy and powerful urban republic of Novgorod, with its vast lands in northern Russia. Much of Novgorod's lands were confiscated and granted to Ivan's loyal supporters, but on conditional tenure or *pomeste*; that is, continued ownership of these lands was conditional on loyal service to the Grand Prince. Ivan thus provided himself with a relatively inexpensive army. This also highlights one of the basic political and social differences between Russia and western Europe. In Russia, the nobility was much more closely linked to the ruler and his service, and it had less of a local or provincial power base than in the west. Therefore, political scheming among Russian nobles was usually over influence in

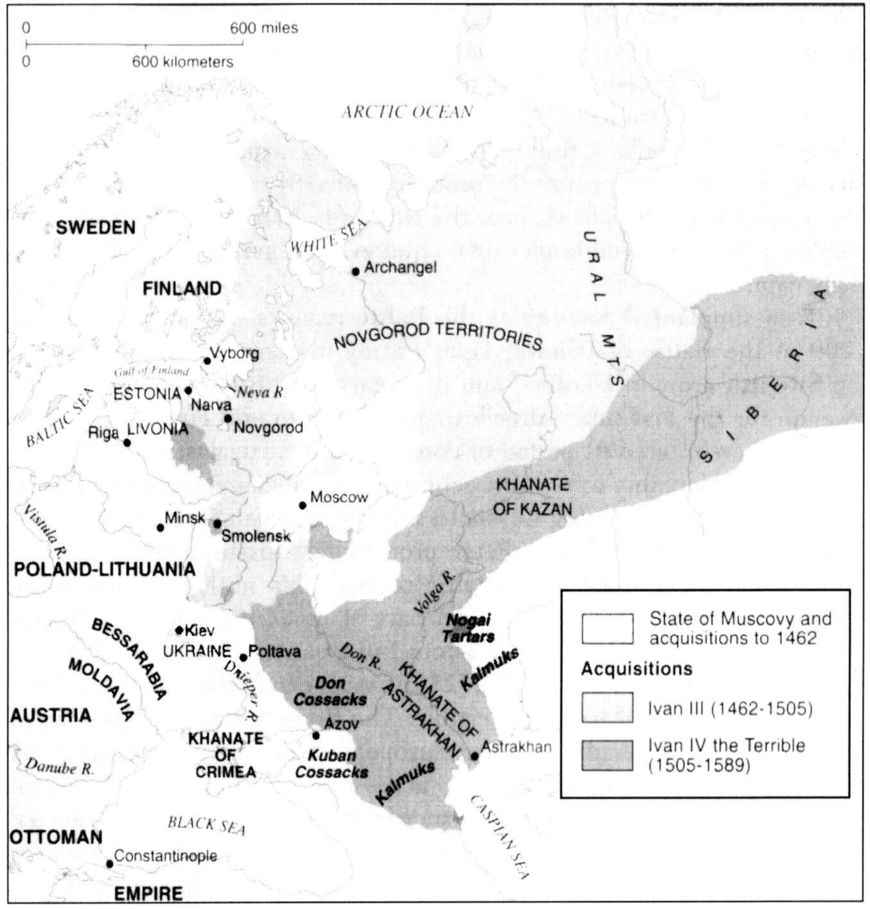

MAP 13.2 ⇶ THE GROWTH OF MUSCOVY IN THE 16TH CENTURY

the government rather than over attempts to establish or maintain local or regional autonomy.

Ivan III was also the first Russian ruler to consistently use the title of tsar, or emperor, derived from the Latin *cæsar*. In doing so, he laid claim to undisputed sovereignty over all the lands occupied by Russian-speaking Orthodox Christians. This inevitably brought conflict with Poland-Lithuania, in which, as we have seen, there was a sizable minority of Orthodox Russians. It was also during Ivan's reign that Russia's independence from the Mongols was finally established, as he refused to pay the tribute demanded by the khans. Furthermore, during Ivan's reign the trend toward autocracy was confirmed. Through his use of conditional tenure, he ensured the loyalty and service of the most important nobles or *boyars*. Like his royal counterparts in western Europe, he made extensive use of commoners without a power base of their own in his administration. Contemporary observers from western Europe noted the contrast to their homelands. As one visitor wrote during Vasilii's reign, "in the sway which he [the Tsar] holds over his people, he surpasses the monarchs of the whole world. ... "

In diplomacy, Ivan clashed repeatedly with the Grand Dukes of Lithuania to the west. Relations were complicated, as we have seen, by the fact that a large number of the Grand Duke's subjects were Orthodox Russians. In addition, Lithuania stood between landlocked Muscovy and an outlet on the Baltic Sea. In a series of conflicts, Ivan III managed eventually to seize the important city of Smolensk, but this was the last Muscovite territorial gain in the west for more than a century.

In all important respects, Ivan's son and successor Vasilii III continued his father's policies. When he died in 1533, he was succeeded by his infant son, Ivan IV, the Terrible (1533–84). During Ivan's childhood, the *boyars* schemed and plotted against each other for domination of the young ruler and the government. Yet, unlike similar crises in western European monarchies, this period of royal weakness never threatened to dismember the state. For unlike the great nobles in France or Spain, for example, the *boyars*' power was centred in the court and central government, rather than in provincial power bases. Nevertheless, the period of confusion and *boyar* domination made an indelible impression on the young Ivan, causing him to fear and resent the nobles. Incidentally, when Ivan was finally crowned in 1547, he was the first Muscovite ruler to be invested with the title of tsar at his coronation.

Ivan the Terrible[2] was a mercurial and temperamental ruler who has gained a largely deserved reputation for cruelty and sadism. It seems likely that a good deal of this irascibility stemmed from chronic illness and the alcohol and drugs in which he indulged to alleviate his pain. Nevertheless, the early years of Ivan's reign were a time of significant achievement. The government was rationalized and streamlined through the creation of a series of bodies or chanceries to administer the various functions of the government. A new legal code was introduced in 1550. The army was strengthened through the creation of six companies of infantry musketeers, or *streltsy*, and the streamlining of command structures to reduce the jousting for precedence among noble commanders. In order to achieve these reforms, Ivan relied on the input and cooperation of a new kind of assembly, made up of ecclesiastical and lay members. This was the *zemskii sobor*, or "assembly of the land," roughly analogous to the various popular assemblies in the states of western Europe, such as the English Parliament, Spanish *cortes*, or French estates.

Ivan's first forays into diplomacy were directed to the south and east, and they were very successful. By 1560, Russian forces had conquered the khanates of Kazan and Astrakhan, which gave Ivan control of the River Volga and access to the Caspian Sea. This opened the door to Russian influence in the Middle East and paved the way for eventual further expansion eastwards into Siberia. This was also the first time that non-Russian and non-Orthodox (and even non-Christian) peoples came under the rule of the tsars. From now on, Russian governments would wrestle with the problems of ruling peoples different in ethnicity, culture, and religion. Rather than pursue this military success further south to the

Crimea and the Black Sea, Ivan decided to pursue westward expansion, a decision that was to have fateful consequences. His target was Livonia (roughly modern Latvia). As we have seen, however, this territory, as well as the whole eastern Baltic, was coveted by both Poland and Sweden as well. Some initial Russian successes prompted Polish intervention, and by the early 1560s Russian conquests had stalled. Seeking a scapegoat for the failure of his foreign policy, Ivan struck out at the *boyars*.

Indeed, Ivan's attitude toward the *boyars* had long been poisonous, given the experiences of his childhood. Relations were further embittered in 1553 when the Tsar fell gravely ill. He attempted to secure the *boyars*' loyalty to his infant son Dmitri, in the event of his death. Many of the *boyars* hesitated, remembering the disorders of an infant ruler during Ivan's childhood, and preferring instead an adult cousin of the Tsar. Now, in the mid-1560s, Ivan lashed out against the *boyars*. A number were imprisoned or executed for supposed collusion with the enemy, including one who was dragged out of a church before being murdered. In 1565, the Tsar made a startling announcement. Faced with the hostility and recalcitrance of the *boyars* who had impeded his goals, he announced his abdication from the throne. Faced with the loss of their ruler and the potential for instability and chaos, the leaders of the government and the church begged Ivan to reconsider. Ivan relented, but at a high price, for he announced his intention to create a separate administration, or *oprichnina*, for the support of the Tsar and his household.

Approximately one half of the country was assigned to Ivan's *oprichnina*, which became in essence the Tsar's personal property. The rest of the country, or *zemshchina*, was to be administered by the *boyar* council, or Duma, with only the most important matters of state to be referred to the Tsar. Ivan's precise reasons for creating the *oprichnina* remain obscure and much debated by historians. In large part, it was intended to punish specific *boyars* for their alleged treason, as their lands were confiscated and incorporated into the *oprichnina*. It also struck at the root of *boyar* power, as lands within the *oprichnina* were held under conditional tenure at the Tsar's pleasure. Ivan used his *oprichnina* lands to reward supporters and punish supposed enemies. Within the *oprichnina*, peasants were forbidden to leave the land and were subject to oppressive conditions. This prompted many to run away, which only worsened conditions for those left behind. Opposition to the *oprichnina* was widespread among both nobles and peasants and was brutally repressed, giving rise to the Tsar's nickname of the "Terrible." The Tsar's opponents, real or imagined, were subject to Ivan's paranoia and cruelty; they included Metropolitan Filipp of the Orthodox Church, who was deposed and strangled on Ivan's orders. Ivan also attacked and sacked the large and prosperous city of Novgorod, supposedly because of its plotting with the King of Poland.

The *oprichnina* was disastrous for Russia. It brought political instability and economic chaos. The existence of two parallel governments made rational administration impossible. The disorders of the *oprichnina* fatally damaged foreign policy as well. In 1571 the Khan of the Crimean Tartars attacked Moscow itself, and most of the city was burned to the ground. Russia was also forced to relinquish its Baltic ambitions in the Treaty of Yam Zapolski (1582) with Poland. Therefore, in 1572, Ivan abolished the *oprichnina* and reintegrated the two realms, but the damage had been done.

Nor was Ivan the Terrible's poisonous legacy complete. His personal life was just as chaotic as his government, and it would plunge Russia into chaos and civil war after his death. He personally killed his eldest surviving son Ivan in a fit of rage. A few hours later, the prince's pregnant wife miscarried. Ivan the Terrible thus destroyed both his son and heir and his grandchild in one fell swoop. His second son and eventual successor Fedor was completely unsuited to rule. His only other child was an infant named Dmitri, the product of a seventh marriage, whose legitimacy was very doubtful.

Ivan the Terrible died in 1584, leaving behind a very troubled country. Despite the promise and achievements of the early part of his reign, his policies, particularly the *oprichnina*, did terrible damage to the fabric of politics and society. From 1584 until 1613, Russia endured a near-complete political, social, and economic collapse known as the Time of Troubles. Ivan's immediate successor was his son Fedor I (1584–98). Fedor was a saintly imbecile and completely unable to rule, so real power was exercised by the Tsar's brother-in-law, Boris Godunov. Godunov had risen to Ivan the Terrible's favour through the *oprichnina* and had been rewarded by his sister's marriage to Fedor. By all accounts, Godunov was an able and intelligent ruler and did what he could to solve the crises that faced the country. He granted the nobles a partial tax exemption in order to enhance their ability to serve in the army; he also further restricted the rights of peasants in order to assist the nobles, further advancing serfdom in Russia. But the severity of the problems he faced very likely would have prevailed over *any* sixteenth-century ruler. War with the Crimean Tartars, Poland, and Sweden all compounded the problems Godunov faced, and in diplomacy and warfare, he was about as successful as could be expected. In the west, there was a virtual stalemate with Poland and Sweden, not an inconsiderable achievement given the dynastic union of the two kingdoms and Russia's dire domestic position. Likewise in the south, Russian forces managed to put an end to the raids of the Crimean Tartars for the time being. In the east, Russian expansion reached well into Siberia.

In 1591, further tragedy struck when Fedor's younger brother Dmitri died in an accident while playing with friends. Boris Godunov was strongly (but in all likelihood, falsely) suspected of having him killed in order to further his own ambitions to be tsar. When Fedor died childless in 1598, Godunov was in fact able to seize the throne and have himself crowned tsar.

Although Godunov was able to rule as Tsar until his death in 1605, his lack of a legitimate connection to the ruling dynasty effectively handicapped him. Moreover, a series of poor harvests led to widespread famine and unrest. Peasants abandoned their land in search of survival, and nobles ceased fulfilling their military and service obligations to the government. For nearly the next decade, political and social order was in a state of collapse. The royal government became the plaything of *boyar* factions. Several pretenders claiming to be the real Dimitri (who miraculously still lived!) laid claim to the throne. The first of these false "Dmitris" actually succeeded in taking power in Moscow for a time. To make matters worse, in 1609 the Poles conquered the important city of Smolensk, and in 1610 occupied Moscow. There was a serious movement to install as tsar Ladislaus, the son of the Polish king Sigismund III, which fell apart over his father's reluctance to see him convert to the Orthodox Church. Russia was confronted by a seemingly insoluble dilemma. One the one hand, the tradition of autocratic rule was so entrenched in Russian consciousness that there was no conceivable alternative. Centuries of historical development of the power of the Grand Princes of Moscow had obliterated any other way of thinking about political power. Yet, on the other hand, there was no obvious candidate for the role of autocratic ruler who could claim a legitimate connection to the former ruling dynasty. A foreign ruler, such as Prince Ladislaus of Poland, was really out of the question, given the inwardness of Russian society and the strong identification of the Muscovite state with Russian Orthodoxy. Selecting a native *boyar* as ruler also posed problems, for inevitably those not chosen and their families would feel resentful at the elevation of one of their number.

Yet this is precisely what happened. In 1612 the Polish garrison that had controlled Moscow was expelled, and a *zemski sobor* was called together to elect a new tsar. The man chosen was Michael Romanov, a teenaged prince of one of the handful of the most distinguished *boyar* clans. Michael's advantages were several. He did have a legitimate connection with the former royal dynasty, as Ivan the Terrible's first and much-loved wife was a Romanov. Michael's father Filaret was therefore a cousin of the last indisputably legitimate tsar, Fedor I. Yet as a youth of sixteen, Michael was not considered a threat to the *boyars*' control of the government. Filaret, Michael's father, was a clergyman and statesman of importance, and in 1618 he was named Patriarch of Moscow. Indeed, until his death in 1633, Filaret was the real ruler of Russia.

All things considered, order was restored to Russian society and government relatively quickly and completely, given the social and political collapse of the Time of Troubles. This is a testament to just how effective the Grand Princes of Moscow had been in their construction of an autocratic state in close alliance with Russian Orthodoxy. When Michael died in 1645, he was succeeded without incident by his son Alexei (1645–76). Internally, Russia continued to develop along the lines laid down by the Grand Princes of Moscow and Ivan the Terrible. The Tsar ruled as autocrat, but he was dependent on the nobility to make his authority effective throughout Russia's vast territory. In turn, the government made no attempt to interfere with the nobility's management of their estates. Indeed, it was in the mid-seventeenth century that serfdom was legally entrenched as the foundation of the Russian economy and society.

Externally, Michael and Filaret made peace with Sweden with the 1617 Treaty of Stolbovo, but at the high cost of recognizing Swedish control over the eastern

Baltic. Russia thus remained cut off from the Baltic and from relatively easy access to western Europe. Peace with Poland was more elusive and the rulers of the two countries remained mutually hostile, fighting two wars in 1632–34 and 1654–67. At the same time, Russia continued to expand eastwards into Siberia, reaching the Pacific coast by 1700.

The close identification of Russian Orthodoxy with political authority was sorely tested in the mid-seventeenth century, causing a long-lived schism with the Orthodox Church and contributing to a very serious rebellion. The roots of this conflict lay in Russia's increasing ties with western Europe and the suspicions they aroused among many Russians. Influenced by increasing contacts with western European scholarship, Patriarch Nikon (1652–66) became convinced that a number of corruptions and variations had crept into Russian Orthodox doctrine and liturgy. These involved such seemingly trivial issues as crossing oneself with three fingers rather than two, bowing only to the waist rather than to the ground, and the proper Russian spelling of the name of Jesus. With the initial support of Tsar Alexei, Nikon was determined to correct them. Nikon, however, was arrogant and headstrong, and he failed to take into account the very traditional nature of the beliefs of many Russians, who saw these innovations as the mark of the Antichrist. Nikon's reforms were strongly resisted by many, despite their official adoption by the government. These "Old Believers" in many cases preferred martyrdom to conformity, and many of them fled to the margins of Russia, where they were basically immune from government power. Ironically, by this time Nikon and Alexei had fallen out over the former's high-handed ways and claims to political power for the Church.

Many of the Old Believers fled to the south, where they joined with the Cossacks of the grasslands, or steppes. While nominal subjects of the Tsar, the various groups of Cossacks had their own chief, or *hetman*, were fiercely independent and obeyed the government (or not) at their leisure. In 1670, Stepan (Stenka) Razin, a leader of the Don Cossacks, launched a rebellion against Moscow. Soon, Razin attracted all sorts of disaffected elements of Russian society to his cause: not only Cossacks, but also serfs and Old Believers, overtaxed townspeople, and soldiers. As his army advanced up the River Volga toward Moscow, serfs rose up in rebellion and drove out or murdered the landlords. The rebel army, however, proved no match for the government's, and Razin was captured and taken to Moscow where he was horribly executed as a traitor. Without its leader, the revolt collapsed and the rebels were brutally suppressed.

Upon Alexei's death in 1676, he was succeeded by his eldest son Fedor, who died himself in 1682. The succession was complicated by the fact that Tsar Alexei had married twice, and the families of his two wives were bitter political rivals. As a compromise, in 1682, Fedor's younger brother Ivan and his younger half-brother Peter were proclaimed co-tsars, with their elder sister Sophia as regent. At the time, no one could have imagined that ten-year-old Peter would one day overthrow his sister in a bloody coup and transform Russia into a European power as Peter the Great.

NOTES

1 Michael Roberts, *Gustavus Adolphus*, 2nd ed. (London: Longman, 1992) 189, 190–91.

2 The Russian word *grozny*, which is usually translated as "terrible" in reference to Ivan, also carries the connotation of "awesome" or "dreaded" in addition to "terrible" in its more usual meaning in English.

CHAPTER FOURTEEN

France under Louis XIV, 1661–1715

The Personal Reign of Louis XIV

When Cardinal Mazarin died in 1661, Louis XIV, then 23 years old, determined that he would not be replaced, that he himself would actually govern as well as reign. And in fact, Louis XIV did just this for the rest of his long reign, until his death in 1715. One of the young king's first acts upon Mazarin's death was the arrest and imprisonment of Nicolas Fouquet. Fouquet had served as finance minister under Mazarin and had been one of the government's staunchest supporters during the Fronde. He was wealthy and highly cultivated, and he patronized some of the leading artists of the day. He had built himself a château at Vaux-le-Vicomte, southeast of Paris, which was a showpiece of architecture, decoration, and landscape design. Fouquet himself, and many others, had assumed that he would take over from Mazarin, and he acted as if he already had. Egged on by Fouquet's rivals, primarily Jean-Baptiste Colbert, and his own fear of being dominated by a chief minister, the young king determined to punish Fouquet in such a way that his fate would underline his determination to rule as well as to reign. Fouquet was tried on trumped-up charges of financial corruption. He was certainly guilty, but then so was everyone involved in the royal fiscal system. For the rest of his life (he died in 1680), he was imprisoned in the remote alpine fortress of Pinerolo. From then on, it was clear to everyone that Louis *did* mean to govern as well as to reign.

Indeed, Louis XIV was ideally suited to fill the role of an absolute monarch. He had an iron constitution, which enabled him to live a long life despite the ministrations of his physicians. He had tremendous endurance, necessary for the mind-numbing rituals demanded by court protocol as well as the day-to-day business of government. Here is one historian's colourful description of the *levée*, the King's ceremonial rising from bed every morning:

> It was perhaps as well that the courtier had no inducement to linger abed of a morning, for it behoved him to make an early start if he was

> to be at his post in the ante-room when the King was awakened at eight o'clock. (We are inclined at this time of the day to envy the ladies, who are still in bed, and will not be making a move until nine.) The courtier had had his own toilet to make, which, if it did not include washing, meant an elaborate powdering and prinking, before attending his patron's *lever* and following him to that of the King. In the King's room the day began at about a quarter to eight, when the First Valet de Chambre, who had slept in the room, would dismantle and put away his folding bed; if it was winter, the two *porte-buchon du roi*, the royal faggot bearers, would next make their appearance to light the King's fire, followed a minute or two later by the King's watchmaker to wind up the royal watch. From a side door would enter the royal wigmaker, coming from the room in which the King's wigs reposed, each on its pedestal, in glass-fronted wardrobes—hunting wigs, council wigs, evening wigs, walking wigs, an endless array of wigs. But at the moment the wigmaker carries two only, the short wig which the King wears whilst dressing, and the first wig of the day. All this time Louis would be in bed asleep, or pretending to be so, with the bedclothes turned down to his hips, as is his uncomfortable custom, winter and summer. On the first stroke of eight his valet would wake him, and the exciting news that His Majesty was awake would pass into the closely packed ante-room to set the courtiers rustling like a field of ripe corn in a summer breeze. At the same moment the First Physician and the First Surgeon entered the room, together with the King's old nurse, who went up to the bed, kissed him, and asked how he had slept, whilst the two medical men rubbed the King down and changed his shirt. At a quarter-past eight the Grand Chamberlain was admitted, together with those courtiers who had the coveted *grandes entrées*, and Louis was presented with Holy Water. Now was the time to ask the King a favour, we are told, which suggests that in this, as in so many other respects, his psychology differed considerably from that of ordinary mortals.[1]

At night, the process was reversed in the *couchée*, or ceremonial retiring of the King to his bed.

Although he was not extremely well educated in a formal sense, he did receive a valuable political education from Cardinal Mazarin. He was smart enough to be able to carry out his functions, but not so smart that he was bored by them. Most of all, he had immense sense of his own worth and dignity. The French word used for this was *gloire*, which is difficult to translate in a way that does justice to its connotations, but "reputation" or "renown" comes close. *Gloire* conveys the sense that not only must Louis be the greatest monarch in Europe; he must also be acknowledged to be so.

The personal reign of Louis XIV is full of contrasts and contradictions. It would bring absolute monarchy in France and French power in Europe to their height, but it would also reveal the fundamental weaknesses both in the French state and in absolute monarchy. Louis's ambitious and egotistical foreign policy would enable France to challenge virtually all the other powers of Europe, but at a very significant cost, both to the royal treasury and government and to ordinary people. The glittering court life at Versailles has sometimes led observers to mistake the illusion for the reality and has overshadowed both the realities of political and social life and the miseries that the King's policies compounded. Nor is Louis's reign notable for any great innovation in his methods of government and administration. Rather, he continued and built upon the foundations laid by Henry IV, and Louis XIII and Cardinal Richelieu.

Although Louis was determined to rule without a chief minister, obviously one man could not do everything alone. He therefore required advisors and ministers on whom he could rely. In this he was particularly fortunate, especially in the earlier part of his reign, when he relied on a group of ministers who had come to political maturity under Richelieu and Mazarin. But Louis was always careful not to let any one minister attain a position of dominance in the government. Indeed, he encouraged rivalry among his ministers and their extended networks of kin and clients. In this way, it was clear that the final decision on any matter rested with Louis, and Louis alone. Once, when Jean-Baptiste Colbert, one of his most important ministers, continued to argue a point after a royal decision had been made, Louis dressed him down with the following words:

> I was master enough of myself the day before yesterday to conceal from you the sorrow I felt in hearing a man whom I had overwhelmed with benefits ... speak to me the way you did. I have been very friendly towards you.... I still have such a feeling, and I believe that I am giving you real proof of it by telling you that I restrained myself for a single moment for your sake.... It is the memory of services that you have rendered me, and my friendship, which have caused me to do so. Profit thereby and do not risk vexing me again, because after I have heard your arguments and those of your colleagues, and have given my opinion on all of your claims, I never wish to hear more about it. ... I am telling you my thoughts so that you may work on an assured basis and so that you will not make any false steps.

Louis selected his ministers from among the elite of the robe nobility, former middle-class families who had been recently ennobled through royal service. This has led to the misconception that he chose his servants from among the "vile bourgeoisie." This phrase comes from the memoirs of the Duke of Saint-Simon, an acid-tongued contemporary who resented his lack of influence and political power. On the other hand, Louis did keep away from the levers of real power: the great nobles of the sword. In other words, Louis's ministers had no provincial power base of their own outside of the King's favour. They were dependent on the King, and should they lose his favour, they were in no position to mount a rebellion such as the Fronde. Among his most important ministers were two he had inherited from Mazarin, Jean-Baptiste Colbert and Michel le Tellier, and later le Tellier's son, the Marquis of Louvois. Significantly, Louis pitted them against each other, to keep either from dominating.

Jean-Baptiste Colbert (1619–83) came from a family of wholesale cloth merchants in Reims. He held several different posts in the bureaucracy before becoming Cardinal Mazarin's personal secretary. After the cardinal's death, he ingratiated himself with the King by leading the campaign against Fouquet. Indeed, after Fouquet's disgrace, Colbert stepped into his shoes as finance minister. In fact, however, Colbert became much more than finance minister. As well as being one of the King's closest advisors, he became a sort of super minister of finance, trade, and industry.

In government finances, Colbert realized the fundamental problems with the system—the tax exemption of the nobility, the sale of offices, and widespread graft and corruption—and he was full of plans for wide-ranging reform. But a thorough reform could be carried out only with the King's whole-hearted support, which he did not get, since Louis was primarily concerned with establishing and burnishing his *gloire* in diplomacy and warfare. As a result, Colbert had to be satisfied with cleaning things up around the edges. For example, he drove harder bargains with tax collectors and financiers, to ensure that more of the revenue collected actually went into the royal treasury, rather than lining the pockets of greedy or corrupt officials. As a result, the burden of the *taille* (the major direct tax, which fell overwhelmingly on peasants) actually went down during Colbert's tenure in office.

As a merchant's son, Colbert understood that the best way to improve government finances was through general prosperity, and so he was an economic reformer as well. His economic reforms were based on the principles of mercantilism, as discussed in Chapter 3. He encouraged and subsidized industries within France in order to discourage imports. High tariff barriers were created to keep imports out. Virtually all trades were intensively regulated and controlled. Colbert also encouraged overseas trade, setting up trading companies to compete with the Dutch and the English in Asia and the New World. It was at this time that the French colonial empire in New France and the West Indies became a reality. To carry and protect this trade he increased the merchant marine and the French navy. In 1661, the French navy possessed only eighteen serviceable ships; by 1683, it had nearly 150. Colbert was keenly conscious of the maritime advantages of the English and Dutch and was anxious to catch up and surpass them.

All of these efforts had mixed results. For one thing, despite the best efforts of Colbert and the bureaucracy, these reforms were met with a great deal of resistance or inertia on the part of ordinary people, and the government simply did not have the wherewithal to rigorously and consistently enforce them. Moreover, government encouragement of industry tended to focus on luxury goods with small markets, rather than basic goods that could have made a real difference in the economy. Thus industries such as silk, porcelain, and tapestries were favoured rather than metallurgy or agriculture. Most importantly, perhaps, Colbert was attempting his economic reforms in an unfavourable climate. As we saw in Chapter 3, the later seventeenth century was in general a time of stagnant or declining economic prospects.

In terms of foreign trade, in one sense Colbert's policies were self-defeating. His mercantilist assumptions made him believe that the only way to increase France's share of commerce was to decrease that of others, primarily the Dutch, who were the dominant commercial power of the day. His anti-Dutch commercial policies were one factor that led to war with the Dutch Republic in 1672. War in turn placed great strain on the economy and fiscal system, which killed any long-term hopes of fundamental reform. Nevertheless, by his death in 1683, Colbert had substantially improved government finances. If he failed to transform the economy in the way he wanted, it was because the King had other priorities, and because of the general economic picture of the later seventeenth century.

Michel le Tellier (1603–85), like Colbert, was descended from a family of merchants who had established themselves in the venal bureaucracy. In 1643 he became minister of war under Mazarin, a post he was to retain when Louis XIV assumed control of the government in 1661. Together with his son, François-Michel le Teller, Marquis of Louvois (1641–91), he succeeded in drastically reforming the French army. Even during his life, le Tellier was closely assisted by his son, who assumed his father's posts when his father died in 1685. In fact, the two worked so closely together that it is difficult to differentiate between them. Prior to these reforms, the French army had been an unwieldy combination of mercenaries and semi-independent units under noble commanders. These commanders in turn had purchased their commissions, without much regard for ability or experience. Once in the field, generals (always powerful nobles) pursued their goals with a great deal of independence from the king or minister of war. Under le Tellier and Louvois, senior commanders were appointed on the basis of seniority rather than birth. Although commissions were still venal in nature, officers were provided with more regular pay, which lessened the temptation or necessity to skim from the money intended for the soldiers. Strict inspections ensured that the soldiers being paid for were actually present. Stricter discipline was prescribed through the publication of codes and enforced through brutal punishments for offenders. The construction of barracks in frontier towns lessened the burden on civilian populations. Likewise, the establishment of storehouses reduced the need for soldiers to live off the countryside and its inhabitants. One mark of this growing, if still imperfect, discipline was the adoption of regular uniforms beginning in the 1670s. In addition, commanders in the field were subject to much stricter central control by the minister of war and the king. The size of the army also increased throughout Louis's reign. In 1667 it consisted of 72,000; in 1703 it reached its greatest size when almost 400,000 men were under arms. It was by far the largest and most powerful army of its day.

To accomplish all these things, to say nothing of carrying out the day-to-day business of government, Louis and his ministers obviously needed some means of enforcing their will throughout France. At the centre of the government were the King and his closest ministers, who met virtually every day and decided the important matters of policy. There were a number of other councils that met regularly to oversee specific government functions: foreign affairs, finance, and so on.

The supreme law courts, or *parlements*, gave Louis little trouble, for the Fronde had demonstrated what happened when they tried to limit the power of the King. Indeed, the King and the *parlements* needed each other. No royal edict was legally effective until registered by the *parlement*; by the same token, the *parlement*'s power was clearly derived from the judicial functions of the King. Louis understood that there was little to be gained by humiliating the *parlements*. For most of the reign, the King and his judges understood each other: each had a legitimate role to play, and neither of them could gain anything by trying to unduly limit the power of the other. This relationship is an excellent example of a king taming the society of orders. The judges of the *parlement* (who had bought or inherited their positions) retained both their important legal functions and their extensive rights, liberties, and social prestige. At the same time, they mostly worked as buttresses rather than as critics of royal authority.

Cities and towns throughout France traditionally had a great deal of independence, with their own elected governments, fortifications, civic militia, and powers of justice and taxation. Here, too, the royal government enhanced its power without entirely eliminating the rights and liberties of towns. In 1692, a royal decree declared that mayors were to be appointed by the king rather than elected. However, this was only partly a measure to enhance administrative efficiency: these posts were sold, very often to the same men who would have been mayors in any case.

This observation highlights the fact that the absolute monarchy of Louis XIV did not in any way replace the personal and haphazard administrative methods derived from the Middle Ages with a modernized, bureaucratic administration. Historians who have maintained that it did have mistaken appearance for reality. This is particularly apparent when we look at the functions of the *intendants*. As we have seen, when widespread use of *intendants* was first made under Louis XIII and Richelieu during the 1630s, they were seen as periodic trouble-shooters and hatchet men. Although abolished during the Fronde, *intendants* gradually came back into use, and during the reign of Louis XIV they were integrated into the regular machinery of government. Even so, they did not supplant or replace the existing administrative structure; their instructions stressed that they were to work within the established system whenever possible. Their primary function was collecting and relaying information to the central government, and relaying royal policies and orders to the local bureaucracy. They represent a tiny step in the bureaucratization of government, not a governmental revolution. This is hardly surprising, since there were only about 30 *intendants*, compared to around 65,000 venal bureaucrats. Moreover, most of the available evidence indicates that the *intendants* operated in much the same way as the more traditional venal office-holders, that is, through building up networks of clients and influence among local elites.

The government of Louis XIV also created the new office of lieutenant-general of police to keep order in Paris. Jurisdiction over the kingdom's capital and largest city was divided between and disputed by a number of different jurisdictions and officials, with the result that law enforcement was irregular at best. Paris could be very disorderly, as Louis no doubt recalled from his experiences as a boy during the Fronde, when a disorderly mob broke into the young king's bedroom in order to reassure themselves that the royal family had not fled the city. The lieutenant-general was appointed as a sort of coordinating official among the various bodies whose jurisdiction included Paris. His duties included not only law enforcement, but also "police" in the French sense of the term: regulation and administration. He was also charged, therefore, with issues such as sanitation, monitoring publications, and lighting the streets. The office was filled first by Nicolas de la Reynie, who held the office from its creation in 1667 until his death in 1697, and then by the Marquis d'Argenson (1697–1718).

However impressive the absolute monarchy of Louis XIV appears on paper, it was strictly limited in practice. France was still a patchwork of provinces with different customs, different laws, and even different languages. Some had their own representative assemblies, which Louis XIV did not eliminate, although in some cases he curtailed their power. In particular, as we have seen, there remained the venal office-holders, who needed to be coerced and cajoled and appeased, since they could not be fired. In fact, the venal bureaucracy was expanded during Louis's reign, much against the better judgement of Colbert and others. But the King's insatiable need for money, driven by his aggressive foreign policy, dictated that long-term reform was sacrificed for immediate revenue. A complete range of useless offices, like inspectors of oysters, was created, only to be sold. As one of Louis's ministers remarked, "every time Your Majesty creates an office, God creates a fool to buy it."

Louis and his agents could usually get their way, but by operating within the system, not by overthrowing it. In large part, absolute monarchy was a cooperative venture of the King and the elites to which the King contributed his prestige and the elites contributed their obedience, at least most of the time. The lubricant that made the system run smoothly was money, in the form of tax revenue. Local elites shared the spoils of power with the King and his government.

Religion: Jansenists and Huguenots

Louis XIV's relations with the Catholic Church were complicated, to say the least. On the one hand, he was "the Most Christian King," the heir of Clovis, Charlemagne, and St. Louis. On the other hand, his kingdom had a legally recognized religious minority of heretics in the Huguenots, or those of "the so-called reformed religion" as it was known (*la religion prétendue réformée*). Louis clearly wanted to restore religious uniformity, believing that religious pluralism detracted from his dignity and *gloire* as king. Yet the Catholic Church in France had a long tradition of gallicanism, or autonomy from Rome in matters of personnel, finance, and administration. This made relations with Rome problematic at best. In fact, the decrees of the Council of Trent had never been formally recognized in France, for fear that doing so might prejudice the "gallican liberties" of the French church.

Louis himself was a devout but conventional Catholic who saw himself as sort of an equal of God. In the royal chapel at Versailles, worshippers sat with their backs to the altar, facing the King. Thus they witnessed not the priest celebrating Mass, but rather the King watching the priest celebrate Mass. In the 1680s he became increasingly devout as he aged, largely under the influence of his mistress (and later his wife), Madame de Maintenon. This led to some complications that are evident in his relations with the Jansenists. Louis disliked the Jansenists for a number of reasons. First of all, they were dissenters; they did not neatly conform to the ideal of *un roi, une loi, une foi* (one king, one law, one faith). As with the Huguenots, Louis believed that they detracted from his reputation as the Most Christian King. They were also opposed by the Jesuits, who flattered Louis and his power, and whose moral casuistry could be used to justify almost anything the King wanted to do. The Jesuits were also very influential with Madame de Maintenon. Moreover, among the Jansenists there were a number of people and families who had been active in the Fronde. It was not that the Fronde had a religious dimension to it, but Jansenism was popular among some of the judges in the Parlement of Paris, and in Louis's mind, anyone or anything associated with the Fronde of his childhood was automatically suspect. Persecution began early in the personal reign but was soon stalled by the King's concern with other more pressing matters. The dispute was papered over by an agreement of 1668 known as the Peace of the Church.

In order to combat the Jansenists, Louis needed the support of the Pope, but there were a number of sore points in their relationship, primarily concerning finances and the Pope's power over the French church. These tensions were exacerbated during the pontificate of Innocent XI (1676–89), who admired the Jansenists' strict morality and was a strident defender of papal power. The bitterest conflict between France and Rome was over the *régale*. According to this practice, in much of northern France, during an episcopal vacancy the revenue from the vacant bishopric went to the royal treasury. During the 1670s the government unilaterally extended the *régale* to all of France. This extension was condemned by the Pope, and Louis convened a special Assembly of the Clergy, which in 1682 pronounced the "Four Articles." These articles summarized the Gallican position and were ordered to be taught in the universities. Pope Innocent responded by refusing to invest French bishops and excommunicating the French ambassador to Rome. However, Innocent died in 1689 and was replaced by a more amenable pope, while Louis himself became involved in a major war, prompting a reconciliation on terms largely favourable to Rome.

With the differences between the King and Rome resolved, persecution of the Jansenists resumed. Now, strangely, Louis and the Pope were cooperating in putting down the Jansenists, among whom were many judges and lawyers of the Parlement of Paris, the traditional stronghold of Gallican sentiment. Already forbidden to receive new novices, in 1709 the twelve nuns who remained at Port-Royal were expelled at swordpoint. In 1711, the convent was razed to the ground. These actions, however, only further inflamed tensions. In 1713, Louis XIV prevailed upon a reluctant pope, who issued the bull *Unigenitus*, decisively rejecting Jansenism as heresy. In its rush to condemn Jansenism, however, the papal bull exceeded its scope, denouncing theology that had long been accepted as orthodox Catholic teaching. The conflict continued long after Louis's death, demonstrating the resilience of the society of orders. Jansenists were well represented in the Parlement and the Sorbonne, two institutions that Louis disciplined and tamed but whose privileges and liberties he could not eliminate.

At the height of his struggle with Innocent XI in 1685, Louis had issued the Edict of Fontainebleau, which revoked the Edict of Nantes, at least partly in order to demonstrate his unimpeachable credentials as a Catholic ruler. Since at least 1678, the Edict of Nantes had been enforced with increasing strictness. Previously, Louis had been held in check by Colbert, who recognized that the Huguenots were a hard-working and valuable minority. Diplomatic considerations also played a role, as Louis needed alliances with foreign Protestant rulers. In addition, unlike the Jansenists, Louis bore the Huguenots no personal animosity. In fact, during the Fronde, the Huguenots had been the only major group who had remained completely loyal. But Colbert's great rival, Michel le Tellier, was gaining the upper hand in the government and was an advocate of harsher policies. When Colbert died in 1683, the last restraint was removed. Soldiers were billeted with Huguenot families, churches and schools closed down, converts were given a tax exemption, and a special fund was established to reward converts. By 1685, Louis had convinced himself that there were so few Huguenots left that the Edict of Nantes was moot.

According to the Edict of Fontainebleau, Huguenot pastors were to accept conversion or go into exile, all remaining Huguenot churches and schools were destroyed, all Protestant worship was to cease, and remaining Huguenots were simply declared to be Catholic. Louis had seemingly restored religious unity, and many (including Louis himself) saw this as the most glorious achievement of his reign. In fact, however, there were still about one million Huguenots left in France, and of these about 200,000 chose exile rather than conversion. Some went to England and its American colonies, while others found their way to the Dutch Republic and its colony in the Cape of Good Hope. Protestant states in Germany, especially Brandenburg-Prussia, also attracted Huguenot refugees.

Historians used to think that the loss of the Huguenots was a severe economic blow to France, since they were a well-educated, hard-working, and relatively wealthy minority. In fact, the economic blow to France was rather slight. On the other hand, the Huguenot refugees did in many cases boost the economy of their new homes more than their absence hurt France. Diplomatically, however, the revocation severely damaged Louis's interests. It made his relations with Protestant states all the more difficult, and it spread abroad a hard core of anti-French and anti-Bourbon activists, many of whom quickly reached positions of influence in their new homes. From 1685 on, Louis XIV appears increasingly in Protestant propaganda as a political and religious tyrant.

Nor did the revocation have the desired effect, for many Huguenot communities survived underground. Indeed, during Louis's last and most desperate war, the War of Spanish Succession, there was a Huguenot revolt in the Cevennes, a remote and mountainous region in south-central France. This was the Revolt of Camisards from 1702–10, which required an army to suppress it, an army that had to be diverted from fighting the King's foreign enemies.

Versailles and the Court

Probably nothing is as indicative of Louis and his reign as the new palace he built for himself at Versailles. Louis hated Paris because of its disorderliness and his experiences during the Fronde. Moreover, the main royal palace in Paris, the Louvre, was a ramshackle medieval fortress and was hardly fitting for so grand a king. Louis did add on to it, but this was not sufficient to satisfy his desire for a fitting monument to his *gloire*. Therefore, beginning in the 1670s, he started construction on a grand new palace at Versailles, just outside of Paris. Mostly completed by the mid-1680s, it became the new capital of France when the King and his court took up permanent residence there.

One of the most important points to note about Versailles is that it was an undefended palace. There were no walls, moats, or battlements. This was intended as a statement of Louis's power and prestige: he had no need of merely physical defences. The architecture of the palace itself was in a relatively restrained and classical style, emphasizing symmetry and harmony. Likewise, vast gardens and an extensive system of canals imposed geometric order on nature, in the same way that Louis purportedly imposed order on France and Europe.

In its decoration as well, we see that Versailles was intended as a monument to Louis XIV's *gloire*. Present everywhere are images of the sun, Louis's royal emblem. By this time, Copernicus's heliocentric universe was widely accepted, and Louis's adoption of the sun as his emblem put him at the centre of the social and political universe. The sun was also the source of all power and light in the same way that Louis brought his power and light to bear on France. Another recurring theme is that of Apollo, the Greco-Roman god of peace, order, and harmony, who was also closely associated with the sun.

Versailles was, however, much more than an architectural statement of power. It was a political tool as well. It has been said that Versailles functioned as a gilded cage for the nobility, but, like most such generalizations, this is only partly true. In fact, the vast majority of French nobles had no desire to live there, nor could they afford to. They remained overwhelmingly concerned with managing their estates, living as noble a lifestyle as their means permitted, and functioning as a local elite. Rather, Versailles served as a magnet for those nobles who were, or sought to be, politically or socially prominent on a national scale. Nor can it be said that Louis XIV "forced" the nobility to live in Versailles. The palace was very large, but it was by no means large enough to house the approximately 400,000 French nobles. Perhaps 10,000 courtiers inhabited the palace and town, living in cramped and unsanitary conditions. Instead of forcing the nobles to relocate there, Louis used the attractions and rewards of court life to entice important and ambitious nobles.

Louis was a master of using the ceremonial gestures of court life to reward or punish his courtiers. Social advancement and monetary rewards in the form of posts or pensions were dependent on physical proximity to the King. The elaborate court rituals and protocol were deliberately used as a means of focussing the courtiers' attention on the person of the King. It is not quite accurate to say the great nobility was politically emasculated by court life at Versailles; rather, they were made to understand that social prominence and the material rewards that accompanied it could be gained through attendance on the King and participation in the glittering social life of Versailles. In the past, great nobles had sought power through their power bases and networks of clients and dependants in their provincial power bases, which could be (and often were) used to launch revolts against the King, or more commonly against his "evil advisors." Through Versailles, Louis ensured that this could no longer happen. Indeed, the Prince of Condé—the "great Condé," one of France's most important nobles, the victor of Rocroi, who had shaken the monarchy to its core during the Fronde and allied with the King of Spain in his revolt against Mazarin in his provincial power base of Guyenne—ended his days rowing ladies around a lake at Versailles.

Versailles can be seen as a sort of secular temple in the cult of absolute monarchy, but it also became the focal point of French cultural life in the later seventeenth century. A vast army of painters, sculptors, musicians, poets, and playwrights were deployed in the glorification of the King and court. The tragedies of Jean Racine and Pierre Corneille were performed regularly, as were the comedies of Molière. Ballets and operas by Lully, Rameau, and Couperin regularly graced the stages and gardens of Versailles. In literature, this was the age of Boileau, Fénélon, Bossuet, La Rochefoucauld, Perreault, and Fontenelle, some of the greatest names in French literature. It was during this period that French styles and culture became the fashion throughout Europe, largely replacing Italian models that had been dominant among European elites since the Renaissance. Increasingly, French became the language of polite society and of European diplomacy. Other European rulers would build scaled-down replicas of Versailles for themselves and seek to imitate its court ritual and protocol.

The Later Years: Warfare, Taxation, and Misery

Of course all of this was very expensive: not only Versailles and the royal court, but also the vast administration, the hundreds of useless officers, and most of all the demands of continuing war. From the beginning of Louis's personal reign in 1661 until his death in 1715, a period of 54 years, France was at war for more than half of the time. Without Colbert (who had died in 1683) to make Louis at least think about the costs of his policies, government expenditure and the tax burden increased enormously. This was especially true from about 1690 until the end of the reign, when France became bogged down in two bitterly exhausting conflicts: the War of the League of Augsburg (1689–97) and the War of Spanish Succession (1702–13). The amount collected through the *taille*, the major direct tax, was ratcheted up, but by the 1690s it had reached the point of diminishing returns. That is, any attempts to raise it higher only produced rebellion, which required costly repression. The basic problem was that the nobility was essentially exempt from paying this tax, as was a good portion of the wealthy middle class. As a result, the major burden of the *taille* fell on the peasants, those who were least able to pay. Moreover, the fiscal system was incredibly inefficient and corrupt, with a large portion of the taxes paid sticking to the fingers of greedy or corrupt officials, who often turned around and lent the money to the government at high rates of interest. Other sources of revenue were also increased to their maximum: new offices were created and sold; future revenues were mortgaged in return for immediate cash. But it was still not enough. Louis's later finance ministers were forced by circumstances to introduce other sorts of taxes from which no one was exempt. Introduced against much opposition, they were never really effective and were repealed as soon as the fiscal demands of warfare abated.

On top of the tremendous demands of taxation, the 1690s and the early 1700s were terrible times in general for ordinary people. There was, however, a good deal of regional variation, with maritime areas faring better than the interior agricultural districts. Poor harvests in 1693 and 1694 as well as in 1709 led to widespread famine and disease. Moreover, peasant indebtedness (in large part a result of heavy taxation) led to widespread foreclosure on their lands, as they were snapped up by nobles or wealthy bourgeois with money to invest. Here is the heart-wrenching description of a contemporary observer in the region around Beauvais in northern France in the spring of 1694:

> An infinite number of poor souls, weak from hunger and wretchedness and dying from want and lack of bread in the streets and squares, in the towns and countryside because, having no work or occupation, they lack the money to buy bread.... Seeking to prolong their lives a little and somewhat to appease their hunger, these poor folk for the most part, lacking bread, eat such unclean things as cats and flesh of horses flayed and cast on to dung heaps, the blood which flows when cows and oxen are slaughtered and the offal and lights and such which cooks throw into the streets.... Other poor

> wretches eat roots and herbs which they boil in water, nettles and weeds of that kind. ... Yet others will grub up the beans and seed corn which were sown in the spring ... and all this breeds corruption in the bodies of men and divers mortal and infectious maladies, such as malignant fevers ... which assail even wealthy and well-provided persons.

At the same time, some serious military reverses in the War of Spanish Succession (1702–13) only reinforced the sense that things had somehow gone drastically wrong. There were numerous revolts that required suppression, further adding to the cost of government and the general misery. Louis himself had changed and become more devout as he aged. He spent less and less time at Versailles, preferred his smaller, more intimate palaces such as the one at neighbouring Marly, where he surrounded himself with his family and closest friends. As a result, court life at Versailles lost some of its glamour, and the centre of cultural life shifted back to Paris and away from the royal court, which a new generation of trendsetters increasingly saw as stuffy and old-fashioned.

Louis was also increasingly concerned with family affairs. In particular, a series of deaths caused him to doubt some of his actions, to wonder if God was punishing him for his arrogance. His eldest son Louis, the Grand Dauphin, died in 1711; the King's grandson, the duke of Burgundy (the Grand Dauphin's son), died in 1712, as did his wife, the Duchess of Burgundy, of whom Louis XIV was very fond. The Duke and Duchess of Burgundy had three sons, of whom the two eldest died as children and the youngest succeeded his great-grandfather, as King Louis XV, in 1715.

In the later years of the reign, there was also increasing questioning of and opposition to the government of Louis XIV. In particular, while he was alive, Louis's grandson the Duke of Burgundy provided a focal point for this opposition, since as far as anyone knew he was likely to become king one day. This oppositional group of thinkers and writers, which included Fénélon, the writer la Bruyère, the noblemen the dukes of Chevreuse and Beauvillier, and the marshall Vauban, proposed a regime that would be more aristocratic, less absolute, and less warlike. They envisioned a thoroughgoing economic and fiscal reform as well.

When Louis finally died in September 1715, just a few days shy of his 77th birthday, his death was greeted by relief more than anything else. Assessment of his reign is difficult. An apt analogy might be that of a holographic image that changes depending upon the angle from which it is viewed. From the perspective of high culture, the arts and literature, and the life of the court, it was a glorious period, the "Splendid Century" as the title of one famous book has it. Likewise from the perspective of royal authority: neither before nor after would a king of France rule as absolutely as Louis XIV did; his reign was indeed the pinnacle of royal authority in French history. As we have seen, however, Louis's achievement in this respect was a culmination of the past, rather than a new departure. Louis governed his kingdom and his subjects in entirely traditional ways, building on and completing the achievements of Henry IV, Louis XIII, and Cardinal Richelieu. Yet all this had significant drawbacks. It was a system that required a hard-working and effective politician as king, and Louis XIV fitted this description. Although it is always dangerous to read history backwards, the fact that neither of his successors, Louis XV (1715–74) or Louis XVI (1774–92), was as committed or as capable must be seen as a contributing cause of the French Revolution.

Diplomatically, Louis XIV brought France to the peak of its international prestige and power (see Chapter 17). Yet his ambitions and arrogance also brought France dangerously close to collapse during the last two decades of the reign, during the darkest days of the War of Spanish Succession. Heavy military expenditure, combined with an unreformed and unfair fiscal system and economic depression, reduced millions of his subjects to abject poverty. Louis XIV was above all a man of his own time, for better and for worse.

NOTE

1 W.H. Lewis, *The Splendid Century* (New York: Doubleday, 1957) 45–47.

CHAPTER FIFTEEN

England: From Restoration to Oligarchy, 1660–1714

Charles II and the Restoration

When Charles II became King of England in 1660, the monarchy was restored with its powers as they had been in 1641, that is in the early days of the revolution, before the civil war had broken out. All the acts to which Charles I had assented were kept, but those passed without the King's assent were rendered null and void. In practical terms, this meant that the prerogative courts such as Star Chamber and High Commission were not restored, extra-Parliamentary taxation was still illegal, and Parliament still had to meet at least every three years. On the other hand, the monarch still had great power, including the exclusive right to choose his own ministers and advisors, command of the armed forces, and control of foreign policy. In other words, the Restoration saw the triumph of the moderates who objected to Charles I's abuse of royal power but who still believed in the necessity of a strong monarch.

Of course, everyone understood that what had happened in the previous twenty years would affect the relations between Charles and Parliament. Nobody understood this better than Charles himself, almost ideally suited for the role he would have to play. Having spent years in exile, he was determined, as he put it, "not to go on his travels again." He was humorous, somewhat lazy, and a dedicated and successful ladies' man. Indeed, he was the original "goodtime Charlie." To his credit, he does not seem to have been overly embittered by the fate of his father, and a quest for vengeance was simply not part of his makeup. He was gracious in victory and magnanimous in defeat. He cautiously refused to punish all but the most intransigent republicans, and only thirteen people were executed for their roles in the Civil War and Revolution. In his government, he found himself having to rely on former rebels, and he did so graciously and without rancour.

What was happening in the later seventeenth century was that the political and social elite of England, as represented in Parliament, were forming a partnership with the King. An aristocratic form of government was taking shape, a system that would govern England into the twentieth century. The exact balance of powers within this partnership was still vague and uncertain, and neither party was willing to press the issue. Parliament had seen what happened when they tried to restrict the power of the monarch too much, and Charles was determined not to go into exile again.

In religion, the Church of England was restored, together with its bishops and with the King as Supreme Head. But without the court of High Commission to enforce royal control, ultimate control of the Church passed into Parliament's hands. The majority of Englishmen accepted the restored church. The more moderate Puritans, the Presbyterians, made their peace with the Church; if it was not precisely what they wanted in a church, it was better than the alternatives they had seen during the Revolution. The more radical Puritans, the Baptists, Quakers, and so on, who refused to accept the restored church became known as Dissenters or non-conformists and were subject to legal hindrances and penalties, known as the Clarendon Code after Charles II's chief minister the Earl of Clarendon.

Charles II's own religious beliefs were relatively tolerant and easy-going. Given his preference, he would likely have converted to Roman Catholicism, as indeed he did on his deathbed. His Queen, the Portuguese princess Catherine of Braganza, was Catholic, as were his mother, sister, and his brother and heir James, the Duke of York. Catholics had been among the keenest defenders of his father. Personally, it is likely that he found the Catholic doctrine of "easy" grace attractive. As the father of at least fourteen bastards, he is supposed to have said, "all appetites are free and ... God will never damn a man for allowing himself a little pleasure." But he clearly recognized that any attempt to restore the Catholic Church would be political (and perhaps literal) suicide. The most he tried to do was insist on greater tolerance for everyone, Protestant dissenters and Catholics, but when he ran into opposition from Parliament, he knew enough to back down. Indeed, Parliament was much more stringent in enforcing conformity to the Church of England than Charles was.

The Parliament that was elected in 1661 became known as the Cavalier Parliament for its sympathy to the new king and royal policies. Indeed, Charles and his advisors figured that a more amenable group could never be elected, and so the Cavalier Parliament remained in existence until 1679. Even so, there were several sources of tension. One was religion, where Charles wanted a more tolerant and comprehensive Church of England, while Parliament insisted on a stricter definition and enforcement of orthodoxy and conformity. Another was money. At the Restoration, as we have seen, extra-Parliamentary taxation such as Ship Money, which had caused so much trouble in the past, remained abolished. Instead, the royal household and government were to be supported by an annual grant from Parliament, to be supplemented by the revenue from excise taxes. In reality, this income was not sufficient even in peacetime. Parliament was reluctant to grant more, unless they had more say in how it was being spent. Many were also put off by what they saw as an extravagant court culture and royal lifestyle, especially the King's generous treatment of his many mistresses.

No one, however, wanted to attack the King directly. Thus, in the time-honoured tradition, opposition to royal policy was focussed on the King's "evil advisors." From his accession in 1660 until 1667, Charles's chief advisor was Edward Hyde, the Earl of Clarendon. Hyde had been a moderate leader in the Long Parliament of the early 1640s, and after the royal defeat he had joined the young Prince Charles in exile and become his political teacher and mentor. It was Clarendon who became the lightning rod for unpopular royal policies. A good deal of this was simply political infighting, but Clarendon declined to build alliances in the court and Parliament, relying exclusively on his close relationship with the King. Ironically, Clarendon's fall was largely due to defeat in a war to which he had been opposed, but which had been forced upon him.

In 1665, England fought its second war against the Dutch Republic in a decade. As before, the issues at stake were maritime and commercial, particularly English efforts to enforce the Navigation Act of 1660, which was a direct assault on Dutch commercial dominance. Despite some initial victories, the war turned out badly for England. In 1667, a Dutch fleet sailed up the Thames, sank three ships at anchor, and towed two others away, including the fleet's flagship, the *Royal Charles*. Not only was the war going badly, but also, in 1665, London was struck by the worst outbreak of bubonic plague in its history, causing approximately 70,000 deaths. In 1666 the Great Fire of London left a quarter of a million people homeless and destroyed 395 acres of the city. Defeat, plague, and fire cause many to wonder if God was not perhaps punishing a sinful nation. Charles, who had grown tired of Clarendon's self-righteousness, offered him as a scapegoat. He was impeached in Parliament and went into exile rather than stay and face trial and possible execution; he died in France in 1674.

Although Clarendon had taken the blame for all that had gone wrong, his removal from office did nothing for long-term stability. He was replaced by a series of advisors who lacked his consistency and especially his conviction to a theory of government in which a strong king governed with respect for law, liberty, and property. His successors, although more popular with the King, were more ambitious and less principled. The same underlying tensions remained in politics and religion.

After Clarendon's fall, Charles II relied on a group of advisors who became known as the "cabal," after their initials: Sir Thomas Clifford, Baron *A*shley, the Duke of *B*uckingham, Lord *A*rlington, and the Earl of *L*auderdale. They never formed a coherent group, but rather the King relied on them individually, which allowed him to pursue his own preferences as he saw fit. These years were notable for two major developments, both dear to the King's heart: closer relations with Louis XIV and France, and increased religious toleration at home. Thus, in the 1670 Treaty of Dover, Charles and Louis concluded an anti-Dutch alliance in preparation for a common war against the Republic. Moreover, in a series of secret articles, and in return for a hefty pension from the French king, Charles committed himself to restoring England to the Roman Catholic Church "as soon as his country's affairs permit." This should not necessarily be taken as proof of

Catholic conviction on Charles's part. Rather, it was a typical piece of political and diplomatic opportunism.

The English and French allies went to war against the Dutch in 1672, the third war in two decades between England and the Dutch Republic. Fighting a fellow Protestant power alongside a Catholic French monarch did not sit well with many in Parliament, especially once French successes led to the overthrow of Johan de Witt and the appointment of Charles's nephew William of Orange as *stadtholder* (see Chapter 12). At the same time that war broke out, Charles issued a Declaration of Indulgence, which effectively repealed much of the legal repression of Catholics and Protestant Dissenters. Anglican opinion in Parliament was outraged, both on religious and political grounds, since in the minds of most, the King had no power to repeal statutes of Parliament. In the minds of many Protestant Parliamentarians, there was an association taking shape comprising support for France, popery, and arbitrary government. This sentiment was only reinforced when the King's younger brother and heir apparent James, the Duke of York, revealed in 1673 that he had converted to the Roman Catholic Church.

The war did not go particularly well for England, and by 1674, lack of financial support from Parliament forced Charles to make peace with the Dutch, abandoning the French alliance. In order to gain financing from Parliament, Charles repealed the Declaration of Indulgence. Parliament then passed a rigorous Test Act, which required all government officials to take communion in the Church of England and to sign a declaration opposing the Catholic doctrine of transubstantiation.

With its two major policies—better relations with France and greater religious toleration—discredited and abandoned, the Cabal gradually lost its influence, and its members either retired from politics completely or went into active opposition to royal policies. The figure who now emerged as Charles II's chief minister was Thomas Osborne, the Earl of Danby. Danby's period of power represented a complete reversal of the policies of the Cabal, for he was a stringent proponent of Anglican conformity and orthodoxy and was anti-French in his international outlook. Danby proved to be an effective politician and manipulator of Parliament. Through careful economizing he built up a slush fund with which to bribe voters and MPs. Indeed, it is in this period that we see the very beginnings of party politics in Parliament. These were not parties in the modern sense of the word; there were no formal organizations with constitutions, conventions, and so on. Rather, they were groups of men who thought alike on most issues, who tended to vote the same way in Parliament, and who tended to frequent the same taverns and clubs. Two main factions emerged during this period, although membership was very fluid. One was the Tories, who were generally the King's supporters in Parliament. These were the men that Danby's patronage organized and supported. In general terms, they supported the idea of divine-right monarchy, although they opposed absolutism (what they called "arbitrary government"). They believed that a just balance of power between king and Parliament had been arrived at, and that any attempt to increase the power of Parliament threatened the very fabric of the monarchy and the social order. They were also staunch supporters of the established Church of England. The Whigs, on the other hand, were much more suspicious both of Charles II in particular and of monarchy in general. Most were not republicans but believed that the power of Parliament was essential in restraining the king. Many were Dissenters, or at least sympathetic to them, and sought greater toleration. They were, however, very much anti-Catholic. In their minds, "popery and arbitrary government" were two sides of the same coin. They were highly suspicious of Charles's sympathies toward France and Catholics.

Indeed, it was the issue of religion that provoked the most serious crisis of the reign. Specifically, Charles's queen Mary of Braganza was unable to have children; therefore, despite having a whole brood of bastards, the King had no legitimate child to succeed him. His brother James, the Duke of York, was therefore heir apparent. As we have seen, in 1673 James had revealed his earlier conversion to the Catholic Church and had had to resign as Lord High Admiral under the Test Act.

Then, in September 1678, two virulent anti-Catholics and pathological liars named Israel Tonge and Titus Oates came forward with details of a widespread Catholic plot. According to Tonge and Oates, this "Popish Plot" involved murdering the King in order to place the Catholic James on the throne, rebellion in Ireland, an invasion from France, and the elimination of both Parliament and Protestantism. That Tonge and Oates were so swiftly and widely believed speaks to the widespread acceptance of the notion that "popery and arbitrary government" were two sides of the same coin. The King's opponents seized on the resulting mass hysteria in order to discredit Danby. Although he was firmly anti-Catholic, he was the major supporter of royal power and therefore must have been secretly sympathetic to the Catholics. Charles offered up Danby as a sacrificial lamb, and he spent five years in the Tower of London, mostly to escape more serious punishment at the hands of the King's opponents. The key figure in the opposition to Charles II was Anthony Ashley Cooper, the Earl of Shaftesbury, who had made a career out of changing sides at the opportune moment. Originally a supporter of Charles I, when he saw which way the Civil War was going he became a supporter of Parliament. When the Protectorate was on its last legs, he worked for the restoration of Charles II. He had been a member of the Cabal until his anti-Catholic sentiments caused the King to dismiss him. Thereafter, he became the King's most vociferous opponent. Now he saw his chance to use the panic over the Popish Plot to enhance his power. In May 1679 Shaftesbury introduced in Parliament an Exclusion Bill, which would have excluded from the succession Charles II's brother, James, Duke of York, because of his Catholic sympathies. In many ways, however, this "Exclusion Crisis" was a symptom, rather than a cause. The root cause was suspicion of "popery and arbitrary government" in the present rather than in the future. Both Shaftesbury and the Whigs (of whom he emerged as the leader) feared that Charles II himself was a danger to Parliament and Protestantism and would try to leave to his brother a firmly established Catholic absolute monarchy. From 1679 until 1681, three successive Parliaments would meet, only to be quickly dismissed by the King in order to prevent passage of the Exclusion bill.

What Shaftesbury and the Whigs did not appreciate, however, was the King's principled opposition to any alteration in the succession. As we have seen, Charles would not fight to the end for his religion, nor even for the power of the king over Parliament, but on the maintenance of the succession in the legitimate Stuart line he was utterly inflexible. For two years, English politics was dominated by this crisis, and memories of the civil war of the 1640s were on everyone's mind. For not only did Charles have a Catholic brother to succeed him, but he also had an illegitimate Protestant son, the Duke of Monmouth, whom many (including Monmouth himself) wanted to see on the throne rather than the Catholic James.

Providing theoretical justification for opposition to the King was the writer and philosopher John Locke (1632–1704). A friend and employee of Shaftesbury, it was during the exclusion crisis that Locke wrote his major work of political theory *Two Treatises of Civil Government*, although it would not be published until 1689. Although it was purportedly written to refute the divine-right theories of Robert Filmer, whose *Patriarcha* had been written in the 1620s, Locke's real target was Thomas Hobbes. Like Hobbes, Locke attempted to deduce the purpose of government by examining its origins. Thus, like Hobbes, he imagined a world without government, a "state of nature." As we saw in Chapter 9, for Hobbes this state of nature was "a war of all against all," and the "greatest evil that can happen in this life," necessitating an absolute sovereign (his "leviathan" or "mortal god") who can terrify men into obedience to the law of nature. Locke's state of nature, on the other hand, was much more benign. People will generally respect each other's natural rights of life, liberty, and property. However, the enjoyment of these rights is uncertain and subject to invasion by others. Therefore, a relatively benign state of nature can be made more secure and even better by the introduction of civil government: "The great and chief end, therefore, of men's uniting into commonwealths and putting themselves under government, is the preservation of their property." If a government is no longer fulfilling its purposes, or is actively working against them, then it may legitimately be overthrown and replaced. Locke, Shaftesbury, and the Whigs argued, therefore, that the spectre of "popery and arbitrary government" was a fundamental threat to the liberties and property of Englishmen, and that, according to the contractual origins and nature of government, they were entitled to protect their natural rights.

At the height of this exclusion crisis, the King fell deathly ill, causing everybody to reflect on the possibility of a new civil war, and eventually cooler heads prevailed. Charles was a master at letting his opponents have just enough rope to hang themselves. In this case, many moderates were uneasy with the vehemence of Shaftesbury and his supporters. In 1681 Charles ordered Shaftesbury's arrest. Completely discredited, he fled the country and died in Amsterdam in 1683.

From 1681 until his death in 1685, Charles II ruled without Parliament. England's trade was booming, and with it the excise taxes that filled the royal treasury. Substantial subsidies from Louis XIV also eased the financial situation.

Charles had no need to call Parliament for money, and so he did not. Some have suggested that Charles was aiming to impose a Louis XIV-style absolute monarchy on England. In fact, however, this is a misreading of the situation. The Whigs were discredited and demoralized after the Exclusion Crisis, but Charles knew enough to limit his actions to what he knew the Tories would support. Therefore, persecution of Protestant dissenters was intensified, and local political arrangements were altered in ways that favoured the Tories. Charles was even able, with only minimal protest, to ignore the Triennial Act. Fundamentally, Charles II was incapable of the kind of singleness of purpose necessary to impose absolute monarchy in England. He was too lazy and too pragmatic; he was only erratically and opportunistically authoritarian, rather than authoritarian out of principle. Moreover, despite a deathbed conversion to the Roman Catholic Church, he had proved his willingness to maintain the Church of England against both Catholics and Protestant dissenters. When he died in 1685, his brother who succeeded him as King James II, was both authoritarian on principle and a confirmed and devoted Catholic. This combination proved disastrous, for within three years James's actions would lead to his overthrow. Indeed, before his death Charles had predicted that James would not last four years on the throne, an extremely prescient prediction.

James II and the Glorious Revolution

When James II came to the throne in 1685, he found that his brother had admirably paved his way. The Whigs were discredited and their leaders either dead or in exile. The Tories were in firm control of the machinery of local government. When Parliament met at the beginning of the reign, James commented, "there were not above forty members but such as he himself had wished for." The Earl of Peterborough remarked, "Everything is very happy here. Never king was proclaimed with more applause than ... James II. He is courted by all men,... and I doubt not but to see a happy reign." Yet, within three years, he had provoked such hostility that he faced an invasion led by his son-in-law and would ignominiously flee into exile. For this unhappy ending, James himself must bear almost all the blame.

He seemingly had learned nothing from the examples of his father and brother. He was hard-working, but stubborn, humourless, and moralistic, convinced that any who opposed his policies were traitors. Above all, with the zeal of an adult convert, he desired to restore England to Roman Catholicism. The social and political elite who made up the political class of England, however, came to the conclusion that he could be tolerated as king for two major reasons. One was that they expected him to keep his religious convictions as private as possible, that he would maintain the Church of England as it stood as the official church. The other reason was that they expected only a short interlude during which there would be a Catholic king. James had two daughters, Mary and Anne, by his first marriage to Anne Hyde, the daughter of the Earl of Clarendon. After announcing his conversion to Roman Catholicism in 1673, James married an Italian Catholic princess, Mary of Modena. But when he became king, James was 53 years old and his second marriage had remained childless. Most therefore expected him to be succeeded on the throne by one of his Protestant daughters. Moreover, Mary was married to Prince William III of Orange, *de facto* ruler of the Dutch Republic, and one of the leading Protestant statesmen in Europe (see Chapter 12). Over his brief reign, James managed to alienate the Tories (whose support was absolutely necessary) on both counts.

Very early in his reign, James faced an abortive Protestant uprising in support of the Duke of Monmouth, Charles II's illegitimate son. Parliament granted him the money to raise an army to suppress the rebellion. The rebellion was easily crushed, but its severe repression raised concerns in the minds of many. Not only was Monmouth executed, but so were 400 of his supporters, most of them peasants. What was worse, he illegally staffed the army with Catholic officers and stationed it around London while he requested that Parliament repeal laws discriminating against nonconformists and Catholics. When Parliament refused, he dismissed it and simply enacted this and other similar measures on his own. He revived the court of High Commission, replaced moderate bishops with those who favoured the Catholic Church, and relied on Catholic advisors. What James had shown was that unlike his brother, he was willing to provoke a confrontation with Parliament over religion. Charles II had known enough to back off when Parliament resisted his attempts to increase religious toleration, but James did not. Moreover, only months earlier, Louis XIV had revoked the Edict of Nantes, and many people in England were suspicious and fearful of their king's plans. They feared that James wanted to imitate his French cousin and establish a Catholic absolute monarchy in England.

The social and political elite also felt that the King's policies threatened not only their political control, but also their personal property. In a famous case, in 1687 the King attempted to impose a Catholic principal upon Magdalen College at the University of Oxford. The Fellows of the College refused and were deprived of their positions, which were regarded as a form of private property. Taking a page from his brother's book, James meddled in local politics. But whereas Charles had put in place loyal Tories, James attempted to pack local governments with Catholics and Dissenters, many whom were uneducated and inexperienced and seemed to threaten the control of the propertied elite.

The final straw came in June 1688, when James's Catholic queen gave birth to a baby boy, who took precedence over his two older half-sisters in the royal succession. This boy would of course be raised as a Catholic, raising the spectre of a Catholic dynasty ruling England indefinitely. Much Protestant propaganda maintained that the baby was not in fact the son of James II but rather had been smuggled into the royal bed. This is significant in that it reflects the Tories' devotion to the ideal of legitimate succession; their only hope seemed to lie in disproving the baby's legitimacy. Nevertheless, recent events had convinced a number of leading figures, both Whigs and Tories, that drastic action was needed.

On June 30, a group of Whig and Tory leaders wrote to William of Orange asking him to come to England to protect the Protestant faith, secure the meeting of a free Parliament, and investigate the legitimacy of James II's newborn heir. Not only was William married to James II's elder daughter Mary, but he also had a genealogical claim to the throne as a grandson of Charles I. Afraid of leaving the Dutch Republic vulnerable to Louis XIV, William waited until Louis became involved in military affairs in Germany. In November the Dutch fleet of 463 ships and 40,000 men landed in the southwest of England. The English Navy had been kept in port by an unfavourable wind; the same "Protestant" wind blew the Dutch fleet off course, ensuring that they landed unopposed by the English army.[1]

By the middle of December, William and his army were in London, their progress across the south of England having been virtually unopposed. The success of the Dutch invasion was due primarily to the miscalculations and bumbling of both Louis XIV and James II himself. Louis had just become embroiled in a major war in Germany provoked by his own aggressive ambitions (see Chapter 17). He was sure that the Dutch invasion of England would provoke a long and bloody civil war that would serve the dual purpose of tying William III down in England and removing England as a potential French enemy. James II, however, suffered from a loss of nerve. He failed completely to capitalize on his advantages as legitimate king, and on his command of a large army. No doubt with his father's fate in mind, he attempted to flee the country, after throwing the Great Seal of England into the Thames, thinking that government could not be conducted without it. He was recognized and brought back to London, only to escape two weeks later into exile in France. His "escape" was engineered with the connivance of William III, who recognized James's presence as a potential rallying point for his opponents. In fact, fleeing was the worst thing that James could have done, for it demoralized his supporters even as it deprived them of their leader. If the King himself was not willing to fight for his throne, why should they? This series of events culminating in the flight of James II and the installation of William and Mary as joint monarchs is known as the Glorious Revolution.

In late December 1688, William summoned an *ad hoc* body of former MPs and others to advise him. This body urged him to call elections for a Convention "for the preservation of our religion, rights, laws, liberty and property ... upon such sure and legal foundations that they may not be in danger of being again subverted." (This body could not be called a Parliament, since Parliament could only meet when called by the king.) The Convention started meeting in January 1689; it eventually managed to hammer out a compromise political settlement that was acceptable to most Whigs and Tories and satisfied all but the most extreme on either end of the spectrum. The throne was declared vacant, James's flight having been construed as abdication. William and Mary were declared joint monarchs, on the basis both of heredity and of having defeated James II in a just war. William, however, made sure that although he shared the title with his wife, he held the power. Their coronation oaths emphasized their duty to govern according to the law and Parliament, "to govern the people of this kingdom of England, and the dominions thereunto belonging, according to the statutes in Parliament agreed on, and the laws and customs of the same." In December 1689, Parliament passed a Bill of Rights, which attempted to define more closely the limitations on royal power. It forbade the arbitrary use of power as exercised by James II, particularly the suspension of statutes of Parliament. It also forbade a standing army during peacetime without Parliament's approval. It provided, somewhat vaguely, for "frequent" Parliaments, and declared that elections to and debates in Parliament were to be free. Catholics were declared ineligible to inherit the throne, and the royal succession was confirmed upon the children of William and Mary or, if they remained childless (as proved to be the case), upon Mary's sister Anne and her heirs.

This constitutional settlement was expressed in several other documents. The Mutiny Act granted the commanders of the army the power to discipline soldiers only for a year at a time, thereby guaranteeing frequent recourse to Parliament. William and Mary were granted an annual income of £1.2 million, not nearly sufficient to run the government even in peacetime. This too meant that frequent Parliaments would be necessary. Parliament also passed a Toleration Act, which allowed Protestant non-conformists the right to worship but still placed legal barriers in their way. Catholics were specifically excluded from the Act, but in practice they were allowed to worship as long as they were not too obvious about it and did not cause trouble.

William and Mary ruled jointly until Mary's death in 1694, and William then ruled on his own until his death in 1702. Mary's sister Anne ruled from 1702 to 1714. Anne, however, was the last monarch of the Stuart dynasty, having been predeceased by all her children. (She was pregnant seventeen times. Of these, only one child survived infancy and he died at the age of ten.) This lack of a direct heir in turn brought the issue of the succession back to the spotlight. The Act of Settlement (1701) had excluded Catholics from the throne, including the heirs of James II. (James II died in Versailles in 1701. His son, the baby whose birth prompted the Glorious Revolution, was known in England as the "Old Pretender" and claimed to be the rightful King of England as James III.) The Act of Settlement passed over the top 57 claimants to the English throne (all Catholics) and settled the succession on a German princess, Electress Sophie of Hanover and her heirs. Therefore, when Queen Anne died in 1714, the new king was the Elector of Hanover, who became George I (1714–27), an overweight, slightly stupid, petty German prince who never learned to speak English but who possessed the single qualification of being Protestant.

Above all, William III had been concerned with military and diplomatic affairs, leading the resistance to Louis XIV. Indeed, his primary motivation in claiming the English throne was to prevent an English-French alliance and to bring England's resources and wealth to the aid of the Dutch Republic. In fact, the late seventeenth and early eighteenth centuries saw England's arrival on the scene as a major European power. England was a full participant in the two major wars of the period: the War of the League of Augsburg (1689–97) and the War of Spanish Succession (1702–13). William was fundamentally uninterested in governing England, except when it came to obtaining the funds necessary to prosecute these wars. Parliament was able, therefore, to further cement its central role in the government. The principle became established that Parliament had the power not only to grant tax revenue, but also to oversee its spending. A number of acts were passed excluding certain government officials from sitting in Parliament who might influence its decisions. During William's long absences, when Mary governed the country, and even more under Anne, the principle of Cabinet government was being established. That is, the monarch relied increasingly on a small, inner group of advisors, who were the primary conduit of information between Crown and Parliament. To look ahead a little, during the course of the eighteenth century, the principle would become established that the Cabinet must normally be able to count on the support of a majority within Parliament. Yet it would be anachronistic to see the monarchs of this period as mere figureheads. They retained very significant power, especially in the areas of warfare and diplomacy. They were still free to choose their own advisors and ministers, and they possessed very significant powers of patronage and influence.

Another significant constitutional development was the permanent political union of England and Scotland in 1707. Since 1603, both countries had been ruled by the same kings of the Stuart dynasty, but they had retained their separate political and institutional identities. The Scots had accepted the Glorious Revolution, but the death of Anne's last surviving child in 1700 brought the possibility that Scotland might eventually be ruled by a different monarch than England. In particular, the Scottish Parliament balked at the Act of Settlement and the Hanoverian succession. To forestall this possibility, the Parliaments of both kingdoms passed the Act of Union in 1707, formally establishing the United Kingdom of Great Britain and Ireland. Scotland was guaranteed the integrity of its legal system and Presbyterian Kirk, but in all other respects the two kingdoms were unified, and Scotland accepted the Hanoverian succession.

By the early eighteenth century, after nearly a century of instability that included two revolutions, a civil war, and the execution of a king, England had arrived at a form of limited monarchy in which the monarch governed in a partnership with the country's social and political elite. The forum for this cooperation was Parliament, which was able to establish itself as a permanent part of government, most notably due to its power to grant tax revenue and oversee its spending. It was an aristocratic form of government that would last in most respects until the democratic reforms of the late nineteenth and early twentieth centuries. It is important to realize that this limited monarchy was not arrived at on the basis of some previous or *a priori* commitment to a theoretical ideal. (Although the ideas of Locke's *Two Treatises* were later used to justify the Glorious Revolution, this was clearly retroactive. It is completely wrong to suggest that William and Mary became monarchs on the basis of Locke's political theories.) Rather, it was the product of revolution and civil war. English monarchs, particularly Charles I and James II, tried (and failed) to make the monarchy more absolute, and in the process, quite by accident, gave birth to a limited monarchy.

On the surface, then, the absolute monarchy of France under Louis XIV and the English limited monarchy look very different. And in many ways these differences are real and important. On the other hand, the differences should not blind us to some important similarities. While Louis XIV did not have to contend with a powerful national representative body such as Parliament, he still relied on the cooperation of elites as expressed in other sorts of bodies, such as the *parlements* and regional assemblies. The primary difference between the two systems was that the rulers of England were dependent on Parliament for revenue, while the kings of France had much more latitude in assessing and collecting taxes, and were certainly less restrained in spending that revenue. On the other hand, it could certainly be argued that Parliamentary consent made the English government more, rather than less, powerful because it ensured the cooperation and participation of the political and social elite. The absolute monarchy of France and the limited monarchy of England should therefore not be seen as polar opposites, but as different arrangements of power between rulers and elites, as variations on a theme rather than as different species.

NOTE

1 This series of events is the origin of the nursery rhyme "Rock-a-bye Baby." (Many nursery rhymes originated as commentaries on contemporary events.) The baby in question was the newborn son of James II. The cradle in the tree-top represents the baby's precarious position as heir to the throne. The wind rocking the cradle is the "Protestant wind" that blew William's invasion force to the west while it kept James's forces in port. The bough breaking and the cradle falling represent James's replacement on the throne by William and Mary.

CHAPTER SIXTEEN

Absolutism in Central and Eastern Europe

As we saw in Chapter 13, dominance in northern and eastern Europe had been contested among several different powers: Sweden, Denmark, Poland, and Russia. Of these, only Russia maintained and enhanced its position as a dominant power in the region. In the second half of the seventeenth century, two new powers came to challenge for dominance in the region. These were the Habsburg monarchy and Brandenburg-Prussia. Although they grew out of previous states, they were so fundamentally renovated that we are justified in thinking of them as new states. All three of these states developed absolutist types of governments. There were, however, important differences both among these three states and between them and the absolutist monarchies further west, especially that of France under Louis XIV.

The major distinction between the governments of these three states and those of western Europe stemmed from a difference in their social structure. Central and eastern European society was much more rural, agrarian, and dominated by the nobility than in the west. Towns were much less important economically and politically. As we have seen, by the end of the Middle Ages, most peasants in western Europe were personally free; that is, they were no longer serfs. In central and eastern Europe, exactly the opposite process took place. Peasants who had once enjoyed greater personal freedom than those in the west now found themselves subject to numerous restrictions on their personal freedom. Landlords throughout the region guaranteed themselves a cheap source of labour on their estates in order to maximize the profits to be made selling their grain on the open market to feed the rapidly growing cities of western Europe. As a corollary of this, urban middle classes in central and eastern Europe were much smaller and weaker than those in the west. Politically, this meant that rulers could not use a wealthy and socially ambitious middle class as a counterweight to the power of the nobility, as rulers did in western Europe. They were faced with a powerfully entrenched nobility with large and profitable estates that in many cases were virtually independent of the ruler's power.

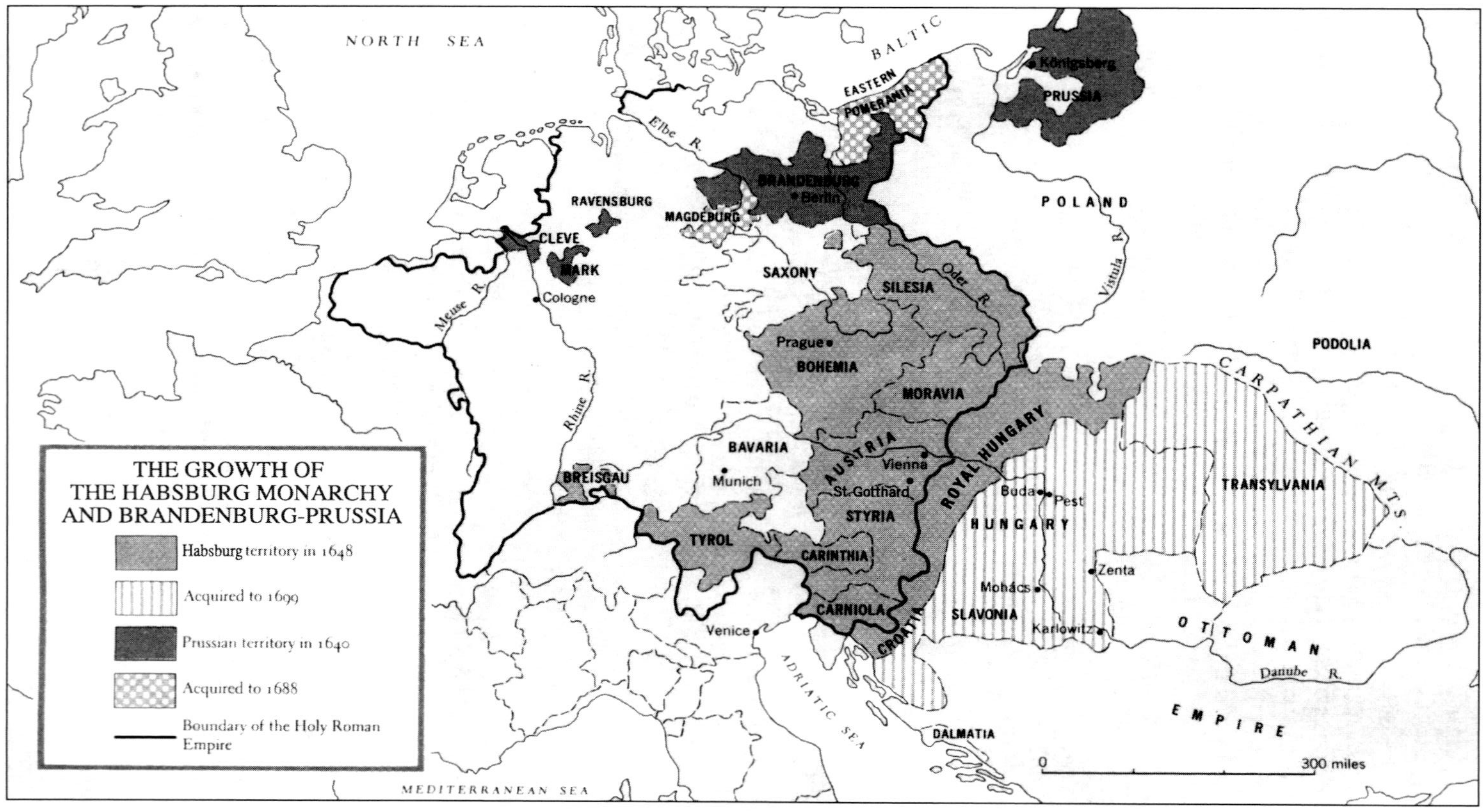

MAP 16.1 THE GROWTH OF THE HABSBURG MONARCHY AND BRANDENBURG-PRUSSIA

The best example of this is Poland, which, as we have seen, devolved into a noble republic in the seventeenth century. But Poland is only an extreme case; the same was true to a greater or lesser degree in all the states of central and eastern Europe. If these rulers were to enhance their power and build up their states, they needed to do so with the cooperation and collusion of the nobility, not in opposition to it. These rulers came to strike a deal with their nobles that enhanced both the power of the monarch and the control of the nobles over their estates and serfs. As long as the nobles supported the monarch and his policies, and served in his army and civil service, they would be virtually independent on their own estates. As a result, the degree of servitude of the serfs actually increased throughout the sixteenth and seventeenth centuries.

What differentiated the Habsburg monarchy, Brandenburg-Prussia, and Russia were the ways in which these rulers assembled their territories and the degree of internal cohesion among their possessions and subjects. The Habsburg monarchy consisted of an assortment of different nationalities and peoples with little internal unity. Although Brandenburg-Prussia was more internally cohesive, consisting overwhelmingly of Germans, its territories were scattered across northern Germany and were without significant economic resources or natural defences. Moreover, absolutism in Brandenburg-Prussia was both driven by and enforced through the army, making it more efficient, bureaucratic, and uniform than in the Habsburg monarchy. Russia, after the tribulations of Ivan the Terrible's reign and the Time of Troubles, emerged as a leading force with no significant challenge to the power of the Tsar and with very significant human and natural resources. These distinctions would all have a significant effect on the development of these three states.

The Growth of Brandenburg-Prussia

At the end of the Thirty Years' War in 1648, nothing indicated that Brandenburg-Prussia would rise to the status of a great power by the mid-eighteenth century. Its territories were small and scattered, determined by inheritance, not logic or geography, and without a common identity except that they were ruled by the same man; they were also without natural defences or resources to speak of. Brandenburg in particular was poor, flat, and marshy, known as "the sandbox of Europe." In addition, the territories were thinly populated: in 1648 there were perhaps 1.5 million people. Moreover, during the Thirty Years' War much of the country had been devastated by rival Imperial and Swedish armies. If one were to have picked a German state that would eventually challenge the Habsburgs for dominance in Germany, Brandenburg-Prussia would surely have been far down the list. Its prospects were certainly less promising than those of Bavaria, Saxony, or the Palatinate. Yet by the mid-eighteenth century Brandenburg-Prussia (or simply Prussia as it was increasingly called) would become one of the great powers of Europe, particularly under its greatest ruler, King Frederick II, the Great (r. 1740–86). And of course, in the nineteenth century, it would be Prussia that would unify Germany under the leadership of its "Iron Chancellor," Otto von Bismarck.

The foundations of Brandenburg-Prussia's rise to power were laid in the late sixteenth century, when the two territories of Brandenburg and Prussia were united under a single ruler of the Hohenzollern dynasty. Brandenburg, in north-central Germany, was within the Holy Roman Empire and its ruler was one of the seven electors who occupied an elite rank among the princes of the Empire and who chose the Emperor. Prussia, on the southern shore of the eastern Baltic, was not part of the Holy Roman Empire and was in fact technically part of the Kingdom of Poland, with its Duke a vassal of the Polish king. In the later Middle Ages, Prussia had been ruled by the order of the Teutonic Knights. In 1525, the Grand Master of the order, Albert of Hohenzollern, converted to Lutheranism and secularized the territory, becoming the first Duke of Prussia. A subsequent marriage between the two branches of the Hohenzollern family led to the union of the two territories under the rule of Elector John Sigismund (1608–19). Prussia was a somewhat more promising and prosperous territory than Brandenburg. It was more populous, with approximately 400,000 inhabitants in the early seventeenth century, compared with Brandenburg's 270,000. It had access to the Baltic Sea, unlike landlocked Brandenburg. It also had larger and more prosperous towns, and more of them. Berlin, the chief city of Brandenburg had at this time, only about 12,000 inhabitants. Prussia, while its towns could not compare to the greatest Baltic ports such as Danzig, Riga, or Reval (Tallin), nevertheless boasted several important Baltic ports, which gave its rulers access to the rich Baltic grain trade. Chief among these towns was Königsberg (modern Kaliningrad).

The rulers of Brandenburg-Prussia also possessed some smaller but important territories in the Rhineland of northwest Germany, near the frontier of the Dutch Republic. These were the territories of Cleves, Mark, and Ravensburg. These had previously been ruled by the Duke of Jülich-Cleves. When he died childless in 1609, control of these territories became crucial for a number of different rulers, and this conflict was crucial in the building of tensions that led to the Thirty Years' War (see Chapter 8). Ultimately, the Elector of Brandenburg was successful in pressing his claim to part of these territories (Cleves, Mark, and Ravensburg), while the other part (Jülich-Berg) went to a Catholic claimant.

The Elector of Brandenburg converted his territories and subjects to Lutheranism in the 1520s, as did his cousin the Duke of Prussia. But these Hohenzollern rulers played a very minor role in German religious politics throughout the sixteenth century, preferring to cautiously follow the lead of Saxony and the other important Lutheran states of northern Germany. In 1613, Elector John Sigismund converted to Calvinism (illegal in Germany according to the 1555 Peace of Augsburg), while agreeing that his subjects could maintain their Lutheran faith. Religious division and suspicion did, however, cause tensions between the ruler and his subjects, especially the nobles on whom he was so dependent.

The Thirty Years' War brought further troubles to Brandenburg-Prussia. Elector George William (1619–40) was overly cautious and indecisive, and lacked any sort of leverage to protect his territories. As a result, Brandenburg-Prussia was repeatedly caught in the crossfire. Large parts of Brandenburg and Prussia were occupied by Sweden, while Wallenstein's army ravaged Brandenburg, and Dutch and Spanish armies occupied Cleves, Mark, and Ravensburg. The prospects seemed bleak indeed for his son and successor, Frederick William, when he succeeded his father at the age of twenty in 1640. Nevertheless, from these very inauspicious beginnings, Frederick William (1640–88), known as the Great Elector, set Brandenburg-Prussia on the road to greatness.

Taking advantage of general war-weariness and changes in the diplomatic situation, Frederick William managed some small but important gains in the Peace of Westphalia. Although he had a dynastic claim to all of the neighbouring duchy of Pomerania, he had to settle for its poorer eastern half, while Sweden took the richer western portion, including the important port city of Stettin. By way of compensation, he did gain the territory of the secularized bishoprics of Halberstadt, Minden, and Kammin, and the right to possess the archbishopric of Magdeburg on its administrator's death. Given his abject weakness in 1640, these were fairly impressive gains for the young elector. The key to these small but significant gains was Frederick William's establishing of a small but effective army. Very early on, he decided that if his territories were to be built into a viable state, they needed a powerful army, both to deter invasion and to protect its small and scattered territories. In 1648, the Elector possessed a force of 2,000 men. At its peak in 1678, his army numbered 45,000, and at his death Frederick William commanded a force of 30,000 men.

The chief obstacle to building up such a force was of course finding the means to pay for it. The Elector's traditional revenues were clearly insufficient, so other sources of revenue had to be found. Over the course of his reign, the Great Elector made alliances with other powers, which included subsidies from other rulers for his army. Utterly ruthless and calculating in his foreign policy, he periodically switched sides, thus managing to profit from both sides in the wars of Louis XIV, which dominated the later seventeenth century (see Chapter 17). Therefore, in the War of Devolution (1667–68) when French armies overran the Spanish Netherlands, Louis XIV bribed Frederick William into neutrality. During the subsequent Dutch War (1672–78), he switched sides no less than three times.

Even foreign subsidies, however, could not completely pay for the Elector's army. Inevitably, he would have to resort to extraordinary taxation. And just as inevitably, these demands for taxation brought conflict with the representative assemblies, or *Landtäge*, of his various territories. His basic strategy was to split the opposition to his taxation demands by siding with the nobles, or *Junkers* as they were known, against the urban middle classes, by at least partially exempting the nobles from taxes and recognizing and enhancing their control over their estates and serfs. In 1653, he managed to obtain from the *Landtag* of Brandenburg a sum of money that enabled him to expand his army to 20,000 men. This money was to be paid by commoners in six annual instalments. The price he paid for this was the recognition of the *Landtag*'s political powers, which he promised not to violate. At the same time he confirmed and expanded the privileges of the nobility. The *Junkers* alone could own land, and their virtually unlimited right to seize land and evict peasants was confirmed. All peasants were assumed to be serfs unless they could prove positively that they were free. When the money granted proved insufficient to support the army, Frederick William ignored his promises to the *Landtag* and simply increased the amount to be paid, using his army to enforce and collect it. In subsequent years, the Elector was able to impose an excise tax without the consent of the *Landtag*.

In Prussia, a similar situation prevailed. The centre of resistance was the important port city of Königsberg. In 1661, there was open revolt in the city, which required military suppression. The Prussian assembly then granted the Duke/Elector a three-year excise tax in return for a promise to respect its right to consent to further taxation. As in Brandenburg, Frederick blatantly violated his promise in the following years, which led to further resistance. In 1674 Königsberg was subjected to military occupation. As in Brandenburg again, this was achieved by siding with the nobility at the expense of the peasants and middle classes, confirming the *Junkers*' control over their estates and serfs. In his western territories of Cleves, Mark, and Ravensburg, however, the Great Elector was rather less successful in eliminating the power of the popular assemblies. These territories were more highly urbanized, with a free peasantry and a correspondingly less powerful nobility.

As the only institution common to all of the Elector's territories, the army increasingly became the core of Brandenburg-Prussia. This is apparent if we look at the development of the General War Commissariat, or *Generalkriegskommissariat*, which increasingly appropriated all the functions of government to itself. Since the primary consumer of tax revenue was the army, it only made sense that the officials of the General War Commissariat should supervise the assessment and collection of taxes. This body also assumed responsibility for economic and fiscal reform, and by the end of the century its officials had largely replaced urban governments and taken over most of their functions. In a very real sense the state of Brandenburg-Prussia was created to serve the army, rather than the other way around. Year after year, the army consumed half of the government's revenue.

Frederick William also had a direct interest in trying to build up the economy of his territories. In doing so, he proceeded on the basic mercantilistic assumptions of his times. He encouraged self-sufficiency in agriculture and industry. He actively recruited foreign immigrants from more advanced areas to settle in his territories, bringing with them their expertise and capital. He welcomed Huguenot refugees from France, with his territories becoming the new home of some 20,000. By 1688 fully a sixth of Brandenburg's population was made up of immigrants. He attempted to encourage foreign trade by building canals and reducing internal tariffs and tolls. Yet the economic base of Brandenburg-Prussia was still too weak for his economic policies to turn his state into an economic leader. Indeed, in economic terms his policies were self-defeating: his political policies weakened and retarded the development of a commercial middle class on which the success of his economic reforms depended. Therefore, the economy remained overwhelmingly rural and agrarian.

By his death in 1688, the Great Elector had taken an assortment of separate territories and welded them into one of the most efficient and effective states of the time, making himself a ruler to be reckoned with on the European diplomatic scene. At the same time, he greatly enhanced his power by relegating the *Landtäge* in Brandenburg and Prussia to virtual impotence and using his army to enforce his policies. He had succeeded in co-opting the nobility into his service by recognizing and expanding their social and economic pre-eminence. Yet it is easy to overstate the modernity of his vision and accomplishment and to see him as the self-conscious founder of a centralized and unified Prussian state that would unify Germany in the nineteenth century. His vision was that of an absolute dynastic ruler of the seventeenth century. Despite all his successes in unifying his territories, in his will of 1680 he carefully divided up his lands and titles among his six sons.[1]

When the Great Elector died in 1688, he was succeeded by his eldest son as Elector Frederick III. History has been rather less kind to the son than to the father, and certainly they were very different personalities. Frederick was very much devoted to the pomp and ceremony of court life and deliberately imitated Louis XIV in these matters. He was also very devoted to literature, poetry, and high culture in general. His chief aim was to obtain the title of king for himself and his family. This, however, was a tricky proposition, since in theory only the Holy Roman Emperor could elevate him to royal status, and the Habsburg emperors were loath to create a king within the empire, let alone a Calvinist king. In the early eighteenth century, however, a constellation of circumstances succeeded in gaining Frederick the title he so coveted. Primarily, Emperor Leopold I sought Frederick's support in the diplomatic manoeuvring for the Spanish succession (see Chapter 17) and thus consented to grant him the title of king. The operative question, however, was of which of his possessions was he to be king? Reluctant to create a Protestant kingdom within the Holy Roman Empire, Prussia became the obvious choice for the royal title, yet Prussia had never been part of the Empire. The dilemma was sidestepped by granting Frederick the title "King in Prussia" rather than "King of Prussia." Therefore, in 1701, Elector Frederick III became King Frederick I.[2] Frederick I has often been criticized for his relentless and costly pursuit of his royal title and for his vast expenditures on palaces and courtly life. Yet this was tremendously important in an age that valued symbolism and ceremony much more than our own. It can be argued that in order to be treated as a king alongside other kings, Frederick needed to behave as a king.

Still, there can be no doubt that as a ruler Frederick was less successful and forceful than his father. On the other hand, at the very least, he did nothing to undo his father's achievements. Indeed, the centralization of these territories continued apace, as did the development of royal absolutism. Upon his death in 1713, he was succeeded by his eldest son, King Frederick William I (1713–40). It was under Frederick William, and even more under his son Frederick II or Frederick the Great (1740–86), that Brandenburg-Prussia would become one of the great powers of Europe.

The Habsburg or Danubian Monarchy

For two centuries prior to the end of the Thirty Years' War in 1648, the main goal of the Habsburg Holy Roman Emperors had been to enhance and enforce imperial power in Germany. The Peace of Westphalia put a decisive end to these ambitions. Though they would remain Holy Roman Emperors and involved in German affairs, from now on the attention of Habsburg rulers was focussed on their hereditary territories, rather than on the Holy Roman Empire. There was thus a fundamental reorientation of Habsburg policy. From their capital of Vienna, instead of looking north and west toward Germany, in the course of the seventeenth century they began to look south and east, along the basin of the Danube river. Hence the name sometimes used by historians to describe their possessions is the Danubian monarchy. Indeed, it is significant that there is no single name that one can apply to these territories, such as "France" or "England," for there was no legal, political, ethnic, or institutional unity in these territories, other than the fact that they were ruled by the Habsburg dynasty. In addition, within the Habsburg dominions there was a bewildering variety of languages, cultures, and ethnic groups: Germans, Czechs, Poles, Slovaks, Hungarians, Slovenes, Croats, and Romanians, to name only the most prominent. Constrained by this institutional and cultural diversity, and also by a central European position that rarely left them free of military threats, the Habsburg emperors did their best to centralize power in their hands. Unlike most of the other countries of Europe, however, in the Habsburg Empire this was accomplished through compromise and the search for consensus among the various national and social groups of which it consisted.

Habsburg attempts to assert and expand control of these territories in the seventeenth century rested upon two pillars: respecting noble control of their estates and peasants, and the enforcement of strict religious unity under the banner of reformed Tridentine Catholicism. As in the other states of central and eastern Europe, a small nobility dominated an overwhelmingly agrarian society made up of unfree peasant labourers or serfs. Because of the enormous diversity of the Habsburg domains, the conditions of serfdom varied quite a bit from place to place, and it is difficult to generalize, but conditions were generally worst in Hungary where an ethnic Magyar nobility dominated a largely Croatian serf class. In Hungary, just 13 great nobles controlled 37 per cent of the villages, while in Bohemia, 82 aristocrats controlled 62 per cent of the peasants. As elsewhere, this small group of noble landowners cultivated their estates as commercial enterprises, and the conditions of serfdom were gradually increased as a means of keeping costs down and maximizing profits. By the middle of the seventeenth century, virtually all Bohemian peasants were serfs, while in Habsburg-ruled Hungary the proportion was around 90 per cent. These peasants had to perform *robot*, or labour-services, on the lord's land up to three days a week. Many, perhaps most, peasants performed this labour service mechanically and without enthusiasm, giving the current meaning of the English word "robot."

The other pillar of Habsburg rule was Tridentine Catholicism. Wherever they were able, Habsburg rulers increased persecution of Protestants while at the same time inculcating Catholic beliefs among ordinary people. Educational institutions were handed over to religious orders, particularly the Jesuits. Political office was limited to Catholics, inducing many Protestant nobles to convert. The Habsburg emperors also enthusiastically embraced the veneration of the Virgin Mary; Emperor Leopold I named seven of his nine daughters after the mother of Christ.

The Habsburg or Danubian monarchy was composed of three major blocs of territories. The heart of the monarchy consisted of the Austrian duchies of Upper and Lower Austria, Tyrol, Styria, Carinthia, and Carniola. The Kingdom of Bohemia comprised the provinces of Bohemia, Moravia, and Silesia. Then there was the Kingdom of Hungary. In 1526 Archduke Ferdinand, brother of Emperor Charles V and later Emperor Ferdinand I, had been elected king of Hungary. For most of this period, however, most of Hungary was occupied by the Ottoman Turks. Habsburg control consisted of a strip along the border with Austria, known as Royal Hungary. Indeed, the Ottoman presence in Hungary was a constant threat and worry for the Habsburgs in particular, and for Christian Europe as a whole. Vienna was in reality a frontier city, with Ottoman forces a mere eighty miles away. Eastern Hungary consisted primarily of the ethnically and religiously diverse principality of Transylvania. The princes of Transylvania, though nominally subject to Turkish rule, in fact enjoyed a precarious independence and were at various times able to challenge Habsburg efforts to reclaim all of Hungary.

In the course of the Thirty Years' War, as we have seen, the Habsburgs gained virtually complete control of Austria and Bohemia. Rebellious Protestant nobles, peasants, and townsmen had been crushed. The once powerful Estates of Bohemia had been rendered impotent, and the lands of rebellious Czech nobles confiscated and given or sold to loyal Catholics, many of them foreigners, mostly Germans. The Crown of Bohemia had been declared hereditary in the Habsburg dynasty. Protestant pastors had been expelled, Protestant worship outlawed, and educational institutions turned over to the Jesuits. The situation in Austria was similar, with the near total triumph of Habsburg power and Counter-Reformation Catholicism.

It was Hungary that was the real obstacle to the expansion of Habsburg control. This kingdom was dominated by a proud and fiercely independent nobility, who were extremely sensitive to their ethnic distinctiveness and political independence. As had been the case in Bohemia, the Crown of Hungary was elective, and the nobles knew how to use this power to extort concessions from their Habsburg kings. The nobles controlled Hungary's assembly, or diet, and enjoyed the *jus resistendi*, or the constitutional right of rebellion against any violation of their rights and liberties. Moreover, a large proportion of the Hungarian nobility were

Protestant, mostly Calvinist, and were determined to use their political power to defend their religious liberty. The situation of Hungary within the Habsburg dominions after the Thirty Years' War was analogous to that of Bohemia before it. That is, there was an ethnically distinct nobility with extensive political power who were determined to use that power to protect their religious liberty and political prerogatives. In the case of Hungary, however, there were several added complications. One was that about two-thirds of the country was occupied by the Turks. This meant that the Habsburg kings of Hungary could not pursue their political and religious agenda too rigorously, for they needed the support of the Hungarian nobles to aid in their defence against the Turks. In fact, many Hungarian nobles actually preferred Turkish rule to Habsburg rule. The Turks allowed them to freely practise their religion and made no efforts to reduce their political autonomy. As long as taxes were paid, the Turks were happy to let each area govern itself as much as possible. Nevertheless, during the reign of Ferdinand II, important steps were taken in the implementation of Counter-Reformation Catholicism in Hungary. The key figure here was Cardinal Peter Pázmány, Archbishop of Esztergom (1570–1637). Although born into a Calvinist family, he was educated by the Jesuits and later joined the order. He sponsored the activities of the Jesuits and other missionary orders in Hungary, with the result that, by his death, virtually all of the hundred or so Hungarian magnate families had converted to Catholicism. The lower nobility, or gentry, however, remained overwhelmingly Calvinist, and in the current circumstances, neither church nor government could do much about it.

Then there was the problem of Transylvania. Ruled by autonomous princes, theoretically subject to Turkish authority, Transylvania was ethnically and religiously diverse and religiously tolerant. The princes of Transylvania on several occasions launched invasions of Royal Hungary in defence of Hungarian religious and political liberties. For Habsburg rulers, then, Hungary presented a difficult dilemma. They wished to apply to Hungary the same solutions that had been worked out in Austria and Bohemia, or, as one of the advisors of Emperor Leopold I put it, "to put the Hungarians into Czech trousers." But the political independence of the Hungarian nobles could not be reduced while their cooperation was needed against the Turks. It was only after the Turkish military threat began to recede that the Habsburgs could attempt to bring Hungary into line with their Austrian and Bohemian lands.

The ruler of the Habsburg lands for the last half of the seventeenth century was Leopold I (Holy Roman Emperor, 1658–1705). Leopold's reputation has suffered in comparison with the other powerful rulers of the day, such as Louis XIV, Frederick William, the Great Elector of Brandenburg, Peter the Great of Russia, and William III of the Dutch Republic and King of England. Like his unfortunate Spanish cousin, Charles II, Leopold suffered from the physical (though not the mental) results of generations of Habsburg inbreeding. His lower jaw and lip jutted out so far that when it rained he could not keep the water out of his mouth. He was typical of his family in his personal morality and integrity, as well as in his religious devotion. He had been educated by the Jesuits for a career in the Church before the untimely death of his older brother cast him into the political limelight. He once stated, "I want to have the most holy Virgin Mary as my commander-in-chief in wartime and my ambassador during peace negotiations." He was also highly cultured and widely read. In his policies he was extremely cautious and had difficulty making hard decisions. Yet it is arguable that these were precisely the qualities required to rule such a disparate and vulnerable constellation of territories. One would certainly have a hard time arguing with the results. By the end of his long reign, the Turkish military threat to central Europe had permanently receded, Hungary had been conquered and the Hungarian nobility tamed and integrated into the Habsburg empire, and the Danubian monarchy was one of the five great powers that would dominate Europe until the early twentieth century.

As we have seen, the major complication in Habsburg rule of Hungary was the presence and power of the Ottoman Turks. In the sixteenth century, the Ottomans had posed a direct and serious threat, several times laying siege to Vienna itself. In the intervening years, however, the threat had waned somewhat. Economic and political turbulence at home, combined with renewed war against Persia in the east, meant that for the first half of the seventeenth century, Ottoman forces were dormant in Europe. This would change in the 1650s with the accession of several members of the Köprülü family as Grand Viziers, or prime ministers. Albanian in origin, Mehmed Köprülü came to power in 1656 and undertook a wide-ranging reform of the Empire's finances and military. Now the sultan's gaze turned back toward Europe. The first victim of Ottoman renewal was the autonomous principality of Transylvania. The prince, George Rákózi II, had alienated the Ottomans with his ambition and independence. In 1660, therefore, Ottoman forces invaded Transylvania and killed the prince in battle. Leopold was timid in his support, but not timid enough to prevent Ottoman retaliation. In 1663, the Sultan declared war, and an Ottoman army under a new Grand Vizier, Fazil Ahmed Köprülü, invaded Royal Hungary. In August 1664, a Habsburg army that was outnumbered 2 to 1 inflicted a decisive defeat on the Ottoman army at St. Gotthard on the Austrian border. Yet Leopold failed to follow up on this victory, outraging many Hungarians who saw this as a supreme opportunity to free their country from Ottoman rule. Leopold was concerned about Louis XIV's growing ambitions and had one eye on the Spanish succession, so he was reluctant to commit himself to all-out war in Hungary. Instead, he signed the humiliating Treaty of Vasvár (1664) in which he surrendered several border fortresses, recognized Ottoman control of Transylvania, and agreed to pay the Sultan an annual "gift" of 200,000 ducats. In return, the Emperor received only the promise of a twenty-year truce with the Ottoman Empire.

The Treaty of Vasvár convinced many prominent Hungarian nobles that Emperor Leopold was subordinating Hungary to his other interests. Therefore, in the 1660s a number of Hungarian magnates invoked the *jus resistendi* and plotted to overthrow Habsburg rule and make Royal Hungary an independent kingdom.

Through their own incompetence and indecisiveness, the plotters were eventually exposed, and in 1670 the three principal ringleaders were executed. Leopold and the government seized the opportunity to enforce a stricter rule on Habsburg Royal Hungary. Although all of the plotters were Catholic, the government used the opportunity to persecute Protestants. The government of Hungary was put into the hands of foreigners, as Leopold ignored the traditional constitutional liberties of the Hungarians. The nobles were forced to pay taxes, which were collected through armed force. These repressive policies soon produced insurrection among Protestants and Hungarian nobles and their peasants. A disaffected Protestant nobleman named Imre Thököly provided leadership. For nearly a decade a guerrilla war was waged before Leopold agreed to compromise, and in 1681 he restored the Hungarian constitution, called a meeting of the Diet, and restored limited toleration to Protestants. Thököly and the rebels rejected these concessions as insufficient. Thököly was in contact with both the French and Turks and hoped to have himself made king of an independent Hungary. At the same time, the new Grand Vizier of the Ottomans, Kara Mustafa (brother-in-law of Ahmed Köprülü), embarked on a renewed aggressive policy in Hungary. The Ottomans recognized Thököly as king of Hungary, and with the expiration of the truce of the Treaty of Vasvár in 1683, the Ottoman Empire declared war on the Habsburg monarchy and launched an invasion along the Danube, laying siege to Vienna in July 1683.

Faced with a Turkish army that was vastly superior in numbers, Leopold and his court hastily fled Vienna for Passau, further to the west, from where he directed military operations and tried to enlist allies. For two months Vienna was besieged by the Turks, with brutal cruelty on both sides. Finally, in September, a force composed primarily of Austrian and Polish troops, with smaller contributions from Leopold's German allies, appeared on the heights of Kahlenberg in the Vienna suburbs. The force was commanded by King John Sobieski of Poland, who feared that Turkish victory in Austria threatened Poland next. On September 12, 1683, the numerically larger Turkish force was decisively defeated and retreated in disorder back down the Danube. Kara Mustafa paid with his life for the failure to take Vienna. The lifting of the siege of Vienna marked the end of the Muslim Ottoman threat to Europe, prompting many to attribute the victory of Christian arms to divine Providence. Many, thinking of King John Sobieski, recalled the words of the Gospel of John in reference to John the Baptist: "There was a man sent from God whose name was John."

In contrast to the battle of St. Gotthard two decades earlier, Leopold seized the opportunity to take the battle to the Turks. The alliance that had led to victory in Vienna was continued and expanded by the addition of Russia and the support of the Pope, and was rechristened the Holy League. By 1687 virtually all of Hungary and Transylvania had been reconquered. Victory followed victory as Habsburg armies reversed 150 years of Turkish rule. Only the prospect of protecting Habsburg interests in continuing manoeuvring over the Spanish succession prompted Leopold to make peace with the Turks in 1699. The Treaty of Karlowitz ratified the Habsburg gains that had been made in Hungary since 1683.

With the end of the Turkish threat, the way was paved for the integration of Hungary into the Habsburg Empire. Many of Leopold's advisors urged a radical policy of repression upon the Emperor, which Leopold resisted. Instead, in 1687, he promised to respect the traditional constitutional liberties of the Hungarian nobles—but at a price: that the nobles give up their right to elect the king. The Hungarian throne was made hereditary in the Habsburg dynasty. In addition, the nobles gave up the *jus resistendi*, the constitutional right of rebellion against a king who violated their privileges and liberties. Hungarian nobles were thus confirmed in their control of their estates and serfs even as they were more closely integrated into the Habsburg Empire. At the same time, however, Hungarians were completely excluded from imperial policy-making, which continued to be the province of a small circle of Austrian and Bohemian advisors. Leopold also agreed to restore religious liberty to the Hungarian nobles, but in practice this liberty was very narrowly defined.

The Treaty of Karlowitz also recognized Habsburg control of Transylvania. The principality was not, however, incorporated into the Kingdom of Hungary, for fear of strengthening the Hungarian nobility with their even more restive Transylvanian brethren. Transylvania was allowed to keep its distinctive political and religious culture.

The Habsburg conquest of Hungary also opened up for settlement vast tracts of underpopulated land that had been under Turkish rule for 150 years. A Commission for the Newly-Acquired Territory or *Commission Neo Acquisitica* (from which Hungarians were excluded), supervised the allocation of this land. In theory, the descendants of those who held it at the time of the Turkish conquest were able to reclaim their families' lands, but they had to produce positive proof of ownership that was in most cases impossible. And even if they could produce the required proof, they had to pay a heavy administrative fee of 10 per cent of the land's value. As a result, much of the land was sold or given to loyal Habsburg supporters, either Catholic Hungarian magnates or German or Bohemian nobles.

These policies caused much resentment, which in 1703 erupted into a rebellion led by Francis Rákózi, a relative of the former princes of Transylvania. Since the Emperor's armies were busy in the west during the War of the Spanish Succession, the rebels met with some initial successes. By 1711, however, the Habsburg emperor was able to divert troops to Hungary and peace was negotiated. The peace confirmed the earlier commitment to respect the rights and liberties of the Hungarian nobles, and this time it proved more lasting. The integration of Hungary was therefore less complete and less repressive than that of Bohemia fifty years earlier. The Hungarian nobility retained more of their rights, including religious liberty, but at the same time were kept away from levers of power in Vienna.

Leopold I died in 1705 after a reign of almost 50 years, with the Habsburg dominions certainly in a much stronger position than they had been at his succession. He was succeeded by his elder son Joseph I (1705–11), a very different figure from his father. Although a devout Catholic, he was less favourable toward the Jesuits and more secular in outlook. How the Habsburg monarchy might have differed had he reigned a long time, we will never know, for he died suddenly of smallpox in 1711. Since he had no children, he was succeeded by his younger brother, who became Emperor Charles VI (1711–40). Charles had been educated in Spain and groomed for the Spanish succession, with little thought that he might one day take charge of the Habsburgs' central European possessions. With his accession, the emphasis on Counter-Reformation Catholicism was renewed, along with the prominence of the Jesuits.

The growth of royal power in the Habsburg monarchy was thus very different than in Brandenburg-Prussia. To a much greater extent, the local functions of government were carried out by local elites rather than by agents of the central government. This was both a strength and a weakness. Given the diverse ethnic and cultural makeup of the monarchy, this way of proceeding gave local nobles an interest in their alliance with the Habsburg monarchy. (Indeed, the Habsburg Empire was about to become even more diverse. In the division of the Spanish possessions that resulted from the Treaty of Utrecht of 1713, the Austrian Habsburgs gained their Spanish cousins' lands in the Netherlands and Italy.) It was a bargain from which both parties benefited. Habsburg "absolutism" was therefore more cooperative than in Brandenburg-Prussia. Or, rather, the base of cooperation was much broader than in Brandenburg-Prussia, where the army and the administration provided the arena for cooperation between ruler and nobility. The strength of the Habsburg system was therefore that it gave noble elites from a number of different nationalities a sense of belonging to a larger enterprise, one that was devoted to Counter-Reformation Catholicism and the perpetuation of the dynasty. This diversity was also a weakness, because of the tenuousness of the ties that held the system together. In the coming Age of Enlightenment, could devotion to a set of religious ideas and practices suffice to hold together such a diverse constellation of territories? And what of the dynasty? If the dynasty should fail to provide an acceptable heir, on what basis could the system continue? Indeed this very question absorbed a great deal of Charles VI's time and energy. In 1713 he promulgated the Pragmatic Sanction, which declared the Habsburg possessions to be indivisible and hereditary. When his only son died in infancy, Charles persuaded the estates of his lands to accept the principle of inheritability in the female line. He was also indefatigable in gaining the assent of other rulers to the Pragmatic Sanction, for he realized that his empire presented a tempting target to other rulers. The other rulers agreed to it, but when Charles died in 1740, leaving his empire to his daughter Maria Theresa, they were quick to disregard their commitments. The very fact that she was able to defend her inheritance (with the loss of only Silesia), and that Habsburg emperors played a vital role in European diplomacy until the early twentieth century, says a great deal about the effectiveness and durability of the system that was put in place in the course of the seventeenth century.

Russia Under Peter The Great

It was during the reign of Tsar Peter I, or Peter the Great (1682–1725), that Russia became a European power. Certainly the Tsar himself was an important factor in this development, yet the process had been underway for some time and was probably inevitable. Even as Russia expanded eastwards and southwards across the steppes and into Siberia, it was still vulnerable to the west. Sweden controlled Finland and the eastern Baltic coast. Poland, with which there was a bitter military rivalry compounded by religious and cultural differences, was still a power to be reckoned with. Further south, the Ottoman Empire controlled the Balkans and the Black Sea. Thus, even before Peter's reign, his predecessors had adopted western military and technological developments in order to better counter these threats. Foreign soldiers and craftsmen were recruited to bring the Russian military up to date.

Economically, too, Russia was growing closer to the rest of Europe by the time of Peter the Great. Muscovy's traditional access to western Europe had been through Poland, Lithuania, and the Baltic, and although these routes remained, Swedish dominance of the eastern Baltic made trade and communication along these lines difficult. In 1553, English ships pioneered the northern White Sea route through the port of Archangel. This trade was largely in the hands of English and Dutch merchants, and although it was increasingly important, it was fraught with difficulties. Archangel was a long way from Moscow and the Russian heartland, and while there were navigable rivers, they were frozen for a large part of the year. The same was true of the White Sea itself. Indeed, the fact that there were already substantial and growing economic contacts with the west is crucial in understanding a vital element of Peter's reign: the quest for an outlet on the Baltic Sea.

By the mid-seventeenth century, there was a substantial foreign community living in Moscow, numbering several thousand people. They were mostly English, Dutch, German, and Scottish and were for the most part soldiers, craftsmen, merchants, and physicians. They lived primarily in the "German Quarter" of the city. Their relationship with their Russian hosts was often uneasy, reflecting fundamental Russian ambivalence toward the outside world. On the one hand, there were elements within Russian society that admired western Europe and sought to emulate it, particularly its military, scientific, and technological achievements. On the other hand, Russian exceptionalism, manifested most strongly in Russian Orthodoxy, feared and suspected foreigners as heretics and a corrupting influence. In any case, the westernizing policies adopted by Peter the Great were by no means a complete novelty in Russian history. On the other hand, Peter's impatience, energy, and mercurial personality accelerated these developments and turned evolutionary change into revolutionary change. In the process, the net effect of Peter's reforms was paradoxically both to strengthen Russia's connection to the rest of Europe and to deepen the Russian ambivalence toward foreign influence.

Peter, born in 1672, was the son of Tsar Alexei by his second marriage. By his first marriage Alexei had two sons, Fedor and Ivan, as well as a daughter

Sophia. In contrast to the sickly and feeble Fedor and Ivan, young Peter was the very picture of health and vitality. When Alexei died in 1676, Fedor succeeded him as tsar and Peter, his mother, and their family were shoved aside as the family of Alexei's first wife took control. When Fedor died childless in 1682, Peter was proclaimed co-tsar with his older half-brother Ivan. As Ivan was blind and mentally retarded, and Peter was a boy of ten, their older sister Sophia was proclaimed regent.

During his boyhood, Peter spent a great deal of time in the German Quarter, or foreigners' district, of Moscow. It was here that he acquired his convictions that Russia was hopelessly backward and that western Europe was culturally and technologically superior. Even as a boy, Peter was intrigued with the way things worked. He was especially fond of anything military. He would organize his playmates in army companies and drill them. He learned to sail and became fascinated with boat building. Peter grew into a giant of a man, even by modern standards, with seemingly limitless reserves of energy and enthusiasm. He and his friends frequently indulged in wild, drunken parties, with no apparent effect on Peter's health or attitude.

As Peter grew into manhood, he became increasingly suspicious of the regent, his older half-sister Sophia. In particular, she was beginning to act as if she were the ruler, and not her two brothers. In 1689, alarmed by false rumours that Sophia's supporters were on their way to seize him, Peter launched a coup against the regent. Using his support within Moscow's foreign community and his "toy soldiers," who had now grown to manhood themselves, several of Sophia's closest advisors were seized and executed, while the regent herself was exiled to a convent. For the next few years, Peter was content to leave the actual government in the hands of his mother and her family, while he returned to his accustomed life of partying and frequenting the German Quarter. This would end, however, when his mother died in 1694. From 1696, with the death of his half-brother and co-tsar Ivan, until his death in 1725, Peter ruled on his own as he attempted to transform Russia.

In 1697, Peter led a group of 250 on a tour of western Europe. The Tsar intended to travel incognito as Peter Mikhailov, an aspiring shipbuilder. In fact, he was widely recognized, and he often became upset when he was not given due courtesy and attention as Tsar. For more than a year, Peter travelled through the Baltic, through Germany, and on to the Dutch Republic and England. For a time he worked as a carpenter in the shipyards of the Dutch Republic. During his trip, Peter became even more convinced of the superiority of western knowledge and technology. He determined that when he returned to Russia, drastic measures would have to be taken in this respect. As a means of introducing western knowledge to Russia, he recruited 750 craftsmen to return to Russia with him.

He was on his way back to Moscow in 1698 when he received word of a revolt against his rule. Indeed, many people were disturbed by the young Tsar's lack of respect for Russian traditions and his impious ways. This resentment found a particular resonance among the *streltsy*. Begun by Ivan the Terrible as a musketeer force to complement the traditional Russian cavalry, the *streltsy* had evolved into something like a Praetorian guard. More than 20,000 in number, they lived at government expense in their own neighbourhood of Moscow. With their privileges, many grew wealthy, and the *streltsy* became the primary defenders of old Muscovy and its ways. Old Belief was strong among them. Peter disdained them as old-fashioned, and regularly humiliated them. In June of 1689, several companies mutinied against their orders and marched on Moscow, where they hoped to enlist their brethren in revolt and possibly restore Sophia to power. (Sophia herself, however, was likely not directly involved in the revolt.) The mutineers were easily crushed by the regular army, and revolt was over by the time Peter got back to Moscow. He nevertheless exacted a terrible revenge. Nearly 1,200 *streltsy* were tortured and executed, and the rest banished to Siberia and their companies disbanded. Sophia was forced to take monastic vows and lived the rest of her life in strict seclusion.

Having returned to Russia and crushed his opposition, Peter began his policy of westernization in earnest. He was interested first and foremost in using western knowledge and technology to strengthen Russia's military. (Indeed Russia was at war for most of Peter's personal reign, first against the Ottoman Empire from 1695 to 1700, then against Sweden from 1700 to 1721, and finally against Persia beginning in 1722.) He had little interest in culture or education for their own sakes. Applying the mercantilistic assumptions then prevalent in the west, Peter used all the resources of his government to direct the Russian economy and Russian society in the paths he wished them to follow.

By the middle of the sixteenth century, Russia had been at least introduced to western European military reforms, largely through foreign commanders who had settled there. With his characteristic impetuousness, in 1700 Peter, along with the kings of Denmark and Poland, declared war on King Charles XII of Sweden (see Chapter 17). A humiliating defeat at Narva in 1700 convinced Peter that yet further western-style military reforms were needed, and quickly. Thereafter, the Russian army was made up of conscripts for life, drawn from the vast population of serfs. As a rule, every twenty households had to provide one recruit. Peter thus created a permanent standing army of 200,000. Likewise, landowners were required to serve as officers. Significant reforms were also undertaken in training, weapons, artillery, and discipline. Peter was also the founder of the Russian navy. Drawing on his enthusiasm for all things maritime, Peter built a fleet in 1696 to conquer the Turkish fortress of Azov on the Black Sea. More significant in the long run was the establishment of a Baltic fleet in the early 1700s in the course of the Great Northern War with Charles XII of Sweden.

Such an ambitious program of military reforms required a fundamental reorientation of the Russian government, economy, and indeed Russian society itself. A previously haphazard and inefficient system of taxation was improved by the introduction of a poll tax in 1717. This required a new census, to which there was enormous grass-roots opposition, and registration in many cases had to be compelled by armed force. When the poll tax finally came into effect in 1724, it brought in significant sums. It was, however, a decidedly regressive tax, as it consisted of a set amount on every male "soul," regardless of wealth or status. It therefore fell disproportionately on the serfs and was yet another factor in their continuing subjugation.

Peter also reformed both the central and local administrations. At the central level, following the Swedish example, he established "colleges" of officials to take over the responsibility for the functioning of the government. Thus there were colleges established for foreign affairs, the army, the navy, finance, the economy, and justice. The colleges were responsible to the Senate, which replaced the council of magnates, or *boyar* Duma. The Senate, a small body (originally there were nine members) appointed by the Tsar, had responsibility for setting policy and overseeing its execution. There was also another layer of officials to serve as Peter's eyes and ears in the colleges and throughout the administration. These were the *fiskals*, headed by an *oberfiskal* or procurator-general. Roughly analogous to French *intendants*, their job was to ensure the proper functioning of the government and to root out inefficiency and corruption.

Peter also attempted a far-reaching reform of provincial and local administration, although this was less successful than the reform of the central administration. In 1719, the country was divided into fifty provinces with elaborate administrative structures, but these were far removed from the realities of Russian life and society and therefore remained mostly confined to paper. Likewise, in 1721, municipal life and governance was the subject of a far-ranging reform edict. Peter hoped to create vibrant and prosperous urban communities such as those he had seen on his European travels. The intense regulation of urban life had, however, exactly the opposite effect of stultifying and paralysing urban development.

Once again taking his cue from western Europe, Peter sought to modernize Russia's economy along the mercantilist lines that were then current. He strove mightily to expand commerce and industry in Russia. Through either direct government involvement or the subsidization of private entrepreneurs, about 180 industrial establishments were set up. Most of these were directly related to military needs: iron mines and foundries for cannons, textile mills for uniforms and sails, sawmills for shipbuilding, and so on. In this program of rapid industrialization, Peter benefited from the vast pool of unfree labour in the serfs, who were drafted into industry in much the same way they were drafted into the army. Peter's efforts also had a significant effect on Russia's commerce. By conquering Swedish Estonia and Livonia and by establishing a port on the Baltic in the new city of St. Petersburg, access to the west was vastly improved. Tariffs were installed to discourage imports, and commercial treaties were signed with a number of countries.

Although Peter was fundamentally concerned with catching up with western Europe in technological and military matters, he was also determined to transform Russian society, although in ways that may seem trivial to us. After his return from western Europe, Peter ordered his nobles to shave their beards; indeed, the Tsar shaved a number himself. Beards were traditional for Russian men and had acquired religious significance. Later regulations allowed men to keep their beards with the payment of a special tax. Likewise, Peter forbade traditional Muscovite dress, at least among the aristocracy. He also encouraged the use of tobacco, partly as means of generating revenue since it was a government monopoly, but also partly because of its prevalence in the west.

More importantly, he sought to westernize Russian education for the elite who served in his military and government. He encouraged and indeed coerced Russian nobles to send their sons to the west to study gunnery, shipbuilding, navigation, and mathematics. At the same time, he broadened educational opportunities at home, at least for the aristocracy. A system of secular schools was established, the first in Russian history. Advanced academies were founded in the new capital of St. Petersburg for the study of engineering, artillery, and navigation. To "encourage" Russian nobles to send their sons to these schools, in 1714 he decreed that no Russian nobleman could marry without proof of having completed school. Resistance was so fervent that this measure was quickly revoked.

Peter viewed all of his subjects as servants of his state: the serfs through their farming and tax paying, and the nobles through their service in the military and government. Indeed, as we saw in Chapter 13, the Russian nobility had always been closely tied to the service of the ruler, at least in theory. Peter the Great succeeded in making theory into reality. In 1722, a Table of Ranks came into effect that would last until the Russian Revolution of 1917. All nobles were required to perform government service, whether in the military or civil service. There were fourteen ranks, with passage from lower to higher ranks achieved through a combination of seniority and merit. Social status was henceforth dependent on service to the state. In return, Peter enhanced the control of landowners over their serfs and did away with conditional tenure (*pomeste*) of noble estates, further cementing the social and economic predominance of the aristocracy.

Such dramatic changes to the fabric of Russian life and society inevitably provoked resentment and resistance. Because so much of the identity of traditional Muscovy was bound up with the Orthodox faith, most of the resistance to Peter's reforms was to be found among the devout. Although Peter himself observed the formalities of the Orthodox faith, his extravagant and excessive lifestyle aroused much hostility among the faithful. For example, in a scathing parody of a church council, he would periodically convoke an "All-Mad, All-Jesting, All-Drunken Assembly" at which he and his friends would drink themselves into a stupor and engage in behaviour deliberately designed to shock the pious. He also neglected the traditional elaborate court ceremonies that imbued the Tsar with a kind of mystical power. In 1721, he abolished the position of patriarch, and replaced it with a "Holy Governing Synod," in essence an administrative college such as those that had been established in the civil government, whose members were appointed by the Tsar. Having transformed the Orthodox Church into a department of the government, Peter used his control to reform and direct the Church in the ways he thought most useful. Entrance into monasteries was strictly limited and monastic discipline strictly enforced. Much church revenue was diverted to the government, and the Church was directed to fulfill its educational and charitable functions.

As was so often case, opposition to a ruler coalesced around the heir to the throne, in this case, the tsarevich Alexei. Born in 1690 to Peter's first wife Eudoxia, Alexei was highly devout, though unintelligent and lazy. Over the years Peter tried to prepare his son for rule by hounding and tormenting him. In 1716 Alexei fled Russia and was granted refuge by the Holy Roman Emperor Charles VI. Persuaded to return to Russia by promises of forgiveness, Alexei was thrown into prison and tortured into confessing to treason against his father. At the same time, a number of his friends and supporters were imprisoned and tortured. Even systematic torture did not reveal an organized opposition to Peter's rule. What it did reveal, however, was in some ways more troubling: widespread resistance to Peter's reforms and the hope that, on his death, Russia would revert to the "good old days." Sentenced to death in 1718, Alexei was spared public execution only by his death in prison under mysterious circumstances.

The problem of Alexei was intimately bound up with the problem of succession. The principle of hereditary succession by the eldest son of the ruler was the norm in Russia, but it was by no means as universally accepted as it was in the other European monarchies. With Alexei dead, Peter declared his heir to be his infant son Peter, son of his second wife Catherine, an illiterate Livonian peasant girl who had been his mistress for a number of years. Young prince Peter died, however, at the age of three in 1719. Catherine had previously borne two daughters, Anna (b. 1708) and Elizabeth (b. 1709), and in 1723 would give birth to another son who died shortly after birth. In 1722, Peter declared the right of the tsar to name his own successor, a step that he never took. After Peter's death, and for most of the eighteenth century, plotting and scheming over the succession would preoccupy and occasionally paralyse Russian rulers and the Russian political system.

Nothing represents the changes that Peter the Great brought to Russia as graphically as the construction of the new capital of St. Petersburg. To Peter, Moscow represented the backwardness of traditional Russia. Begun in 1702 on land wrested from Sweden, St. Petersburg was to be both a grand city in western styles and Peter's "window to the west"—a port city on the Baltic with direct access to western Europe. The land, however, was marshy, and thousands of serfs laboured and died in the construction of Peter's grandest monument. Peter insisted that anyone who wanted his ear and favour had to be physically present in St. Petersburg. And so the aristocracy reluctantly and unhappily followed the Tsar to the northern marshes, far removed from their estates and traditional haunts. From then until the Russian Revolution of 1917, and in some ways to the present day, the dichotomy of St. Petersburg (renamed Leningrad after the Revolution and since reverted to its original name) and Moscow has represented the fundamental ambivalence of Russian history. Moscow was situated in a central position to govern a vast empire that straddled Eurasia. St. Petersburg, on the other hand, was situated at the far western extremity of the empire, but in a position that reflected Peter's overarching ambition to remake Russia into a European power.

The legacy of Peter the Great is indeed mixed and complex. He did strengthen Russia's ties to western Europe, although this was a process that was already underway and would likely have occurred with or without him. On the other hand, the pace and nature of Peter's reforms make this change more revolutionary and wrenching than it might otherwise have been, creating and exposing deep rifts in Russian society. Much of the Russian aristocracy would become increasingly westernized in their cultural outlook, while the vast majority, who were of course their serfs, remained entirely and traditionally Russian in their outlook. Peter's reforms of the Church increased the suspicion and hostility of those who believed that foreign influence was an evil and corrupting force.

Peter also accelerated and enhanced the longstanding trend toward autocracy in the Russian monarchy. Indeed, it could be said that he created an absolute monarchy that Louis XIV could only dream of, with a subservient service nobility and masses of serfs. In fact, most western observers considered Russia a despotism rather than a monarchy like those of France, England, or Spain. But this dependence on the will of one man would prove problematic. The system could work reasonably well with an intelligent, capable, and energetic ruler such as Peter; in the hands of less capable rulers, however, it did not function nearly as well. Combined with confusion and infighting over succession after Peter's death, this meant that much of Russia's ability to participate in the European balance of power in the eighteenth century remained latent rather than actual. Only during the reign of Catherine II, or Catherine the Great (1762–96), would Russia actually play a vital role in European warfare and diplomacy.

At the heart of Peter's legacy is an even deeper ambiguity. Although he successfully turned Russia toward the west, and although a large portion of the elite adopted western fashions and culture, these things were possible only because Russian society was very different from western European society. Indeed, these things were accomplished in ways that profoundly accentuated the differences between Russia and the west. To be precise, most of Peter the Great's accomplishments were possible only because Russia was a serf society. The concept of the service nobility was possible only because Peter agreed to allow Russian nobles continued and enhanced control over their estates and serfs. The tremendous growth in Russian military power was possible only because of the vast pool of serfs who not only served as soldiers and sailors, but who also mined the iron and worked in the factories that supplied the military with weapons, ammunition, sails, and uniforms. Even St. Petersburg, Peter's western capital, was possible only because hundreds of thousands of serfs, many thousands of whom died, were conscripted to drain the marshes and dig the canals that made the city the "Venice of the North."

NOTES

1 That the Great Elector's territories survived as a unit under his eldest surviving son, Elector Frederick III, is attributable to the latter's annulling the terms of his father's testament after his death.

2 The dynastic history of Brandenburg-Prussia is thus complicated not only by the fact that every ruler from the Great Elector to the end of the monarchy in 1918 was named Frederick, William, or Frederick William, but also by the fact that they started renumbering themselves in the middle, when Elector Frederick III became King Frederick I in 1701.

CHAPTER SEVENTEEN

Establishing the Balance of Power: The Wars of Louis XIV

At the same time that Emperor Leopold I was struggling to evict the Ottoman Turks from Hungary (see Chapter 16), the diplomacy and foreign affairs of western Europe in the later seventeenth century were dominated by a series of wars provoked in large part by the ambitions and aggressions of Louis XIV. Meanwhile, in northern and eastern Europe, Peter the Great and Charles XII of Sweden were contending for control of the Baltic in the Great Northern War of 1700–21. By the early eighteenth century, these conflicts had been resolved in ways that established a general balance among the powers of Europe, a balance that would endure until the upheavals of the French Revolution in the 1790s.

Diplomacy and international relations in this period were in a transitional phase. Relations between states and rulers were no longer determined by religion, but religion continued to complicate them. For example, England and the Dutch Republic were fellow Protestant powers, but they found themselves fighting three wars in the mid-seventeenth century over commercial and naval issues. On the other hand, France and England were both opposed to the naval and commercial dominance of the Dutch but were separated by deep hostility over religion. In central and eastern Europe, the threat of the Muslim Ottoman Empire was on occasion sufficient to cause European powers, Catholic and Protestant, to put aside their religious and political differences in order to defeat the "infidel" threat. If religion had ceased to be a driving force in international affairs since the Peace of Westphalia in 1648, it still had the power to complicate things.

On the other hand, diplomacy was still not yet purely national in character. Not only were things complicated by religion, they were also complicated by the dynastic relations among the various ruling families of Europe. Rulers conducted their foreign policy in large part on the basis of their dynastic claims rather than any rational calculation of abstract national interest. Or, to be more precise, the two were inseparable in their minds. They did not, indeed could not, separate what was good for themselves, their dynasty, and their kingdom. In a famous phrase, Louis XIV of France is supposed to have said, "I am the State." Whether or not he actually said this is open to debate, but clearly he could have said it, for it accurately reflects his attitude. What was good for Louis and his Bourbon dynasty was by definition good for France. It is fundamentally anachronistic to think of rulers of this period acting on the basis of the interests of some abstract national identity called "France" or "England" or "Spain," separate and apart from themselves and their dynasties.

In the later seventeenth century in western Europe, Louis XIV attempted to become the dominant, hegemonic power. There were of course other tensions and rivalries, but Louis's ambition overshadowed them and forced other rulers to combine against him. So the threat from France caused England and the Dutch Republic to put aside their differences, a process greatly aided by the fact that they were both ruled by William III after 1689. Likewise, the Austrian Habsburgs and Brandenburg-Prussia put aside their rivalry in Germany in order to fight Louis XIV's aggressive policies there.

The Wars of Louis XIV in Western Europe

Since most of the diplomacy and warfare of this period revolved around the policies and ambitions of Louis XIV, it is necessary to evaluate what drove the foreign policy of the Sun King. Over the years, historians have advanced a number of different views. Some French historians of the nineteenth century maintained that he was attempting to give France its "natural" boundaries: the Rhine, the Alps, and the Pyrenees. This view has been largely refuted by subsequent research. To the extent that Louis XIV was driven by concern over boundaries, it was over defensible boundaries, especially in the northeast, adjacent to the Spanish Netherlands. This was especially the concern of Sebastien le Prestre, maréchal de Vauban, Louis XIV's chief military engineer who built a number of new-style fortresses and renovated many others in order to protect France's vulnerable northeastern frontier. Louis XIV also went to war because that was what a king was expected to do, especially a young and vigorous king such as Louis was at the beginning of his personal reign. He had before him the role models of his father, Louis XIII, and his grandfather, Henry IV, both of whom had distinguished themselves on the battlefield. Part of the contemporary image of kingship was the ideal of the chief warrior of the kingdom.

Above all, however, Louis was driven to war by concern for his reputation, his renown, his *gloire*. That is, Louis believed deeply that it was his due to be recognized as the greatest monarch in Europe. He needed not only to be the most powerful monarch, but also to be *seen* to be the most powerful monarch. In 1661, at the very outset of Louis's personal reign, there was a diplomatic incident in London that highlights this concern for his *gloire*. French ambassadors had been instructed not to cede precedence in any diplomatic functions, upsetting a century's worth of tradition according to which Spanish ambassadors had taken precedence. There was a riot in the streets of London between the retinues of the rival ambassadors. When Louis XIV threatened war over the issue, Philip IV of

Spain (Louis's father-in-law) gave way and agreed that French ambassadors would precede Spanish everywhere except Vienna. Though seemingly trivial in itself, this incident speaks volumes about Louis XIV and his foreign policy.

Besides the *gloire* of Louis XIV, the other pole around which later seventeenth-century diplomacy revolved was the prospect of the Spanish succession. As we saw in Chapter 11, Charles II, the last Habsburg king of Spain, was incapable of producing an heir. Therefore, upon his death, the vast Spanish Empire in Europe and the New World would be up for grabs. The unfortunate Charles II defeated everyone's expectations merely by continuing to breathe until 1700, but the issue of the Spanish succession was continually on the minds of the statesmen and rulers of Europe. It was a question of when, not if, and all were concerned to position themselves for a piece of the Spanish succession, or at least to deny it to others. All of the ruling families of Europe were closely interrelated through generations of dynastic marriage alliances; there were thus at least ten potential claimants for the Spanish throne. The strongest claims to the Spanish throne were those of Louis XIV and of Holy Roman Emperor Leopold I, each of whom were both the sons and husbands of Spanish Habsburg princesses. Furthermore, if the Spanish Empire fell undivided into one ruler's hands, that ruler would inevitably emerge as the dominant ruler in Europe. So all European rulers had an interest in who would succeed Charles II.

We see all these elements at work in Louis XIV's first war, the so-called War of Devolution against Spain in the Netherlands in 1667–68. When Philip IV of Spain died in 1665, Louis claimed that parts of the Spanish Netherlands should be inherited by his wife, Maria Theresa, rather than by her younger half-brother Charles II. French lawyers argued that according to the laws of these territories, female children of a first marriage took precedence over male children of a second in matters of inheritance, and so by right these territories belonged to Louis XIV's queen. In addition, although Louis XIV had putatively given up his wife's claims on Spanish possessions in the Peace of the Pyrenees of 1659, it was also claimed that this provision of the treaty was inoperative, since Maria Theresa's large dowry had not yet been paid in full. It simply never occurred to anyone to think about what the Netherlanders themselves might want, which says much about the dynastic nature of international relations.

After painstaking military and diplomatic preparations, a French army of some 20,000 men invaded the Spanish Netherlands in the spring of 1667. Spain, still dealing with the revolt in Portugal, was in no position to put up a strong defence. Town after town fell to French sieges, even as another French army occupied Franche-Comté. The prospect of French domination in the southern Netherlands quickly alarmed the other powers. England and the Dutch Republic, still enmeshed in the Second Anglo-Dutch War, soon reached a peace treaty and formed a Triple Alliance, along with Sweden, to impose an arbitrated settlement on Louis, failing which they would go to war against him. Johan de Witt and the Dutch government preferred to have a powerful France as an ally rather than as a neighbour, while the English feared French control of the entire Channel coast.

Meanwhile, Spain had recognized Portugal's independence and was therefore in a better position to strike back against the French invaders.

Faced with the possibility of having to fight numerous enemies at the same time, Louis agreed to a peace treaty in May 1668. According to the Treaty of Aix-la-Chapelle, France returned Franche-Comté to Spanish rule but held on to a number of small but significant gains along the boundary with the Spanish Netherlands. These included the city of Lille and a handful of important fortresses. Despite the intervention of the Triple Alliance, therefore, Louis XIV realized several small but significant gains from the brief War of Devolution. Although the boundary with the Spanish Netherlands could by no means be described as rational or secure, the possession of border fortresses at least made it more defensible than it had been. Perhaps more importantly, Louis had established the principle that he was in line for at least a portion of the Spanish succession.

Indeed, even before the war itself was formally concluded, Louis and Emperor Leopold had signed a secret treaty that partitioned the Spanish Empire upon the death of Charles II. Louis or his heirs were to receive the Spanish Netherlands, Franche-Comté, the Spanish portion of Navarre, as well as Naples and Sicily, while the rest—the Spanish kingdoms, the overseas possessions, Sardinia, and Milan—were to go to Leopold or his heirs.

Another legacy of the War of Devolution was that it poisoned Louis's attitude toward the Dutch. Traditional allies against Spain, Louis now felt betrayed by the perfidy of a nation of republican cheese-merchants and shopkeepers. He would write, "Rather than be interested in my good fortune, they wished to impose their law upon me and oblige me to make peace. They even dared threaten me in case I should refuse to accept their mediation." For once, Louis's primary ministers and rivals the Le Telliers and Colbert were in agreement that the Dutch had to be punished. For the next four years, French foreign policy was preoccupied with punishing the Dutch Republic. Sweden was bribed to abandon the Triple Alliance in order to harass France's potential enemies in northern Germany, in particular the Elector of Brandenburg. Charles II of England was brought onside in the Treaty of Dover 1670 (see Chapter 15). Alliances were made with various German rulers to allow passage to French armies and deny the same to Spanish or Imperial armies, and Emperor Leopold himself was intimidated into neutrality. In 1670, the independent Duchy of Lorraine, technically within the boundaries of the Holy Roman Empire, was occupied by French troops with hardly a voice raised in protest.

In the spring of 1672, a massive French force of 120,000 men invaded the Dutch Republic and met with huge initial successes. They quickly crossed the Rhine, capturing the important cities of Arnhem and Utrecht. In a panic, the Dutch government offered huge concessions. Buoyed by his initial success, however, Louis rejected these proposals. He believed that it was possible that he might not only take the Spanish Netherlands, but annex the Dutch Republic as well. Or, at the very least, the Republic could be neutralized as a diplomatic and commercial force to the benefit of France. The way seemed clear all the way to Amsterdam, but Louis ordered his armies to halt in order not to outrun their supplies. The

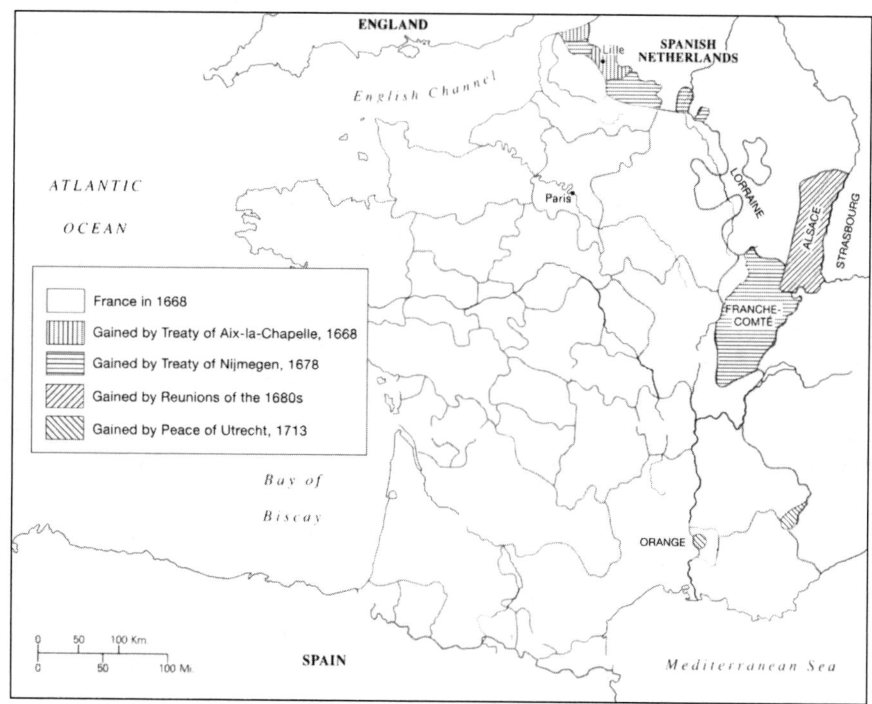

MAP 17.1 ⇛ TERRITORIAL GAINS OF LOUIS XIV

Dutch used this reprieve to open dikes, which turned Holland into an archipelago of towns surrounded by water. In the meantime, de Witt and the regents were forcibly overthrown and William III, Prince of Orange, assumed control of the Dutch Republic (see Chapter 12). In the coming years, William of Orange would prove to be Louis XIV's most implacable and effective foe.

With the invasion at a standstill, William worked tirelessly to dismantle the system of French alliances that threatened his country. Already in 1672, the Emperor and the Elector of Brandenburg had come to the Republic's assistance. In a stunning reversal of a century's worth of hostility, Spain declared war on France in alliance with the Dutch. In 1674, Charles II of England signed the Treaty of Westminster, abandoning the French alliance. Peace negotiations opened in 1676, but without a ceasefire they only intensified the fighting as each side sought to strengthen its bargaining position.

In 1678, the combatants finally signed the Treaty of Nijmegen that ended the Dutch War. In this treaty, Louis strengthened his northeastern frontier through the acquisition of several more border towns and fortresses and gained possession of Franche-Comté from Spain. Although Louis and his ministers put a positive spin on the outcome, the Dutch War was largely a failure. The Dutch were still independent and commercially powerful, and indeed were now led by Louis's most determined opponent. Louis's aggression had also raised up a coalition of rulers and powers who were rightly suspicious of the Sun King's ultimate ambitions to dominate Europe. In many ways, the Dutch War represents both the apogee and the turning point in Louis XIV's foreign policy. Although he would wage two more long and brutal wars, they gained France very little in the way of territory and cost much in the way of economic sacrifice and human misery.

Having strengthened his northeastern frontier, Louis turned his sights eastwards toward Germany. A series of special courts were set up to investigate French claims on territories along France's boundary with the Holy Roman Empire. These were called *Chambres de réunion* and were really a rubber stamp that legalized French military seizure of these territories. This area in particular was a conglomeration of small territories and cities with extremely tangled dynastic and historical ties. According to the *Chambres de réunion*, any territory that had ever been a dependent of another ruled by the King of France was fair game. Then, once the initial territory was occupied, any territories that had ever been dependent on it were in turn open to conquest. In this way, French forces occupied most of Alsace, as well as most of Luxembourg and a number of other territories. In addition, the important city of Strasbourg was taken through naked military seizure in 1681, as was the fortress of Luxembourg in 1684. Louis was able to pursue this aggressive policy in Germany because his opponents were once again divided and distracted. Emperor Leopold was preoccupied with the Ottoman threat that produced the siege of Vienna in 1683 and thereafter with the conquest of Hungary (see Chapter 16). William III of the Dutch Republic could not mobilize the cumbersome machinery of that country to oppose Louis XIV. Charles II of England was studiously avoiding any undertaking that might lead to war, which would require the calling of Parliament.

Eventually, however, Louis's aggressive policies in Germany aroused a united opposition. In 1686, the rulers of Saxony, the Palatinate, as well as the King of Spain and the Holy Roman Emperor formed the League of Augsburg to defend the territorial settlements arrived at in Westphalia in 1648 and Nijmegen in 1678. This was, in effect, a warning shot across Louis XIV's bow.

War was triggered in 1688 by Louis's attempt to install his candidate as Bishop of Cologne, who also ruled a strategically important territory in northwestern Germany. French forces invaded in September, hoping that a quick strike would lead to a swift and favourable settlement. Instead, just the opposite happened. Louis's enemies united against him as never before. The unity of the German rulers was strengthened by French conduct in the Palatinate, where soldiers ransacked the countryside and pillaged the towns in order to make it impossible to use the territory as the base for an invasion of France. Louis also lost a calculated gamble when he failed to oppose William III's invasion of England to claim the English throne from his father-in-law James II (see Chapter 15). Louis thought that James would fight back, and that England would once again become ensnared in civil and religious war. As we have seen, however, William easily took the English throne, and henceforth England's vast and growing financial resources were at the command of Louis XIV's most inveterate foe.

The so-called Nine Years' War, or War of the League of Augsburg (as it is also known), would drag on until 1697. At first the war went quite well for France, and French armies captured several important fortresses in the Netherlands. Eventually, however, the military tide turned as English naval might began to prevail and France fell victim to a series of poor harvests that led to famine in much of the country. By the later 1690s both sides were exhausted, and it appeared that the long-awaited death of Charles II of Spain was drawing nigh. In the Treaty of Ryswick of 1697, Louis surrendered almost all of his territorial gains of the previous twenty years, with the exception of Strasbourg. The Dutch were allowed to occupy a series of fortresses in the Spanish Netherlands to serve as a sort of seventeenth-century distant early warning system of French aggression.

With the looming death of Charles II of Spain, the question of the Spanish succession was once again first and foremost in the minds of European rulers and statesmen. Although a secret partition treaty had been signed by Louis XIV and Leopold I in 1668, it remained inoperative due to its very secrecy: such an arrangement inevitably required the agreement of the other interested powers of Europe. Moreover, Emperor Leopold was in a stronger position in the late 1690s than he had been in 1668, having steadily driven the Turks out of Hungary. Some new way of handling this complex and tricky question was therefore required.

In 1698, following a suggestion by William III, the interested parties agreed to divide the Spanish Empire upon the death of Charles III in the following way: Spain itself, its American colonies, the Spanish Netherlands, and the island of Sardinia were to go to the Emperor's grandson, Joseph Ferdinand of Bavaria, then still a small boy. The rest would go to Louis XIV's son, except for the Duchy of Milan, which was to go the Emperor's younger son, Archduke Charles. This solution might have worked, for it did divide up the Spanish Empire in a way that kept any one ruler from domination. There were two things that worked against it, however: first, Charles II of Spain, and the Spanish elite in general, were adamantly opposed to their empire being divvied up without their consent; second, no one thought that the Spaniards ought to have some say in who ruled them, not to mention the Netherlanders or Italians, or even the American natives. Charles II rewrote his will such that the whole of his possessions were to go undivided to Joseph Ferdinand. But in 1699 the young prince died at the age of seven, rendering this treaty null and void.

In 1700, therefore, England, France, and the Dutch Republic signed a new partition treaty. Spain and its colonies and the Netherlands were to go to Archduke Charles, while Louis XIV's son, the dauphin, was to get Naples, Sicily, and Lorraine. (The Duke of Lorraine was to be induced to trade Lorraine for Milan.) Emperor Leopold refused to countenance such a partition, feeling that the time was right to restore the empire of Charles V, while Charles II and the Spaniards once again objected to their empire being divided behind their backs. Accordingly, Charles II changed his will once again, leaving the entirety of his empire to one of Louis XIV's grandsons, Philip of Anjou. His appeal was that with the support of his grandfather he could defend the integrity of the Spanish Empire, but that as a younger grandson of Louis XIV he was unlikely to ever become king of France, thereby preserving Spanish independence.

In November 1700, the long-awaited death of Charles II finally came to pass. Louis XIV then faced a serious dilemma: should he abide by the terms of the partition treaty he had signed in 1700? Or should he uphold the will of Charles II and claim the entire Spanish Empire for his grandson Philip? Faced with such a tempting prize, Louis decided on the latter course of action, and young King Philip V of Spain entered his capital of Madrid in the spring of 1701. Although William III, Emperor Leopold, and the Dutch were upset by these events, this solution would have had a better-than-even chance of lasting had it not been for the rash actions of Louis XIV. He had the Parlement of Paris affirm the traditional order of succession for the French crown, meaning that Philip or his successor(s) might one day be king of both France and Spain. Then, having persuaded his grandson to name him regent for the Spanish Netherlands, Louis ordered the Dutch to vacate the border fortresses they had won in the Peace of Ryswick.

Given Louis's high-handed actions, and the mistrust and fear built up over the previous thirty years, war was now inevitable. In September 1701, a Grand Alliance was formed by England, the Dutch Republic, and the Holy Roman Emperor. Its goals were threefold: first, to prevent the union of the French and Spanish crowns in the same person; second, to secure Dutch possession of their border fortresses; and third, to secure something of the Spanish Empire for the Emperor in the Netherlands and Italy. Also, the Dutch and English had the additional, if undeclared, war aim of securing for themselves pieces of the valuable commerce of the Spanish Empire.

The War of Spanish Succession broke out in 1702 and was a long, bloody, and exhausting conflict that would drag on until 1713 and feature a number of savage and costly battles. In 1704, the English commander John Churchill, Duke of Marlborough, soundly thrashed a French army in Bavaria at the Battle of Blenheim. Then, in 1706, he drove the French from the Netherlands at Ramillies. The same year, Leopold I's great commander, Eugene of Savoy, drove the French from Italy at the Battle of Turin. Further allied victories at Oudenarde (1708) and Malplaquet (1709), combined with crushing taxation and widespread famine in France, drove Louis XIV to offer generous concessions in return for peace. He offered to return all his conquests, including Strasbourg, and to withdraw French armies from Spain. Not trusting him, however, the allies heightened their demands, insisting that Louis help to drive his grandson from the Spanish throne if necessary. This Louis simply could not do, so the war continued.

In the meantime, young Philip V of Spain was proving to be a popular and effective ruler. He supplied the political will to reform Spain that had been lacking under the later Habsburgs. Therefore, when an allied force landed in Spain in 1702, it met with no support. Although a force led by Archduke Charles invaded Catalonia and occupied Barcelona, it was unable to dislodge Philip V, and eventually Bourbon forces recovered Catalonia. By this time, the situation had changed somewhat. Most importantly, with the death of his older brother Holy Roman

Emperor Joseph I (1705–11), Archduke Charles, the putative claimant to the Spanish throne, had himself become Holy Roman Emperor. The Dutch and English allies were no more ready to see a revival of Charles V's empire than they were to see the French in control of Spain. The Dutch especially were feeling the strains of decades of war, and in England a palace revolution replaced Marlborough and his supporters with ministers more inclined to peace.

Philip V of Spain opened the way for a peace settlement when he agreed to forgo any claim on the French throne for himself or his heirs. In 1713 and 1714 the various combatants signed a series of treaties known collectively as the Peace of Utrecht. Philip V was recognized as King of Spain and its overseas colonies. The Emperor gained the southern Netherlands (henceforth known as the Austrian Netherlands), Milan, Naples, and Sardinia. France was to keep Alsace and Strasbourg, the Franche-Comté, as well as the gains it had previously made along her northeastern boundary. England gained the fortress of Gibraltar at the southern tip of Spain, as well as some French territories in the New World: Newfoundland, Acadia, and St. Kitts. England also gained an advantageous position in the trade of the Spanish Empire. France recognized George I's legitimacy as English monarch, bringing to an end French support for the exiled James II and his successors (see Chapter 15). The Dutch maintained their border fortresses in the (now) Austrian Netherlands, but in a weaker state than before. The Dutch also found themselves blocked out of the lucrative Spanish colonial trade, which the English had snapped up. Indeed, the Peace of Utrecht can be seen as the end of the Dutch Republic as an international power of the first rank.

The Peace of Utrecht may be seen as the definitive end of Louis XIV's and France's ambitions to dominate European diplomacy. Indeed, the last two of Louis's wars (the Nine Years' War and the War of Spanish Succession) had gained France virtually nothing in the way of territory and cost her an enormous amount in terms of money, men, and human misery. Yet in some senses, in the War of Spanish Succession Louis managed to snatch, if not victory, then survival, from the jaws of defeat. His armies had fought off a formidable alliance, and he had managed to place a grandson on the Spanish throne and keep most of the gains made in previous wars.

The net result of the Peace of Utrecht was that the Spanish Empire was divided so that all the interested parties got something, but no one got so much that they could threaten to dominate as Louis XIV had threatened to. It did indeed establish a balance among the powers of Europe that was to last until the ideological upheavals of the French Revolution at the end of the eighteenth century. In the meantime, the wars in the eighteenth century would be fought for more practical and limited aims. Whereas wars had previously been waged in the name of the true faith, or to establish European hegemony, eighteenth-century wars were fought over territories, colonies or resources, aims that were more attainable and therefore of rational cost-benefit analysis. Warfare in the eighteenth century would become a more refined and limited affair than in the age that had come to a close with the Peace of Utrecht.

Sweden, Russia, and the Struggle for Baltic Supremacy

King Charles XI (r. 1660–97) of Sweden attained the age of majority in 1672 and within several years managed to break the stranglehold the nobles had exercised on the royal government since the death of his father Charles X in 1660. In this he was greatly aided by the fact that the noble oligarchs had made themselves extremely unpopular through their greed in further alienating royal lands to their own benefit. Furthermore, in 1675 they went to war against Brandenburg in alliance with France, a war that ended in a humiliating defeat for the fabled Swedish army. Even worse, Swedish forces were driven from their possessions along the southern shore of the Baltic. The oligarchs who ran Sweden were saved from complete humiliation only by the intervention of Louis XIV, which restored the status quo in the 1679 Treaty of Fontainebleau.

Charles XI used the widespread dissatisfaction with the noble regime to establish a much more absolutist regime than had ever existed in Sweden. Yet it was an absolutism built on the explicit consent and agreement of the *Riksdag*, or at least the non-noble elements of it. In the *Riksdag* of 1680, the estates of the clergy, townsmen, and peasants demanded an absolute monarchy as a means of checking noble excess and incompetence. Charles seized on this support to effect a further "reduction," that is, restoration of crown lands that had found their way into noble hands. Noble holdings were reduced from two-thirds of the land to one-third. A Great Commission investigated noble conduct during the regency and forced many nobles to cough up their ill-gotten gains. With the money and resources gained in this way, Charles effected a thorough and much-needed reform of the government, army, and navy. He also freed himself from the need for foreign subsidies, such as those required by his neighbour and rival, Frederick William of Brandenburg, the Great Elector. In the 1693 Declaration of Sovereignty, the *Riksdag* declared that the king was "by God, Nature, and the crown's high hereditary right ... an absolute sovereign king, whose commands are binding on all, and who is responsible to no one on earth for his actions, but has power and might at his pleasure, as a Christian king, to rule and govern his kingdom."

Yet for all his success internally, Charles maintained a cautious foreign policy, for, as he said, "a war is soon begun, but as to its ending—that is in God's hands." The Swedish army and navy were efficient and kept in a high state of readiness, but Charles preferred not to use them if possible. Thus, he adroitly manoeuvred between France and her enemies, helping to establish a balance of power in which Sweden could play an important part. The inescapable fact was that Sweden's brief career as a great power, which had been brought about by the gains of Gustavus Adolphus, was now coming to a close. Brandenburg-Prussia threatened her territories in northern Germany, while Russia under Peter the Great posed a dire threat to her territories in the eastern Baltic. Poland, although declining, was still in a position to cause trouble for Sweden, as was her ancient enemy Denmark. Maintaining at least the appearance of a great power required the delicate fending off of all these threats, a task at which Charles XI was very successful. It was only during the reign of his son Charles XII (1697–1718) that the great power wrapping was ripped away, exposing the weakness beneath.

Charles XII's great nemesis would prove to be Tsar Peter the Great of Russia who, as we have seen, had dramatic ambitions to change his country. Peter's first foray into warfare came against the Ottoman Empire in 1695, when Russian forces attacked the fortress of Azov, which controlled the mouth of the River Don into the Black Sea. The attempt failed because the Russians could not counter Ottoman naval power. The very next year, Peter, with his usual enthusiastic and energetic approach, had a fleet built on the Don and successfully attacked Azov. Peter had hoped to spearhead a grand alliance against the Turks but was circumvented by the Treaty of Karlowitz between the Emperor and the Turks in 1699, and by the preoccupation of European rulers with the Spanish succession.

Besides, Peter soon became involved in the schemes of King Augustus of Poland to dismember Sweden's Baltic empire. Russia thus formed an alliance with Poland and Denmark to attack Sweden while Charles XII was still an inexperienced youth and would be an easy target, or so they thought. Charles, however, soon proved more than a match for the three allies. Physically courageous to the point of insanity, he had few interests outside of warfare and hunting. Thus, when the three allies launched the Great Northern War in 1700 by invading Swedish-ruled territory, Charles quickly turned the tables on the invaders, making good use of the efficient military forces bequeathed him by his father. Copenhagen was besieged in the summer of 1700, and King Frederick of Denmark signed a humiliating peace treaty. In the autumn, Charles's army of 6,000 met a Russian force of 40,000 men in a blinding snowstorm at Narva, in Ingria in the eastern Baltic. The disorganized and ill-disciplined Russian troops soon wilted under Swedish attack, and their foreign generals quickly surrendered. The humiliation at Narva only redoubled Peter's conviction that the westernization of Russia needed to be accelerated (see Chapter 16). Charles XII, however, failed to follow up his crushing victory. He was convinced that Narva had as good as driven Russia out of the war, and turned to attack Poland instead. By January 1702, the Swedish army had occupied Warsaw, and in 1705 Charles managed to replace Augustus on the Polish throne with a ruler more amenable to Swedish interests. This was an undistinguished Polish nobleman, Stanislas Leszczynski. Augustus, however, fought on and found increasing support among many Polish nobles who found Swedish manipulation unacceptable. Before he was elected king of Poland, Augustus had been Elector of Saxony, and Charles XII now prepared to invade Saxony in order to drive Augustus to make peace. In 1706, Augustus made peace with Sweden, recognizing Leszczynski as king of Poland.

Having driven Denmark and Poland out of the war, Charles now turned his attention to Peter the Great and Russia. In early 1708, he led an army of over 40,000 in an invasion of Russia from the west. By this time, however, Peter's efforts to update the Russian army had begun to bear fruit. Following a pattern used on several subsequent invasions (such as Napoleon's invasion in 1812 and Hitler's in 1941), the Russians drew the Swedish army into the vast Russian inte-

MAP 17.2 ⁂ EUROPE IN 1715

rior, destroying supplies as they retreated. Charles was forced to turn south into the Ukraine, which had not been devastated, in order to supply his army. He also hoped to link up with a rebellious group of Cossacks in the south. The harsh winter of 1708-09 took a heavy toll on the Swedish occupiers. In the summer of 1709, the Swedes attacked the fortress of Poltava, which lay between them and Moscow, and suffered a devastating defeat at the hands of the Russian defenders. Of the Swedish troops, 7,000 were killed and another 2,000 were taken prisoner. Forced to abandon the advance on Moscow, Charles led his remaining troops south into the Ottoman Empire, where he was given refuge by the Sultan.

In hindsight, we can see that the Great Northern War was essentially decided at Poltava in 1709, although the fighting would drag on until 1721, outlasting even Charles XII, who died in 1718. With the Swedish defeat, Charles's enemies regained their confidence. Augustus re-asserted his claim to the Polish throne, and Denmark invaded southern Sweden. By 1713, all of Charles XII's military gains had been reversed. Charles, meanwhile, was marooned in Turkey and was able to return to Sweden only in 1715. With the death of Charles XII and surrounded by enemies who had regained the advantage, the Swedes signed the Treaty of Nystad in 1721.

The Treaty of Nystad heralded a new phase in international relations in northern Europe. It reduced Sweden to the status of a minor power and inaugurated a period of Russian domination. Peter the Great gained possession of Sweden's eastern Baltic territories of Estonia, Livonia, eastern Karelia, and Ingria, where the construction of St. Petersburg was already well advanced. Denmark took over the disputed territory of Holstein. In an earlier treaty, the German state of Hanover (whose ruler had recently become King George I of England) bought the Swedish possessions of Bremen and Verden in northern Germany, while Prussia gained Swedish Pomerania. Of the empire that had turned the Baltic into a Swedish lake following the Thirty Years' War, only a small fragment remained: the port cities of Stralsund and Wismar and the island of Rugen.

PART FOUR

Toward a New World-View

CHAPTER EIGHTEEN

Intellectual Life: The Quest for Certainty

The sixteenth and seventeenth centuries were a time of profound change in the mental outlook of Europeans, especially among the elites of society. Looking at the period backwards, from the vantage point of the present, the most significant development was the construction of what we know as modern science. These developments have been labelled the "Scientific Revolution," but as we shall see, this label is fraught with problems. Yet seeing this period only through the lens of the "Scientific Revolution" considerably distorts the reality of the past, for this was a time of tremendous intellectual and cultural turmoil, in which various and sometimes contradictory impulses confronted each other in a picture that was at times messy and complex. Just about the only constant was the search for order, for reliable authority, in a world where all the old authorities and reliable truths were called into question. Different people at different times sought certainty in the experiences of the senses, in the processes of the human mind, in religious enthusiasm, and in revivals of ancient philosophies. It is impossible in the space available here to give anything approaching a comprehensive treatment of the intellectual life of this period. (It may well be impossible in any amount of space.) So, rather than attempt the impossible and inevitably fall short, what follows is an examination of some of the major figures and trends of the period that tries to strike a balance between outlining the major developments while still trying to do justice to its enormous variety and productivity.

The Scientific Revolution

In recent years, a number of historians of science have come to question the usefulness of the notion of a "Scientific Revolution" in the sixteenth and seventeenth centuries. Their objections to the term are based on several arguments. First, the very notion of a revolution implies a swift and dramatic change. Can a "revolution" truly last a century and a half? Second, the notion of a Scientific Revolution crudely conceived can convey the impression that there was a total break with the past. Rather, these historians argue, developments in science were firmly rooted in the past. The term "revolution" can also imply a deliberate intention to break with the past, an intention that was not always present. Finally, many historians dispute the idea that the figures involved in the "Scientific Revolution" were engaged in "science" in the modern sense, a sense that did not come into being until the nineteenth century. Rather, these men (and a very, very few women) were engaged in "natural philosophy." That is, they were enquiring into the workings of nature in the same ways in which moral philosophers enquired into what constituted the good life and theologians enquired into the nature of God and religion. There was as yet no "science" in our sense of the word, that is, a separate and distinct mode of inquiry with its own rules and procedures for establishing facts and truth. Indeed, this very notion of "science" was a creation of this period.

Is the concept of a "Scientific Revolution" then completely worthless? Surely not, for these developments were revolutionary in their impact and consequences, if not in their intent. While it is anachronistic to view the past only with reference to the present, it is just as mistaken to ignore the present in our approach to the past. Part of the historian's job is to understand how the past gave birth to the present; it is mere antiquarianism to deal with the past with no reference at all to the present. It is beyond debate that science is a dominant influence, perhaps *the* dominant influence, in our modern western world. This was not inevitable or "natural," since most past societies have had comparatively little interest in uncovering the workings of the natural world. Instead, it is a product of history, one that has its origins in the sixteenth and seventeenth centuries.

We must approach this topic with care, then, if we are to avoid the conceptual pitfalls that have often confused understanding. One such pitfall can be characterized as a "whiggish" and triumphal "march of progress" view of the Scientific Revolution. That is, the emergence of modern science was the product of a few brave individual geniuses throwing off the shackles of the ignorance and superstition of the past. For one thing, this approach artificially divides people into "progressives" on the side of truth and knowledge, and "reactionaries" devoted to perpetuating the darkness of the past. This can be accomplished only through a very selective reading of the past: whatever turns out to be "true" is put on the side of the progressives, while the dead ends are ignored. It also ignores the fact that many of the "heroes" of this story held views that are distinctly unscientific to our minds. These awkward facts must be explained away by the patronizing view that in certain areas, these people were still subject to the ignorance of the past. Part and parcel of this approach is what may be called a "relay-race" view, where the baton of scientific progress is passed from one scientist to another, while ignoring disagreements among scientists and the dead ends.

Closely allied to this (mis)understanding of the Scientific Revolution is the image of the scientist as an impartial observer of nature, closeted away in his laboratory where he derives his ideas without reference to the world outside. Much recent research has revealed the intricate and complex ways in which natural philosophers responded to political, religious, economic, and cultural developments in the broader society of early modern Europe. All or almost all of these natural philosophers were Christians, and most of them were notably devout Christians. Indeed, many were explicit in their views that they were attempting to better comprehend the divine creation and thus its Creator. Natural philosophy was for most a worship of a sort, so it is thus completely wrong to see a fundamental hostility between the science and the Christian churches of the age. There were conflicts, most famously in the case of Galileo, but they were exceptional rather than normative, and in most cases attributable to external factors rather than any inherent conflict between science and Christianity.

It is also important to understand that the Scientific Revolution did not come about through a prior revolution in method, nor was there (or is there today) a single accepted "scientific method" equally applicable to all sciences, problems, and situations. In fact, not only were there divergent views of the proper methods for investigating nature, but these only emerged in the course of the Scientific Revolution itself as scientists sought to explain and come to grips with the implications of their ideas.

Perhaps most importantly, we need to dispel the myth that what emerged from the Scientific Revolution was "Truth" as opposed to errors of the past. What emerged eventually were better explanations for observed phenomena, not necessarily eternal truths. Even today most scientists will acknowledge that they seek to advance better explanations rather than arrive at universal truths. We must also acknowledge that the old scientific "truths" were not self-evidently false or stupid. In fact, they explained observable phenomena almost as well as the new explanations. They were mathematically sophisticated, aesthetically pleasing and conformed more closely to common-sense observations than the new explanations that eventually took their place.

Indeed, many of the natural philosophers whose ideas contributed to the breakdown of the old explanations were trying to improve them, or perhaps even rescue them, from the difficulties and contradictions that had emerged. Thus it was in the sciences of astronomy and physics that the old explanations were first "improved," then challenged, and eventually discarded, for the old explanations of the movements of the heavens and of movement on earth suffered from significant weaknesses. These sciences are also essentially mathematical in nature, and the later Middle Ages had become relatively sophisticated mathematically. The development of more precise instruments also aided scientists as they sought to measure and quantify their observations.

The Old Explanations

For most of human history, people have not been fundamentally interested in theoretical science, that is, in pure science simply for the sake of understanding the natural world. Before the Scientific Revolution of the sixteenth and seventeenth centuries, the last civilization to have been so interested were the ancient Greeks.

The Romans were interested primarily in applied science or technology, but as long as things worked, they thought little about theory. As a result, they adopted and continued Greek views of theoretical science that explained things well enough.

With the medieval emphasis on spirituality and the afterlife, one would not expect great advances in theoretical science in the Middle Ages. Nevertheless, researchers are increasingly finding that there were original scientists in the Middle Ages, challenging the view of that period as a scientific wasteland. Nevertheless, these medieval scientists still worked within the assumptions of Greek science.

The Renaissance contributed only indirectly to the Scientific Revolution. The humanists' emphasis on this world naturally turned people's attention toward the study of nature, but there was little "scientific" about this. Humanist efforts uncovered more and more ancient manuscripts, revealing that ancient Greek thinkers had not agreed among themselves. In particular, Renaissance humanists' rediscovery of ancient scientific manuscripts lay behind many of the developments of the sixteenth and seventeenth centuries. Renaissance artists, through their close observations of nature and of the human body, undermined many of the tenets of ancient medicine. At about the same time, although not part of the cultural movement of the Renaissance, navigators and tradesmen came up with better and more accurate instruments and observations, which were eventually put to use by scientists in their investigations. In mathematics as well, the period of the later Middle Ages and Renaissance saw considerable advances, most notably the introduction of the Arabic number system and of algebra, both transmitted to Europe through contact with Muslim civilization in Spain and the Middle East.

It is also clear, although it is difficult or impossible to delineate a direct connection, that European scholars benefitted from the achievements of non-Europeans. Indeed, in the understanding of the natural world, European scholars of the Renaissance lagged far behind their counterparts in the Middle East, India, and China. Certainly increased contact with the older and more advanced civilizations to the east at the time of the Renaissance contributed to the origins of modern European science. For example, the Muslim astronomer Ibn al-Shatir (1304–75) arrived at conclusions similar to those reached by Copernicus almost two centuries later, although there is no positive proof that Copernicus knew of his work.

Nevertheless, for more than 1500 years, Greek science was accepted and "true." As in most other fields, Aristotle was the pre-eminent authority in science. He posited a finite geocentric universe, with the Moon, Sun, planets, and stars revolving around an earth that remains motionless in the centre. The heavenly bodies were embedded in crystalline spheres which themselves rotated in perfect circles at uniform speeds. It must be emphasized that this is not a stupid view: it conforms with common sense, for even today we talk about the Sun rising and setting, even though we know that it is the Earth and not the Sun that is moving.

For Aristotle, there was a fundamental distinction between the Earth and the heavens. Everything on Earth (or more accurately, inside the sphere of the Moon—the sublunary sphere) was corrupt and imperfect, subject to change. In contrast, everything above the sphere of the Moon was perfect and unchanging.

FIGURE 18.1 ⇛ ARISTOTLE'S UNIVERSE

A Medieval rendering of Aristotle's Universe, showing the earth in the center, surrounded by the spheres of water, air, and fire, then the spheres of the planets, and finally the sphere of the fixed starts, represented by the figures of the zodiac.

The Moon, stars, and planets revolved around the Earth in perfect circles at regular and uniform speeds. Following the views of matter established by Empedocles, in the sublunar sphere everything was composed of a combination of the four elements: the two heavy elements of earth and water, and the two light elements of air and fire. According to Aristotle, sublunar motion is explained by the composition of the moving thing. Thus an "earthy" object such as a stone, if dropped into a pond, will fall to the bottom. It seeks its "natural" place or its "home" at the centre of the earth. Light things, like fire, seek their natural places at the circumference of the sublunar sphere. Motion is thus explained by the composition of the moving object.

But this explains only one type of motion: natural motion, or motion in a straight line up or down or, more accurately, toward or away from the centre of the Earth. Unnatural or "violent" motion, the flight of an arrow for example, also required an explanation. According to Aristotle, "everything that is moved, is moved by something else." That is, for every object moving in this way, there had to be a mover causing it to move. The biggest problem in Aristotelian physics was its inadequacy in explaining projectile motion. According to Aristotle's view, an arrow (an "earthy" thing) should drop to the ground the instant it leaves the bowstring. Throughout the centuries, a number of explanations were advanced for projectile motion, but none was completely satisfactory. Nevertheless, Aristotelian physics explained motion well enough to be accepted for many centuries.

Outside the sphere of the Moon, in the celestial spheres things were very different. Since the heavens were perfect, Aristotle posited uniform circular motion, and a perfect fifth element, æther or quintessence. Thus the Sun, Moon, and planets revolve around the Earth in uniform circular orbits, embedded in their crystalline spheres. Outside the outer sphere was the domain of the Prime Mover, the *primum mobile*, the unmoving mover. Medieval Christian philosophers interpreted this Prime Mover as God. For Aristotle, however, this was not God in any Judeo-Christian sense, since it was itself part of, and not outside, the natural order.

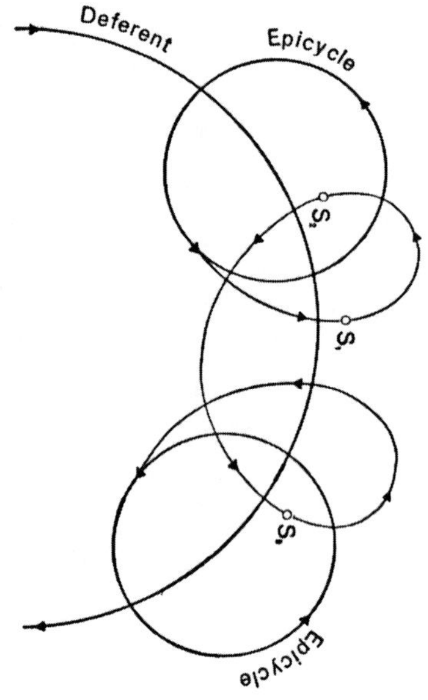

FIGURE 18.2 EPICYCLES

Aristotle's views, however, were intended only to explain motion, not to describe the structure of the heavens. Specifically, a universe constructed according to Aristotle's views could not explain the motion of the planets. If the planets did revolve in perfect circles around the Earth, this motion should be observable from Earth. The planets, however, wandered all over the sky (hence the name planet, from the Greek for wanderer). Specifically, they seemed to stop, back up, and then continue on their original course. This was called the retrograde motion of the planets, and was most pronounced and observable in the case of Mars.

When it came to understanding motion in the heavens, the most important ancient authority was Ptolemy, a Greek living in Egypt in the second century. Ptolemy saved the basic assumptions of Aristotle (a geocentric universe with uniform circular motion in the heavens) by introducing epicycles. An epicycle is a circle within a larger circle (the deferent). It must be emphasized once again that this is not a stupid or ignorant system. It describes planetary motion almost as well as our modern view of elliptical orbits around the sun. It is a mathematically complex and sophisticated system, conforming to observable data. Ptolemy figured out how large the epicycles needed to be and the speeds at which the planets revolved, both around the deferent and around the epicycle. In the end, approximately 300 epicycles were required to explain observable motion in the heavens. For all their sophistication, however, Ptolemy did not intend his theories to be taken as a physical description of the heavens, nor did later astronomers understand them that way. Rather, they were explanations that "saved the phenomena";

that is, they did an excellent job of describing and predicting celestial motion without claiming to describe physical reality. For instance, it was apparent that epicycles could not coexist with the crystalline spheres in which the planets and stars were embedded. As long as people could accept it as an explanatory framework only, it could coexist with Aristotle's apparently contradictory cosmology. When, however, astronomers began to maintain that what they sought was a description of physical reality, the first cracks began to appear in Ptolemy's edifice.

The Revolution in Astronomy and Physics

Any account of the development of modern astronomy must begin with the Polish clergyman Nicolaus Copernicus (1473–1543). Copernicus was very much a figure of the Renaissance, and he studied in Italy for a time where he was influenced by the view of natural magic current among Renaissance neo-Platonists: that material objects had hidden or occult properties, which the proper knowledge could manipulate to produce a desired result. Closely allied to Renaissance neo-Platonism were the so-called Hermetic writings. These writings were purported to be the very ancient works of an Egyptian demigod and magician, Hermes Trismegestis ("thrice-blessed Hermes"). Many people during the Renaissance believed that this Hermetic corpus represented the lost and original wisdom of ancient Egypt. Central to the Hermetic writings was the importance of the Sun as the giver of light and life, and so the secrets of controlling nature and its hidden magic lay in uncovering the Sun's mathematical harmonies. Indeed, during his studies in Italy, Copernicus became aware of the work of a recently rediscovered Greek astronomer named Aristarchus of Samos (310–ca. 230 BCE). Aristarchus had postulated a heliocentric (Sun-centred) universe rather than the Earth-centred or geocentric universe of Aristotle and Ptolemy. In an earlier version of his famous work *De revolutionibus*, Copernicus mentions Aristarchus by name, but this reference was omitted when the work was published.

In 1543, shortly before his death, Copernicus published his great work, *De revolutionibus cœlestium orbium* (*On the Revolution of Heavenly Bodies*). Although this is usually taken as the opening shot in the Scientific Revolution, it is clear that Copernicus was anything but a bold pioneer setting out to disprove the ignorant superstitions of the past. In fact, his intention was to improve Ptolemy's system, to rescue it from its weaknesses, while still preserving its basic assumptions. By putting the Sun rather than the Earth in the centre of the universe, he was able to greatly simplify the Ptolemaic universe. The number of epicycles was greatly reduced, although not eliminated, for Copernicus maintained the notion of perfect circular motion. To explain day and night without the sun revolving around the earth, he introduced the diurnal rotation of the earth. Thus, not only was the Earth not immobile at the centre of the universe, but it also spun on its axis as it revolved around the Sun.

It must be stressed that Copernicus was a very reluctant revolutionary, if in fact he was a revolutionary at all. His conclusions were purely a result of mathematical procedure, not of any new observations. Copernicus was a mathematician who studied movement in the heavens, rather than an astronomer who observed and recorded that motion. It is also clear that, mathematical procedures aside, he was led to put the Sun in the centre of the universe in large part by his Hermetic and neo-Platonist beliefs. As he wrote,

> In the middle of all sits the Sun enthroned. In this most beautiful temple could we place this luminary in any better position from which he can illuminate the whole at once? He is rightly calls the Lamp, the Mind, the Ruler of the Universe; Hermes Trismigestus names him the visible God, Sophocles' Electra calls him the All-seeing. So the sun sits as upon a royal throne ruling his children the planets which circle around him.

Copernicus's work met with mixed reactions. Indeed, it is likely that he knew his ideas would meet with great opposition, which is why he delayed publishing his book until just before his death. It is also difficult to see why the Copernican universe should have been met with anything but skepticism. Not only did it contradict the accepted beliefs of more than 1500 years, but it also violated common sense and people's perceptions. The Aristotelian/Ptolemaic universe had been closely integrated into Christian theology during the Middle Ages, and Copernicus's views seemed to call into question humankind's central place in God's creation. Both Protestant and Catholic church leaders and theologians denounced Copernicus's views, but their condemnations were mollified somewhat by a preface, not written by Copernicus himself, which claimed his work was a mathematical hypothesis only, even though Copernicus himself believed his theories to be the physical truth. One historian states that before 1600, only ten scholars accepted the Copernican universe, and that their belief was motivated more by their Hermetic and neo-Platonic orientation than by a commitment to "science."[1]

Despite this near-universal resistance to a heliocentric universe, Copernicus's views were the beginning of the end for the Aristotelian/Ptolemaic universe. Copernicus maintained, despite the preface appended to his work, that his was a description of the physical reality of the heavens, not just an attempt to "save the phenomena." If this were so, turning the Earth into a body that orbited the Sun made nonsense of Aristotle's physics, which demanded an immobile Earth at the centre of the universe. Moreover, if the geocentricity of the universe could be questioned, why could not the other assumptions of the Aristotelian/Ptolemaic universe?

Another weakness of the old view was its distinction between the sublunary and celestial spheres, in particular the assertion that the celestial sphere was perfect and unchanging. To the extent that people thought about obvious changes in the heavens—comets, shooting stars or meteorites, for example—they attributed them to the sublunary sphere, where all was imperfect and subject to change and flux. In 1572 a supernova and in 1577 a comet, both visible to the naked eye, prompted the observations of Tycho Brahe (1546–1601), a Danish nobleman, mathematician, and astrologer. Brahe built for himself at Uraniborg in Denmark the most

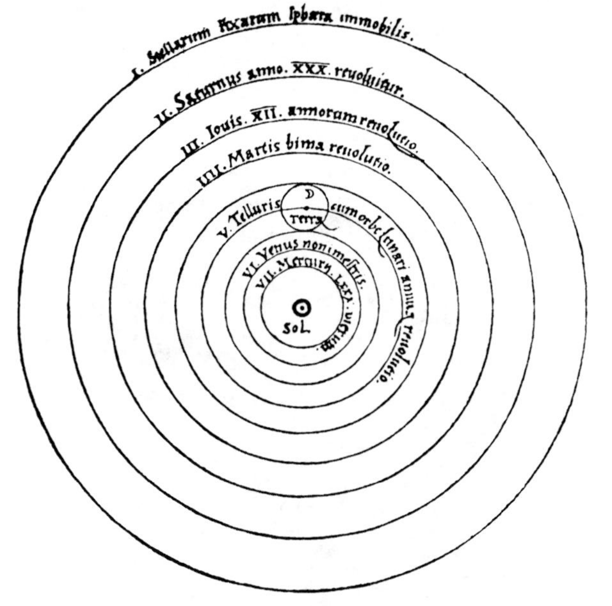

FIGURE 18.3 ⥱ THE COPERNICAN UNIVERSE

from *De Revolutionibus* (1543)

advanced and sophisticated astronomical observatory of the time. With his precise instruments and detailed observations, he demonstrated that both the supernova and the comet were celestial and not sublunary phenomena. These conclusions shattered two of the major assumptions of the Aristotelian/Ptolemaic universe, for if the heavens were perfect and unchanging, how could there be a new star? If the planets were embedded in crystalline spheres, how could a comet travel a path that clearly took it through these spheres?

Brahe, however, could not accept a fully Copernican universe. Rather, in his view, the Earth remained at the centre of the universe, while the planets and stars revolved around the Sun which itself circled the Earth. It is also noteworthy that Brahe's chief interest was in astrology. His goal was not the advancement of scientific knowledge in any modern sense, but rather casting more accurate horoscopes. We see the same mixture of what seem to us "scientific" and "magical" motivations in the very important person and work of Johannes Kepler (1571–1630), who worked for a time as Brahe's research assistant, largely in order to gain access to the Danish astronomer's vast collection of extremely accurate and detailed observations and calculations.

Kepler was a strange figure, reclusive and enigmatic. He too was deeply influenced by neo-Platonism and especially with the numerological mysticism associated with Pythagoras. For example, in an early work called *Mysterium Cosmographicum*, he attempted to explain why there were six planets, rather than

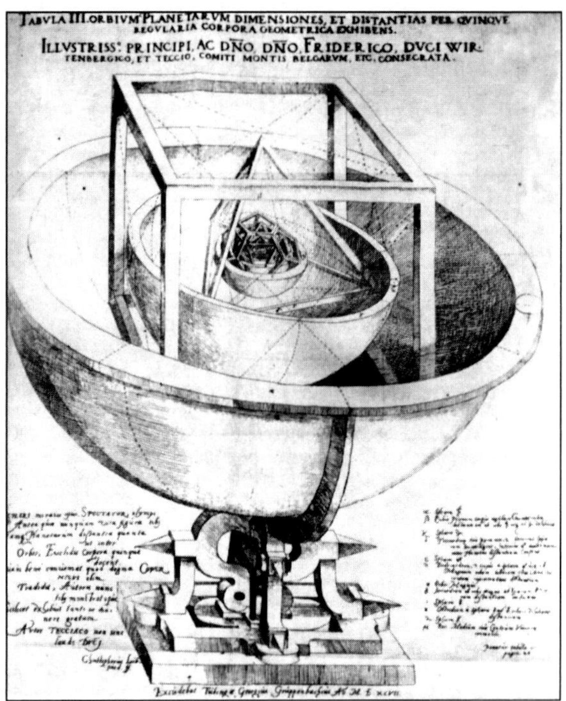

FIGURE 18.4 ⇛ KEPLER'S ORBS

Kepler's Orbs, showing the five perfect Euclidean solids which determined the number and placement of the planets.

five or eight or nine. (Only six planets were known to astronomers at the time. It is also worth noting that for Kepler the Earth was one of the six planets, which shows he had accepted Copernicus, part of a still tiny minority.) His answer to the question was that each of the planets was nestled in a sphere that corresponded with one of the five Euclidean perfect solids. That is, there are only five closed three-dimensional shapes with their sides all the same. When God had used the last of these to inscribe the sphere of the last planet, there was no other shape that could be used. In addition, the distances between the planets demanded by this scheme corresponded almost exactly with the actual distances between their orbits as established by the calculations of Copernicus. God had created the heavens according to the properties of geometry.

Kepler spent years manipulating Brahe's data, at first trying to describe Brahe's solar system mathematically . After years of diligent calculation, he published his *Astronomia Nova* (*New Astronomy*) in 1609, in which he outlined his first two laws of planetary motion. The first was that the planets move around the Sun not in circular orbits, but in elliptical ones. Further, the Sun was not in the centre of the ellipse, but toward one end, at a focus of the ellipse. The second law was that a line drawn between the planet and the Sun would sweep equal areas in

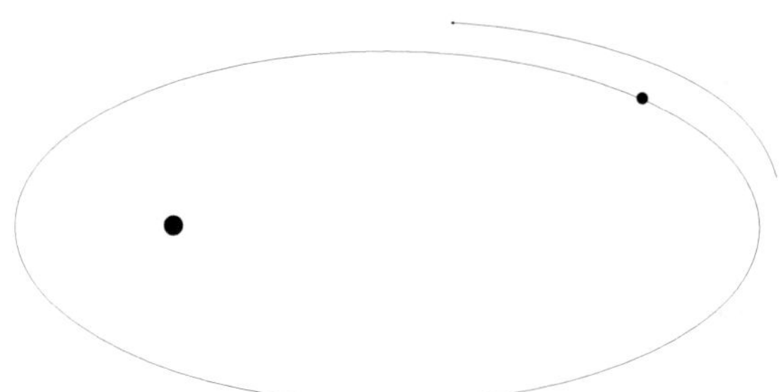

Keplers Fi rst Law. The planet orbits the sun in an ellipse, with the sun at one focus of the ellipse.

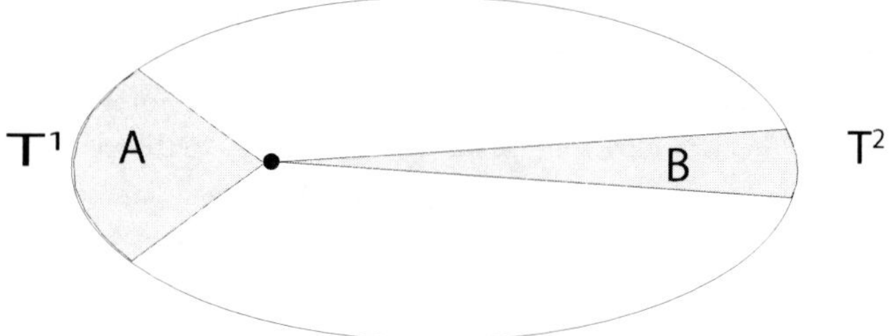

Kepler's Second Law. In equal periods of time (T^1 and T^2), a line drawn from the planet to the sun will sweep equal areas (Area A = Area B).

FIGURE 18.5 ⇛ KEPLER'S LAWS

equal times. Practically, this meant that the speed of the planet was not uniform: that it moved faster when it was nearer the Sun and more slowly when it was farther away. Kepler's third law would only emerge with his later work, *Harmonice Mundi* (1619), and was directly related to Kepler's abiding belief that God had created a universe governed by the mathematical laws of geometry and harmony. His third law stated that there is a constant relation between the square of the period of the planet's revolution and the cube of the planet's mean distance from the sun ($T^2=R^3$). This only confirmed his belief in the harmony of the planets, that as they revolved they produced their own musical scales. For Kepler, the universe was not an impersonal machine, but was animated by entities that sang as they orbited the sun.

Kepler's laws finally destroyed the Ptolemaic universe: none of its basic assumptions—geocentrism or uniform circular motion—survived. What Kepler had done, however, was describe the motion of the planets rather than explain it. To explain it, he resorted to the recent work of an English natural philosopher named William Gilbert. Gilbert had conducted a series of experiments on magnetism and had concluded that the Earth itself was a giant magnet, and further, in neo-Platonic and Hermetic fashion, that the Earth was animated by a soul. Kepler adopted and adapted Gilbert's theory of magnetism and applied it to the

Sun. This was the force that kept the planets in their elliptical orbits and propelled them along, much like spokes in a wheel. Although he had destroyed Ptolemy's astronomy, he was still bound by Aristotle's physics, in which anything that moved must be moved by something else. Kepler's views and laws, however, did not meet with wide or immediate acceptance. Even other natural philosophers, such as Galileo and René Descartes, persisted in maintaining perfect circular motion in the heavens. It was not until the time of Isaac Newton (1640–1727) that Kepler's views would gain wide acceptance.

One of Kepler's few contemporaries who subscribed to the Copernican view was an Italian mathematician named Galileo Galilei (1564–1642). Galileo's significance is twofold: as a natural philosopher who made original contributions in the science of motion, and as a popularizer of the Copernican system. The latter got him into the trouble with the Roman Catholic Church for which he is best known, but ultimately it was the former that proved more important.

Galileo first became prominent in 1610 with the publication of his book *Siderius Nuncius* (*The Starry Messenger*), written in vernacular Italian rather than academic Latin. Having heard of a telescope invented by a Dutchman, Galileo made one for himself and turned it skyward. He observed peaks and valleys on the Moon, and sunspots, which he took as evidence that the celestial sphere was not perfect and unchanging, qualitatively different from the sublunar sphere, but rather was made of the same kind of matter as the Earth itself. Further, he discovered four moons of Jupiter, which showed that the Earth could not be the sole centre around which all else revolved. He observed the phases of Venus, which could only be explained if both Earth and Venus revolved around the Sun.

He was still, however, no closer than Kepler to explaining the motion of the planets. It was his research in physics that provided the breakthrough here. If the heavens are really no different than the Earth, why should not the laws that govern motion be the same? In his subsequent books, *Dialogue Concerning the Two Chief World Systems* (1632) and *Discourses on Two New Sciences* (1638), Galileo established the basis of modern physics. His great achievement was the conclusion that the same laws govern motion on the Earth and in the heavens. He shifted the terms of inquiry from the composition of the moving object to the forces acting on it, finally destroying Aristotelian physics, which required that "unnatural" or "violent" motion be explained by continual contact between a mover and the moving object. In other words, motion itself no longer required explanation, only changes in motion. He established the law of uniform acceleration, that falling bodies accelerated at the same rate no matter what their size or composition, and further that this rate of acceleration was governed by a mathematical formula. He discovered that projectiles (an arrow or a cannonball, for example) travelled in parabolic motion, as their flight was a continuous combination of forces. He came very close to the law of inertia as it would later be formulated by René Descartes and Pierre Gassendi: a body in motion will remain in motion until acted on by other forces, and a body at rest will remain at rest until acted on by other forces. He did, however, reject Kepler's elliptical orbits purely on the basis of logical reasoning. He assumed, as did Copernicus (although on a different basis), that the circle was the fundamental principle of cosmic order:

> straight motion being by nature infinite (because a straight line is infinite and indeterminate), it is impossible that anything should have by nature the principle of moving in a straight line; or, in other words towards a place where it is impossible to arrive, there being no finite end. For nature, as Aristotle well says..., never undertakes to do that which cannot be done, nor endeavours to move whither it is impossible to arrive.

While Galileo did measure and experiment, his originality in this regard has been greatly exaggerated. He was not the originator of an "experimental method" that was a radical break with the past; he undertook his experiments primarily to demonstrate the conclusions at which he had already arrived. In his *Dialogue*, he stated regarding one of his conclusions, "I, without observation, know that the result must be as I say, because it is necessary." Moreover, many of his experiments were "thought experiments"; there is no evidence that he actually dropped objects of different weights from the Leaning Tower of Pisa. Rather, he described what would happen if one were to do this.

Galileo's fame over the centuries has stemmed principally from his conflict with the Roman Catholic Church. Although he did get into trouble with the Church, it is highly inaccurate to see this episode as the product of an inevitable conflict between science and religion, or Galileo as a brave genius confronting the forces of superstition and ignorance. In fact, Galileo was and remained a devout and loyal Christian and Catholic, and he maintained that he was simply seeking to understand God's creation. He did, however, argue that investigation of nature could not be constrained by the dictates of theology, that in fact they were different pursuits, each with its own proper procedures. Galileo's advocacy of the Copernican model brought him to the attention of the Roman Inquisition in 1616, but he found supporters within the Church who maintained, in the words of one, that Scripture teaches "how to go to heaven, not how the heavens go." In particular, he obtained support from Cardinal Robert Bellarmine, one of the most influential theologians of the day, and from Cardinal Barberini, later Pope Urban VIII (r. 1623–44). In return, Galileo agreed to treat the Copernican system as a mathematical hypothesis rather than as an accurate description of natural reality. In publishing his *Dialogue Concerning the Two Chief World Systems* (1632), Galileo miscalculated his political support in violating the spirit, if not the letter, of his agreement. As the title implies, the book (published in Italian to reach the widest possible audience) is presented as a dialogue between supporters of the Ptolemaic and Copernican systems. The defender of the Ptolemaic system is made to look like an idiot, leaving no question that Galileo believed in the physical reality of the Copernican model. His book was placed on the Index of Forbidden Books, and in 1633, in a famous scene before the Inquisition, Galileo recanted his beliefs as heretical and contrary to the teachings of Scripture. Galileo spent the rest of his life in failing health under house arrest. He nevertheless continued to conduct his research and write, publishing his *Discourses on Two New Sciences* in 1638.

The conflict between Galileo and the Church was therefore a political conflict. It was also a philosophical conflict between Galileo and the supporters of Aristotelian natural philosophy. Throughout the Middle Ages, Aristotelian philosophy had been closely integrated into Catholic theology. The Council of Trent had elevated the philosophies of Aristotle and his medieval synthesizer Thomas Aquinas to the level of religious truth. Besides challenging Ptolemaic astronomy, Galileo's ideas also laid waste to Aristotle's philosophy that things were to be known by their inner essences. For Galileo what counted was what could be quantified and measured: size, weight, speed, and direction, not the "secondary" qualities such as colour, smell, and taste. His opponents perceived, correctly, that Galileo's universe was a machine that operated according to mathematical laws, independent of God's sustaining presence and guidance.

With the advantage of hindsight, once more, we see that by the middle of the seventeenth century, then, the old explanations in physics and astronomy had been effectively destroyed, and the framework of a new system had been roughly sketched out. On the other hand, there were still many unanswered questions, and the new explanations were by no means universally accepted, as we have seen. The new universe that was coming into being was a heliocentric universe, with elliptical orbits, and uniformity of physical laws on the Earth and in the heavens. No one, however, had yet been able to explain why things moved as they did, as opposed to describing that motion. This was the significance of the greatest figure of the Scientific Revolution, Sir Isaac Newton (1642–1727). A mathematician of genius, he invented calculus simultaneously with his German contemporary and bitter rival Gottfried Wilhelm Leibniz (1646–1716). Newton also conducted research in optics, using prisms to break light down into its component colours of the spectrum. But his fame rests squarely on his masterwork of 1687, *Principia mathematica philosophiæ naturalis* (*Mathematical Principles of Natural Philosophy*, usually referred to as *Principia*), perhaps the most important scientific work ever written. In it, Newton combined the unified physics of Galileo with the heliocentric universe, and with Kepler's elliptical orbits. According to Newton, the planets' elliptical orbits were explained as the combination of two different motions. First, he adapted from Galileo the notion of inertial motion, by which objects in motion will remain in motion until acted on by other forces. For Newton, however, inertial force was not circular, but linear. That is, left unchecked, the inertial motion of the planets would carry them along a straight line into infinite space. This did not happen, however, because inertial motion was counterbalanced by the force of gravity. According to Newton, every object in the universe exerts an attraction on every other object. Moreover, the force exerted by this gravitational pull was subject to precise mathematical formulation. It was equal to the product of the masses of the two objects, and inversely proportional to the square of the distance between them. Thus, larger objects exerted a greater pull than smaller, and closer greater than farther. He further discovered that

Galileo's calculation of the rate of acceleration of falling bodies applied to the motion of the planets as well. Thus, the same force that causes apples to fall to the ground also keeps the planets from flying off into infinite space.

Newton's synthesis, however, was neither immediately nor universally accepted. For one thing, although Newton could describe gravity's effects, he could not convincingly explain what gravity was. He thus contradicted the mechanical view of the universe that had been constructed by Galileo, Descartes, and others. It seemed to many, including Leibniz, that Newton was reintroducing an occult force into physics. How could gravity work across the vast distances of space unless there was some sort of previously undiscovered physical connection? For many years, especially in continental Europe, the mechanistic or Cartesian view (after René Descartes) dominated thinking about physics.

Indeed, Newton himself was hardly the supremely rational and detached scientist he has often been portrayed as. He was deeply, and in some ways unconventionally, religious. He spent large parts of his career calculating biblical chronologies and in speculative writings about the end times. It has become increasingly clear that many of his "scientific" insights were directly related to his thinking and writing about alchemy and neo-Platonic mathematical mysticism. Indeed, he was heavily influenced by a group of neo-Platonist thinkers at Cambridge University in his youth. In a very great irony, since Newtonian physics was later taken as the cornerstone of a mechanistic universe, Newton himself was horrified by the idea that the universe functioned like a huge machine, independent of God's sustaining presence: "This most beautiful system of sun, planets and comets could only proceed from the counsel and dominion an intelligent and powerful Being." To Newton, God was not just the supreme mechanic who designed and built the universe according to mathematical principles; He was also the supreme artist who endowed it with beauty and harmony and preserved it through His eternal presence and oversight.

Medicine and Chemistry

Although they did not compare with the magnitude of the changes in the study of physics and astronomy, our period also witnessed a number of important developments in medicine and chemistry. The academic medical thought of the sixteenth and seventeenth centuries was, like that in physics and astronomy, heavily influenced by ancient authorities. The leading authorities were the ancient Greek physicians and writers Hippocrates (ca. 460–ca. 377 BCE) and especially Galen (129–ca. 199 CE). The dominant theory of disease was the humoral theory. Health was thought of as the balance of the four bodily humours: blood, phlegm, black bile, and yellow bile. Illness was therefore caused by an imbalance in the humours. The task of the physician was then to restore the proper humoral balance through various methods such as bleeding, purging, vomiting, sweating, and so on. The liver was seen as the major organ of the body, and especially as the creator of blood. Blood flowed outward from the liver where it nourished the body and was itself consumed in the process. There were also two separate and virtually self-contained blood systems. The arteries carried bright red blood to nourish the muscles and flesh, while the veins carried dark red blood to control digestion.

The Flemish physician and anatomist Andreas Vesalius (1514–64) struck an early blow against the authority of Galen, who had based his anatomy on dissections of animals rather than of human cadavers. Vesalius, who taught at the University of Padua (which would later be home to Galileo as well), performed his own dissections of human cadavers, proving the error of many of Galen's assertions. His book *De humani corporis fabrica* (*On the Fabric of the Human Body*) of 1543 was a meticulously illustrated and complete demonstration of his findings. The authority of Galen and ancient medicine was further shaken by the discoveries of William Harvey (1578–1657). As a student in Padua, he was taught by students of Vesalius. In his 1628 book *De motu cordis et sanguinis* (*On the Motion of the Heart and Blood*), he demonstrated that the blood in the arteries is the same blood as in the veins. That is, there are not two separate systems, as Galen had thought, but one only, and that blood circulates between them. He was, however, unable to explain precisely how the blood got from the arteries to the veins. This would have to wait until 1661, when the Italian Marcello Malpighi (1628–94) used a microscope to discover the existence of previously invisible capillaries.

A much more radical challenge to prevailing knowledge was posed by the Swiss physician Theophrastus Bombastus von Hohenheim (1493?–1591), better known as Paracelsus or "beyond Celsus." (Celsus was an ancient Roman medical writer.) Paracelsus lived the life of an itinerant scholar and outcast, alienating almost everybody with his quick temper and arrogance. He rejected received medical authority and the humoral theory, maintaining that disease was caused by external agents that attacked organs in particular ways, rather than by imbalance of the humours. Influenced by neo-Platonism, he further believed that the human body was a microcosm of the universe (the macrocosm). That is, the human body replicated all the qualities of the physical world. Diseases were to be diagnosed and treated by observing the correspondences of the microcosm and macrocosm. For example, the stars and planets were linked to certain parts of the body, and observing the heavens would lead to proper treatment of disease. To the traditional four elements of earth, water, air, and fire, Paracelsus added sulphur, mercury, and salt. His operative principle was that "like cures like"; that is, small amounts of otherwise toxic materials administered in the proper way were the means of curing disease. Indeed, this is not so different from modern chemotherapy or radiation therapy, where controlled doses of toxic substances are administered in a precise fashion. Natural substances had hidden or occult qualities that could be manipulated by the properly trained practitioner. Thus, Paracelsus brought together the worlds of medicine and alchemy, for it was the alchemist who dealt in the occult qualities of natural substances. Despite several well-publicized cures, Paracelsian medicine did not catch on during his lifetime. This was partly due to Paracelsus's prickly personality and contempt for all established authority. After his death, however, he did attract a group of followers who influenced the evolution of both medicine and chemistry. Although many of his ideas seem far-fetched to us (to say the least), his devotion to experimentation and observation does constitute one of the foundations of modern medicine.

Paracelsus's ideas were also important in the development of chemistry. Unlike physics and astronomy, chemistry underwent no revolutionary transformation in the early modern period. Chemistry was the province, on the one hand, of artisans such as miners and metallurgists who dealt with the properties of materials as a matter of practical experience, and on the other, of the alchemist, who was concerned with the inner essences of matter, with refining and purifying matter so that its occult qualities could emerge and be manipulated. Paracelsus forms a bridge between the worlds of alchemy and practical chemistry, and the world of scientific chemistry that was to emerge in the eighteenth century. The mechanical philosophers such as Galileo, Descartes, and Gassendi were concerned above all with those aspects of matter that could be measured and quantified, such as size, weight, and speed. It scarcely mattered what the thing was made of. The influence of Paracelsus and his followers was twofold: first, their emphasis on the qualities of matter eventually led others to focus on the nature and composition of the matter being studied, rather than just its quantifiable aspects; second, they paid a great deal of attention to observation and experimentation, both in the diagnosis of disease and in the preparation of their medicines.

We see the impact of both these in the work of the Robert Boyle (1627–91). As one of the founders and moving spirits of the English Royal Society, he was a colleague and friend of Isaac Newton. More than anyone else, Boyle was responsible for the empirical and experimental orientation of the Royal Society. A wealthy gentleman of leisure, Boyle conducted a number of very famous experiments, one of which led to the formulation of the law that bears his name. Boyle was also dissatisfied with the mechanical philosophy that was then prominent in scientific circles. In what he termed the "corpuscular philosophy," he believed that chemical processes could not be reduced entirely to mechanical terms. Rather, they were the product of specialized particles or corpuscles that reacted with each other in ways that could be understood only by something other than strict mechanical effect. Although he dispensed with the traditional four elements, and with Paracelsus's additional three, he did believe that matter was composed of elements that were capable of combining with each other in different ways. Thus, although neither medicine nor chemistry experienced the revolutionary changes we have examined in astronomy and physics, there were important developments that would lead, in the eighteenth and nineteenth centuries, to revolutions in those sciences as well.

Impact of the Scientific Revolution

In thinking about the impact of the Scientific Revolution, we need to be careful to avoid historical "tunnel vision." That is, it is all too easy to concentrate on the end product, on the origins of modern science and all that it has meant in the last several centuries. Rather, we need to think more about the consequences for the sixteenth and seventeenth centuries. Until the Newtonian synthesis was widely accepted in the early eighteenth century, the main consequence of the Scientific Revolution was doubt and uncertainty. As we have seen, in science or "natural philosophy," this was a period of creative destruction. It is too easy for us to concentrate on the creative part of the equation and to forget the impact that the destruction of the old certainties had on contemporaries. As the poet John Donne wrote,

> And new Philosophy calls all in doubt,
> The Element of fire is quite put out;
> the Sun is lost, and th'earth, and no man's wit
> Can well direct him where to look for it.
> And freely men confess that this world's spent,
> When in the Planets, and the Firmament
> They seek so many new; they see that this
> Is crumbled out again to his Atomies.
> Tis all in pieces, all coherence gone;
> All just supply, and all Relation.

One of the more immediate consequences of the developments in science was the dethroning of classical Greek and Roman writers from their positions of authority. Since the early Middle Ages, it had been assumed that classical civilization represented the pinnacle of human achievement, and that the goal of intellectual pursuit was to revive it. Now, by the middle of the seventeenth century, previously unimpeachable ancient authorities had been proven horribly wrong about the very structure of the universe. What else might they have been wrong about? Where was certainty now to be found? What authorities could one turn to for reliable knowledge? How could people be certain that their "new" knowledge of the universe was in fact reliable? Indeed, it was some time before contemporary thinkers and scientists arrived at methods for determining the accuracy of their theories. And even then, there was (and still is) no single accepted "scientific method."

One of the first people to think systematically about a new theoretical basis for natural philosophy was the English writer and politician Sir Francis Bacon (1561–1626). A philosopher and theorist rather than a scientist in his own right, Bacon argued that the scientific knowledge of the past was hopelessly handicapped by an improper method. In his *Organon Novum* (*New Instrument*) of 1620, he set out what he believed to be the true path to knowledge. Unlike the ancients (particularly Aristotle), who began with theories and then sought the facts to support them, the true path was an empirical one that stressed observation and experimentation. The proper scientific method was an inductive one, in which the scientist carefully experimented and observed, building a mass of data. Only then was it proper to attempt a general explanation:

> There are and can be only two ways of searching into and discovering truth. The one flies from the senses and particulars to the most general axioms, and from these principles, the truth of which it takes for settled and immovable, proceeds to judgement and to the discovery of middle axioms. And this way is now in fashion. The other derives axioms from the senses and particulars, rising by a gradual and unbroken ascent, so that it arrives at the most general axioms last of all. This is the true way, but as yet untried.

Moreover, for Bacon, the true goal of science was not abstract knowledge, but the improvement of the human condition: "Now the true and lawful goal of the sciences is none other than this: that human life be endowed with new discoveries and powers." In his *New Atlantis* (1627), Bacon described an ideal land, where teams of scientists collaborated and cooperated in uncovering nature's secrets. But Bacon had only the vaguest understanding of how scientists actually worked. His extreme emphasis on collecting masses of data overlooked the role of intuition and hypothesis. His was a naive faith that truth would somehow emerge on its own, almost independent of human interpretation.

On the other hand, his belief that science would ultimately lead to human progress was profoundly important for the future, although not in Bacon's lifetime. Of more immediate importance was his insistence that science was a collaborative and cooperative endeavour. Scientific societies and academies sprung up all over Europe during the seventeenth century, and although Bacon cannot be said to have inspired them all, certainly his influence was important in their spread. One of the first was the *Accademia de Lincei* (Academy of the Lynx-Eyed), which was founded in Italy in 1603 and counted Galileo among its members. Similar academies were founded elsewhere, usually under aristocratic patronage. The two most important scientific societies were the English Royal Society, founded in 1662, and the French Académie des sciences, sponsored by Colbert and founded in 1666. Although Charles II lent his support to the Royal Society, it was essentially an independent and self-supporting body. As a result, it cultivated the support of interested laymen, including the King himself. The Académie des sciences, on the other hand, was under strict government control and was a body devoted more exclusively to professional scientists. Whatever their differences, however, scientific societies played a large role in publicizing new discoveries among the literate elite, and in facilitating communication among scientists. As such, they are an important marker of the acceptance both of new scientific discoveries and of science as a legitimate and important intellectual pursuit.

Another sort of answer in the quest for certainty was supplied by the French mathematician and philosopher René Descartes (1596–1650). Descartes was a mathematician of genius, inventing analytical geometry. After a spell as a soldier, Descartes devoted himself to science and philosophy. Disillusioned by the blatant absurdities and contradictions of accepted authorities, he sought a new method of thinking that would bring certainty. In his *Discourse on Method* of 1637, he recounted his procedure. First, he decided to reject as false anything of which he could conceive the least doubt, in order to see what would be left. Thus, unlike Bacon, he dismissed the experiences of his senses, since senses could deceive. The only thing that he could not doubt was that he was thinking or doubting. Since nothing could not think, he must exist, hence his famous statement *cogito ergo sum* (I think; therefore I am). Further, he was a being whose nature it was to think. Once he arrived at this conclusion, he had a clear idea what certainty felt like. Anything that he perceived with the same degree of certainty and clarity must therefore also be true. This was the firm foundation upon which knowledge could be built. From this he deduced the existence of God. He knew himself to be imperfect. He must therefore have some standard of comparison, some notion of perfection with which to contrast his own imperfection. Since an imperfect being such as he could not generate an idea of perfection, there must therefore be a perfect being: in a word, God. Since God is perfect, He does not deceive us, and the world is therefore orderly and rational, susceptible to human understanding.

Descartes's deductive method led him inexorably to a radical dualism, a separation of mind and matter. Since he was a substance "whose whole essence or nature consists in thinking, and which, that it may exist, has no need of space, nor is dependent on any material thing," it therefore followed that mind (or soul, or thinking substance) was wholly distinct from matter, or extended substance. For Descartes, therefore, the physical world was a machine that operated according to physical laws that were accessible to the human through his deductive method, and describable in mathematical language. Descartes was therefore one of the key figures, if not the leading one, in the "mechanical philosophy" that dominated seventeenth-century thinking about nature.

Descartes's views on physics were widely influential in his day, especially on the continent, until they were eclipsed by Newton's in the early eighteenth century. For Descartes, the universe was completely full of infinitely divisible matter. (This is in contrast to Newton's later view of matter exerting a gravitational attraction across empty space.) In this way, Descartes was still somewhat bound to Aristotle's physics in which a direct physical connection was necessary to explain motion. If the universe is full, how then can anything move at all? For Descartes, the universe consisted of innumerable swirling vortices or whirlpools of matter. The centrifugal force of matter within the vortices was matched by the pressure exerted by neighbouring vortices in such a way that a balance was achieved. In this way, Descartes extended Galileo's views into something very close to the modern idea of inertia.

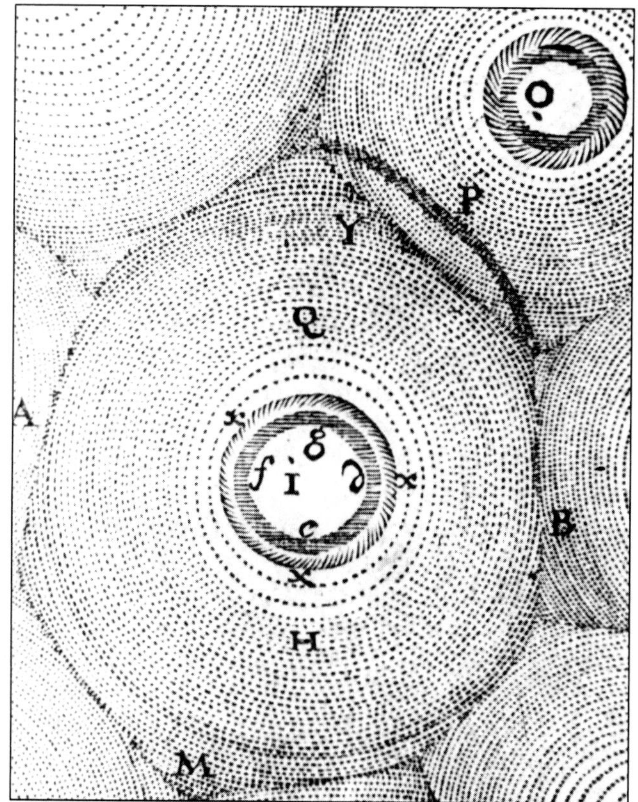

FIGURE 18.6 ⇶ DESCARTES'S VORTICES

From our perspective, the difficulties in his thinking are obvious. It was based primarily on *a priori* reasoning as to how the universe must work, with little experimental or observational support. Yet contemporaries found Descartes's philosophy deeply compelling, for it seemed to many to offer an account of a mechanical physical world that nevertheless had room for the Christian God and man's immortal soul. It is also clear that Descartes's method differs dramatically from Bacon's, and that scientists actually operated in both modes, benefiting from the rational deduction of Descartes, but verified by the experimental empiricism of Bacon.

Although Descartes and his followers insisted that their philosophy in no way contradicted orthodox Christian doctrine, this claim was not universally accepted. In fact, many found Descartes's treatment of God especially troubling. God seemed to be a necessary step in his logical reasoning, rather than the Creator of the universe and Redeemer of mankind, who had sent His Son to die on a cross. His mechanistic view of the universe seemed to many to lead straight to atheism. His works were placed on the Index of Forbidden Books by the Roman Catholic Church, and subsequent thinkers wrestled mightily with his philosophy.

The horrifying implications of a mechanistic universe were fulfilled for many in the political philosophy of Thomas Hobbes, who saw human beings as machines, motivated entirely by their appetites (see Chapter 9). It was, however, John Locke, who was also Hobbes's chief adversary in political theory, who supplied the common-sense answer to questions of knowledge and certainty (see Chapter 15). In his *Essay Concerning Human Understanding* (1690), Locke applied a basically Baconian method to the problems of ascertaining certainty. According to Locke, humans came into the world with no innate ideas. At birth, their minds were a blank slate or *tabula rasa*. In this he was concerned primarily to refute Descartes, whose entire epistemology was based on innate ideas. Locke was concerned that Cartesian philosophy ultimately provided no certainty, for its standard of truth was what was clearly and distinctly perceived to be true by the mind. Different people clearly and distinctly perceived contrary ideas. How then could one arrive at the truth? For Locke, the experience of the senses was paramount. All knowledge, he asserted, was the product of sensation and reflection, that is, the experience of the senses as processed by the mind. But did not people process the same sensory information in different ways? Locke believed that people were basically rational, and given the proper education and environment, their reason would ultimately lead them to the truth.

To us, Locke's philosophy suffers from a number of difficulties. What was this "reason" that governed reflection, if not an innate quality of the mind? Logically, his philosophy excluded divine revelation as a source of certain knowledge. This, in turn, should logically have excluded miracles, original sin, the incarnation of Christ, and most accepted Christian doctrine. Yet he tried, unconvincingly, to maintain a role for divine revelation. Certainly other philosophers of the time supplied more compelling and deeper answers to these questions than those of Locke. Yet, along with Newton's views on the physical universe, it was Locke's ideas on human nature and knowledge that were ultimately and broadly accepted by the literate elites by the early eighteenth century. More than any other thinkers, Locke and Newton were the apostles of the Enlightenment of the eighteenth century. As historian Theodore Rabb points out in a study of the "general crisis" of the seventeenth century,

> Society took Newton and Locke to heart primarily because they offered a far less troubling and difficult message than did Descartes, Pascal or Hobbes—none of whom, after all, had been inherently less impressive or "scientific" in their arguments. What the age wanted to hear was that the world was harmonious and sensible; that human beings were marvellously capable, endowed with an orderly Reason that could solve all problems. Believing that their problems had indeed *been* solved, contemporaries demanded an epistemology that would allow them to relax and enjoy life, and this was exactly the soothing reassurance that Locke provided.[2]

While Bacon, Descartes, Hobbes, Locke, and others were seeking certainty in knowledge, others denied that certainty could ever be attained, that all human knowledge was ultimately uncertain and all certainty illusory. Among these was the French nobleman and judge Michel de Montaigne (1533–92). He was heavily influenced by a revived interest in the ancient philosophy of Pyrrhonism, which maintained that both man's senses and his reason were fallible and likely to deceive. It was therefore foolish to believe that humans could know the truth about anything. Revolted by the violence and disorders of the Wars of Religion, he retired to his country estate to write and think, pioneering the literary form of the essay. (Derived from the French verb *essayer*, to try, his essays are literally trials, that is, his musings on various subjects, his trying out of his thoughts.) Having seen more than enough of what certainty in religious belief brought to his native land, he adopted an attitude that was at once calmly rational and skeptical of all human knowledge and wisdom. His motto and guiding principle was the French phrase "Que sais-je?" or "What do I know?" His answer to this question was that, in the end, he knew nothing for sure: "I shall leave here ignorant of everything except my ignorance."

> Is it possible to imagine anything so ridiculous as that wretched and puny creature, who is not even master of himself, exposed to offenses from all things, and who yet proclaims himself master and emperor of the universe, concerning which it is not within his power to know the slightest part, let alone to govern it?

If knowledge is so uncertain, Montaigne maintained, then it is only prudent to withhold judgement and rely on God's goodness, and to leave in His hands ultimate judgement, an approach that has been characterized as fideism, or reliance on faith where human reason and knowledge fail: "Now there can be no universally valid principles for men unless the divinity has revealed them to them; all the rest, the beginning, the middle, and the end, is only dream and smoke." His comments on the new science that was shaking the old certainties are especially revealing:

> The sky and the stars revolved for three thousand years; everyone had believed so until Cleanthes of Samos, or according to Theophrastus, Nicetas of Syracuse took it into his head to maintain that it was the earth which moved around the oblique circle of the Zodiac, spinning on its axis; and, in our own day, Copernicus has so well established that doctrine that he uses it in quite a systematic way for all astronomical calculations. What shall we draw from that, if not that we should not worry which of the two systems is true? And who knows that a third opinion, a thousand years from now, may not overthrow the two previous ones?

For himself, Montaigne was content to rely on the judgement of the Catholic Church in matters of faith. He declared, "Either we must submit entirely to the authority of our ecclesiastical establishment, or we must dispense with it altogether." He clearly opted for the former, but it must also be recognized that he left the door open for the latter.

Montaigne's detached skepticism, however, was not for most an ultimately satisfying solution to the burning questions of the time. One of the most profound attempts to bring together the new developments in science and the tenets of Christianity was that of Blaise Pascal (1623–62). A scientist and mathematician of genius himself, Pascal could not simply dismiss the new science as had Montaigne. As a young man, he conducted ingenious experiments on barometric pressure, further discrediting Aristotelian physics. He wrote a treatise on conic sections, and invented a primitive mechanical computer. Of a delicate constitution, he suffered throughout his short life from debilitating migraines. But in November 1654, he underwent an ecstatic religious experience that he called his "night of fire." He recorded it in his journal:

> GOD of Abraham, GOD of Isaac, GOD of Jacob not of the philosophers and of the learned. Certitude. Certitude. Feeling. Joy. Peace. GOD of Jesus Christ. My God and your God. Your GOD will be my God. Forgetfulness of the world and of everything, except GOD. He is only found by the ways taught in the Gospel. Grandeur of the human soul. Righteous Father, the world has not known you, but I have known you. Joy, joy, joy, tears of joy. I have departed from him: They have forsaken me, the fount of living water. My God, will you leave me? Let me not be separated from him forever. This is eternal life, that they know you, the one true God, and the one that you sent, Jesus Christ. Jesus Christ. Jesus Christ. I left him; I fled him, renounced, crucified. Let me never be separated from him. He is only kept securely by the ways taught in the Gospel: Renunciation, total and sweet. Complete submission to Jesus Christ and to my director. Eternally in joy for a day's exercise on the earth. Not to forget your words. Amen.

Henceforth, Pascal would devote his life to his faith. He was attracted to the morality and austerity of the Jansenists and spent a good deal of time at Port-Royal. His *Provincial Letters* (1657) is a strident defence of the Jansenists against their critics, especially the Jesuits (see Chapter 4).

Pascal was concerned above all to show people that the new science was not irreconcilable with the Christian faith. He was especially concerned that the mechanistic view of the universe would lead people astray. His was also a mechanistic universe, but one that had room for the Christian God and the miraculous. As a scientist himself, he did not reject science, but rather conceded that it was essential for knowledge of the universe. On the other hand, science did not and could not provide answers for the most important questions. Over the last years of his life, he began making notes on what he hoped would be his masterpiece and would ultimately convince people of his views. Although he died before he could write this work, about one thousand of his notes survived and were later published as *Pensées* (*Thoughts*). Probably the best known of these aphorisms, and one that aptly captures his overall philosophy, is "The heart has its reasons, which reason cannot know." Further: "It is the heart which experiences God, and not the reason. This, then, is faith: God felt by the heart, not by the reason." On the nature of man, he drew attention to the paradox of the Christian view, that man is at once God's special creation and also a weak and sinful being:

> Knowledge of God without knowledge of man's wretchedness leads to pride. Knowledge of man's wretchedness without knowledge of God leads to despair. Knowledge of Jesus Christ is the middle course, because by it we discover both God and our wretched state.
>
> Incapable of absolute ignorance and of certain knowledge, we have thus been manifestly in a degree of perfection from which we have unhappily fallen.
>
> Man is but a reed, the most feeble thing in nature, but he is a thinking reed. ... But if the universe were to crush him, man would still be more noble than that which killed him, because he knows that he dies and the advantage which the universe has over him; the universe knows nothing of this.

But Pascal's was a minority voice. Most who thought about such questions believed that the Christian God and faith could best be understood by applying to them the same reason that had seemingly unlocked the secrets of the universe.

Yet another sort of answer to these questions of God, man, and the universe was provided by the eccentric Dutch Jew Benedict (or Baruch) Spinoza (1632–77). As we saw in Chapter 12, Spinoza was born in the Jewish community in Amsterdam, but he was ostracized because of his unusual and controversial views. Supporting himself by grinding lenses, he operated on the fringes of respectable intellectual society, even turning down a position at the University of Heidelberg so as not to interfere with his freedom to think and write as he wished. He was reviled equally by Jews, Catholics, and Protestants, so it is extremely difficult to encapsulate his philosophy. Spinoza rejected the distinction between mind and matter so rigidly established by Descartes, although he did accept Descartes's geometrical and mathematical approach to knowledge. In 1670, he published his *Tractatus Theologico-Politicus* (*Theological-Political Treatise*), the only one of his works to be published in his lifetime. In it, he argued against current anthropomorphic conceptions of God, and for religious toleration. According to Spinoza, stability was not threatened by religious toleration, but rather strengthened by it. He condemned the political power of the clergy, which, he argued, they used to enforce and expand their power. It was also a work of Biblical criticism, in which he analyzed the Bible as one would any other historical document, discounting its miraculous elements and emphasizing its human authors and their foibles. Although published anonymously, the *Tractatus* met with immediate and vituperative condemnation.

His major work was not published until after his death, although he had completed it some years earlier, and manuscripts of it had circulated among his friends. This was *Ethica Ordine Geometrico Demonstrata* (*Ethics Demonstrated with Geometrical Order*), in which he stated his views on God, man, and the universe. For Spinoza, God was all and in all, and what we perceive as disparate parts of the universe are in fact modes or expressions of divinity. God was not a transcendent Creator who stood outside nature, but rather was *in* nature. Man, too, was part of this pantheistic universe. Everything is the way it is out of necessity. Although seemingly deterministic, Spinoza felt that recognition of the interconnectedness of the universe held the key to human happiness, for people could learn to master one passion with another nobler passion. Knowledge of "God or nature," as Spinoza termed the divinity, was the highest good, and true freedom lay in knowledge of what determines our actions and devotion to reason over passion. Spinoza's was a unique voice, and he found few followers in his lifetime. His philosophy does, however, illustrate several of the themes under discussion here: the evaporation of the old certainties, the quest for a new order and authority, and the effort to deal with the implications of the mechanistic view of the universe.

Yet others found the sought-after certainty and authority in religious enthusiasm or revival of ancient pagan philosophies. The basis of religious enthusiasm is that all human wisdom is foolishness. Efforts to understand the physical world are completely irrelevant; the only thing to do is to lose oneself in God. For such people, there is no need of church or scriptural authority. God reveals himself directly, surpassing Scripture, clergy, and religious institutions. These groups have their predecessors and ancestors in the radical groups that sprang up at the time of the Reformation earlier in the sixteenth century. In this connection, we may mention many of the groups that emerged during the English Revolution: the Quakers, who literally shook with the Holy Ghost; the Fifth Monarchy Men, the Ranters, Muggletonians, and so on (see Chapter 10). In Spain, there were the Illuminists or *Alumbrados*, an unorganized tendency more than a movement, who maintained that external religious forms were superfluous in light of direct divine revelation and inspiration. Along with "Lutherans," *conversos*, and *moriscos*, the *Alumbrados* were one of the chief targets of the Spanish Inquisition. In more normal times, these enthusiasts either kept a very low profile or were coerced into silence or conformity by religious and political authorities. In times of disorder and instability, however, they emerged into the open. The fears of governments and churches were generally out of all proportion to the actual threat or influence of these groups, so severely were they believed to threaten the established order in church and state.

We have already noted the blurred lines between what we would consider "science" and "magic," including various forms of mysticism, astrology, alchemy, and numerology. In addition, as the humanists of the Renaissance unearthed more and more ancient texts, many Europeans found solace for the disorders and uncertainties of their times in revivals and adaptations of pagan philosophies. Whereas earlier scholars had attempted to accommodate these pagan philosophies within Christianity, to force them into a Christian mould, increasingly now the process was reversed. That is, more and more, Christianity was being accommodated to pagan philosophy. One of the strongest currents of this sort of thought was the persistence of neo-Platonism and the associated hermetic tradition, which, as we have seen, were closely bound up with the heliocentric view of the universe. One of the most famous thinkers in this vein was the Italian Dominican friar Giordano Bruno (1548–1600). Bruno went beyond many thinkers influenced by neo-Platonism and the hermetic tradition in discarding the elements of Christianity that did not fit his frankly pagan religious and philosophical views. According to Bruno, not only did the Earth revolve around the Sun (which he accepted on philosophical rather than scientific grounds), the universe itself was infinite and alive and divine in nature. Much as Spinoza would later do, Bruno insisted that God was immanent in nature, not transcendent over it. Nature was God, and vice versa. Since God was not beyond and above the universe, and the universe itself was infinite (as of course was God), God could not help but create an infinite number of worlds with their own forms of life. Bruno led the life of a wandering scholar and philosopher, propounding his beliefs with enthusiasm as he travelled the continent. In the end, Bruno was tried by the Roman Inquisition and burned at the stake for heresy in 1600. Some scholars have tended to include Bruno among the "martyrs" of science to superstitious religious ignorance, largely because of his support for the heliocentric theory. In fact, however, it was his extremely radical religious and philosophical views for which he was executed. That is, he was condemned for the conclusions he drew from the heliocentric theory that arose from his reading of pagan philosophers, rather than for his support for the heliocentric theory itself.

Neo-Platonic influence continued into the seventeenth century, most notably at Cambridge University where a group of writers, poets, and philosophers gathered, including Henry More (1614–87). They believed that although human reason was imperfect, it could nevertheless divine the outlines of God's will through contemplation of ancient philosophies. Their chief target was the materialism of Descartes and Hobbes and the concomitant mechanistic view of the universe. For them, the universe was not a soulless machine, but rather it was possessed of a divine soul. In his youth, Isaac Newton was involved with the Cambridge neo-Platonists, and his later idea of gravity operating across vast distances of space owes much to their influence.

The ancient philosophies of Epicureanism and Stoicism also witnessed revivals in this period, and like neo-Platonism played an important role in the development of natural philosophy. Both Epicureanism and Stoicism were not only moral philosophies, which prescribed a way of life, but they were also natural philosophies that had specific views of the universe. Indeed, the way they taught their followers to live was closely linked to their views of matter and the physical universe. Epicurus (341–270 BCE) had taught that the universe was infinite and uncreated. It was composed of an infinite number of indivisible particles or atoms, which were in continual motion in an infinite void. These atoms were continually combining and dissolving to form an infinite number of worlds, some like ours, some not. His material universe avoided mechanical determinism, however, in postulating occasional random motion of atoms, which left room for the human will. Faced with a universe that was basically meaningless, composed of matter in motion, the proper response was maximizing pleasure and minimizing pain. This did not mean, however, that one should abandon oneself to sensual pleasure, as the term "epicurean" has come to mean. Rather, it is the product of rational calculation, in which moderation is to be preferred over excess.

The ancient Stoics, on the other hand, had taught that the universe, including mankind, although material in nature, was pervaded by a divine principle and was continually evolving toward a state of goodness. The mechanism for this purpose or intelligence was an all-pervading substance, or *pneuma*, which filled the universe. The proper response to this view of the physical universe was to accommodate oneself to this purpose, and to work toward it, accepting with equanimity the pains and pleasures of life, since they were both unavoidable and part of the universe's unfolding.

The sixteenth- and seventeenth-century revivals of Epicureanism and Stoicism saw a number of ancient works of both philosophies recovered and publicized by humanists. Moreover, these philosophies gave thinkers and philosophers (including natural philosophers) new conceptual tools with which to think about the universe and man's place in it. Of the two, it was Epicureanism that both posed the greater challenge to traditional thought and made the clearest contribution to natural philosophy. Above all, it was the French philosopher and priest Pierre Gassendi (1592–1655) who made Epicurean natural philosophy safe for Christian Europeans. For there were a number of very important areas in which Epicurean physics contradicted accepted Christian theology. Most notably, it stated that the universe was infinite and uncreated, with an infinite number of atoms, the movement of which was entirely random. There were gods, but they were part of nature, not above it. Gassendi was attracted by the atomistic elements of Epicurean natural philosophy because it was easily conformable to the mechanistic view that was then being worked out, most notably by Descartes. Gassendi managed to "baptize"—to Christianize—Epicurus by putting God outside the natural order, making Him the creator of the atoms. Moreover, Gassendi's God had created a finite number of atoms and continued to play a role in nature through His divine providence.

The impact of the revival of Stoicism on natural philosophy was less obvious and less direct than that of Epicureanism. Indeed, its impact is much more noticeable in the realm of ethical philosophy than that of natural philosophy. One of the key figures here was the Flemish humanist and writer Justus Lipsius (1547–1606). Lipsius was able to do for Stoicism what Gassendi would for Epicureanism, that is, to make it safe for Christian consumption. Admittedly, this was a less onerous task, for much of Stoic philosophy accorded reasonably well with Christian theology, and there was a long tradition, going back to St. Augustine, of incorporating Stoic thought into Christianity. Lipsius argued that what we see as ill fortune is in fact part of God's providential activity and should be met with equanimity and constancy (*constantia*). He did, however, have to modify Stoic natural philosophy to make it consonant with Christianity. He saw fate as the expression of God's will, rather than a natural force to which even God or the gods are subject. The Stoics had taught that events have only natural causes, which ruled out miracles, and that the universe is deterministic in nature and does not permit the operation of free will, positions that Lipsius rejected.

The influences of Stoicism on natural philosophy are oblique rather than direct. Stoic physics was mechanistic, as was Epicurean, although in a different way. The Stoic *pneuma* was an explanation for the transmission of movement from body to body. So, for example, Johannes Kepler displayed some Stoic influence when he postulated that the movement of the planets could be explained by the transmission of the Sun's magnetic attraction through something very much like the Stoic *pneuma*. Isaac Newton was also heavily influenced by the Stoic revival. He believed that the universe was filled with an invisible and insensible *æther*. At one time, he believed that this was the vehicle through which gravity exerted its force. He eventually discarded its role in gravitation but maintained his belief in *æther*, which for him became the medium through which God sustained and preserved the universe.

* * *

It is extremely hazardous to generalize about the thought of any period, let alone one so fertile and diverse as early modern Europe. If there was any unifying principle, it was the quest for order and certainty in an age when all order and certainty seemed lost, in politics, religion, and philosophy. The old certainties had been discarded, but not yet replaced. By the end of the seventeenth century, the calm and harmonious answers supplied by Newton and Locke would come to be accepted, laying the foundation for the Enlightenment. As the poet Alexander Pope would write in the eighteenth century,

> Nature and Nature's laws
> lay hid in night;
> God said, Let Newton be!
> and all was light.

In the meantime however, different thinkers sought certainty in a variety of places. For some, such as Bacon and Locke, the experience of the senses was paramount. For others, such as Descartes, certainty was to be found in the processes of the mind. Those such as Montaigne denied that certainty was possible at all, while Pascal found it in the embrace of a loving and beneficent God. Still others sought refuge in mysticism and religious enthusiasm, or in revivals of ancient philosophies, some made compatible with Christian doctrine, others not. European thought in this period is a rich and varied tapestry that defies easy analysis and labelling.

In the period under examination in this book, European society and culture changed a great deal. Nowhere is this more evident than in the realm of intellectual life where the foundations were laid for modern science. By 1715, the educated elites of Europe were living in a different mental universe than a century and a half earlier. To them, based on the discoveries and philosophies of Locke and Newton, the universe was rational and orderly, with little room for the "superstitious" beliefs of earlier generations. As we have seen, this shift in mental outlook is perhaps the most important single explanation for the disappearance of the great witch hunts that punctuated the sixteenth and seventeenth centuries. By the early eighteenth century, however, the full implications of this mental and intellectual shift were apparent only in vague outline. Indeed, much of the intellectual and cultural history of the eighteenth century can be seen as the working out of these implications, in the intellectual and cultural movement of the Enlightenment.

In the realms of politics and government, too, this period saw important developments, though not as precedent-shattering as those in intellectual life. Indeed, these developments built upon patterns and precedents inherited from the Middle Ages. The two key themes here are centralization and absolutism, that is, the tendency of central governments to amass greater and greater control over their territory and inhabitants, and within that central government for rulers to increasingly concentrate power in their hands alone. Indeed, it is probably no exaggeration to say that at some point during this period, the point of no return was passed. That is, in 1559, it is possible to imagine that the political development of Europe could have evolved differently, that the future could have looked more like decentralized and noble-dominated Poland or the Holy Roman Empire than France or Great Britain. By 1715, though, large, centrally controlled monarchies had won the day. The apparent and important differences between France, Great Britain, Brandenburg-Prussia, the Habsburg monarchy, and Russia should not blind us to their commonalities. Likewise, the apparent and important differences between the various absolute monarchies (primarily France, Brandenburg-Prussia, the Habsburg monarchy, and Russia) and the limited governments of Great Britain and the Dutch Republic should not obscure the fact that in all these states, central governments were in more effective control in 1715 than they had been in 1559.

In diplomacy and international relations, the key feature of this period is the impact of religious division on relations between states and rulers. As we have seen, at least until the latter stages of the Thirty Years' War, religion was the single most important factor in diplomacy and warfare. This period of nearly continual war interacted directly with the evolution of governments discussed above. The constant need for more and more money in order to pay for this warfare is an extremely important factor in the continuing processes of centralization and absolutism, in creating the "warfare state" where the rights and liberties of the society of orders are subjected to the onslaught of the ruler and his tax collectors. By the later stages of the Thirty Years' War, religious passion had lost its central role in international affairs. Yet the influence of religious conflict lingered in several different ways. First, religious division and the concomitant warfare did result in the "warfare state," which lasted beyond the period of religious warfare, and in the sustained attack on the rights and privileges of the society of orders. Although no one can say for certain, without the religious division resulting from the Reformation and the subsequent century of religious war, it is very likely that European states would have developed very differently than was actually the case. Second, even after religion ceased to be the driving factor in diplomacy, the residue of religious warfare still complicated international relations, dividing potential allies and bringing together potential enemies. Thus, as we have seen, England and the Dutch Republic were commercial and naval rivals but found themselves on the same side of the religious divide, while France and England had a common interest in weakening Dutch commerce but were divided by deep religious hostility.

Other facets of history do not fit quite as neatly into the relatively short timeframe of this book. Economic life did not change dramatically in this period. In 1715 as in 1559, the vast majority of people continued to derive their livelihood from agriculture. Most manufactured goods continued to be made on a handicraft basis for local consumption. On the other hand, important changes continued beneath the surface. The most important was the continuing and growing importance of the market in agriculture. By 1715 it was much more common for peasants to grow food for sale on the open market than for their own subsistence alone. During the course of the eighteenth century, this development would ultimately lead to a transformation in European agriculture that would lay the foundation for the Industrial Revolution.

European society also seemed to change very little in this period. The daily lives of most people and the routines of birth, marriage, family, and death remained essentially the same. The demographic pattern of early modern Europe was established in the wake of the Black Death of the fourteenth century and persisted until the impact of the Industrial Revolution was widely felt in the nineteenth. In 1715, as in 1559, a society composed overwhelmingly of agrarian peasants was dominated by an aristocracy whose power was based on their control of the land and was supported by the twin pillars of monarchy and the Church. Beneath the surface, however, important changes were taking place. For one thing, the nature of the aristocracy was changing, due largely to greater social mobility. That is, increasing numbers of bourgeois were either becoming noble, mostly through royal bureaucracies, or were living the leisurely life of a *rentier*. At the same time, the increasing importance of the market in agriculture changed the way that aristocratic landowners and peasants related to each other. In western

Europe, these relations became more impersonal and commercial, while in eastern Europe serfdom was imposed and strengthened as a way of guaranteeing a cheap and captive labour force. Changing agricultural economics, increased taxation, and the depredations of war combined to produce social tension and frequent rebellions.

In religious life, as we have seen, the key feature of this period was the religious division produced by the Protestant Reformation. Yet this division between the Roman Catholic Church and the various Protestant churches should not blind us to some important common trends and developments. First, even as religion receded as a force in international relations, most rulers and governments continued to stress the vital importance of religious uniformity within their territories. At the same time, there was a concerted effort to "improve" the religious lives and devotion of ordinary people. This project was many-faceted. It involved better education for clergy and laity alike, teaching people the essential tenets of their faith. It involved the reform of popular culture, purging it of what the reformers saw as pagan vestiges as well as immoral and impious practices.

This endeavour to "improve" the religious lives of ordinary people had consequences very different from those envisioned by governments and the "godly" reformers. At one level, these efforts were quite successful in teaching more people than ever before to read and write. On the other hand, ordinary people, once literate, put this literacy to work in ways that had not been foreseen. At the same time, efforts to "clean up" popular culture drove a wedge between ordinary people and cultural elites. As long as rulers and elites remained committed to enforcing religious uniformity, ordinary people could be made to conform, but nothing could make them like it. Once this commitment began to waver, as happened in the course of the eighteenth century, the seemingly solid foundations of European churches were shown to be rather weak.

So, there is no doubt that European society was more secular in 1715 than in 1559, although this would become apparent only in the years to come. It is somewhat ironic, then, that the outcome of a century and a half of largely religious war, of efforts to impose religious uniformity and to educate people in the basic tenets of their faith, was ultimately a society and culture in which Christianity would be much less central to people's lives than it had been for over a thousand years before.

NOTES

1 John Henry, *The Scientific Revolution and the Origins of Modern Science* (New York: St. Martin's, 1997) 12.

2 Theodore K. Rabb, *The Struggle for Stability in Early Modern Europe* (New York: Oxford University Press, 1975) 114–15.

FURTHER READINGS

What follows is not intended as a comprehensive bibliography. Rather, it is intended as a tool for students, enabling them to further explore the events and topics treated in this book. Accordingly, it lists only books published in, or translated into, English. There is also, of course, a vast periodical literature that is omitted here. Moreover, given the volume of material that continues to be published on early modern Europe, it is no doubt possible to compile a completely different list many times as long as what follows. I have tried to include a judicious selection of the more important recent works as well as some acknowledged older "classics" of historical literature.

General Works

Aston, Trevor, ed. *Crisis in Europe 1560–1660: Essays from Past and Present.* London: Routledge and Kegan Paul, 1965.

Bonney, Richard, ed. *The Rise of the Fiscal State in Europe c. 1200–1815.* New York: Oxford University Press, 1999.

Bonney, Richard. *The European Dynastic States, 1494–1660.* Oxford: Oxford University Press, 1991.

Brady, Thomas A., H.A. Oberman, and James D. Tracy, eds. *Handbook of European History 1400–1600: Late Middle Ages, Renaissance, and Reformation.* 2 vols. Leiden: E.J. Brill, 1994.

Cameron, Euan, ed. *Early Modern Europe.* New York: Oxford University Press, 1999.

Elliott, J.H. *Europe Divided 1559–1598.* Oxford: Blackwell, 2000.

Lockyer, Roger. *Habsburg and Bourbon Europe.* London: Longman, 1974.

Morris, T.A. *England and Europe in the Sixteenth Century.* New York: Routledge, 1998.

Munck, Thomas. *Seventeenth Century Europe: State, Conflict and the Social Order in Europe 1598–1700*. London: Macmillan, 1990.

Parker, Geoffrey. *Europe in Crisis, 1598–1648*. London: Blackwell, 2001.

Pettegree, Andrew. *Europe in the Sixteenth Century*. Oxford: Blackwell, 2002.

CHAPTER 1 ⥲ POPULATION AND DEMOGRAPHY

Anderson, Michael. *Approaches to the History of the Western Family, 1500–1914*. London: Macmillan, 1980.

Baumgartner, Frederic. *From Spear to Flintlock: A History of War in Europe and the Middle East to the French Revolution*. New York: Praeger, 1991.

Black, Jeremy. *A Military Revolution? Military Change and European Society 1550–1800*. Atlantic Highlands, NJ: Humanities Press International, 1991.

——. *War and Society in Early Modern Europe, 1494–1715*. New York: Routledge, 1997.

Clark, Peter, ed. *Small Towns in Early Modern Europe*. Cambridge: Cambridge University Press, 1995.

Clark, Peter, and Paul Slack. *English Towns in Transition, 1500–1700*. Oxford: Oxford University Press, 1976.

Corvisier, A. *Armies and Societies in Europe, 1494–1789*. Trans. A.T. Siddall. Bloomington: Indiana University Press, 1979.

Cowan, Alexander. *Urban Europe, 1500–1700*. London: Arnold, 1998.

De Vries, Jan. *European Urbanization, 1500–1800*. New York: Cambridge University Press, 1984.

Dobson, Mary J. *Contours of Death and Disease in Early Modern England*. Cambridge: Cambridge University Press, 1997.

Duffy, Christopher. *Siege Warfare: The Fortress in the Early Modern World, 1494–1660*. New York: Routledge, 1996.

Eltis, David. *The Military Revolution in Sixteenth-Century Europe*. New York: I.B. Taurus Publishers, 1995.

Epstein, S.R., ed. *Town and Country in Pre-Modern Europe*. Cambridge: Cambridge University Press, 2001.

Flandrin, J.L. *Families in Former Times: Kinship, Household and Sexuality*. Trans. R. Southern. Cambridge: Cambridge University Press, 1979.

Friedrichs, Christopher R. *The Early Modern City, 1450–1750*. London and New York: Longman, 1995.

Gordon, Bruce, and Peter Marshall, eds. *The Place of the Dead: Death and Remembrance in Late Medieval and Early Modern Europe*. Cambridge: Cambridge University Press, 2000.

Grigg, David B. *Population Growth and Agrarian Change: An Historical Perspective*. Cambridge: Cambridge University Press, 1980.

Gottlieb, Beatrice. *The Family in the Western World from the Black Death to the Industrial Age*. Oxford: Oxford University Press, 1993.

Gutmann, M.P. *War and Rural Life in the Early Modern Low Countries*. Princeton, NJ: Princeton University Press, 1980.

Hale, J.R. *War and Society in Renaissance Europe, 1450–1620*. Leicester: Leicester University Press, 1985.

Hall, Bert S. *Weapons and Warfare in Renaissance Europe: Gunpowder, Technology and Tactics*. Baltimore: Johns Hopkins University Press, 2002.

Harding, Vanessa. *The Dead and the Living in Paris and London, 1500–1670*. Cambridge and New York: Cambridge University Press, 2002.

Houlbrooke, R.A. *The English Family, 1450–1700*. London: Longman, 1984.

Hunt, David. *Parents and Children in History: The Psychology of Family Life in Early Modern France*. New York: Harper and Row, 1972.

Kertzer, David I., and Marzio Barbagli, eds. *The History of the European Family, vol. 1: Family Life in Early Modern Times*. New Haven, CT: Yale University Press, 2001.

Knox, MacGregor, and Williamson Murray, eds. *The Dynamics of Military Revolution, 1300–2050*. Cambridge: Cambridge University Press, 2002.

Laslett, Peter. *The World We Have Lost*. London: Methuen, 1983.

Lynn, John A., ed. *Feeding Mars: Logistics in Western Warfare from the Middle Ages to the Present*. Boulder, CO: Westview Press, 1993.

Mitterauer, Michael, and Reinhard Sieder. *The European Family*. Chicago: University of Chicago Press, 1982.

O'Brien, Patrick, Marjolein Hart, Derek Keene, and Herman van der Wee, eds. *Urban Achievement in Early Modern Europe: Golden Ages in Antwerp, Amsterdam and London*. Cambridge: Cambridge University Press, 2001.

Parker, Geoffrey. *The Military Revolution: Military Innovation and the Rise of the West, 1500–1800*. Cambridge: Cambridge University Press, 1986.

Stone, Lawrence. *The Family, Sex, and Marriage in England, 1500–1800*. New York: Harper and Row, 1979.

Tallet, Frank. *War and Society in Early Modern Europe, 1495–1715*. London: Routledge, 1992.

Tittler, Robert. *Townspeople and Nation: English Urban Experiences, c. 1540–1640.* Stanford, CA: Stanford University Press, 2001.

Walter, John, and Roger Schofield, eds. *Famine, Disease and the Social Order in Early Modern Society.* New York: Cambridge University Press, 1989.

Wrightson, Keith. *English Society, 1580–1680.* London: Hutchinson, 1982.

CHAPTER 2 ⭆ SOCIAL RELATIONS AND THE STRUCTURE OF SOCIETY

Adamson, John, ed. *The Princely Courts of Europe: Ritual, Politics and Culture under the Ancien Régime, 1500–1750.* London: Weidenfeld and Nicolson, 1999.

Amussen, Susan. *An Ordered Society: Gender and Class in Early Modern England.* London: Blackwell, 1988.

Ankarloo, Bengt, and Gustav Henningsen, eds. *Early Modern European Witchcraft.* Oxford: Clarendon Press, 1990.

Asch, R.G., ed. *Prince, Patronage and the Nobility: The Court at the Beginning of the Modern Age.* Oxford: Oxford University Press, 1991.

Barry, Jonathan, Marianne Hester, and Gareth Roberts, eds. *Witchcraft in Early Modern Europe: Culture and Belief.* New York: Cambridge University Press, 1996.

Behringer, Wolfgang. *Witchcraft Persecutions in Bavaria: Popular Magic, Religious Zealotry and Reason of State in Early Modern Europe.* Trans. J.C. Grayson and David Lederer. New York: Cambridge University Press, 1997.

Bercé, Yves-Marie. *History of Peasant Revolts: The Social Origins of Rebellion in Early Modern France.* Trans. Amanda Whitmore. Ithaca, NY: Cornell University Press, 1989.

Billacois, François. *The Duel: Its Rise and Fall in Early Modern France.* Trans. Trista Selous. New Haven, CT: Yale University Press, 1990.

Bitton, Davis. *The French Nobility in Crisis, 1560–1640.* Stanford, CA: Stanford University Press, 1969.

Bush, M.L. *Noble Privilege.* Manchester: Manchester University Press, 1983.

Bush, Michael. *Social Orders and Social Classes in Europe since 1500.* White Plains, NY: Longman, 1991.

Briggs, Robin. *Communities of Belief: Cultural and social tensions in early modern France.* Oxford: Clarendon Press, 1989.

Cavallo, Sandra, and Lyndan Warner, eds. *Widowhood in Medieval and Early Modern Europe.* London: Longman, 1999.

Chojnacka, Monica. *Working Women of Early Modern Venice.* Baltimore: Johns Hopkins University Press, 2000.

Clark, S. *Thinking with Demons: The Idea of Witchcraft in Early Modern Europe.* Oxford: Clarendon Press, 1997.

Cohn, N. *Europe's Inner Demons: An Enquiry Inspired by the Great Witch-Hunt.* Chicago: University of Chicago Press, 2000.

Collins, James B. *Classes, Estates, and Order in Early Modern Brittany.* Cambridge: Cambridge University Press, 1994.

Crawford, Patricia. *Women in Religion in England 1500–1720.* New York: Routledge, 1993.

Critchlow, Donald T., and Charles H. Parker, eds. *With Us Always: A History of Private Charity and Public Welfare.* Lanham, MD: Rowman and Littlefield, 1998.

Davis, Natalie Zemon. *Society and Culture in Early Modern France.* Stanford, CA: Stanford University Press, 1975.

——. *Women on the Margins: Three Seventeenth-Century Lives.* Cambridge, MA: Harvard University Press, 1995.

Davis, Natalie Zemon, and Arlette Farge, eds. *A History of Women in the West, vol. 3: Renaissance and Enlightenment Paradoxes.* Cambridge, MA: Belknap, 1993.

Dewald, Jonathan. *The European Nobility, 1400–1800.* Cambridge: Cambridge University Press, 1996.

Eisenstein, Elizabeth L. *The Printing Revolution in Early Modern Europe.* Cambridge: Cambridge University Press, 1993.

Farr, James R. *Hands of Honor: Artisans and their World in Early Modern France.* Ithaca, NY: Cornell University Press, 1988.

——. *Authority and Sexuality in Early Modern Burgundy, 1550–1730.* New York: Oxford University Press, 1994.

——. *Artisans in Europe, 1300–1914.* New York: Cambridge University Press, 2000.

Friedrichs, Christopher R. *Urban Politics in Early Modern Europe.* New York: Routledge, 2000.

Gibson, Wendy. *Women in Seventeenth-Century France.* New York: St. Martin's Press, 1989.

Ginzburg, Carlo. *The Night Battles: Witchcraft and Agrarian Cults in the Sixteenth and Seventeenth Centuries.* Trans. John and Anne Tedeschi. Baltimore: Johns Hopkins University Press, 1983.

——. *Ecstasies: Deciphering the Witches' Sabbath*. Trans. R. Rosenthal. New York: Random House, 1991.

Goldstone, Jack A. *Revolution and Rebellion in the Early Modern World*. Berkeley and Los Angeles: University of California Press, 1983.

Goubert, Pierre. *The Ancien Régime: French Society, 1600–1750*. Trans. Steve Cox. New York: Harper Torchbooks, 1974.

——. *The French Peasantry in the Seventeenth Century*. Trans. Ian Patterson. Cambridge: Cambridge University Press, 1986.

Graves, Rolande. *Born to Procreate: Women and Childbirth in France from the Middle Ages to the Eighteenth Century*. New York: Peter Lang, 2001.

Hafter, Daryl M., ed. *European Women and Preindustrial Craft*. Bloomington: Indiana University Press, 1995.

Hanawalt, Barbara. *Women and Work in Preindustrial Europe*. Bloomington: Indiana University Press, 1986.

Hardwick, Julie. *The Practice of Patriarchy: Gender and the Politics of Household Authority in Early Modern France*. State College, PA: Penn State University Press, 1998.

Harrington, Joel F. *Reordering Marriage and Society in Reformation Germany*. New York: Cambridge University Press, 1994.

Houston, R.A. *Literacy in Early Modern Europe: Culture and Education 1500–1800*. London: Longman, 1989.

Huppert, George. *Les Bourgeois Gentilshommes: An Essay of the Definition of Elites in Renaissance France*. Chicago: University of Chicago Press, 1977.

——. *After the Black Death: A Social History of Early Modern Europe*. Bloomington: Indiana University Press, 1998.

Jutte, Robert. *Poverty and Deviance in Early Modern Europe*. Cambridge: Cambridge University Press, 1994.

Kamen, Henry. *The Iron Century: social change in Europe 1550–1660*. London: Weidenfeld & Nicolson, 1971.

——. *Early Modern European Society*. New York: Routledge, 2000.

Kieckhefer, R. *European Witchtrials: Their Foundation in Popular and Learned Culture, 1300–1500*. Berkeley: University of California Press, 1976.

Klaits, Joseph. *Servants of Satan: The Age of the Witch Hunts*. Bloomington: Indiana University Press, 1985.

Larner, Christina. *Witchcraft and Religion: The Politics of Popular Belief*. Oxford: Blackwell, 1984.

Laurence, Anne. *Women in England 1500–1760: A Social History*. New York: St. Martin's Press, 1994.

Le Roy Ladurie, E. *The Peasants of Languedoc*. Trans. John Day. Urbana: University of Illinois Press, 1974.

——. *Carnival in Romans*. Trans. Mary Feeney. New York: George Braziller, 1979.

——. *The French Peasantry 1450–1660*. Berkeley and Los Angeles: University of California Press, 1987.

Levack, Brian. *The Witch-Hunt in Early Modern Europe*, 2nd ed. London: Longman, 1994.

Marshall, Sherrin. *The Dutch Gentry, 1500–1650: Family, Faith, and Fortune*. New York: Greenwood Press, 1987.

Marshall, Sherrin, ed. *Women in Reformation and Counter-Reformation Europe: Private and Public Worlds*. Bloomington: Indiana University Press, 1989.

Martin, Ruth. *Witchcraft and the Inquisition in Venice, 1550–1650*. Oxford: Blackwell, 1989.

Martz, L. *Poverty and Welfare in Habsburg Spain: The Example of Toledo*. Cambridge: Cambridge University Press, 1983.

Meek, Christine, ed. *Women in Renaissance and Early Modern Europe*. Portland, OR: Four Courts Press, 2000.

Mendelson, Sara, and Patricia Crawford. *Women in Early Modern England*. New York: Oxford University Press, 1998.

Midelfort, H.C. Erik. *Witch-Hunting in Southwestern Germany, 1562–1684: The Social and Intellectual Foundations*. Stanford, CA: Stanford University Press, 1972.

Monter, E.W. *Witchcraft in France and Switzerland*. Ithaca, NY: Cornell University Press, 1976.

Mora, George, ed. *Witches, Devils, and Doctors in the Renaissance: Johann de Weyer, De praestigiis daemonum*. Binghamton: MRTS, 1991.

Mousnier, Roland. *Social Hierarchies, 1450 to the Present*. Trans. P. Evans. New York: Schocken, 1973.

Ozment, Steven. *When Fathers Ruled: Family Life in Reformation Europe*. Cambridge, MA: Harvard University Press, 1983.

Peterson, E.L. *The Crisis of the Danish Nobility, 1580–1660*. Odense: Odense Universitetsforlag, 1967.

Pullan, Brian. *Rich and Poor in Renaissance Venice: The Social Institutions of a Catholic State to 1620*. Cambridge, MA: Harvard University Press, 1971.

Rapley, Robert. *A Case of Witchcraft: The trial of Urbain Granider.* Manchester: Manchester University Press, 1998.

Roper, Lyndal. *The Holy Household: Women and Morals in Reformation Augsburg.* Oxford: Oxford University Press, 1989.

——. *Oedipus and the Devil: Witchcraft, Religion and Sexuality in Early Modern Europe.* London: Routledge, 1994.

Rublack, Ursula, ed. *Gender in Early Modern German History.* New York: Cambridge University Press, 2002.

Schalk, Ellery. *From Valor to Pedigree: Ideas of Nobility in France in the Sixteenth and Seventeenth Centuries.* Princeton, NJ: Princeton University Press, 1986.

Sommerville, Margaret. *Sex and Subjection: Attitudes to Women in Early Modern Society.* London: Arnold, 1995.

Stone, Lawrence. *The Crisis of the Aristocracy, 1558–1641.* Oxford: Clarendon Press, 1967.

Weisser, M.R. *The Peasants of the Montes: The Roots of Rural Rebellion in Spain.* Chicago: University of Chicago Press, 1976.

Wiesner, Merry. *Working Women in Renaissance Germany.* New Brunswick, NJ: Rutgers University Press, 1986.

——. *Gender, Church and State in Early Modern Germany.* London and New York: Longman, 1998.

——. *Women and Gender in Early Modern Europe.* New York: Cambridge University Press, 2000.

Wunder, Heide. *He is the Sun, She is the Moon: Women in Early Modern* Germany. Trans. Thomas Dunlap. Cambridge, MA: Harvard University Press, 1998.

CHAPTER 3 ⭆ THE ECONOMY OF EARLY MODERN EUROPE

Barbour, V. *Capitalism in Amsterdam in the Seventeenth Century.* Baltimore: Johns Hopkins University Press, 1950.

Braudel, Fernand. *The Mediterranean and the Mediterranean World in the Age of Philip II.* 2 vols. Trans. S. Reynolds. New York: Harper and Row, 1972.

——. *Capitalism and Material Life, 1400–1800.* London: Weidenfeld & Nicolson, 1973.

——. *Civilization and Capitalism, 15th–18th Centuries.* 3 vols. Trans. Sian Reynolds. London: Collins, 1981.

Burke, Peter, ed. *Economy and Society in Early Modern Europe: Essays from Annales.* London: Routledge, 1972.

Cipolla, Carlo M. *The Fontana Economic History of Europe. Vol. 2: The Sixteenth and Seventeenth Centuries*. Glasgow: Collins/Fontana, 1974.

——. *Before the Industrial Revolution: European Society and Economy, 1000–1700.* London: Routledge, 1993.

Coleman, D.C. *Revisions in Mercantilism.* London: Methuen, 1969.

Davis, J.C. *The Decline of the Venetian Nobility as a Ruling Class.* Baltimore: Johns Hopkins University Press, 1962.

Davis, Ralph. *The Rise of the Atlantic Economies.* Ithaca, NY: Cornell University Press, 1973.

De Vries, Jan. *The Dutch Rural Economy in the Golden Age, 1500–1700.* New Haven, CT: Yale University Press, 1974.

——. *The Economy of Europe in an Age of Crisis.* Cambridge: Cambridge University Press, 1976.

De Vries, Jan, and Ad van der Woude. *The First Modern Economy: Success, Failure, and Perseverance of the Dutch Economy, 1500–1815.* New York: Cambridge University Press, 1996.

DuPlessis, Robert S. *Transitions to Capitalism in Early Modern Europe.* New York: Cambridge University Press, 1997.

Goodman, Jordan, and Katrina Honeyman. *Gainful Pursuits: The Making of Industrial Europe, 1600–1914.* London: Edwin Arnold, 1988.

Hoffman, Philip T. *Growth in a Traditional Society.* Princeton, NJ: Princeton University Press, 1996.

Lachmann, Richard. *Capitalists in Spite of Themselves: Elite Conflict and European Transitions in Early Modern Europe.* New York: Oxford University Press, 1999.

Miskimin, H.A. *The Economy of Later Renaissance Europe, 1460–1600.* Cambridge: Cambridge University Press, 1977.

Pullan, Brian. *Crisis and Change in the Venetian Economy in the Sixteenth and Seventeenth Centuries.* London: Methuen, 1968.

Rich, E.E. and C.H. Wilson, *Cambridge Economic History of Europe, vol. 4: The Economy of Expanding Europe in the Sixteenth and Seventeenth Centuries.* Cambridge: Cambridge University Press, 1977.

Sacks, David Harris. *The Widening Gate: Bristol and the Atlantic Economy 1450–1700.* Berkeley and Los Angeles: University of California Press, 1991.

Safley, Thomas Max, Jr., and Leonard N. Rosenband, eds. *The Workplace before the Factory: Artisans and Proletarians, 1500–1800.* Ithaca, NY: Cornell University Press, 1993.

Tracy, James D., ed. *The Rise of Merchant Empires: Long Distance Trade in the Early Modern World, 1350-1750.* Cambridge: Cambridge University Press, 1990.

Van der Wee, H. *The Growth of the Antwerp Market and the European Economy, Fourteenth-Sixteenth Centuries.* The Hague: Nijhoff, 1963.

Wallerstein, I. *The Modern World-System.* 2 vols. New York: Academic Press, 1974, 1980.

Wrightson, Keith. *Earthly Necessities: Economic Lives in Early Modern Britain.* New Haven, CT: Yale University Press, 2000.

CHAPTER 4 Religion and the People

Bangs, C. *Arminius: A Study in the Dutch Reformation.* Nashville: Abingdon Press, 1971.

Benedict, Philip. *Christ's Churches Purely Reformed.* New Haven, CT: Yale University Press, 2002.

Bireley, Robert. *Religion and Politics in the Age of the Counter-Reformation: Emperor Ferdinand II, William Lamormaini SJ, and the Formulation of Imperial Policy.* Chapel Hill: University of North Carolina Press, 1981.

——. *The Jesuits and the Thirty Years War: Kings, Courts, and Confessors.* Cambridge: Cambridge University Press, 2003.

Bossy, John. *Christianity in the West.* Oxford: Oxford University Press, 1985.

Bouwsma, William. *John Calvin: A Sixteenth-Century Portrait.* New York: Oxford University Press, 1988.

Burke, Peter. *Popular Culture in Early Modern Europe.* New York: Harper Torchbooks, 1978.

Carlson, Eric Joseph, ed. *Religion and the English People, 1500–1640: New Voices, New Perspectives.* Kirksville, MO: Thomas Jefferson University Press, 1998.

Chatellier, Louis. *The Europe of the Devout: the Catholic Reformation and the Formation of a New Society.* Cambridge: Cambridge University Press, 1989.

——. *The Religion of the Poor: Rural Missions in Europe and the Formation of Modern Catholicism, c. 1500–1800.* New York: Cambridge University Press, 1997.

Delumeau, J. *Catholicism between Luther and Voltaire: A New View of the Counter-Reformation.* Philadelphia: Westminster Press, 1977.

Ditchfield, Simon. *Christianity and Community in the West: Essays for John Bossy.* Burlington, VT: Ashgate, 2001.

Evennett, H.O. *The Spirit of the Counter-Reformation.* Notre Dame, IN: Notre Dame University Press, 1970.

Forster, Marc R. *The Counter-Reformation in the Villages: Religion and Reform in the Bishopric of Speyer, 1560–1720.* Ithaca, NY: Cornell University Press, 1992.

——. *Catholic Revival in the Age of the Baroque: Religious Identity in Southwest Germany.* New York: Cambridge University Press, 2001

Ginzburg, Carlo. *The Cheese and the Worms: The Cosmos of a Sixteenth-Century Miller.* Trans. John and Anne Tedeschi. Baltimore: Johns Hopkins University Press, 1980.

Green, Ian. *The Christian's ABC: Catechisms and Catechizing in England c. 1530–1740.* New York: Oxford University Press, 1996.

Hsia, R. Pochia. *The World of Catholic Renewal, 1540–1770.* Cambridge: Cambridge University Press, 1998.

Israel, Jonathan. *European Jewry in the Age of Mercantilism, 1550–1750.* Oxford: Clarendon Press, 1985.

Jones, Martin. *The Counter Reformation: Religion and Society in Early Modern Europe.* Cambridge: Cambridge University Press, 1995.

Kingdon, Robert M. *Adultery and Divorce in Calvin's Geneva.* Cambridge, MA: Harvard University Press, 1995.

Mack, Phyllis. *Visionary Women: Ecstatic Prophecy in Seventeenth-Century England.* Berkeley and Los Angeles: University of California Press, 1994.

Maltby, Judith. *Prayer Book and People in Elizabethan and Early Stuart England.* New York: Cambridge University Press, 1997.

Marsh, Christopher. *Popular Religion in Sixteenth-Century England: Holding their Peace.* New York: St. Martin's Press, 1998.

Marshall, Peter, ed. *The Impact of the English Reformation 1500–1640.* London: Arnold, 1994.

Martin, A. Lynn. *The Jesuit Mind: The Mentality of an Elite in Early Modern France.* Ithaca, NY: Cornell University Press, 1988.

Mentzer, Raymond A., ed. *Sin and the Calvinists: Morals, Control, and the Consistory in the Reformed Tradition.* Kirksville, MO: Sixteenth Century Journal Publishers, 1994.

Monter, E.W. *Ritual, Myth and Magic in Early Modern Europe.* Athens: Ohio University Press, 1983.

Muchembled, R. *Popular Culture and Elite Culture in France, 1400–1750.* Trans. L. Cochrane. Baton Rouge: Louisiana State University Press, 1985.

Mullett, Michael A. *The Catholic Reformation.* New York: Routledge, 1999.

Myers, W. David. *"Poor Sinning Folk": Confession and Conscience in Counter-Reformation Germany.* Ithaca, NY: Cornell University Press, 1996.

Nischan, Bodo. *Prince, People, and Confession: The Second Reformation in Brandenburg.* Philadelphia: University of Pennsylvania Press, 1994.

——. *Lutherans and Calvinists in the Age of Confessionalism.* Brookfield, VT: Variorum, 1999.

O'Connell, Marvin. *The Counter Reformation, 1559–1610.* New York: Harper and Row, 1974.

O'Malley, John W. *The First Jesuits.* Cambridge, Mass: Harvard University Press, 1993.

——. *Trent and All That: Renaming Catholicism in the Early Modern Era.* Cambridge, MA: Harvard University Press, 2000.

Oldridge, D.J. *Religion and Society in Early Stuart England.* Brookfield, VT: Ashgate, 1998.

Parker, T.H.L. *John Calvin: A Biography.* London: Dent, 1975.

Pettegree, A., A. Duke, and G. Lewis, eds. *Calvinism in Europe, 1540–1620.* New York: Cambridge University Press, 1994.

Poska, Allyson M. *Regulating the People: The Catholic Reformation in Seventeenth-Century Spain.* Leiden: E.J. Brill, 1998.

Prestwich, Menna, ed. *International Calvinism, 1541–1715.* Oxford: Clarendon Press, 1985.

Slack, Paul. *From Reformation to Improvement: Public Welfare in Early Modern England.* New York: Oxford University Press, 1997.

Solt, Leo F. *Church and State in Early Modern England.* New York: Oxford University Press, 1990.

Thomas, Keith. *Religion and the Decline of Magic.* Harmondsworth: Penguin, 1973.

von Greyerz, Kaspar, ed. *Religion and Society in Early Modern Europe, 1500–1800.* London: George Allen and Unwin, 1984.

Wendel, François. *Calvin: the Origins and Development of his Religious Thought.* Trans. Philippe Mairet. London: Collins, 1963.

CHAPTER 5 ⇜ THE WARS OF RELIGION IN FRANCE

Baumgartner, Frederic J. *France in the Sixteenth Century.* New York: St. Martin's Press, 1995.

Briggs, Robin. *Early Modern France, 1560–1715.* 2nd ed. New York: Oxford University Press, 1998.

Diefendorf, Barbara. *Beneath the Cross: Catholics and Huguenots in Sixteenth-Century Paris.* Oxford: Oxford University Press, 1991.

Garrisson, Janine. *A History of Sixteenth-Century France, 1483–1598.* London: Macmillan, 1995.

Holt, Mack P. *The French Wars of Religion, 1562–1629.* Cambridge: Cambridge University Press, 1995.

Kingdon, Robert M. *Geneva and the Coming of the Wars of Religion in France.* Geneva: Droz, 1957.

——. *Geneva and the Consolidation of the French Protestant Movement.* Madison: University of Wisconsin Press, 1967.

——. *Myths about the St. Bartholomew's Day Massacres.* Cambridge, MA: Harvard University Press, 1988.

Knecht, Robert J. *The Rise and Fall of Renaissance France.* London: Blackwell, 1996.

——. *Catherine de' Medici.* London: Longman, 1998.

Le Roy Ladurie, E. *The Royal French State, 1460–1610.* Trans. Juliet Vale. Oxford: Blackwell, 1994.

Love, Ronald S. *Blood and Religion: The Conscience of Henry IV.* Toronto: McGill-Queen's University Press, 2001.

Martin, A. Lynn. *Henry III and the Jesuit Politicians.* Geneva: Droz, 1973.

Salmon, J.H.M. *Society in Crisis: France in the Sixteenth Century.* New York: St. Martin's Press, 1975.

Sutherland, N.M. *The Massacre of St. Bartholomew and the European Conflict 1559–1572.* London: Macmillan, 1973.

——. *The Huguenot Struggle for Recognition.* New Haven, CT: Yale University Press, 1980.

Wolfe, Michael. *The Conversion of Henri IV: Politics, Power, and Religious Belief in Early Modern France.* Cambridge, MA: Harvard University Press, 1993.

Wood, James B. *The King's Army: Warfare, Soldiers and Society during the Wars of Religion in France, 1562–76.* New York: Cambridge University Press, 1996.

CHAPTER 6 ⥱ SPAIN AND THE NETHERLANDS

Spain

Boyden, James M. *The Courtier and the King: Ruy de Gomez Silva, Philip II, and the Court of Spain.* Berkeley and Los Angeles: University of California Press, 1994.

Casey, James. *Early Modern Spain: A Social History.* London: Routledge, 1999.

Elliott, J.H. *Imperial Spain, 1469–1716.* New York: Penguin, 1964.

——. *Spain and its World, 1500–1700: Selected Essays.* New Haven, CT: Yale University Press, 1989.

Haliczer, Stephen. *Inquisition and Society in the Kingdom of Valencia, 1478–1834.* Berkeley: University of California Press, 1990.

Kagan, Richard L., and Geoffrey Parker, eds. *Spain, Europe and the Atlantic World: Essays in Honour of John H. Elliott.* Cambridge: Cambridge University Press, 1995.

Kamen, Henry. *Inquisition and Society in Spain in the Sixteenth and Seventeenth Centuries.* London: Weidenfeld and Nicolson, 1985.

——. *Spain, 1469–1714.* 2nd ed. White Plains, NY: Longman, 1991.

——. *Crisis and Change in Early Modern Spain.* Brookfield, VT: Variorum, 1993.

——. *The Phoenix and the Flame: Catalonia and the Counter-Reformation.* New Haven: Yale University Press, 1993.

——. *The Spanish Inquisition: A Historical Revision.* New Haven, CT: Yale University Press, 1998.

Lovett, A.W. *Early Habsburg Spain, 1517–1598.* Oxford: Oxford University Press, 1986.

Lynch, John. *Spain under the Hapsburgs, 1516–1700.* 2nd ed. 2 vols. New York: New York University Press, 1981.

——. *Spain 1516–1598: From Nation State to World Empire.* Cambridge, MA: Blackwell, 1992.

Monter, E. William. *Frontiers of Heresy: The Spanish Inquisition from the Basque Lands to Sicily.* Cambridge: Cambridge University Press, 1990.

Nader, Helen. *Liberty in Absolutist Spain: The Habsburg Sale of Towns, 1516–1700.* Baltimore: Johns Hopkins University Press, 1993.

Parker, Geoffrey. *Philip II.* London: Hutchinson, 1979.

——. *The Grand Strategy of Philip II.* New Haven, CT: Yale University Press, 1998.

Peters, Edward. *Inquisition*. Berkeley: University of California Press, 1988.

Pierson, Peter. *Philip II*. London: Thames and Hudson, 1989.

Rodriguez-Salgado, M.J. *The Changing Face of Empire: Charles V, Philip II and Habsburg Authority, 1551–1559*. Cambridge: Cambridge University Press, 1988.

The Netherlands and the Dutch Revolt

Duke, Alastair. *Reformation and Revolt in the Low Countries*. London: Hambledon Press, 1990.

Geyl, Pieter. *The Revolt of the Netherlands, 1555–1609*. New York: Barnes and Noble, 1958.

Koenigsberger, H.G. *Monarchies, States Generals and Parliaments: The Netherlands in the Fifteenth and Sixteenth Centuries*. Cambridge: Cambridge University Press, 2002.

Parker, Geoffrey. *The Dutch Revolt*. Ithaca, NY: Cornell University Press, 1977.

——. *Spain and the Netherlands*. London: Collins, 1979.

Swart, K.W. *William the Silent and the Revolt of the Netherlands*. London: Historical Association, 1978.

Tracy, James. *Holland under Habsburg Rule 1505–1566: the Formation of a Body Politic*. Berkeley: University of California Press, 1990.

Van Gelderen, Martin. *The Political Thought of the Dutch Revolt, 1555–1590*. Cambridge: Cambridge University Press, 1992.

Van Gelderen, Martin, ed. *The Dutch Revolt*. Cambridge: Cambridge University Press, 1993.

Wedgwood, C.V. *William the Silent*. London: Norton, 1944.

CHAPTER 7 ⅏ ELIZABETHAN ENGLAND

Bassnett, Susan. *Elizabeth I: A Feminist Perspective*. Oxford: Berg, 1988.

Collinson, Patrick. *The Religion of Protestants: The Church in English Society 1559–1625*. Oxford: Clarendon Press, 1982.

——. *The Elizabethan Puritan Movement*. Berkeley: University of California Press, 1990.

Collinson, Patrick, and John Craig, eds. *The Reformation in English Towns, 1500–1640*. New York: St. Martin's Press, 1998.

Donaldson, Gordon. *The Scottish Reformation*. Cambridge: Cambridge University Press, 1960.

——. *Mary, Queen of Scots*. London: English Universities Press, 1974.

Durston, Christopher, and Jacqueline Eales, eds. *The Culture of English Puritanism, 1560–1700*. New York: St. Martin's Press, 1996.

Erickson, Carolly. *The First Elizabeth*. New York: St. Martin's Press, 1997.

Fernandez-Armesto, F. *The Spanish Armada: The Experience of War in 1588*. Oxford: Oxford University Press, 1988.

Fraser, Antonia. *Mary Queen of Scots*. London: Weidenfeld and Nicolson, 1969.

Greaves, Richard. *Religion and Society in Elizabethan England*. Minneapolis: University of Minnesota Press, 1981.

Hartley, T.E. *Elizabeth's Parliaments: Queen, Lords, and Commons*. Manchester and New York: Manchester University Press, 1992.

Hopkins, Lisa. *Elizabeth I and Her Court*. New York: St. Martin's Press, 1990.

Hurstfield, Joel. *Elizabeth I and the Unity of England*. Harmondsworth: Penguin, 1971.

Kelsey, Henry. *Sir Francis Drake: The Queen's Pirate*. New Haven, CT: Yale University Press, 1998.

Levin, Carole. *The Heart and Stomach of a King: Elizabeth I and the Politics of Sex and Power*. Philadelphia: University of Pennsylvania Press, 1994.

——. *The Reign of Elizabeth I*. New York: Palgrave, 2002.

Lewis, Jayne Elizabeth. *The Trial of Mary Queen of Scots: A Brief History with Documents*. New York: St. Martin's Press, 1999.

Loades, David. *The Tudor Court*. New York: Barnes and Noble, 1986.

——. *The Mid-Tudor Crisis, 1545–1565*. New York: St. Martin's Press, 1992.

——. *Power in Tudor England*. New York: St. Martin's Press, 1996.

——. *Elizabeth I*. New York: Palgrave, 2003.

MacCaffrey, Wallace T. *Elizabeth I*. London: Edwin Arnold, 1992.

——. *Elizabeth I: War and Politics, 1588–1603*. Princeton, NJ: Princeton University Press, 1992.

MacCulloch, Diarmaid. *The Later Reformation in England 1547–1603*. New York: St. Martin's Press, 1990.

MacRobert, A.E. *Mary Queen of Scots and the Casket Letters*. New York: I.B. Tauris, 2002.

Martin, Colin, and Geoffrey Parker. *The Spanish Armada.* New York: Palgrave, 2003.

Mattingly, Garrett. *The Armada.* Boston: Houghton Mifflin Sentry, 1959.

McLaren, Anne. *Political Culture in the Reign of Elizabeth I: Queen and Commonwealth 1558–1585.* Cambridge: Cambridge University Press, 2000.

Starkey, David. *Elizabeth: The Struggle for the Throne.* New York: HarperCollins, 2000.

Walker, Julia M., ed. *Dissing Elizabeth: Negative Representations of Gloriana.* Durham, NC: Duke University Press, 1998.

Williams, Penry. *The Later Tudors: England 1547–1603.* Oxford: Oxford University Press, 1995.

CHAPTER 8 ⥲ GERMANY AND THE THIRTY YEARS' WAR

Asch, Ronald G. *The Thirty Years War: the Holy Roman Empire and Europe, 1618–1648.* New York: St. Martin's Press, 1997.

Dixon, C. Scott. *The Reformation in Germany.* Oxford: Blackwell, 2000.

Evans, R.J.W. *Rudolf II and His World.* Oxford: Clarendon Press, 1973.

Fichtner, Paula Sutter. *Emperor Maximilian II.* New Haven, CT: Yale University Press, 2001.

Holborn, Hajo. *A History of Modern Germany, vol.1: The Reformation.* Princeton, NJ: Princeton University Press, 1964.

Hughes, Michael. *Early Modern Germany, 1477–1806.* Philadelphia: University of Pennsylvania Press, 1992.

Koenigsberger, H.G. *The Habsburgs and Europe, 1516–1660.* Ithaca, NY: Cornell University Press, 1971.

Mann, G. *Wallenstein.* New York: Holt, Rinehart, and Winston, 1976.

Pages, Georges. *The Thirty Years' War.* Trans. David Maland and John Hooper. London: Adam and Charles Black, 1939.

Parker, Geoffrey. *The Thirty Years' War.* 2nd ed. London: Routledge, 1996.

Polisensky, J.V. *The Thirty Years War.* Trans. R.J.W. Evans. Berkeley: University of California Press, 1971.

Steinberg, S.H. *The Thirty Years' War and the Conflict for European Hegemony.* London: Edward Arnold, 1966.

Wedgwood, C.V. *The Thirty Years War.* London: Jonathan Cape, 1938.

Wilson, Peter H. *The Holy Roman Empire, 14951806*. New York: St. Martin's, 1999.

PART III ⥼ The General Crisis of the Seventeenth Century

Allen, J.W. *Political Thought in the Sixteenth Century*. London: Methuen, 1928.

Church, W.F. *Constitutional Thought in Sixteenth-Century France*. Cambridge, MA: Harvard University Press, 1941.

Duindam, Jeroen. *Vienna and Versailles: The Courts of Europe's Dynastic Rivals, 1550–1780*. Cambridge and New York: Cambridge University Press, 2003.

Franklin, J.H. *Constitutionalism and Resistance in the Sixteenth Century: Three Treatises by Hotman, Beza and Mornay*. New York: Pegasus, 1969.

——. *Jean Bodin and the Rise of Absolutist Theory*. New York: Cambridge University Press, 1973.

Greengrass, Mark, ed. *Conquest and Coalescence: The Shaping of the State in Early Modern Europe*. London: Longmans, 1991.

Hoffman, Philip T., and Kathryn Norberg, eds. *Fiscal Crises, Liberty, and Representative Government, 1450–1789*. Stanford, CA: Stanford University Press, 1994.

Monod, Paul Kléber. *The Power of Kings: Monarchy and Religion in Europe, 1589–1715*. New Haven, CT: Yale University Press, 1999.

Parker, Geoffrey, and Lesley M. Smith, eds. *The General Crisis of the Seventeenth Century*, 2nd ed. London: Routledge, 1997.

Rabb, Theodore K. *The Struggle for Stability in Early Modern Europe*. New York: Oxford University Press, 1975.

Skinner, Q. *The Foundations of Modern Political Thought*. 2 vols. Cambridge: Cambridge University Press, 1978.

Zagorin, P. *Rebels and Rulers, 1500–1660*. Cambridge: Cambridge University Press, 1982.

CHAPTER 9 ⥼ The Construction of Royal Absolutism in France, 1598–1661

Benedict, Philip. *The Faith and Fortunes of France's Huguenots, 1600–85*. Burlington, VT: Ashgate, 2001.

Bercé, Yves-Marie. *The Birth of Absolutism: A History of France, 1598–1661*. London: Macmillan, 1995.

Bergin, Joseph. *Cardinal Richelieu: Power and the Pursuit of Wealth.* New Haven, CT: Yale University Press, 1985.

——. *The Rise of Richelieu.* New Haven, CT: Yale University Press, 1991.

Bohanan, Donna. *Crown and Nobility in Early Modern France.* Basingstoke and New York: Palgrave, 2001.

Bonney, Richard. *Political Change in France under Richelieu and Mazarin.* Oxford: Oxford University Press, 1978.

——. *The King's Debts: Finance and Politics in France, 1598–1661.* Oxford: Clarendon Press, 1981.

——. *The Limits of Absolutism in Ancien Régime France.* Brookfield, VT: Ashgate, 1995.

Buisseret, David. *Sully and the Growth of Centralized Government in France.* London: Eyre and Spottiswoode, 1968.

——. *Henry IV.* London: Allen and Unwin, 1984.

Collins, James B. *Fiscal Limits of Absolutism: Direct Taxation in Early Seventeenth-Century France.* Berkeley and Los Angeles: University of California Press, 1988.

——. *The State in Early Modern France.* Cambridge: Cambridge University Press, 1995.

Greengrass, Mark. *Henri IV.* London: Longman, 1995.

Hayden, J. Michael. *France and the Estates-General of 1614.* London: Cambridge University Press, 1974.

Knecht, R.J. *Richelieu.* White Plains, NY: Longman, 1991.

Marvick, Elizabeth. *The Young Richelieu.* Chicago: University of Chicago Press, 1983.

——. *Louis XIII: The Making of a King.* New Haven, CT: Yale University Press, 1986.

Moote, A. Lloyd. *The Revolt of the Judges: The Parlement of Paris and the Fronde, 1643–52.* Princeton, NJ: Princeton University Press, 1971.

——. *Louis XIII, the Just.* Berkeley and Los Angeles: The University of California Press, 1989.

Mousnier, Roland. *The Assassination of Henry IV.* Trans. Joan Spencer. New York: Scribner, 1973.

Parker, David. *The Making of French Absolutism.* London: Edwin Arnold, 1983.

——. *Class and State in Early Modern France: The Road to Modernity.* New York: Routledge, 1996.

Parrott, David. *Richelieu's Army: War, Government and Society in France, 1624–1642.* New York: Cambridge University Press, 2001.

Ranum, Orest A. *Richelieu and the Councillors of Louis XIII.* New York: Oxford University Press, 1963.

Tapie, Victor-L. *France in the Age of Louis XIII and Richelieu.* London: Macmillan, 1974.

Treasure, Geoffrey. *Mazarin: The Crisis of Absolutism in France.* New York: Routledge, 1995.

——. *Richelieu and Mazarin.* London: Routledge, 1997.

CHAPTER 10 ⇛ ENGLAND, 1603–60: REBELLION AND REVOLUTION

Bennett, Martyn. *The Civil Wars in Britain and Ireland, 1638–1651.* London: Blackwell, 1996.

Braddick, Michael J. *State Formation in Early Modern England, c. 1550–1700.* Cambridge: Cambridge University Press, 2000.

Burgess, Glenn. *Absolute Monarchy and the Stuart Constitution.* New Haven, CT: Yale University Press, 1996.

Coward, Barry. *The Stuart Age: England, 1603–1714.* London: Longman, 1994.

Croft, Paula. *King James.* New York: Palgrave, 2003.

Fincham, Kenneth, ed. *The Early Stuart Church, 1603–1642.* Stanford, CA: Stanford University Press, 1993.

Fletcher, Anthony, and Peter Roberts, eds. *Religion, Culture, and Society in Early Modern Britain: Essays in Honour of Patrick Collinson.* New York: Cambridge University Press, 1994.

Hill, Christopher. *The Century of Revolution, 1603–1714.* London: Norton, 1961.

——. *God's Englishman: Oliver Cromwell and the English Revolution.* New York: Dial Press, 1970.

——. *The World Turned Upside Down: Radical Ideas during the English Revolution.* London: Temple Smith, 1972.

Kishlansky, Mark. *A Monarchy Transformed: Britain 1603–1714.* London: Penguin, 1997.

MacLachlan, Alastair. *The Rise and Fall of Revolutionary England: An Essay in the Fabrication of Seventeenth-Century History.* New York: St. Martin's Press, 1996.

Patterson, W.B. *King James VI and I and the Reunion of Christendom.* New York: Cambridge University Press, 1998.

Richardson, R.C. *The Debate on the English Revolution.* 3rd ed. New York: St. Martin's Press, 1999.

Russell, Conrad. *The Crisis of Parliaments.* New York: Oxford, 1971.

——. *The Fall of the British Monarchies.* Oxford: Oxford University Press, 1995.

Scott, Jonathan. *England's Troubles: Seventeenth-Century English Political Instability in European Context.* Cambridge: Cambridge University Press, 2000.

Sharpe, Kevin. *Remapping Early Modern England: The Culture of Seventeenth-Century Politics.* Cambridge: Cambridge University Press, 2000.

Sharpe, Kevin, and Peter Lake, eds. *Culture and Politics in Early Stuart England.* Stanford: Stanford University Press, 1994.

Smith, Daniel. *A History of the Modern British Isles, 1603–1707: The Double Crown.* Oxford: Blackwell, 1998.

Stone, Lawrence. *The Causes of the English Revolution, 1529–1642.* New York: Harper Torchbook, 1972.

Underdown, David. *A Freeborn People: Politics and the Nation in Seventeenth-Century England.* New York: Oxford University Press, 1996.

Wall, Alison. *Power and Protest in England, 1525–1640.* New York: Oxford University Press, 2001.

Webster, Tom. *Godly Clergy in Early Stuart England: The Caroline Puritan Movement, c. 1620–1643.* New York: Cambridge University Press, 1997.

White, Peter. *Predestination, Policy and Polemic: Conflict and Consensus in the English Church from the Reformation to the Civil War.* Cambridge: Cambridge University Press, 1992.

CHAPTER 11 ⊭ SPAIN IN DECLINE

Elliott, J.H. *The Revolt of the Catalans.* Cambridge: Cambridge University Press, 1963.

——. *Richelieu and Olivares.* Cambridge: Cambridge University Press, 1984.

——. *The Count-Duke of Olivares: The Statesman in an Age of Decline.* New Haven, CT: Yale University Press, 1986.

Feros, Antonio. *Kingship and Favoritism in the Spain of Philip III, 1598–1621.* New York: Cambridge University Press, 2000.

Kamen, Henry. *Spain in the Later Seventeenth Century, 1665–1700.* London: Longman, 1980.

——. *Golden Age Spain*. London: Macmillan, 1988.

Lynch, John. *The Hispanic World in Crisis and Change, 1598–1700*. Cambridge, MA: Blackwell, 1992.

MacKay, Ruth. *The Limits of Royal Authority: Resistance and Obedience in Seventeenth-Century Castile*. New York: Cambridge University Press, 1999.

Parker, Geoffrey. *The Army of Flanders and the Spanish Road, 1567–1659*. New York: Cambridge, 1972.

Parry, J.H. *The Spanish Seaborne Empire*. New York: Knopf, 1966.

Stradling, R.A. *Europe and the Decline of Spain: a Study of the Spanish System, 1580–1720*. London: Allen Unwin, 1981.

——. *Philip IV and the Government of Spain, 1621–1665*. Cambridge: Cambridge University Press, 1988.

—-. *The Armada of Flanders: Spanish Maritime Policy and European War, 1568–1668*. Cambridge: Cambridge University Press, 1992.

——. *Spain's Struggle for Europe, 1598–1668*. London: The Hambledon Press, 1994.

Thompson, I.A.A. *War and Society in Habsburg Spain*. Brookfield, VT: Variorum, 1992.

——. *Crown and Cortes: Government, Institutions and Representations in Early Modern Castile*. Brookfield, VT: Variorum, 1993.

Thompson, I.A.A., and Bartolome Yun, eds. *The Castilian Crisis of the Seventeenth Century*. New York: Cambridge University Press, 1994.

CHAPTER 12 ⥼ THE GOLDEN AGE OF THE DUTCH REPUBLIC

Boxer, C.R. *The Dutch Seaborne Empire, 1600–1800*. New York: Knopf, 1965.

Davids, Karel, and Jan Lucassen, eds. *A Miracle Mirrored: The Dutch Republic in European Perspective*. Cambridge: Cambridge University Press, 1995.

Geyl, Pieter. *The Netherlands in the Seventeenth Century*. 2 vols. London: Ernest Benn, 1961–64.

Haley, K.H.D. *The Dutch in the Seventeenth Century*. London: Thames and Hudson, 1972.

Israel, Jonathan. *The Dutch Republic: Its Rise, Greatness, and Fall 1477–1806*. Oxford: Oxford University Press, 1995.

Price, J.L. *Culture and Society in the Dutch Republic during the Seventeenth Century*. London: Batsford, 1974.

——. *Holland and the Dutch Republic in the Seventeenth Century: the Politics of Particularism.* Oxford: Oxford University Press, 1994.

Rowen, Herbert H. *John de Witt.* Princeton, NJ: Princeton University Press, 1977.

——. *The Princes of Orange: The Stadholders in the Dutch Republic.* Cambridge: Cambridge University Press, 1988.

Schama, Simon. *The Embarrassment of Riches: An Interpretation of Dutch Culture in the Golden Age.* New York: Knopf, 1987.

Thart, Marjolein C. *The Making of a Bourgeois State: War, Politics, and Finance during the Dutch Revolution.* New York: St. Martin's Press, 1993.

van der Wee, Herman. *The Low Countries in the Early Modern World.* Aldershot: Variorum, 1994.

Wilson, Charles. *The Dutch Republic.* New York: McGraw-Hill, 1968.

CHAPTER 13 ⇜ NORTHERN AND EASTERN EUROPE

Blum, Jerome. *Lord and Peasant in Russia from the Ninth to the Nineteenth Century.* Princeton, NJ: Princeton University Press, 1961.

Crummey, R.O. *The Formation of Muscovy, 1304–1614.* London: Longman, 1987.

Davies, N. *God's Playground: A History of Poland, vol. i: The Origins to 1795.* New York: Columbia University Press, 1982.

Fennell, J.L.I. *Ivan the Great of Moscow.* London: Macmillan, 1961.

Fuhrmann, J.T. *Tsar Alexis: His Reign and His Russia.* Gulf Breeze, FL: Academic International Press, 1981.

Grey, I. *Ivan the Terrible.* Philadelphia: Lipincott, 1964.

Kirby, David. *Northern Europe in the Early Modern Period: The Baltic World 1492–1772.* London: Longman, 1990.

Lockhart, Paul Douglas. *Denmark in the Thirty Years' War, 1618–1648: King Christian IV and the Decline of the Oldenburg State.* Selinsgrove, PA: Susquehanna University Press, 1996.

Pipes, R. *Russia under the Old Regime.* New York: Scribner, 1974.

Platonov, S.F. *The Time of Troubles.* Trans. J.T. Alexander. Lawrence: University Press of Kansas, 1970.

Porshnev, Boris F. *Muscovy and Sweden in the Thirty Years' War, 1630–1655.* Trans. Brian Pearce. Cambridge: Cambridge University Press, 1997.

Riasanovsky, N.V. *A History of Russia.* Oxford: Oxford University Press, 1963.

Roberts, Michael. *The Early Vasas: a history of Sweden, 1523–1611*. Cambridge: Cambridge University Press, 1968.

——. *Gustavus Adolphus and the Rise of Sweden*. London: English Universities Press, 1973.

——. *Gustavus Adolphus, 1611–1632*. London: Longman, 1992.

Skrynnikov, R.G. *Ivan the Terrible*. Trans. H.F. Graham. Gulf Breeze, FL: Academic International Press, 1981.

Smith, R.E.F. *The Enserfment of the Russian Peasantry*. Cambridge: Cambridge University Press, 1968.

Zamoyski, A. *The Polish Way: A Thousand-Year History of the Poles and Their Culture*. New York: F. Watts, 1987.

CHAPTER 14 ⥼ FRANCE UNDER LOUIS XIV: 1661–1715

Beik, W.H. *Absolutism and Society in Seventeenth-Century France: State Power and Provincial Aristocracy in Languedoc*. Cambridge: Cambridge University Press, 1985.

Burke, Peter. *The Fabrication of Louis XIV*. New Haven, CT: Yale University Press, 1992.

Goubert, Pierre. *Louis XIV and Twenty Million Frenchmen*. New York: Random, 1972.

Hurt, John J. *Louis XIV and the Parlements: The Assertion of Royal Authority*. Manchester and New York: Manchester University Press, 2002.

Kettering, S. *Patrons, Brokers and Clients in Seventeenth-Century France*. Oxford: Oxford University Press, 1986.

Kierstead, R., ed. *State and Society in Seventeenth-Century France*. New York: New Viewpoints, 1975.

Le Roy Ladurie, E. *The Ancien Régime: France 1610–1774*. Trans. Mark Greengrass. Oxford: Blackwell, 1995.

Lewis, W.H. *The Splendid Century: Life in the France of Louis XIV*. New York: Morrow, 1953.

Major, J. Russell. *From Renaissance Monarchy to Absolute Monarchy: French Kings, Nobles, and Estates*. Baltimore: Johns Hopkins University Press, 1994.

Ranum, Orest A. *Paris in the Age of Absolutism*. University Park, PA: Pennsylvania State University Press, 2002.

Rule, John C., ed. *Louis XIV and the Craft of Kingship*. Columbus: Ohio State University Press, 1969.

Wolf, John B. *Louis XIV*. New York: Norton. 1968.

CHAPTER 15 ⥼ ENGLAND: FROM RESTORATION TO OLIGARCHY, 1660–1714

Ashley, Maurice. *England in the Seventeenth Century*. Baltimore: Penguin, 1975.

Baxter, Stephen B. *William III*. London: Longman, 1966.

——. *William III and the Defense of European Liberty*. Westport, CT: Greenwood, 1976.

Beddard, R., ed. *The Revolutions of 1688*. Oxford: Clarendon Press, 1988.

Clark, George N. *The Later Stuarts, 1661–1714*. Oxford: Oxford University Press, 1971.

Claydon, Tony. *William III and the Godly Revolution*. Cambridge: Cambridge University Press, 1996.

Davies, Godfrey. *The Restoration of Charles II, 1658–1660*. San Marino, CA: The Huntington Library, 1955.

Haley, K.H.D. *Charles II*. London: Historical Association, 1966.

Holmes, Geoffrey. *The making of a great power: late Stuart and early Georgian Britain, 1660–1722*. London: Longman, 1993.

Holmes, Geoffrey, ed. *Britain after the Glorious Revolution*. London: Macmillan, 1969.

Hutton, Ronald. *The Restoration : a political and religious history of England and Wales, 1658–1667*. Oxford: Clarendon Press, 1985.

——. *Charles II: King of England, Scotland, and Ireland*. Oxford: Clarendon Press, 1989.

Jones, J.R. *Country and Court: England, 1658–1714*. London: Edward Arnold, 1978.

Jones, J.R., ed. *Liberty Secured? Britain before and after 1668*. Stanford, CA: Stanford University Press, 1992.

Miller, John. *James II: A Study in Kingship*. Hove: Wayland, 1977.

Mullett, Michael. *James II and English Politics, 1678–1688*. London: Routledge, 1994.

Plumb, J.H. *The Growth of Political Stability in England, 1675–1720*. London: Macmillan, 1967.

Prest, Wilfred. *Albion Ascendant: English History, 1660–1815*. Oxford: Oxford University Press, 1998.

Schwoerer, Lois G., ed. *The Revolution of 1688–89: Changing Perspectives*. Cambridge: Cambridge University Press, 1992.

Seaward, Paul. *The Restoration, 1660-1688*. London: Macmillan, 1991.

Speck, W.A. *Reluctant Revolutionaries: Englishmen and the Revolution of 1688–89.* Oxford: Oxford University Press, 1988.

Turner, F.C. *James II.* London: Eyre & Spottiswoode, 1948.

CHAPTER 16 ABSOLUTISM IN CENTRAL AND EASTERN EUROPE

Anderson, M.S. *The Eastern Question, 1423–1774.* London: Macmillan, 1966.

Carsten, F.L. *The Origins of Prussia.* Oxford: Clarendon Press, 1954.

——. *Princes and Parliaments in Germany from the Fifteenth to the Eighteenth Century.* Oxford: Oxford University Press, 1959.

Dukes, P. *The Making of Russian Absolutism, 1613–1801.* London: Longman, 1990.

Evans, R.J.W. *The Making of the Habsburg Monarchy, 1550–1700.* Oxford: Clarendon Press, 1985.

Evans, R.J.W., and T.V. Thomas, eds. *Crown, Church and Estates: Central European Politics in the Sixteenth and Seventeenth Centuries.* New York: St. Martin's Press, 1991.

Fay, S.B. *The Rise of Brandenburg-Prussia to 1786.* New York: Holt, Rinehart & Winston, 1965.

Hagen, William W. *Ordinary Prussians: Brandenburg Junkers and Villagers, 1500–1840.* Cambridge: Cambridge University Press, 2002.

Hatton, R. *Charles XII of Sweden.* London: Weidenfeld & Nicolson, 1968.

Holborn, Hajo. *History of Modern Germany, vol. 2: the Age of Absolutism.* Princeton, NJ: Princeton University Press, 1964.

Hughes, Lindsey. *Russia in the Age of Peter the Great.* New Haven, CT: Yale University Press, 1998.

——. *Peter the Great: A Biography.* New Haven, CT: Yale University Press, 2002.

Ingrao, Charles W., ed. *State and Society in Early Modern Austria.* West Lafayette, IN: Purdue University Press, 1994.

Kann, Robert A. *A History of the Habsburg Empire 1526–1918.* Berkeley: University of California Press, 1975.

Klyuchevsky, Vasili. *Peter the Great.* London: Macmillan, 1958.

Macartney, C.A. *Hungary: a short history.* Edinburgh: Edinburgh University Press, 1966.

Roberts, Michael. *Sweden as a Great Power, 1611–97.* London: Edward Arnold, 1968.

——. *The Swedish Imperial Experience, 1560–1718*. Cambridge: Cambridge University Press, 1979.

Setton, Kenneth M. *Venice, Austria and the Turks in the Seventeenth Century*. Philadelphia: American Philosophical Society, 1992.

Sumner, B.H. *Peter the Great and the Ottoman Empire*. Oxford: Blackwell, 1950.

——. *Peter the Great and the Emergence of Russia*. London: English Universities Press, 1970.

Upton, A.F. *Charles XI and Swedish Absolutism*. New York: Cambridge University Press, 1998.

CHAPTER 17 ⥼ ESTABLISHING THE BALANCE OF POWER: THE WARS OF LOUIS XIV

Anderson, M.S. *War and Society in Europe of the Old Regime 1618–1789*. London and Buffalo: McGill-Queen's University Press, 1998.

Black, Jeremy. *The Rise of the European Powers, 1679–1793*. London: Edward Arnold, 1990.

Ekberg, C.J. *The Failure of Louis XIV's Dutch War*. Chapel Hill: University of North Carolina Press, 1979.

Hatton, R. *Louis XIV and Europe*. London: Macmillan, 1976.

Hatton, R., and J.S. Bromley, eds. *William III and Louis XIV, 1680–1720*. Liverpool: Liverpool Univerity Press, 1968.

Kamen, Henry. *The War of Succession in Spain, 1700–1715*. Bloomington: Indiana University Press, 1969.

Lynn, John A. *Giant of the Grand Siècle: The French Army, 1610–1715*. New York: Cambridge University Press, 1997.

——. *The Wars of Louis XIV*. London: Longman, 1999.

McKay, Derek, and H.M. Scott. *The Rise of the Great Powers, 1648–1815*. London: Longman, 1983.

Sonnino, Paul. *Louis XIV and the Origins of the Dutch War*. Cambridge: Cambridge University Press, 1988.

CHAPTER 18 ⊱ INTELLECTUAL LIFE: THE QUEST FOR CERTAINTY

Artigas, Mariano, and W.R. Shea. *Galileo in Rome: the Rise and Fall of a Troublesome Genius*. New York: Oxford University Press, 2003.

Brooke, J.H. *Science and Religion: Some Historical Perspectives*. Cambridge: Cambridge University Press, 1991.

Burtt, E.A. *The Metaphysical Foundations of Modern Science*. Atlantic Highlands, NJ: Humanities Press, 1952.

Butterfield, Herbert. *The Origins of Modern Science, 1300–1800*. London: Bell, 1949.

Butts, R.E., and J.C. Pitt, eds. *New Perspectives on Galileo*. Dordrecht: Reidel, 1978.

Clarke, D.M. *Descartes' Philosophy of Science*. Manchester: Manchester University Press, 1982.

Crombie, A.C. *Augustine to Galileo: II. Science in the Middle Ages and early Modern Times, 13th to 17th Centuries*. Harmondsworth: Penguin, 1969.

Easlea, B. *Witch Hunting, Magic and the New Philosophy: An Introduction to the Debates of the Scientific Revolution, 1450–1750*. Brighton: Harvester, 1980.

Field, J.V. *Kepler's Geometrical Cosmology*. Chicago: University of Chicago Press, 1988.

Finocchiaro, M.A. *Galileo and the Art of Reasoning: Rhetorical Foundations of Logic and Scientific Method*. Dordrecht: Reidel, 1980.

Hazard, Paul. *The European Mind 1680–1715*. Harmondsworth: Penguin, 1964.

Henry, J. *The Scientific Revolution and the Origins of Modern Science*. New York: St. Martin's Press, 1997.

Hunter, M. *Science and Society in Restoration England*. Cambridge: Cambridge University Press, 1981.

Jacob, James. *The Scientific Revolution: Aspirations and Achievements, 1500–1700*. Atlantic Highlands, NJ: Humanities Press, 1998.

Kearney, H. *Origins of the Scientific Revolution*. London: Longmans, 1964.

——. *Science and Change, 1500–1700*. London: Weidenfeld & Nicolson, 1971.

Kenny, A. *Descartes: A Study of His Philosophy*. New York: Random House, 1968.

Koestler, A. *The Sleepwalkers*. Harmondsworth: Penguin, 1970.

Koyre, Alexandre. *From the Closed World to the Infinite Universe*. Baltimore: Johns Hopkins Press, 1957.

Kuhn, T.S. *The Copernican Revoultion: Planetary Astronomy in the Development of Western Thought*. Cambridge, MA: Harvard University Press, 1957.

——. *The Structure of Scientific Revolutions.* Chicago: University of Chicago Press, 1962.

Lindberg, D.C., and R.S. Westman. *Reappraisals of the Scientific Revolution.* Cambridge: Cambridge University Press, 1990.

Osler, Margaret. *Divine will and the mechanical philosophy: Gassendi and Descartes on contingency and necessity in the created world.* Cambridge: Cambridge University Press, 1994.

——. *Rethinking the Scientific Revolution.* Cambridge: Cambridge University Press, 2000.

Shapin, Steven. *The Scientific Revolution.* Chicago: University of Chicago Press, 1996.

Shea, W.R. *Galileo's Intellectual Revolution.* New York: Science History Publications, 1972.

Webster, C. *The Great Instauration: Science, Medicine and Reform 1626–1660.* London: Duckworth, 1975.

Westfall, R.S. *Never at Rest: A Biography of Isaac Newton.* Cambridge: Cambridge University Press, 1980.

Williams, B. *Descartes: The Project of Pure Enquiry.* Hassocks, England: Harvester, 1978.

INDEX